Dancing Women

Dancing Women

*Choreographing Corporeal Histories
of Hindi Cinema*

USHA IYER

OXFORD
UNIVERSITY PRESS

Oxford University Press is a department of the University of Oxford. It furthers
the University's objective of excellence in research, scholarship, and education
by publishing worldwide. Oxford is a registered trade mark of Oxford University
Press in the UK and certain other countries.

Published in the United States of America by Oxford University Press
198 Madison Avenue, New York, NY 10016, United States of America.

© Oxford University Press 2020

All rights reserved. No part of this publication may be reproduced, stored in
a retrieval system, or transmitted, in any form or by any means, without the
prior permission in writing of Oxford University Press, or as expressly permitted
by law, by license, or under terms agreed with the appropriate reproduction
rights organization. Inquiries concerning reproduction outside the scope of the
above should be sent to the Rights Department, Oxford University Press, at the
address above.

You must not circulate this work in any other form
and you must impose this same condition on any acquirer.

CIP data is on file at the Library of Congress
ISBN 978-0-19-093874-1 (pbk.)
ISBN 978-0-19-093873-4 (hbk.)

1 3 5 7 9 8 6 4 2

Paperback printed by Marquis, Canada
Hardback printed by Bridgeport National Bindery, Inc., United States of America

A part of Chapter 1 was previously published as "Dance Musicalization: Proposing a
Choreomusicological Approach to Hindi Film Song-and-dance Sequences" in *The Evolution
of Song and Dance in Hindi Cinema*, edited by Ajay Gehlawat and Rajinder Dudrah, Routledge, 2019.

For Kamala, with gratitude

Contents

About the Companion Website   ix

Acknowledgments   xi

Introduction: A Corporeal History of Hindi Film Dance   1

1. Dance Musicalization and the Choreomusicking Body: Corporealizing Theoretical Frameworks of Film Dance and Music   27

2. Choreographing Architectures of Public Intimacy: A Spatio-Corporeal Approach to Hindi Film Dance   59

3. Corporealizing Colonial Modernities: Azurie and Sadhona Bose as Co-Choreographers of New Mobilities in the 1930s and 1940s   91

4. From the Cabaret Number to the Melodrama of Dance Reform: Folded Corporeal Histories of the Dancer-Actress in the 1950s and 1960s   139

5. Stardom *Ke Peeche Kya Hai* (What Is behind the Stardom)? Saroj Khan and Madhuri Dixit as Co-Choreographers of 1990s Bollywood Femininity   179

Epilogue: An Intermedial History of Hindi Film, Dance, and Music   199

Notes   209
Glossary   249
Index   253

About the Companion Website

www.oup.com/us/dancingwomen

Oxford has created a password-protected website to accompany *Dancing Women: Choreographing Corporeal Histories of Hindi Cinema*. The website contains short clips of many of the dance numbers discussed in the book. The reader is encouraged to consult this resource in conjunction with each chapter. Examples available online are indicated in the text with Oxford's symbol ⏵.

Acknowledgments

As with the women that dance across these pages, this book also has many co-choreographers that I owe deep debts to. It is only fitting that I begin a book that foregrounds collaboration and labor by acknowledging the intellectual and emotional support of numerous mentors, friends, and family members that have been part of this journey. Through its earlier avatar as a PhD dissertation, this project owes much to my formidable all-woman dissertation committee comprising Neepa Majumdar, Marcia Landy, Lucy Fischer, and Ranjani Mazumdar. The work of these foundational figures in feminist film scholarship—on female stardom, melodrama, performance, and reading history through cinema—has greatly informed the methodology of this book. I feel their shadow presence, like that of the choreographer around the on-screen dancer, in much of what I write and teach. As dissertation chair and indefatigable supporter of students, Neepa Majumdar has modeled the intellectual generosity that makes academic work rewarding and grounded in an everyday politics of care and solidarity. I could not have asked for a better mentor.

In its post-dissertation life, this book has benefited enormously from conversations with scholars of cinema, dance, and music. Davesh Soneji's vital scholarship on South Indian dance and music, which excavates the labor and virtuosity of hereditary performers and reveals the complex caste and religious politics that produce homogenous "classical" performance cultures, has been central to my reconfiguring of this book from a study of dancing heroines to a broader exploration of dancing women across Hindi cinema. The manuscript review workshop at the Stanford Humanities Center was invaluable as well in helping me consider the final form of this book, and I owe a deep debt of gratitude to Priya Jaikumar, Adrienne McLean, Jisha Menon, Anna Schultz, and Scott Bukatman for their insightful and astute feedback. These are scholars whose work I highly admire and friendship I greatly cherish. The compelling and thrilling work of Hari Krishnan, Pavitra Sundar, Rumya Putcha, Kareem Khubchandani, and Shikha Jhingan, among many others, has contributed to an impressive body of scholarship on Indian film music and dance, building on the foundational work of Sangita Gopal, Ira

Bhaskar, Lalita Gopalan, and others. I am grateful to be part of a scholarly community that, through this close attention to the production and reception of music and dance, produces a rich intermedial history of film in the Indian subcontinent.

Stanford's Department of Art and Art History is a most supportive and convivial professional home. Conversations with Jean Ma, Pavle Levi, Karla Oeler, Alexander Nemerov, Bissera Pentcheva, Marci Kwon, Shane Denson, and at the department's faculty salons, where I workshopped some of this material, have furthered my appreciation of lyrical writing, visual analysis, and interdisciplinary thinking. Stanford's Center for South Asia has offered a most intellectually rewarding community, and the talks and symposia there have informed many of the questions raised in this book. Thank you Janice Ross and Heather Rastovac Akbarzadeh for enthusiastically welcoming me into the dance studies community at Stanford.

I thank Norm Hirschy at Oxford University Press for his ready enthusiasm for this project and his supportive stewardship throughout. His editorial work across film, dance, and music has produced some of the most exciting work in these areas at OUP. I am grateful to the three anonymous reviewers of the manuscript for their close reading and constructive feedback, which spurred some significant edits. Prabhu Chinnasamy has been a most efficient and responsive project manager through the production phase. Pritha Chakrabarti's Bengali-English translations of Sadhona and Modhu Bose's autobiographies and expert sourcing of publicity materials of their films contributed significantly to Chapter 3 of the book. Alexandria Brown-Hejazi has been a most able and skillful research assistant in the final stages of the book. I look forward to reading their work when published in the next few years.

I am most grateful for the personal interviews with Waheeda Rehman and Madhuri Dixit. Determined early on to not write a purely textual analysis of film dance, but to engage with questions of training and labor, I was moved by these incredible dancing stars' accounts of their negotiations of the film industry. Dayanita Singh's photograph of Saroj Khan and Dixit from her "Masterji" series prompted an examination of training, rehearsal, and collaboration in Chapter 5. I thank her for the use of the photograph from a masterful series. Where archival traces of dancing women like Azurie and Edwina Lyons barely remain, I turned to online fan blogs such as "Dances on the Footpath," "Cinema Nritya Gharana," and "Dusted Off," among many others which, in their impassioned fandom, produce the only archive for dancing women erased in official accounts of female pioneers in popular entertainment. The staff at the National Film Archives of India, the Sangeet Natak Akademi, Doordarshan, and the Nehru Memorial Library were most helpful and resourceful.

A year-long fellowship at the Michelle R. Clayman Institute for Gender Research helped me engage with a wide range of research on gender across disciplines, and faculty writing retreats at the Hume Center at Stanford provided a community of fellow writers. Prior to Stanford, I benefited greatly from feedback from colleagues at Clark University, the University of the West Indies, and Jawaharlal Nehru University. I owe my return to academia and my interest in film studies to many remarkable mentors over the years, including Madhava Prasad, Ravi Vasudevan, Alok Bhalla, Samar Nakhate, Aniket Jaaware, Sangeeta Dutta, and Eunice De Souza. Thank you Monika Mehta, Madhuja Mukherjee, Kyle Stevens, Rajinder Dudrah, Ajay Gehlawat, Meheli Sen, and Anustup Basu for your valuable editorial inputs on earlier publications, some of which are related to the material in this book. The broader field of South Asian film and media studies is an incredibly welcoming and supportive community, and I'd like to thank so many for their intellectual generosity and camaraderie, including but not limited to Debashree Mukherjee, Manishita Dass, Kuhu Tanvir, Rochona Majumdar, Samhita Sunya, Kartik Nair, Lotte Hoek, Gohar Siddiqui, Veena Hariharan, Priyadarshini Shanker, Nitin Govil, Swarnavel Eswaran Pillai, Anupama Kapse, Anuja Jain, Bhaskar Sarkar, and Salma Siddique. All of you make our conferences *addas* to look forward to!

As I write this alone at home during the coronavirus lockdown, I value more than ever the soul-sustaining joy, mirth, and comfort that a sparkling constellation of friends brings to my life. From those closest home, all as dazzlingly bright as the California sun, to those further away, but never too far for a quick enlivening visit, to those in my other home, in India, to whom many decades of my life belong, you—who would take up pages if I were to name each one of you—are my family. As for my family, who are also my friends (and easier to name in one paragraph!), I can't thank enough my sister Renu for her ready wit and our shared nostalgia for a childhood filled with mischief on hot afternoons in suburban Bombay. My parents-in-law, Lucy and Sebastian, opened their verdant Kerala home and large hearts to me from the moment we met. My parents, Geeta and Swaminathan, have been indulgent, patient, curious, flummoxed, and proud by turn at my many career and life transitions. Thanks to my mum for daily phone calls that keep me grounded in the everyday rhythms of life in India. My father's passion for

Hindi film music has bestowed upon my memories of childhood and home a pervading soundtrack of songs by Saigal, Talat Mahmood, Geeta Dutt, and Lata Mangeshkar. His cinephilic presence suffuses many parts of this book. Cyril, my untiring companion through the many adventures of the past fifteen years, encyclopedia of Hindi cinema and popular culture, indefatigable motivator and detractor, has assiduously kept things real—"bhot hard"—for both of us. Thank you for the hours upon hours of belly-shaking laughter, passionate arguments, and that unique combination of sarcasm and sentimentality. And now, brace yourself for the travails of the next project!

I dedicate this book to my first mother, Kamala. In the three decades that she has been gone, I have constantly felt her fearless and formidable presence, her Carnatic and Hindustani singing booming through the air, her restless intelligence captured in urgent writing in numerous notebooks. This is for her and for her mother, my *paati*, Lakshmi—a lineage of remarkable, unconventional women who never quite fit in and taught us not to as well.

Introduction

A Corporeal History of Hindi Film Dance

The dance number opens with a close-up of a *mridangam* drum and zooms out to show us three Carnatic musicians playing percussive music.[1] Cut to a long shot of the dancer-actress Vyjayanthimala executing a *namaskaram*, the opening movement of obeisance in the *Bharatanatyam* repertoire, followed by a dynamically-edited sequence of close-ups of her footwork, *mukhaja abhinaya* (facial gestures), and *hasta mudras* (hand gestures).[2] As she moves, she mobilizes the camera to track from her vigorous *Bharatanatyam* routine to Hindi cinema's favorite "vamp," Helen, performing her trademark "cabaret" dance moves in a bustier, mini skirt, tights, and heels.[3] As both dancing women spurn the film's hero, played by Shammi Kapoor, he swings his Elvis quiff and sings, "*Muqabla humse na karo*" ("Don't compete with me"), his arms swaying, his head jolting frenetically (see ⏵ video 00.01). This scintillating dance-off between Bombay cinema's three best-known dancer-actors of the time is the central attraction of *Prince* (Lekh Tandon, 1969). Its staging of a techno-spectacle of cine-choreographic innovations, dazzling costume and set design, and an array of musical and dance styles alerts us to questions of virtuosity, labor, and pleasure undergirding the production and reception of popular Hindi film dance. While the film's narrative undertakes many contortions to stage this dance number, when we shift our focus from plot to bodily performance, to the corporeal competence and protracted training required for dancing, and to the spectatorial desires that screen-dancing bodies activate, we may discern that spectacle *is* the narrative when Vyjayanthimala, Shammi Kapoor, and Helen come together on screen (see Figure I.1).

Taking a cue from Jane Desmond's discussion of the dancing body "as a ground for the inscription of meaning, a tool for its enactment, and a medium for its continual creation and re-creation,"[4] we may read Vyjayanthimala, Shammi Kapoor, and Helen's bodies as writing and written upon, as interpellated materializations of biology, history, technology. Helen's supple, twisting torso, mobile mouth, and splayed legs, Vyjayanthimala's large, kohl-lined

Figure I.1. Helen, Shammi Kapoor, Vyjayanthimala in *Prince* (Lekh Tandon, 1969).
Credit: Screen capture.

eyes, straight-backed stance, and the crisp *mudras* (codified gestures) of her *Bharatanatyam*-trained body, and Kapoor's seemingly un-choreographed, loose-limbed insouciance disclose the accumulated somatic experiences of each performer, disciplined into certain styles of comportment that have sedimented layers of gestures in each body. "Gestural systems," Henri Lefebvre notes, "embody ideology and bind it to practice. Through gestures, ideology escapes from pure abstraction and performs actions."[5] Helen's cabaret and Vyjayanthimala's "classical" dance routines bear the traces of long histories of the performing arts and of gendered performativity in the Indian subcontinent, folding in figurations of hybrid "oriental dances" from the 1930s, the Anglo-Indian dancing girl in Bombay cinema, and the newly-anointed "classical" dancer who emerges in the 1940s and 1950s through a concerted marginalization of traditional performers (the production of the category of the "classical" is discussed in detail in Chapters 3 and 4). Each performer in this dance number mobilizes a gestural history, not just of their own star bodies and the production thereof, but also of popular Hindi cinema's borrowings from other performance traditions and cinematic idioms. Vyjayanthimala's *Bharatanatyam* routine and the accompanying Carnatic musicians are a nod to the South Indian actress's early career in the Tamil film industry, while her *Kathak* routine puts us in mind of the Muslim courtesan film.[6] Helen's flagrantly hybrid flamenco and belly-dance routines, with accompanying musicians in sombrero and fez hats, respectively, evince Hindi cinema's long-standing engagement with foreign dance forms and the enduring networks of exchange of movement vocabularies, while Kapoor earns his description as India's Elvis Presley in the 1950s and 1960s with his pelvic thrusts, loose-limbed rock and roll moves, and an aura of youthful rebellion and defiance.[7] Attending to Vyjayanthimala's fingers and feet, Helen's waist, or Shammi Kapoor's tremulous head, as indeed the choreography, cinematography, and editing pointedly invite us to, provides a means of constructing a historiography of popular cultural forms and trans-regional exchanges through the dancing body. Analyzing the collision and coalescence of cultural forms in the bodies of dancer-actors illuminates how the planes of the popular and the classical, the regional, the national, and the global are negotiated and articulated by popular Hindi cinema.

In addition to the social practices that construct bodies, dance forces us to attend to the corporeal materiality of performing bodies. Adrienne McLean asks, "Which parts of the body (are allowed to) speak and perform, and in what contexts? Which parts of the body repeat the discursive meaning already placed upon bodies by culture? What kinds of physical training and competence produce what effects?"[8] In *"Muqabla humse na karo,"* Vyjayanthimala's *Bharatanatyam*, *Kathak*, and *Kathakali* routines, Helen's cabaret, flamenco, and belly-dance responses, and Shammi Kapoor's "loose" Elvis moves map all too easily along the axes of tradition and modernity, Indian and Western movement vocabularies, and trained and spontaneous gestural articulations.[9] The dance-off in popular Hindi cinema has typically been read as "corpo-realizing" the post-colonial conflict of modernity and tradition through its binary of Western and state-sanctioned "Indian" dance styles. However, by placing Vyjayanthimala's "Indian" and Helen's "Western" dancing bodies next to, rather than in opposition to each other, by showing us their delight in each other's performance, and by sharing performance space and time equally between the heroine, vamp, and hero, *"Muqabla humse na karo"* moves away from tired clichés, presenting instead a radical celebration of the performative repertoire of each of these dancing bodies. In evenly showcasing different dance vocabularies, the dance-off figures the three performers as agential collaborators in the production of cinematic spectacle. It also enables a reading of the hybridity of both its Indian and Western dance forms, which gestures in turn to the continuous processes of corporeal figurations through the colonial and post-colonial periods, rather than presenting them as discrete and bound by rigid discourses of authenticity. Even if the close-ups of Vyjayanthimala's footwork and hand gestures versus those of Helen's gyrating torso conform to the visual iconography of the heroine-vamp moral binary, these representational codes are queered when we notice that Vyjayanthimala's *Bharatanatyam* costume is constructed in figure-hugging diaphanous red chiffon, her navel and waist left bare, while Helen's brazenly swaying waist is covered in a flesh-colored body stocking, which she customarily donned under her skimpy costumes.[10] By moving easily between the chiffon-draped *Bharatanatyam*-dancing heroine and the vamp with reservations about showing skin, "*Muqabla humse na karo*" hints at the shifting registers of agency and desire articulated by film dance and its female practitioners. A focus on the materiality of dancing bodies draws our attention as well to the spaces between bodies. By the time she was shooting for *Prince* in the late 1960s, Vyjayanthimala had decided to quit acting in films, disheartened by the failure of her magnum opus dance film, *Amrapali* (1966), also directed by Lekh Tandon.[11] Shammi Kapoor reports that she did not exchange a word with him on the shoot. Of her relationship with Helen, on the other hand, Vyjayanthimala remarks in her memoir: "[Helen] is one person with whom I really got along in the industry, as we were both equally reticent—no talking—just working on the sets."[12] This account of the bond between the hard-working dancer-actresses prompts us to consider flows and linkages between performing bodies and to revise our assumptions about relations between the supposedly taciturn heroine, the immodest vamp, and the flamboyant hero.

The three dancing stars—each a particular assemblage of gestures and intensities, bearing traces of their own earlier films as well as those of cinematic and other performing forebears—are, by the time of the production of this number, mature performers at the height of their dancing powers. As the song's refrain declares, "*muqabla humse na karo*" ("don't compete with us"), they indeed have no competition in the Bombay film industry. But the affective force of the dance number is produced not only by the on-screen dancing body. In examining relationships between the insides of the

body drawing our gaze to both anatomical surface and ideological depth—or indeed the reverse, to the depth of the performing body beneath its ideological inscriptions (as, for instance, chaste, salacious, traditional, modern, etc.). Reading the dancing woman through cultural and material lenses directs our attention not only to social norms for female public performance, but also to the specific gestural idiolects of individual dancer-actresses that may challenge or subvert these through their movement vocabulary. Why women? Quite simply, because they were the primary performers of dance in Hindi cinema until the late 1990s, and a focus on the routine picturization of solo dance numbers with female performers reveals how gender plays a central role in the discourses of censorship and spectacle that animate film dance.[17] By charting discursive shifts through figurations of dancing women, their publicly performed movements, private training, and the cinematic and extra-diegetic narratives woven around their dancing bodies, *Dancing Women* considers the "women's question" via female mobility, afforded by the physical movement of dance and the social movement that dancing engenders.[18]

Some of the central figures through whom I analyze Hindi film dance from the 1930s to the 1990s are Azurie, Sadhona Bose, Vyjayanthimala, Helen, Waheeda Rehman, Madhuri Dixit, and Saroj Khan. This selection is not meant to be strictly chronological or comprehensive, but serves rather to highlight certain key moments in the articulation of Bombay cinema's formal and ideological logics and their relation to the problematic of female representation through dance. By reading upper-caste, upper-class, classical-dance-trained heroines alongside mixed-race vamps, "cultured ladies" alongside "sex sirens," this book aims to not just disrupt official histories of dance and female stardom but, through a material history of the labor of producing on-screen dance, to demonstrate how dancing women of various caste, race, religious, and class configurations *co-choreograph* the dance-scape of Bombay cinema.[19] The various stages of writing this book made this collaborative framework apparent as one way to capture a complex intermedial, corporeal history of film dance production. Initially conceptualized as an examination of the role of dance in the construction of the stardom of particular dancer-actresses, the book's sustained focus on the material history of film dance made apparent the bodies whose labor is rendered immaterial. These ghost or shadow figures, whose labor is central to the production of the dancing star but often is pushed to the background, throw a long dark shadow on the spotlighted histories of acclaimed film stars. Ghost figures marginalized at various historical junctures include the silenced bodies of lower-caste traditional performers such as *tawaif*s (courtesans) and *devadasi*s (temple, court, and salon dancers);[20] the cinematic vamp who resided mainly in dance numbers and was erased from the film's narrative as well as the industry's accounts of female stardom; the behind-the-scenes choreographer, rarely credited for the dance performances of stars; and the numerous nameless "background dancers" who performed behind the dancing stars, the spatial praxis of the dance number highlighting the unique *figure* of the star against the *ground* of their uniform "background" bodies.

This book's close historical attention to these various dancing figures over the nineteenth and twentieth centuries, however, began to displace the binarized foreground-background, star-shadow relationship, highlighting instead the protean nature of alternating shifts in the visibility and agency of dancing women. Rather than repeating the routinely drawn linear trajectory of the prominence of performing elites and their eventual decline or marginalization—including of *devadasi*s and *tawaif*s, Anglo-Indian and other Eurasian actresses, oriental dancers, vamps like Helen, or choreographers like Saroj Khan—what became apparent was that one could not tell the story of dancing heroines without invoking all these other dancing women. The Anglo-Indian backup dancer Edwina Lyons remembers in her memoir that her sister Philomena's "legs were used for Madhubala's legs in a couple of films" and that the star came "to her personally and [thanked] her for it."[21] In *Pakeezah*'s (Kamal Amrohi, 1972) final dance number, "*Teer-e-nazar dekhenge*," Meena Kumari's *Kathak* footwork on broken glass was performed by her dancing double, Padma Khanna (see ⓥ video 00.02). In these instances, the figure of the on-screen dancing woman quite literally folds in the limbs, torsos, and gestures of various and variously coded dancing bodies. Helen and Vyjayanthimala co-choreographed the varied attractions of "*Muqabla humse na karo*." Also, analyzing the construction of Vyjayanthimala's star text as a classical dancer-actress through her interactions with choreographers like the traditional *Bharatanatyam nattuvanar* V. S. Muthuswami Pillai, or the *Kathak*-trained Hiralal and Sohanlal, whom she introduced to the Bombay film industry, produces a richer account of the labor involved in the production of the film dance number. Typically having a longer career span than the star, the figure of the choreographer gestures to the longue durée of industry practices and logics. Madhuri Dixit has been credited with marking a momentous shift in the idiom of popular Hindi film dance in the 1980s and 1990s. When we read her sensational dance moves as skilled copies of those conceived by her ingenious choreographer doppelgänger, Saroj Khan, we begin to formulate a corporeal history that is peopled by many bodies, with agency and authorship dispersed over numerous acknowledged and invisibilized actors.

Reading these dancing women alongside each other produces a history shot through with insurgencies and digressions that often proliferate within the dancing heroine's body itself, which narrates an approved linear history but also divulges the mutinous ones always associated with publicly performing women. Rather than posit a straightforward subversion or resistance hypothesis in relation to dancing women in twentieth-century India, *Dancing Women* explores how power shifts and circulates among multiple agents at different historical moments, between *devadasi* and brahmin reformer, *tawaif* and film director, dancer-actress and choreographer, heroine and vamp. In their movement through changing registers of performance, dancing women produce a shifting terrain of agency, subjection, visibility, and erasure. Mirroring the mobility of dancing women, their history also resists stability, traversing multiple intertwined enunciations of gendered modes of being and moving. By placing Azurie and Sadhona Bose, Waheeda Rehman and Vyjayanthimala, Madhuri Dixit and Saroj Khan alongside each other in the following chapters, with frequent digressions to Balasaraswati, Rukmini Devi Arundale, Fearless Nadia, Cuckoo, Helen, Sridevi, various choreographers and assistant choreographers, this book emphasizes how the performative repertoires of these dancing women fold upon each other in varied manifestations that contain overt and subterranean traces of dancing women before and beside them. Tracing the gestural genealogies of film dance produces a very different narrative of Bombay cinema and indeed of South Asian cultural modernities, by way of a corporeal history produced through an interlinked network of remarkable dancing women, co-creating from multiple locations.

"When I think of Dancers, I think of their Bodies": Cine-Corporeal Frameworks of Film Dance

In her book *Dancefilm*, Erin Brannigan remarks on the need for more dialogue between film studies and dance studies: "Dance theory offers understandings of the moving body and its ability to produce and express meanings that are particularly useful for addressing both popular film genres and other categories of dancefilm."²² The corporeal specificity of dancer-actors, what Brannigan describes as their "idiogest," defines the gestural parameters not just of that performer, but also the overall character of the films in which they appear,²³ encouraging us to read cinema as a kinesthetic field that mobilizes moving bodies and technologies to move the spectator in particular ways. Reading film corporeally fundamentally alters our theorization of cinematic performance, spatial organization, and labor networks. Dance scholar Sally Ness remarks, "When I think of dancers, I think of their bodies," elaborating that "[i]n dance, the mind's 'I' can become variable, and may inhabit the person in an infinite number of ways, investing the authority of the first person in different body parts, or in the whole body simultaneously in any number of spatio-temporal relationships."²⁴ When we consider film performance through the lens of movement and dance, acting becomes reconfigured as a choreographic phenomenon. Attention to the thick materiality of laboring, moving bodies reinvests theories of performance with corporeal presence. In the case of popular Indian cinema, while it is routinely acknowledged that performance is self-aware, rather than driven by the realist goal of a performer's full immersion in a role, theories of dance are centrally important for understanding why and how these acting traditions developed in a cinema marked by its mix of presentational and representational styles, where actors are required to move through a range of performance modalities: naturalistic and non-naturalistic, transparent and opaque, individuated and mythic. In Chapter 4, to parse responses to Vyjayanthimala's acting, I turn to performance treatises like the *Natya Shastra* and the *Abhinaya Darpana* to trace cultural theorizations of embodiment.²⁵ Without erasing the complicated history of this textual tradition or essentializing older performative traditions, one may find ways to engage with them for their hermeneutic potential to reveal certain cultural and social attitudes toward performance, especially when we read these texts' body-centered aesthetics translated through the evolving embodied knowledges of *devadasi*s, *tawaif*s, dancer-actresses, choreographers, backup dancers, reality TV show participants, and the like. The delineation, in Indian aesthetic treatises, of the production of affect through a series of physical actions provides clues to the corporeally grounded conventions of performance and reception that inform, however tangentially, dance-trained actors in Indian cinema. When dancer-actors bring to film these conventions of representation from codified styles of dance, they deeply alter the melodramatic-realist mode of acting in popular film and indeed the very structuring of the film's narrative content and affective architecture. Vyjayanthimala, trained in a recently textualized Bharatanatyam in the 1940s, marshals the language of this dance training in describing her own experience with film acting: "I never had any training in theater. Dance has been the most crucial component in my evolving as an actress. Dancing is so much of *bhava* (mood) and *abhinaya* (expression of emotion)."[26] Her contemporary, Waheeda Rehman, ascribes her famed emotive abilities to her training in *Bharatanatyam*, recalling the director Guru Dutt's comment, "She did the song in *Pyaasa* well because she is a dancer. She knows how to give silent expressions."[27] While focused on Indian dancer-actors in particular, a conceptual framework built around moving bodies can extend to other cinemas and other kinds of bodies undergirded by movement, whether acrobatic, vaudevillian, comic, or sporting.

Much of the study of Hindi film song-and-dance numbers has focused on music, mise-en-scène, the relationship of the musical number to the narrative, and has treated the song-and-dance sequence as a combined entity.[28] *Dancing Women*'s focus on the display and mobilization of the dancing body proposes new models for theorizing the Hindi film song-and-dance sequence. It advances questions asked less often of the song-and-dance composite form, such as: How do dancer-actors impact the cinematic narratives and the music composed for them? What is the difference in our spectatorial engagement with dance numbers and with song sequences? How is the on-screen mobility and stardom of the dancer-actress constructed differently than that of actresses not renowned for their dancing skills? These inquiries are generative of new frameworks for analyzing labor, production economies, cultural memory of the cinema, and taste hierarchies. In Chapter 1, I outline a body-centered taxonomy of song-and-dance sequences, and through a choreomusicological approach that studies music and dance as being in a state of mutual implication or possession, propose that in the case of certain famed dancer-actors, a desired dance vocabulary precedes and influences the conceptualization of the song. This proposal for a process that I term *dance musicalization* suggests that the inclusion of dancer-actors may alter the music composed in popular Hindi films so that it responds to their dancing skills and bodily comportment. The dancer-actor thus impacts the choice of music composer, playback singer(s), song lyrics, broad musical influences (Western, Indian, classical, folk, etc.), the structure of the musical composition (melody, beat, vocals and instrumentation, solo and chorus sections), and through these, the affective figurations of the composed music. Relatedly, I advance the notion of a multi-bodied *choreomusicking body* that draws our attention not only to the on-screen performers' gestural repertoire, but also to off-screen music production, art direction, costume, makeup, and other industry practices.

Each chapter attends to the ways in which the presence of the dancer-actress provides an impetus for technological changes (only song-and-dance sequences being shot in color in the early 1950s, for example), production innovations (cinematography, makeup and costume, sets and props, editing), and emphasis on the significance of certain industry personnel (music composers, playback singers, choreographers). While a number of the films considered in the book are conceptualized in order to "exploit" the dancing skills of dancer-actresses, the female performers in turn wrest cinematic authorship by producing narratives that reflect the power of their performing bodies, and by defining regimes of cinematic representation that are not circumscribed by male desire and intent alone. What these dancing women propose is that we cannot read them with a unitary gaze, but that the production of gender and of spectacle happens in complex, multi-sensory ways. By analyzing how the dancing woman's harnessing of cinematic technologies to capture her moving body renders the dance number a site of maximal formal innovation, a "techno-spectacle," *Dancing Women* calls for a reconsideration of spectacle within film studies. Rather than limit the reading of the techno-spectacle of the dancing woman to the framework of ideological suspicion (in relation to the male gaze, industrial exploitation, and the like), a corporeally grounded critical gaze notices how these techno-spectacles work to generate pleasure, determining the very comportment of our bodies as we watch films, and remaining often as our only memories of certain films. Far from being extraneous interruptions to the filmic narrative, dance and music are central to the cinematic staging of techno-spectacle, with oriental dance spectaculars, courtesan films, and dance melodramas especially conceived to showcase new technologies, including color stock, special effects, and cinematographic and editing innovations.

Attention to the industrial organization of labor in producing different parts of the disaggregated popular film form, and, in Chapter 2, a focus on spatial configurations of film dance make apparent that the dancing body is not only a biological object, but also a mode of perception and expression that operates as a site of encounter with spaces and objects, producing a textured system of folds between subjectivities, surfaces, and sensations. Intermedial theorizations of cinema, music, and dance help us understand the production of and our responses to dermal, architectural, audiovisual folds where multiple performance and labor practices conjoin their materialities and intensities. The methodological import of such an intermedial reading practice is not limited to analyzing musical sequences in films. It can alert us to kinesthetic articulations of gesture—in actors, but also as expressed in cinematographic, editing, and other production *gestures* that develop and change in different industrial formations. A focus on dance can thus help us read genre codes as corporeal, generating affects as embodied phenomena.

Reading the dancing body as scripting and scripted by Hindi cinema's signifying practices advances new histories of the female body in the Bombay film industry—corporeal histories not necessarily forged by coherent visions and unified social groups, but relationally, across axes of caste, class, religion, and region. Corporeal histories disrupt linear narratives of movement—from salon to stage to screen dance—and of hierarchies—between performer and choreographer, heroine and vamp. An account of the careers of Sadhona Bose, Azurie, and Vyjayanthimala has to take into account their constant movement between screen and stage, and the respectability accorded to each at different historical junctures. Rather than ossified histories of media as following one after the other, we follow their pleating through the bodies that inhabit and enliven these media. Saroj Khan's continuing six-decade-plus career in Bombay cinema, or Madhuri Dixit's career over three decades as heroine, item dancer, and reality television star alert us to the power of dancing women in mobilizing a range of media for displaying their corporeal expressivities and intensities. Corporeal histories, by their nature, are unfinished histories. Moving bodies, after all, are slippery, and embodiment is a complex mode of inhabitation of performance traditions that does not always leave clear textual or archival traces. *Dancing Women* offers, then, a provisional, gap-filled history that invites additional or counter archives in the form of other bodies that destabilize this narrative, that enter into this choreography of corporeal histories with their own moves. The dancing women who choreograph this narrative through movement vocabularies they introduce into the cinema or remove from it, who are acclaimed and written off at different moments, hailed and forgotten, are protean figures, shape-shifting through the webs of patriarchal, industrial practices, traversing foreground and background spaces, producing in the process a variegated, textured history of dance, music, theater, and cinema. In the following two sections, I provide a brief history of the cine-corporeal transformations wrought by dance in Indian cinema, and responses to these new mobilities corpo-realized by dancing women.

Pre-Playback Dance in Indian Cinema

As forms invested in the exploration and exhibition of movement, cinema and dance have had a long history of engagement. Cinema enlisted dance from its very beginnings. In films like *Dickson Experimental Sound Film* (William K. L. Dickson, 1894) and *Annabelle the Dancer* (William K. L. Dickson, William Heise, 1895), the Edison Manufacturing Company used dancers to demonstrate to first-time spectators cinema's propensity for the spectacular display of movement (see ⊙ video 00.03). The shared investment in movement ensured a "spontaneous intermediality" between early cinema and dance, with traditional or exotic dances frequently featured during the first decade of cinema.[29] Laurent Guido situates the emergence of cinema in a context of intense aesthetic and scientific preoccupation with bodily movement: "Dance, just as sports and gymnastics, imposed itself at the beginning of the 20th century as a harmonious way of organizing body movement. It was considered that the muscular mimicry put into motion by physical performance would position [film] spectators under an irresistible rhythmic spell."[30] Dance, along with acrobatics and other forms of physical display, was employed to showcase the immense kinesthetic potential of the new medium of film. Douglas Rosenberg delineates the relationship of dance and the architectural specificity of the film camera through a discussion of how Eadweard Muybridge, Thomas Edison, the Lumière brothers, Etienne-Jules Marey, Thomas Eakins, and others in the late nineteenth and early twentieth centuries were primarily concerned with the phenomenology of bodies in motion as apprehended by optical technologies.[31] Since Edison's camera was unmoving and anchored to a tripod, he employed dancers to supply motion to the frame. "The visualization of choreography on film reinforces that what we are a witness to is indeed the passing of time. This sort of concrete use of dance as a metronome to prove cinema is the earliest incarnation of the relationship of dance to the moving image," notes Rosenberg.[32] Nell Andrew and Tom Gunning discuss early cinema's fascination with Loie Fuller's serpentine dance, which enables what Andrew terms the "serpentine films," of which more than thirty were made between 1894 and 1910,[33] to demonstrate the shifts between two and three dimensions, motion and stillness, the foundations of what Gunning terms the "cinema of attractions" that delights in movement and rhythm.

In India, the titles of early films such as *Dancing Scenes from the Flower of Persia* (Hiralal Sen, 1898), *Dances from Alibaba* (Hiralal Sen, 1903), and *Dancing of Indian Nautch Girls* (Elphinston Bioscope, 1906) suggest a similar interest in capturing dance on celluloid, even if the films no longer exist. In *Raja Harishchandra* (D. G. Phalke, 1917), the surviving remake of D. G. Phalke's 1913 version of the same film, considered to be the first Indian narrative film, we see an instance of devotional singing and dancing, while D. G. Phalke's later films, *Lanka Dahan* (1917) and *Kaliya Mardan* (1919), feature more elaborate dances, drawing from folk dance forms. In the surviving segment of *Lanka Dahan*, we see the *asura* (demon) women dance around the kidnapped Sita with spears in their hands, while *Kaliya Mardan* features multiple instances of dance. In the episode where Krishna plays the flute, boys prance around trees, and women (male actors dressed as women) perform a *raas*-style dance with sticks (see ⏵ video 00.04). Group dances in these early silent films draw from folk dance idioms to produce a sense of community. While the films do not survive, there are reports of dance segments and dancing girl characters in films from the 1920s such as *Andhare Alo* (*The Influence of Love*, Sisir Bhaduri, Naresh Mitra, 1922), *Pati Bhakti* (*Human Emotions*, J. J. Madan, 1922), *Nartaki Tara* (Jyotish Banerjee, 1922), and *Kalyan Khajina* (*The Treasures of Kalyan*, Baburao Painter, 1925).[34] The recently recovered segments of *Bilwamangal* (Rustomji Dhotiwala, 1919) provide a thrilling glimpse of cinematic engagement with musical and dance performance. The extended salon sequence showcasing the film's courtesan protagonist, Chintamani, played by popular stage actress Miss Gohar, includes a seated song performance (Figure I.2), followed by her dance. The carefully staged tableau that centers Miss Gohar amidst her musicians and her appreciative audience produces what Anupama Kapse refers to as "aural images" that emphasize gestures, facial expressions, and bodily movements to capture "the musical mode, or melos, of Indian theatrical precedents."[35] Even though we cannot hear the music, the sequence palpably vibrates with the moving energies of song and dance performance.

By the time we get to the late silent film, *Diler Jigar* (*Gallant Hearts*, G. P. Pawar, 1931), one of the few surviving pre-sound Indian films, we notice a movement away from the tableau presentation, and multiple dynamization techniques employed to present the heroine, Saranga's (Lalita Pawar) dance performance (see ⏵ video 00.05). Along with her brother, Balbheem, and her

Figure I.2. Still from *Bilwamangal* (Rustomji Dhotiwala, 1919).
Credit: Screen capture.

friend, Hameer, Saranga is part of a traveling acrobat troupe. The intertitle announces: "Witness our unique dance, marvelous and unsurpassed." In a long shot, we see Saranga's dance and the spectating audience circled around the three performers. The scene cuts to a medium close-up of her shimmying with a knife and a tambourine, followed by a dissolve to the audience. We see close-ups of her face with the tambourine, and medium shots of her shaking her hips and tapping the tambourine on her shoulders seductively. The transitions between performer and audience, and between long, medium, and close-up shots set up a grammar for the display of the dancing body. The camera is static, but Saranga constantly moves toward and away from it to generate dynamism within the frame. Despite the absence of sound, we get a sense of rhythm from her movements, her tambourine and the drum that Balbheem plays, and the frequent intercutting between shots at varying camera distance. The ideological import of a dancing heroine is already in evidence, provoking the rest of the film's events. A corrupt army chief tries to take Saranga away from her street performance, claiming he has paid her price, to which Hameer retorts, "You have paid for the dance. How dare you take liberties with her?" Saranga is soon kidnapped by the tyrannical king, evoking associations between dance, spectacle, and sexual labor mobilized by the late nineteenth-century anti-*nautch* movement. Belonging to the stunt film genre popularized in part by the phenomenal success in India of Douglas Fairbanks's *The Thief of Baghdad* (Raoul Walsh, 1924),[36] *Diler Jigar* adds dance to the mix of swashbuckling action, elaborately choreographed swordfights, and acrobatics to generate a hectic spectacle of attractions that would come to define the masala film form of popular Hindi cinema.

With the introduction of sound in 1931, the song-and-dance sequence was publicized as a standard attraction of popular film narratives. Like the early talkies in Hollywood, advertisements from Indian film magazines in the 1930s show that many films were marketed as "all talking, singing, dancing" films. For instance, advertisements for the first sound film, *Alam Ara* (Ardeshir Irani, 1931), describe it as "100% talking, singing, dancing."[37] While talking and singing demonstrate the new aural capacities of sound cinema, the inclusion of dance in the trio of talkie descriptors promises the added dynamism that the movement vocabulary of dance would bring to the sound film, combining pre-sound cinema's preoccupation with capturing movement and the novelty of synchronized sound-image relations. In reality, most of the sound films made between 1931 and 1935 (when the playback system was introduced) featured very static song-and-dance sequences since image and sound had to be recorded simultaneously, which restricted the movement of performers.[38] Until the introduction of playback singing, the on-screen comportment of dancing bodies was determined by sound recording technologies that required musicians to lurk off-screen but close to the microphones, and actors to remain absolutely static as they sang into these hidden microphones. Music composer Naushad Ali describes song picturization during this period: "Not only microphones, but musicians were also hidden from the camera view. On location . . . at Powai Lake, some musicians were perched on the trees with their instruments and some sat at the very edge of the lake."[39] Gregory Booth pays close attention to this liminal, technologically defined period between silent film and playback in India, noting that the need to simultaneously record sound and image resulted in a relative lack of movement by the camera and actors, as well as in long shot durations, as cutting would produce aural discontinuity. This is especially evident in a dance sequence he discusses from *Ayodhyecha Raja* (V. Shantaram, 1932), where a dancing girl performing for the gods first sings a short song in a medium long shot, and then dances to accompanying music (but does not sing) in an extreme long shot. "[T]he dancer either sings or dances; she never does both," remarks Booth, adding that, "[b]ecause the singing portions of her performance were constrained by microphone placement issues, she moves her arms and her head, but remains rooted in her designated position near the microphone. Once she shifts from song to dance, she becomes more completely mobile."[40] The contrast between this static song-and-dance sequence in a sound film and Saranga's dynamic dancing in the silent film *Diler Jigar*, released a year prior to *Ayodhyecha Raja*, highlights the restrictions placed upon the dancing body by new sound technologies.

It is with the introduction of the playback system in 1935, when songs began to be pre-recorded and played back while the actors "lip-synched" the lyrics for the camera, that popular Indian film dance begins to form its contours.[41] The playback system, an important technological and cultural phenomenon for Indian cinema and its figurations, impacted film dance in two ways. The separation of aural and visual tracks allowed actors greater mobility, which eventually enabled the production of elaborately staged dance numbers.[42] Additionally, it enabled, by the 1940s, the separation of acting and singing so that a set of off-screen playback singers (also known as "ghost voices" until the late 1940s) became the voice for a range of actors, some of whom came to prominence for their dancing abilities. In Hollywood, as McLean notes, the musical star had to conform to two largely antithetical regimes, "one concerned with the production of the star voice, and another engaged with producing an idealized star body to mime that production,"[43] which could produce fractured texts for stars like Judy Garland, tormented by simultaneous aural and visual ideals of perfect singing and dancing bodies. In popular Indian cinema, on the other hand, playback singing allowed for the construction of what Neepa Majumdar describes as a dual star text, produced through the combination of the playback singer's voice and multiple actors' bodies.[44] Shikha Jhingan discusses how the technology of playback contributed to the independent but related construction of aural and visual stardom "as the playback singer spent considerable amount of time in rehearsing a song, working on the diction, the expressions, the breathing and the tonal quality that a song demanded" while the on-screen actors used the recorded song as a referent, emoting according to the expressive registers of the pre-recorded voice.[45] "It has also been pointed out that the female star could now concentrate more on her make-up and her looks and not worry about the '*sur*,'" remarks Jhingan.[46] In the following chapters, the focus on dance in the construction of female stardom from the 1930s to the 1990s will call our attention to significant differences in the dual star text when the on-screen actress is also an acclaimed dancer. When combined with an on-screen dancing body, the playback singer's persona may be mobilized to attenuate or intensify the display of the female body and its attendant meanings.

Chapter 1 includes a discussion of how dancing bodies call for different genres of song and registers of voice, pointing to altered constructions of the dual star text and of female presence on and off the screen.

"Seductive, Spectacular, and Fast": Attitudes toward Hindi Film Dance

Like the other elements of the Hindi film form, including melodrama, comedy, music, and action sequences, film dance draws from a range of popular cultural forms circulating in the late nineteenth and early twentieth centuries. The popular theatrical forms of this period—the *Nautanki*, Parsi theater, and *Tamasha*—as well as the folk form of *Jatra* all feature a combination of romance, melodrama, comic sequences, and song-and-dance numbers.[47] Additionally, various regional folk dance forms like *Bhangra*, *Raas Lila*, *Lavani*, *Ghoomar*, *Garba*, and *Dandiya*, among others, have inspired the dance idioms of popular Hindi cinema. The two most common classical dance influences on Hindi film dance come from the North Indian *Kathak* and the South Indian *Bharatanatyam*. In rewriting the content, style, and intent of classical and folk dances and through its adaptation of various local and foreign movement vocabularies, film dance articulated new affective registers to respond to a growing film viewing public from the 1930s. Foreign dance forms such as belly dancing, the waltz, the cha-cha-cha, the twist, and swing featured extensively in Hindi film dance from the 1930s through the 1960s, disco through the 1970s and 1980s, while post-90s Bollywood incorporates elements of jazz, hip hop, salsa, etc.[48] The Hollywood musical has been a significant influence on popular Indian film dance, and song-and-dance sequences in Hindi cinema manifest a range of borrowings and departures from it.

The adroit and hectic heterogeneity of Hindi film dance makes it a profoundly modern dance form that counters accounts of the absence of modern dance in India. However, the promiscuity of Hindi film dance's borrowings and its alleged corruption of dance forms provoked a range of reactions from a variety of commentators. In *Indian Talkies 1931–1956* (published by the Film Federation of India to mark the twenty-fifth anniversary of the Indian talkie), the cultural revivalist E. Krishna Iyer, a key figure in the gentrification of the *devadasi* dance form of *Sadirattam* into the "classical" dance form *Bharatanatyam*, complains that in its use of music and dance, "the screen has vitiated and even vulgarised the tastes of the masses, ... regaling them with exotic, or hybrid or other types of art with scant regard for national traditions."[49] In the same publication, the acclaimed *Kathak* dancer, Sitara Devi, who began her career by dancing a range of "hybrid" numbers in Hindi films from the mid-1930s to the mid-1940s, remarks,

> In films ... dancing, especially that of the classical variety had little expression. Any type of hip-movement passed for dancing ... our choreographers put Rambha [sic] and Samba or mixed the western system with distorted "Mudras" [hand or facial gestures] of our classical forms. Sometimes it becomes difficult to classify a dance number in a film. It neither appears classical nor folk.[50]

The always unflattering comparison with classical dance is a regular feature in the critical reception of Hindi film dance. In a 1957 issue of the popular film magazine *Filmfare*, the writer notes, "the classical dance is like pure mathematics, calculus, for example, and the film dance is like the simple proposition that two and two make four."[51] It is worth noting that the anxiety regarding the hybridity of film dance and its effect on public taste is most marked in journalistic discourse of the 1950s and 1960s, when the impetus to canonize national dance forms was at its zenith. In a 1952 *Filmfare* article titled "Dance Forms of West Corrupt Our Films," the classical dancer Satyavaty declaims, "A glance at one of the dances exhibited in our Indian films is enough to make an intelligent person recoil in sheer disgust."[52] This divide in the figuration of the "intelligent person," that is, the classical dance *rasika* or informed viewer, and the lumpenized film spectator abets the construction of an elite cultural class, and produces hierarchies of taste in the public realm in these formative decades. Mohan Khokar, a dance scholar who, through his books on Indian classical and folk dance forms, became a central figure in the pedagogical project of educating a new citizenry on its cultural heritage, notes of film dance: "The style of the dance was on very rare occasions classical; mostly it was a mixture of glamour and tinsel, often leaning heavily towards vulgarity. In fact, the dance in the Indian film came to be associated with a lack of purpose and a certain cheapness in taste, designated in common parlance as 'filmi.'"[53] The vernacular adjective *filmi*, regularly employed in fan magazines as well, is used to designate popular Hindi cinema's inflated rhetoric and aesthetic of excess, standing in pejorative opposition to the classical, the realistic, the tasteful.

Another set of responses to Hindi film dance center around the place of dance in the film narrative:

> In films, dances are merely "inserts." They are meant to further the story (this they rarely do), but mainly they are in the nature of embellishment to the picture for the purposes of the box-office. As embellishment, therefore, film dance must primarily appeal to the eye. It must be seductive, spectacular and fast in movement.... The film dance pleases the eye, titillates the mind, and is forgotten in a little while.[54]

The writer enlists here a set of descriptors of film dance that continue to circulate to this day—as a spectacular distraction from the main narrative, recruiting the body for visual pleasure, and as a forgettable low art form that is primarily directed at commercial success. On account of the predominance of female on-screen dancers, discussions of film dance also often revolve around questions of sexuality, gender norms, and body cultures. In a 1966 feature titled "Dance in Cinema: Gimmick or Necessity," the writer summarizes anxieties about the plurality of styles that marks the realm of popular entertainment and the participation of the heroine within this system: "In most films it is the heroine herself who is called upon to perform the dance.... The dance is usually a rehash of movements picked at random from Indian and western dances—hardly in tune with the dignity and purpose of the heroine's role.... a serious film-maker must understand that the heroine is not a mere entertainer."[55] Discourses around popular film dance underscore fraught relations between the elite and the popular, the respectable and the disreputable, highlighting the drive toward homogeneity by the nation-state and the radical heterogeneity of popular cultural forms. *Dancing Women* analyzes these discursive formations around gender, female mobility, and public presence by theorizing and historicizing Indian film dance within multiple intersecting frameworks. Grounded in a close reading of female performers' skills, training, labor, and socio-cinematic figurations, the book reads these star texts with reference to shifting relations of gender and respectability, theorizing them in relation to dramatic theories of dance and performance that are responsive to historical shifts themselves, and historicizing them within the trajectory of the nation and certain modes of cultural institutionalization, for instance, through a discussion of the anti-*nautch* movement (Chapter 3), the setting up of organizations like the *Sangeet Natak Akademi* (Chapter 4), and economic deregulation in the 1990s (Chapter 5).

The first two chapters outline the conceptual frameworks that will be employed to undertake the analyses of particular dancer-actresses in the latter three chapters. In Chapter 1, a dance-centered taxonomy of musical numbers, as well as a discussion of how dance enables agency and authorship, lead to a reconsideration of the term *song picturization*, which suggests the primacy of the song as setting the agenda for the on-screen images. I propose instead that in the case of certain dance numbers or famed dancer-actors, a reverse process of *dance musicalization* may be at work, where a desired dance vocabulary precedes and influences the composition of the song. This disruption of the given logics of production and authorship spurs the conceptualization of a multi-bodied *choreomusicking body*, which directs our attention to the many on- and off-screen bodies laboring to produce the song-and-dance number, and fundamentally shifts ideological readings of narrative and spectacle in popular Hindi cinema. Employing choreomusicological theory, historical accounts of dancer-actors' influence on musical composition, and spectatorial responses to the music-dance composite, this chapter proposes new models for theorizing the Hindi film song-and-dance sequence.

Chapter 2 develops a body-space-movement framework that studies the spaces of dance, the movement vocabularies used, and the resulting construction of star bodies to engage in a broader discussion of cinematic representation and the production of gender. This framework is employed to uncover the production processes behind the fetishized space of the Hindi film cabaret, an "architecture of public intimacy" whose spatial and choreographic operations arouse intense sensorial stimulation, with audiences experiencing a gamut of ocular, acoustic, haptic, and gustatory affects. Through a focus on cabaret numbers featuring the dancing star Helen, this chapter discusses the cine-choreographic practices that produce a particular collision of infrastructures, bodies, and spaces, rendering the mediated sensorium of the cabaret an intensely experimental cinematic and performative space. This chapter also employs the body-space-movement framework to analyze Hindi film dance in relation to Indian classical and folk dance forms. Borrowing from the elaborate lexicon of dance movements in Indian treatises like the *Natya Shastra* and *Abhinaya Darpana*, I deconstruct the dancing female body into three broad categories—the face, the torso, and the limbs. Each of these *body zones* is capable of a variety of addresses, depending on the deployment of their constituent parts, and the social connotations of those gestural articulations at certain historical moments.

Chapter 3 focuses on Azurie and Sadhona Bose, once-famous, now-forgotten dancing stars of the 1930s–1940s, to excavate a dense, intersecting, global history of early twentieth-century discourses on dance and on dancing women that features oriental dancers like Ruth St. Denis, the prima ballerina Anna Pavlova, and cultural reformers in the subcontinent, including Rabindranath Tagore, Uday Shankar, and Rukmini Devi Arundale, among many others. Situating Bose, the Bengali *bhadramahila*, and Azurie, an Indo-German "dancing girl," as co-choreographers of new mobilities throws light on cosmopolitan, transnational dance networks that intersected with nationalist projects of modernity. The 1930s and 1940s are a critical period for studying discursive formations around dance, with the so-called revival of classical dance forms, which involved an appropriation of the cultural practices of traditional performers like *devadasi*s and *tawaif*s by upper-caste, upper-class performers. Reading Bose and Azurie's performing bodies and careers alongside each other dislodges unitary accounts of the impulses and controversies around dance on film by a new class of urban performers. In their spirited and skillful production of and participation in a global circuit of entertainment economies, Azurie and Bose marshal dance to co-choreograph new mobilities in this late colonial period.

A focus on two *Bharatanatyam*-trained stars in the 1950s and 1960s, the Tamil Hindu Vyjayanthimala and the Tamil Muslim Waheeda Rehman, sets up, in Chapter 4, an analysis of film dance in relation to the newly independent Indian state's canonization and marginalization of what come to be categorized as "classical" and "folk" dance forms through the *Sangeet Natak Akademi*, Republic Day parades, and other canon-defining mechanisms. The encounter between a newly Sanskritized *Bharatanatyam* and a Hindi film industry newly encountering South Indian actresses trained in this dance form produces certain corporeal and expressive diagrams of ideal femininity along linguistic and religious lines, with Vyjayanthimala figured as an accomplished dancer who needed to prove her acting abilities and all-India appeal, and Waheeda Rehman as a "natural" Hindi film actress who did not fit the mold of a *Bharatanatyam* dancer. By studying how dance training influences acting repertoires, this chapter calls attention to movement, gesture, and bodily comportment to alter our understanding of virtuosity and technique, proposing a movement-based analysis of film acting that accords value to kinesthetic performance and spectatorship. This account of film dance in the 1950s and 60s is populated as well by the many off-screen bodies laboring to stage dance spectacle, including *nattuvanar*s, assistant choreographers, and backup dancers who constitute the extensive choreomusicking body at work on production numbers. Rehman and Vyjayanthimala's most ambitious dance numbers speak to their own performative desires as trained dancers, even as within the film narratives, these spectacular sequences reveal the sustained tensions between public performance and constructions of ideal femininity. Films featuring these A-list actresses as dancing protagonists evince a generic tendency I refer to as the *melodrama of dance reform*, which, like Sadhona Bose's "dance socials" in the 1940s, combine the dance spectacular with the "social problem" film, producing in the process cinematic figurations riven with aspirations and anxieties around female sexuality, bodily movement, and economic independence. In narrativizing dance as work, these films deploy the dichotomies of *devi* and *bai* (wife and courtesan) to negotiate the figure of the dancing woman, who is a source of both pleasure and danger, fascination and revulsion.

With her vigorously libidinous dancing, her infamous "*jhatkas* and *matkas*" (breast pulses, hip and waist undulations), Madhuri Dixit, the leading Hindi film actress of the late 1980s and the 1990s, initiated the consolidation of the figures of the brazen vamp and the coy heroine, sparking censorship controversies and an entirely new movement vocabulary for the Hindi film heroine. Dixit's moves carried the unmistakable imprint of the choreographer who led her to stardom, Saroj Khan. Moving from backup dancer in the 1950s to assistant choreographer in the 1960s and 1970s, to an independent, famed choreographer from the 1980s to the present, Khan's body constitutes a remarkable, embodied archive of Bombay cinema's industrial practices in relation to dance performance and choreography. Chapter 5 delves into Khan and Dixit's co-choreography of a new style of movement, reading choreography as an archival-corporeal system of transmission and transformation that articulates body cultures, industrial systems, and labor networks. A focus on training, rehearsal, and collaboration foregrounds the creative processes in their co-choreography that produced new techniques of the body, which both women continue to build on with richly intermedial careers in film, reality TV dance shows, and on web platforms.

Through dancing women from Bengal (Sadhona Bose), Tamil Nadu (Vyjayanthimala and Rehman), and Maharashtra (Dixit), we may apprehend the logics of regionality and how they impact the form and idiom of the purportedly "all-India" Hindi film. The book's focus on these performers facilitates the mapping of pivotal moments in Hindi film dance—the 1930s and 1940s, when the introduction of sound initiates an enduring song-and-dance vocabulary and when classical dance is appropriated by middle- and upper-class practitioners; the decades of the 1950s and 1960s, during which the newly independent nation canonizes dance forms even as films with dancer protagonists reveal recurrent tensions that illuminate the tenuous place of the female dancer and the film actress in the national imaginary; and the initiation in the 1990s of a new movement vocabulary for the heroine that marks the collapse of the coy heroine–salacious vamp binary and provokes outrage, extended censorship battles, and hectic strategies of recuperation of the iconic woman of the nation. The regulation of dance practices and movement vocabularies often mark attitudes toward and anxieties about women's visibility, mobility, and participation in the public sphere, allowing for an analysis of the place of the female protagonist within the film narrative, as well as that of the actress in public discourse. The introduction of dance into the performance repertoire of the Hindi film heroine repeatedly produced fractured narratives, split characters, and doubled personas. Through a focus on genealogical and professional histories, training, and labor, this book adopts this formal fracturing and doubling as a methodological invitation to produce a different kind of narrative about female labor in the Bombay film industry, one that centers experimentation, collaboration, and mastery in the careers of Hindi cinema's dancing women.

1
Dance Musicalization and the Choreomusicking Body

Corporealizing Theoretical Frameworks of Film Dance and Music

On a dusky Bombay evening, I sit with my father, listening to the personally curated cassette tape compilation of songs by his favorite male playback singer: "Top Hits of Talat Mahmood."[1] Yet again, as one of his best-loved songs, "*Jalte hain jiske liye*" from *Sujata* (Bimal Roy, 1959) comes on, he expresses his annoyance that this poignant *ghazal* is transmitted through the prosaic medium of a telephone. He carps peevishly at one of Mahmood's finest songs being "wasted" on the up-and-coming actor Sunil Dutt, with his simpering smile: "Oh, only Dilip Kumar could have done justice to Talat in that song" (see ⓥ video 01.01). As a result of what he deems a banal song picturization, his verdict is that this song, which perfectly showcases the mellifluous cadences of Mahmood's voice, is better *heard* than *watched*. My father's cinephilic response points to issues of crucial import for the study of the Hindi film song-and-dance sequence regarding the importance of song picturization for the appreciation of film music, and the "matching" of bodies and voices to produce the perfect dual-star text of playback singer and on-screen performer.[2] Pondering his judgment about "*Jalte hain jiske liye*" (even as for me the point of cathexis in that song picturization is the actress Nutan's ability to cry so movingly on-screen, the tears welling up in the first cutaway to her and finally running down her cheek in the next), I wonder aloud if such a purely aural engagement ("better heard than watched") is possible with *dance* numbers. Tellingly, this is not a category that many serious-minded, old-school Hindi film music aficionados like my father pay much heed to. It prompts me, however, to think about what we hear and see when we engage with songs as compared to dance numbers, and what this might suggest about modes of production and reception. Even when we *listen to* rather than watch, for example, dance numbers like "*Hoton pe aisi baat*" (*Jewel Thief,* 1967), "*Choli ke peeche kya hai*" (*Khal Nayak,* 1993), or "*Dard-e-disco*" (*Om Shanti Om,* 2007), our memory is likely to conjure up, respectively, Vyjayanthimala's vigorous movements and swirling red skirt, Madhuri Dixit's rhythmically heaving bosom, and Shah Rukh Khan's sinuous gyrations and hands pumping toward the low-angle camera. These wide-ranging examples raise questions asked less often of the Hindi film song-and-dance composite form (and indeed of musical numbers in other cinematic contexts): Is our spectatorial engagement with dance numbers and song sequences qualitatively different? How do on-screen dancing bodies impact the music composed for them, as well as our reception of this music? Much of the analysis of song-and-dance numbers has treated the song-and-dance sequence as a combined entity. In this chapter, I explore ways in which a focus on dance in the popular Hindi film song-and-dance sequence can provide new models for theorizing this cinematic attraction.

Through a focus on the display and mobilization of the dancing body, I call for a reconsideration of the process of *song picturization*, a term commonly used in Hindi film production and in studies of this industry to reference the practice of recording the song first and then "adding" visuals to it. While "song picturization" suggests the primacy of the song as driving the image and our relationship to it, in the case of certain dance numbers or famed dancer-actors, a reverse process may instead be at work, where a desired dance vocabulary precedes and influences the composition of the song. While scholars have discussed song picturization as a central practice in the production of song-and-dance sequences,[3] this chapter proposes an alternate mode—of *dance musicalization*—to address differences in production and reception modalities when a dancer-actor is featured in a film or a musical number. Employing choreomusicological theory, historical accounts of dancer-actors' influence on musical composition, and spectatorial responses to the music-dance composite, I argue that the inclusion of dancer-actors may alter the music composed in popular Hindi films so that it responds to their dancing skills and bodily comportment. This may impact the choice of music composer, playback singer(s), song lyrics, broad musical influences (Western, Indian, classical, folk, etc.), the structure of the musical composition (melody, beat, vocals and instrumentation, solo and chorus sections), and thus the affective figurations of the composed music. The larger aim of attending to dance in this manner is to trouble the binary of music and dance in the song-and-dance sequence, whether in terms of expressive propensities or processual temporalities (i.e., what comes first).

Musical Numbers and the Cinematic Narrative

Studies of the Hollywood musical have categorized the genre into backstage and integrated musicals. The backstage musical is constructed around the staging of a musical performance or putting on a show, typically with protagonists who are professional entertainers. The musical numbers accumulate serially and are often standalone spectacles connected only loosely, if at all, to the narrative in which they are embedded. In the integrated musical, on the other hand, the numbers are woven into the narrative and are motivated by plot development and character psychology. The performers express their emotions to each other or to the audience through song and dance without the self-conscious invocation of a performance situation.[4] Popular Hindi cinema is both influenced by the Hollywood musical and markedly different from it in terms of generic configurations. Given the development of popular Hindi film as a multi-genre *masala* form, song-and-dance sequences feature as one of the many attractions in social melodramas, historical, horror, war, and gangster films, and in mythological and devotional genres specific to the sub-continent. Indeed, the genre of the musical does not exist separately in a popular cinema that is saturated with music and dance. The grammar of the Hindi film song-and-dance number and its relationship to the rest of the narrative is thus not always similar to that of the Hollywood musical number. This renders scholarship on the Hollywood musical useful but not entirely sufficient to discuss Hindi film music and dance. Unlike the Hollywood musical's adoption of the backstage or integrated form, for instance, the Hindi film is simply not as invested in the rationalization of the insertion of song-and-dance numbers into the film narrative. Adapting the performance modes of backstage and integrated musicals (that is, the foregrounding of singing and dancing skills or the expression of inner states of mind respectively in this binary formulation) to the expressive modes of the Hindi film, I propose a movement-based taxonomy of song-and-dance sequences that considers how singing and dancing bodies profoundly determine the organization and address of popular Indian cinema.[5]

The extensive and vital scholarship on song-and-dance sequences in Indian cinema has featured an emphasis on music, mise-en-scène, and the relationship of the song-and-dance sequence to the narrative.[6] In her analysis of Hindi film songs, Anna Morcom notes that some songs "are *overtly* situational, lacking coherence in their audio dimension, whereas others are more *implicitly* situational, working well on their own as well as working well with the film."[7] While Morcom's typology helps to think about the status of song sequences outside of the film narrative as stand-alone segments on television, CDs, and online platforms like YouTube, its focus is on the aural, semantic, and contextual dimensions of the song-and-dance sequence and the integration of the musical number into the narrative. Lalitha Gopalan offers an elaborate taxonomy of song-and-dance sequences in relation to Mani Ratnam's films, outlining five ways in which the director employs musical numbers to negotiate spatial and temporal discontinuities. Gopalan identifies song-and-dance sequences that regulate spatial disjunctions by propelling the narrative through multiple diegetic spaces in the space of the song, and those that condense or smooth over various events or temporal shifts in the narrative. A third type, which she terms the "Indian backstage musical," features a diegetic audience, and the coincidence between performance time and real time weaves the number into the narrative. The fourth and fifth categories concern the integration of the musical number into the narrative, with some numbers deliberately linked to it and others functioning as extra-diegetic sequences that abruptly break its spatial continuity.[8] Given Gopalan's focus on cinematic "interruptions," as well as Ratnam's conscious engagement with the question of narrative and song-and-dance integration, this taxonomy emphasizes the management of the anachronous song-and-dance sequence in relation to narrative space and time.

Commenting on the function of the song sequence in Hindi cinema, Sangita Gopal argues that the musical number is a critical device for accommodating the competing demands of pleasure and pedagogy placed upon popular Hindi cinema. Focusing on the romantic, conjugal couple, Gopal contends that the song sequence allows for the expression of desires proscribed by the narrative, which prohibits and curtails certain modes of enjoyment.[9] Where the narrative accommodates the demands of tradition, the song sequence affords the couple sovereignty and autonomous mobility, however temporary. While "the *narrative* relocation of the couple within the extended family/community is a sign of ideological closure," she points out that "the successful nucleation of the couple in the romantic duet and the intrusion of song and dance into the larger culture indicate Hindi film's social effectivity."[10] Hindi cinema thus employs this dual enunciation of the couple—in the narrative and the song sequence—not only to comply with current and dominant interests, but also to suggest emergent formations, respectively. In an article on film music and dance, Gopal and Biswarup Sen elaborate on these emergent formations, arguing that the song sequence "posits scenarios of modernity that the narrative is unable to depict, [...] envisions ways of acting and behaving not coded into the text, [...] registers the shock of the new not recordable by the prose of the film, and [...] affords the possibility of *jouissance* or joyous release that cannot be spoken by any character or voice."[11] Gopal and Sen's analysis provides a nuanced examination of the textual bifurcation between the narrative, which is the space of family and convention, and the song-and-dance sequence, in which a more radical and "modern" expression of freedom and desire can erupt.

A Movement-based Taxonomy of Song-and-Dance Sequences

While deeply valuable in theorizing the formal characteristics of popular Hindi cinema and relating these to the ideological construction of the narrative, most discussions of the song-and-dance sequence primarily focus on the aural dimension of the sequence, i.e., the song and its dissemination in the public realm, and on visual mise-en-scène elements such as foreign locations, lavish costumes, and the like.[12] This chapter employs and adapts these various typologies, but seeks to demonstrate in particular how figurations of the on-screen body fashioned by *dance* are critical to understanding the ideological project and spectatorial pleasures of popular Hindi cinema. Calling specific attention to dance (which includes a consideration of movement vocabulary, music, star bodies, mise-en-scène, cinematography, and editing) is necessary, as it is often the comportment of the dancing body in the song-and-dance sequence that is incommensurate with the construction and representation of performing bodies in the narrative. A focus on the dancing body highlights how dance movements interrupt narrative modes of being and moving, and how attention to this physical interruption or alteration of movement vocabulary is key to understanding production and reception modalities and economies. In the narrative, for instance, the performing body has a certain valence, but in the dance and "action" sequences of the film (corresponding typically, until the 1990s, to the female and male performers in the film), the same body is mobilized and displayed differently. In these sequences, the body is spectacularized through choreographed movements, costume, makeup, and particular cinematographic and editing techniques. The regime of performance, including facial expressions and physical movement, is significantly altered, as is the mode of reception.

Audiences pay much more attention, suddenly, to limbs and torsos and their movement through space. This immanence of the star body—of body as body, rather than as a vehicle for a diegetic character—makes dance numbers and action sequences central devices in constructing the iconicity of certain star bodies.[13] Calling specific attention to dance foregrounds differences between the narrative and song-and-dance sequences in terms of *movements* (walking/sitting/standing, etc., in the narrative vs. swaying, "running around trees," and other forms of dancing in the song-and-dance sequence), *spaces* (realistic vs. fantastic spaces or diegetic spaces vs. extra-diegetic excursions to the Swiss alps, for example), and *bodies* (diegetic protagonists vs. standalone dance performers, including vamps, "item girls," background dancers, etc.).[14] Consequently, a focus on dance extends the taxonomies discussed in the preceding section by not only addressing questions of song-and-dance integration into narrative space and time, but also engaging centrally with issues of stardom, gender, virtuosity, and labor.

While any attempt at classification runs the risk of being read as producing stable and fixed categories, the intention of this taxonomy is not to solidify the often fluid forms of musical numbers into restrictive categorizations, but rather, by outlining some common and recurrent modalities, to help elucidate the production logics and spectatorial pleasures of popular Hindi cinema. A taxonomy like this encourages, for instance, a closer analysis of the various spaces that Hindi cinema constructs in different kinds of song-and-dance sequences, the affective and economic investments in these spaces, and the gendering of these spaces through various categories of performative display. It also enables a sharp focus on film dance through a close examination of various bodily movements that may or may not be designated as dance. In effect, this categorization is driven by the following questions: What is construed as dance in Hindi cinema? Who dances and how? What are the spaces in which dance takes place?

At a fundamental level, this taxonomy differentiates between "song sequences" and "song-and-dance sequences," where the former do not feature dance at all, while the latter may feature various kinds of movements that may be described as dance. Song sequences may further be categorized into the "background" song and the "lip-synchronized" song. In the "background" song sequence, no on-screen character sings the song. Even when non-diegetic in character, it is detached from the background score on account of its aural status as an independent song and its visual treatment as a musical interlude. An example of a background song is "*Chalo dildar chalo*" ("Come, my beloved") from the Muslim courtesan film *Pakeezah* (Kamal Amrohi, 1972) (see ▶ video 01.02). This is the only song in the film that does not feature dance, but it is also tellingly not voiced by either of the protagonists, Salim or Sahibjaan, suggesting thus the freedom of Sahibjaan (Meena Kumari), the courtesan protagonist, from a performance regime that she has fled, and conveying their conjoined interiority and conjugal bliss. It is rumored that the song had to be picturized in this fashion because of lead actress Meena Kumari's failing health and altered appearance over the fourteen-year period in which the film was shot, pointing to the centrality of the performing body in determining the construction of Bombay cinema's attractions. A number of devotional songs in Hindi cinema are also constructed as "background" sequences in order to suggest the collective subjectivity of the devotees and their address to an omnipresent, invisible god. An example is the *bhajan* (devotional Hindu song), "*Aa ja re*" ("Come to us, Oh Lord"), from *Roop Ki Rani Choron Ka Raja* (H. S. Rawail, 1961), the only "background song" in yet another film featuring a courtesan, played by Waheeda Rehman (see ▶ video 01.03).

In a "lip-synched" song sequence, one or more on-screen characters' lip movements are synchronized with the pre-recorded song, but the characters do not move in a manner that may be described as dance, i.e., their movements are not strictly and continuously coordinated with the rhythm of the song. The opening example of "*Jalte hain jiske liye*" features a stationary Adhir (Sunil Dutt) lip-synching to Talat Mahmood's rendition of the song. While the characters in a lip-synched song sequence may be sitting, standing, lying down, or walking, movements not generally characterized as dance, these could become dance-like if synchronized with the song's rhythm. An example from the same period is "*Ae mere dil kahin aur chal*" ("Oh my heart, let's go elsewhere") from *Daag* (Amiya Chakravarty, 1952), where Shankar (Dilip Kumar) strides along to the song's rhythm as he lip-synchs to the lyrics. This brings us to the category of song-and-dance sequences.

Narrative Numbers and Production Numbers

I propose two broad subcategories of song-and-dance sequences: the *production number* and the *narrative number*, both featuring physical movements that may be designated as dance. The narrative number, as the name suggests, is a song-and-dance sequence that is integrated, to various degrees, with the narrative in terms of the lyrical content of the song, the spaces in which the sequence is performed, the characters performing it, and the movement vocabulary employed by these characters. A narrative number typically features diegetic characters and involves movements that range from languid swaying to walking or skipping along rhythmically, with intermittently choreographed dance moves. The point of differentiation from what I call the production number is that movements in the narrative number are not *strictly* and *continuously* coordinated with the melody and rhythm of the song. The dancer-actress Waheeda Rehman describes romantic narrative numbers in Hindi cinema: "In a love song the couple would usually hold hands, or run through fields. So no dance steps were required" (see Figure 1.1 for her narrative number in *Guide* (Vijay Anand, 1965), "*Aaj phir jeene ki tamanna hai*").[15]

More commonly, the narrative number features more "free-flowing," internally focused dancing, rather than the codified, outwardly focused, presentational, posed, and controlled dancing of the production number. Ravi

Figure 1.1. Waheeda Rehman and Dev Anand in *Guide* (Vijay Anand, 1965).
Credit: Screen capture.

Vasudevan briefly discusses the difference between the "narrational song," which occurs at "the point in the narrative when music is used to interpret the significance of a sequence," and "those performances which are specifically marked as spectacular and non-narrative in the basic structure of their address,"[16] citing the cabaret and comic interlude as examples of the latter. The world of the narrative number is usually a self-enclosed one in which bodily movement is meant to express inner emotions, often set to a romantic song. Additionally, in narrative numbers, characters may not be obviously centered on screen, unlike the proscenium-like performance space of many production numbers. Rather than codified gestures, and repetitive and replicable dance steps, the narrative number is often marked by minimal or naturalistic gestural articulation.

In the narrative number "*Manzil wahi hai pyaar ki rahi badal gaye*" ("The journey of love is the same but the travelers have changed") from *Kathputli* (Amiya Chakravarty, Nitin Bose, 1957), the male protagonist, Loknath (played by Balraj Sahni), is seated at a piano within the domestic space of his living room, while the film's heroine, Pushpa (played by Vyjayanthimala) sways intermittently but does not perform dance moves that are strictly coordinated with the song (see ⏵ video 01.04). Where an actress not particularly known for her dancing skills would stand gracefully by the piano or restrict herself to a twirl or two, Vyjayanthimala's *Bharatanatyam*-trained dancing body refuses to stay still in this rather undemanding narrative number, with the resultant impression of her body, head, and eye movements being in spectacular excess of the song's expressive demands. Loknath, like most leading men until the 1970s and 1980s, resolutely stays at the piano and sings. The narrative number, more generally, is choreographed to appear as a spontaneous expression of inner emotions in a space not designated as one for paid performance.[17]

In contrast to the narrative number, the production number is structured around a display of dancing bodies, highlighting the experiential rather than narrational pleasures of the text, emphasizing spectacle over narrative, performance over characterization (even accounting for the especially blurry lines between these categories in popular Indian cinema). In the production number, performers' bodies and the spaces of performance are accorded an aura and representational valence that exceeds the libidinal economy of the more-or-less linear narrative. Steven Cohan notes of Fred Astaire, that famed performer of show numbers or production numbers or "show numbers," "Once he begins performing, twirling around the shiny parquet floors, his body's energy and motion redefine narrative space in completely visual terms as spectacle. His musical numbers exert a non-narrative, extradiegetic pressure."[18] The production number shifts spectatorial engagement from investment in the narrative to a visceral pleasure in bodies and their movement. Unlike the narrative number, in the production number, the dancing is *obviously* choreographed, often frontally presented to an internal audience, and marked by distinctive moves that are strictly and continuously coordinated with the melody and rhythm of the song. The production number may feature dance performed in public and private spaces such as the street, the stage, the bedroom, etc. Another point of differentiation from the self-enclosed world of the narrative number is the mode of *looking* in the production number, where the performer explicitly invites and often returns the gaze of the internal as well as external audience, overtly coding this type of song-and-dance sequence as performance and spectacle. Indeed, it is this mode of looking (by the camera, the characters, and the audience) that marks a song-and-dance sequence as a production number even when the space of performance is private, as seen in the discussion of the production number, "*Main kya karoon Ram, mujhe buddha mil gaya*" (*Sangam*, Raj Kapoor, 1964) in the following section.

It is in the production number that the most spectacular display of dancing ability occurs, and the singing and dancing are not limited to an external manifestation of internal feelings centered around heterosexual conjugality. Like Busby Berkeley numbers in the Hollywood musical, the Hindi film production number is marked as a coded spectacle that often functions as an enclosed unit within the narrative, and halts the forward movement of the story.[19] The production number is markedly set off from the narrative by a system of visual and aural brackets created by the dramatically altered movement vocabulary produced by dance, and the transition from speech to song in the song-and-dance sequence. In the climactic production number in *Kathputli*, the heroine, Pushpa, performs an intricately choreographed dance on the theater stage to the song "*Bol ri kathputli dori kaun sang baandhe*" ("Tell me, oh puppet, who holds your strings") (see ⊙ video 01.05). In contrast to her loosely choreographed movements in the narrative number "*Manzil wahi hai pyaar ki*," here we encounter the full force of Vyjayanthimala's dancing talent and decades of training as she performs a spectacular *Kathakali*-inspired routine.[20]

Common to production numbers is the performance before an internal audience, frontal presentation of the dancing body, and frequent direct addresses to the camera, all of which make visible the star persona that transcends the narrative-bound fictional character played by the actor. Thomas Schatz observes that when performing a number, musical stars generally "shift their identities from being actors in a drama to entertainers addressing the audience directly."[21] With its frontal address and emphatic focus on dance performance, it is the production number that allows for this explicit recognition of the dancing star's presence. I refer to this kind of song-and-dance sequence as the *production* number for a variety of reasons. For one, as the most lavishly produced attraction in a film, it brings to the fore the economics of the production of song-and-dance sequences, and the considerable financial investment in these stand-alone segments that call for the creation of separate spaces, costumes, and indeed, performing bodies (see a production still from *Guide* in Figure 1.2). It is rumored, for example, that Bollywood's preeminent star Shah Rukh Khan had to undergo rigorous physical training to build the six-pack abs that are the central, fetishized feature of the production number "*Dard-e-disco*," but are not

Figure 1.2. Production still from *Guide* (Vijay Anand, 1965).
Credit: National Film Archives of India.

otherwise exhibited in the film. For another, the term *production* makes evident the explicitly constructed nature of this musical sequence, which, unlike the narrative number, makes no attempt to be imbricated in the story, but draws attention to the overt production of a different space, time, and order of performance. The *Encyclopedia of Indian Cinema*'s entry for *Kathputli*—"A Vyjayanthimala vehicle, the film consists of expensively staged dance sequences loosely strung together"[22]—reflects, for example, the difference in narrative organization when a dancing star and production numbers are the primary attractions. Indeed, when the presence of a dancing star occasions a string of production numbers, the film's narrative is deeply destabilized, resulting sometimes in delightfully choppy, lurching narratives as for instance, in the series of Vyjayanthimala-Kishore Kumar dance comedies in the 1950s, or it may result in an approximation of the backstage musical, like in *Kathputli*.[23] Finally, as I argue throughout this book, the production number foregrounds the *production* of gender by articulating an economy of spectacle based on certain bodies, their comportment, and the spaces in which these spectacularized bodies may circulate.

The difference in the movement vocabularies of the narrative and the production number configures spaces as private or public, which in turn defines the spectatorial gaze to be directed at the performing body. Gopal and Sen note that the romantic duet provides the central heterosexual couple of the Hindi film with a space for private expression, and for the expression of privacy.[24] Additionally, they describe how song sequences posit an "interior scenario of modernity" where characters are individualized through the creation of interiority and private space, and "singing, rather than dialogue, expresses the innermost aspects of heroes, heroines, and even sidekicks."[25] They argue that this individualizing function explains the focus on romance in most song-and-dance sequences. This perceptive reading of the function of the romantic duet applies to narrative numbers that feature the romantic couple or even one member of the romantic dyad (expressing joy, expectations, or sorrow at separation from the partner in solo narrative numbers). However, the production number—performed for an audience, even if comprising one person (typically, the hero or the villain)—articulates very different configurations of desire than the narrative number. To illustrate their point about the song-and-dance sequence serving to express interiority, Gopal and Sen incisively discuss the romantic duet "*Yeh mera prem patra padhkar*" ("When you read my love letter") from *Sangam* (Raj Kapoor, 1964) as a performance of *private* love between Radha (Vyjayanthimala) and

Gopal (Rajendra Kumar) in a *public* space as they cavort in a large garden that is absolutely empty. I extend this analysis to what I argue is a production number in the same film, "*Main kya karoon Ram, mujhe buddha mil gaya*" ("What am I to do, Ram, I married an old fogey") (see ⓥ video 01.06). The heroine, Radha, addresses this song to Sundar (Raj Kapoor), the man she has been forced to marry but is now learning to love. While the space is private—Radha and Sundar's bedroom—the performance is focused not on expressing Radha's interiority but highlighting her masquerade as a French showgirl. She stops Sundar from going to a cabaret in Paris—because he will not take her with him—and mimics the performance herself. His discomfort at this flagrantly sexualized performance by his wife is palpable, and hence her refrain, "what am I to do, I married an old fogey." This is the only sequence in which Radha wears Western clothes, and in fact creates a sartorial bricolage from the elements of the room's décor, producing an illusion of spontaneity through what Jane Feuer describes as a prop dance or a tinkering solo.[26] She thus constructs, in real time, the persona of a publicly dancing woman. It is the quality of the dance performed that marks the difference between the public and the private, and the kinds of bodily movements, gestural vocabularies, and appearance (costuming, makeup) that are appropriate to each. The difference between this sequence and "*Yeh mera prem patra padhkar*" maps to the private nature of Radha's relationship with Gopal (a secret love) and the public one with Sundar (sanctified by marriage). As evident within the same film, the private enactment of interiority can take place in a public space (the garden), and alternately, a private space (the bedroom) can become an arena for public performance. As discussed in Chapter 2, this has relevance for the kinds of spaces employed in Hindi cinema's production numbers, especially for the staging of dance performances by female characters, typically split between the publicly performing vamp and the more private, domestic routines of the heroine.

A further taxonomic category is that of "pure dance" sequences, which are not accompanied by a song and hence do not convey the semantic content of a song's lyrics but function primarily to display the performer's dancing skills. This may be likened to the concept of *nrtta* in Indian classical dance, where certain segments are choreographed to show off the physical skills of the dancer and serve as *alankara* or ornamentation.[27] These segments in the Indian classical dance repertoire that demonstrate high valuation of gestural articulation and embellishment produce *rasa*s, or spectatorial affects of awe, delight, pleasure, and amazement.[28] In popular Hindi cinema, "pure dance" sequences are often found in films featuring dancer-protagonists. Some examples from the periods discussed in this book include, the courtesan Indrani's (Sadhona Bose) *Manipuri*-inspired court dance in *Raj Nartaki* (Court Dancer, Modhu Bose, 1941);[29] the stage dancer Jimmy's (Mithun Chakraborty) rehearsal of his disco moves to recorded music in *Disco Dancer* (B. Subhash, 1982); the backup dancer Mili's (Urmila Matondkar) gyrations on the beach to the percussive "Spirit of *Rangeela*" score (*Rangeela*/Colorful, Ram Gopal Varma, 1995); and the vigorous "dance-off" between two professional dancers, Nisha (Karisma Kapoor) and Pooja (Madhuri Dixit), in *Dil toh Pagal Hai* (The Heart Is Crazy, Yash Chopra, 1997).[30]

Dance and the Production of Gender

As may be evident from this taxonomy and the examples cited, the comportment and configuration of the performing body significantly alters as we move from the pure song sequence to the pure dance sequence. Dance movements and the modalities of their display emerge as central mechanisms in the gendering of performance in Hindi cinema, where, as we move from the song sequence to the production number and the pure dance sequence, the presence of male performers is dramatically diminished. While the romantic duet in the Hindi film typically features the central heterosexual couple, the modality of display and performance in the production number typically genders it as a space for female performance. Indeed, with a few exceptions, the production number was the domain of the female performer until the late 1990s.[31] In Laura Mulvey's defining discussion of the male gaze, mainstream popular cinema highlights a woman's "to-be-looked-at-ness," equating femininity with spectacle, and in fact building "the way she is to be looked at into the spectacle itself."[32] In popular Hindi cinema, the production number has been the predominant arena for the display of the female body as an icon of male desire. Indeed, certain female roles are constructed purely to function as agents of spectacle, put on display through the production number. The key examples of this are the figures of the vamp and the contemporary item girl, female performers who appear only in production numbers, exit their marginal role in the narrative without ceremony, or are dispensed with in order to clarify the desire of the hero for the heroine. The vamp and the item girl have no place in the narrative number as they are outside the sphere of sociality of the protagonists and their only role is as public performers. The (typically male) comic sidekick, on the other hand, may feature in narrative numbers as he is an active participant in the narrative and in the social relations between characters.

For these reasons, while dancing is a desirable or even necessary attribute for Hindi film actresses, until recently, it has not been a requirement for male actors, highlighting the tendency to display and spectacularize the female body through dance.[33] That this is a commonplace is evident in film critic Partha Chatterjee's nostalgia for a time when heroes did not engage in the vigorous thrust-and-heave gyrations that he finds objectionable in post-1990s actors like Govinda:

> In the good old days, dancing was not considered a masculine pursuit and the likes of Dilip Kumar, Dev Anand and Motilal, of an earlier generation, would have taken exception to the very suggestion that they did more than a few rudimentary steps in their films as an accompaniment to the songs they picturised.[34]

In other words, male actors may be featured in song sequences and in narrative numbers that demand minimal or "rudimentary" dancing, but the production number, especially, is the proper domain of the female performer. Unlike in the Hollywood musical, where the star status of male performers like Fred Astaire and Gene Kelly owes almost entirely to production numbers specially designed to show off their dancing skills, in popular Hindi cinema, dance is much more crucial to the construction of the female star text. Dance, in fact, is often the legitimized form of mobility for the female performer, while action or fight sequences typically perform that function for the male performer. Both these "attractions" involve carefully choreographed movements but are gendered along the heteronormative trajectory of the narrative. Accordingly, action requires the (usually) male protagonist to demonstrate strength, nobility, agility, and musculature, while dance becomes a means for the (usually) female protagonist to display the requisite feminine characteristics of beauty, grace, and sexual attractiveness through her dancing skills. While keeping in mind that there are, of course, exceptions to these rules, this movement-based taxonomy demonstrates that a focused analysis of dance provides insights into the material and representational histories of Hindi cinema's song-and-dance sequences. An examination of the spaces and bodies in these sequences is critical for understanding the different narratives and histories of male and female stardom.[35]

As an illustrative example of the choreography of male and female performance, consider the introduction of the male and female protagonists in *Tezaab* (N. Chandra, 1988). In a film culture where the on-screen introduction of a movie's stars (colloquially known as their "entry") is an elaborately choreographed attraction, the difference in the entry of the two protagonists in *Tezaab* points to the disparate investments in male and female performance. While the female protagonist Mohini's (Madhuri Dixit) production number version of "*Ek do teen*" marks her spectacular entry in the film, prompting wild applause from the diegetic and extra-diegetic audience, the male protagonist, Munna's (Anil Kapoor) entry is styled through the genre codes of film noir and the gangster movie (see ⓥ video 01.07 and ⓥ video 01.08 for Dixit and Kapoor's versions of "*Ek do teen*"). The dancing female protagonist is on full and fully-illuminated display as she performs an elaborately-choreographed production number. Where she sashays onto the linear ramp on stage, he struts along a city street and is greeted and saluted. We are initially only given glimpses of his body – his striding feet, his strong hands, his glinting knife, and backlit face as he launches into a punchy dialog that would elicit applause from the audience.[36] This gendered entry—the hero through the tropes of action, the heroine through the attractions of song and dance—sets up their performance spaces and attitudes for the rest of the film, with shots of her swaying hips and dancing limbs on the professional stage finding their gendered alternate in his muscled torso and fighting limbs on the street. Dance and action sequences thus allow for highly theatricalized performances of gender, both modes of spectacle evoking visceral excitement and exhilaration through the dynamic presentation of movement. In the context of contemporary Hollywood blockbusters, Marc O'Day describes the action sequence as the "rarely achieved sublime spectacle of the human body in motion comparable to musical numbers at their best."[37] In *Tezaab*, this choreography of gendered performance involved parallel regimes of training and rehearsal for the two actors: Anil Kapoor with the stunt coordinator, Ravi Dewan, with whom he shared a long working relationship starting from his Hindi film debut, *Mashaal* (Yash Chopra, 1984), and Dixit with her dance choreographer, Saroj Khan, with whom she would co-choreograph her star body across twenty-one films over more than three decades (see Chapter 5).

Dance and the Film Spectator

While song-and-dance sequences have been theorized as interruptions and attractions by various scholars (Gopalan, Gopal, and Moorti), a focus on dance reveals that some types of song-and-dance sequences (e.g., production numbers) function differently as interruptions or attractions than others, such as narrative numbers or song sequences with no dance component. Narrative numbers and song sequences tend to be more imbricated in the narrative and its more-or-less homogeneous time, while in halting the narrative for their sensational attractions, production numbers inhabit a different temporality, pulling away into a heterogeneous time of spectacle. Within scholarship and popular film criticism, there is mention of audiences walking out for a snack or a smoke during song-and-dance sequences.[38] However, because the production number's attractions exceed its function in the narrative, it offers heterogeneous pleasures which often prompt repeat viewings of the film or of that particular song-and-dance sequence, especially in more recent decades, on television and online streaming services. As discussed earlier, dance sequences choreograph the body differently than the rest of the narrative, producing a repeated attraction through the dazzling skills of solo performers, the euphoric production of community through group dances, or of the couple through a duet, provoking and responding to a variety of spectatorial desires.[39] One example—from Tamil and Telugu cinema of the 1980s and 1990s—is the inclusion of titillating dance numbers by the dancer-actress Silk Smitha, which were guaranteed to draw audiences back for multiple repeat viewings. Dance, in this case, produces the heterogeneous time of stimulation and engagement with the number that is quite separate from, and often more compelling than spectatorial investments in the narrative. A rather different example of the particular attraction of dance numbers is evident in the audience interest in the semi-classical film dance performances of actresses like Vyjayanthimala, Padmini, and Shobhana in Tamil, Hindi, and Malayalam cinema.[40]

A specific study of dance also demonstrates differences in spectatorial engagement with song sequences and with song-and-dance sequences, especially production numbers. In the latter, spectators are likely to *watch* the sequence again and again, rather than just listen to it, since the primary attraction is often the visual element of dance. Whereas, in the repeated *listening* of film songs, audiences become familiar with the style of music directors, playback singers, and lyricists, recurrent *viewing* of dance sequences focuses attention on the on-screen performer(s), and the behind-the-scenes choreographers, art directors, and costume designers. This reveals the differing investments—of filmmakers and viewers—in song sequences and in dance numbers. Hindi cinema's heterogeneous form of manufacture reflects this in the amount of time and money set aside from the film schedule and budget for the shooting of song-and-dance sequences, as well as the appointment of particular singers, music composers, stars, and choreographers.[41] This is especially evident in the contemporary Bollywood item number, where a particular choreographer may be called upon to design and often direct only the item number on account of their expertise in the form, and an item girl (a female star or a lower-rung performer, depending on the film's budget) is recruited for a specific deployment of her body, characterized by moves referred to in the Hindi vernacular as *jhatkas* and *matkas*, or vigorous heaving of the torso and swaying of the waist.

More broadly, film dance produces a mode of participatory spectatorship through a gestural contagion from performer to spectator. Vivian Sobchack's formulation of the "cinesthetic subject" for whom cinema is "somatically intelligible," so that the film experience is meaningful "not to the side of my body, but because of my body,"[42] offers a corporeal grounding for the kinesthetic reception of film dance. Susan Foster articulates the concept of kinesthetic empathy where "perception simulates action, [and the] viewer, watching a dance, is literally dancing along."[43] The spectator's body empathizes with the movements of on-screen bodies, dancing along with the performer, and also with the film's gestures. Our somatic response to dance numbers is not restricted to the gestural repertoire of on-screen performers only, but includes the cine-choreographic operations of the film's music, cinematography, editing, and mise-en-scène. Janet Adshead-Lansdale discusses the co-creation by performer and spectator of "dancing texts," in which "the reader is not . . . a parasite upon a fixed object, sucking its life blood, but a co-creator of a mobile text, breathing new life into (it)."[44] Positing both dancer and spectators' bodies as moving and movable, affected and affecting, allows for a theorizing of performance and reception that is somatically agentive, and counters the one-way logics of many accounts of film spectatorship. Dance numbers produce a reciprocal and intimate intersubjectivity between performers and spectators. Film dance spectators employ an embodied, empathetic reading of gesture, and, as discussed in Chapter 5, this takes on marked qualities of mimicry and adaptation in contemporary televised dance competition shows, where spectator-performers produce virtuosic recreations of Saroj Khan and Madhuri Dixit's signature dance steps, among many others.

Song Picturization

In categorizing musical sequences according to the presence or absence of dance, the taxonomy proposed in this book points to differences in the semantic and semiotic content of the dance number (including references to the external world, generalized address, repetitive vocalized sounds for rhythm) and of the song sequence (expression of personal emotions, interiority, address to beloved/offspring/god, etc.), but also, crucially, reveals distinctions in the *musical* structure and *sonic* quality of the dance number (rhythm-based, percussive, featuring chorus sections for background dancers) and the song sequence (melody-based, typically displaying less orchestration, featuring solos or duets). These divergences point to temporal and motivic structures in dance and music so that narrative numbers' emphasis on melody and lyricism fulfills their function in expressing inner feelings, while production numbers' foregrounding of rhythm, a faster tempo, and extended instrumental sections allows for *nrtta*, or "pure dance" display. The qualities of the musical structure and the comportment of on-screen bodies are closely imbricated and calibrated to generate the affective propensities of each type of musical number.

Differentiating between song sequences and dance numbers complicates the term *song picturization*. Gregory Booth describes the term as "used most frequently by the Indian press to identify both the process of adding visual images to a song and the resultant product."[45] Neepa Majumdar notes that the use of the term *song picturization* to describe the production of song sequences "shows a certain tendency toward defining the image in the terms set out by the song."[46] In their analyses of the Hindi film song sequence, Booth, Majumdar, and Richard Dyer point out that since the term *song picturization* indicates that songs are recorded first and then "picturized," this suggests the primacy of the song, which sets the agenda for the visuals.[47] In the context of the American film musical, Rick Altman highlights the genre's ability to reverse what he calls the "normal" image-sound hierarchy of classical Hollywood cinema, arguing that in the musical number, sound generates the movement within the image, and the image becomes subordinate to sound as tempo and melody lead the dancers' movements as well as the editing decisions.[48]

The formal reversal of the image-sound hierarchy is argued to produce ideological reversals of narrative and spectacle, which scholars of music and dance have read as moments with liberatory potential. For Sangita Gopal, the phrase *song picturization* reverses the primacy enjoyed not only by the image in relation to sound but also the diegesis in relation to the soundtrack: "Entrusted with putting into visual terms the world evoked by the song, the film narrative had to create 'situations' into which the song could be inserted and picturized. As such, the songs did not emanate from the story world but had to be *accommodated* by it."[49] McLean, in her discussion of Rita Hayworth's dance numbers in *Gilda* (Charles Vidor, 1946) and *Affair in Trinidad* (Vincent Sherman, 1952), argues that the primacy of song over narrative in the musical number allows for the insertion of dance, which in turn allows the female body to speak in a register of its own choice: "The musical number is . . . Mulvey's 'no-man's-land,' a regime different both from narrative and from pure spectacle. For where music rules, dance can enter, to join in enlivening the passive, still, inactive female image through . . . the 'dimensionalizing force' of the body in motion."[50] While the interruptive force of song-and-dance sequences upon the narrative indeed allows for a radical rupturing of hegemonic structures of cause-and-effect driven narrative and of gender performance, examining the presumed process of song picturization more deeply alerts us to the complex relations at work between music and dance, image and sound. In *Music in Contemporary Indian Film: Memory, Voice, Identity*, Jayson Beaster-Jones and Natalie Sarrazin note: "Many scholars of Indian film have analyzed the picturization of song sequences with minimal analysis of the musical features."[51] Through attention to dance, the aim is to look more closely at musical features even as we examine how dance exists not only in the realm of image, but also in the realm of sound, through its relations with beat and rhythm.

Dance Musicalization

While the procedural logic of song picturization may apply to most nondance song sequences and to narrative numbers, where, say, a romantic duet is first recorded, and then the director, choreographer, cinematographer, and others determine what the characters on-screen are to do with themselves while the song plays out, for many production numbers that foreground dance moves, it is the movement vocabulary planned for the sequence that influences the kind of song to be recorded. Thus, in the pre-production stages of films starring accomplished dancer-actresses such as Vyjayanthimala or Madhuri Dixit, for example, filmmakers may often decided to include one or more dance-heavy production numbers to showcase these actresses' talent, which in turn prompted them to commission songs to match the desired movement vocabulary. In a television show on dancer-actresses, *Baaje Payal*, film producer and director Mohan Kumar exclaims, "If we didn't exploit [*sic*] Vyjayanthimala in one or two dances, which is her strong point, it would be our *badnaseebi* (folly)," while another producer-director, J. Omprakash, remarks of Vyjayanthimala, "Having a dancer as an actress is great for a producer as music is much better and there is grace in the dance picturization."[52] The improvement in a film's *music* with the inclusion of a dancer-actress suggests that dance vocabulary significantly influences the music of a film, often calling for enhanced rhythmic structures to accompany the dance. Consider, for instance, how the film *New Delhi* (Mohan Segal, 1956), which features Vyjayanthimala as a professional dancer, creates a number of narrative situations to put on display the actress's considerable dancing skills. The songs to which she dances foreground qualities such as rhythm and speed, and include extended non-vocal, instrumental sections to complement the "pure dance" segments of the performance. As Janaki Devi, a South Indian professor of music and dance, Vyjayanthimala performs an *allaripu* item from the *Bharatanatyam* repertoire, set to percussive instrumentation and *sollukattu* or rhythmic enunciations. Later in the film, the Tamil Janaki Devi play-acts as Mohini, a girl from the northern state of Punjab, in what may be read as a cross-regional, North-South double role. Sure enough, a key aspect of this role-play, when the actress in question is Vyjayanthimala, is a performance of the dance of that state, in this case, the folk-dance form of *Gidda*. By depicting Vyjayanthimala as a South Indian *Bharatanatyam*-trained dancer who can also adeptly perform the vigorous moves of *Gidda*, the film reinforces its message of national integration centrally through dance (through recently-anointed "classical" and "folk" forms) and the accompanying music. It would not be a stretch to surmise that it is Vyjayanthimala's ability to convincingly perform both types of dance forms that motivates the inclusion of diverse musical idioms from Punjab and Tamil Nadu in the film's soundtrack.

Commenting on Hollywood's Fred Astaire–Ginger Rogers series of dance films, Steven Cohan observes that the musical scores, often written by leading Broadway talents such as Irving Berlin, were composed to showcase certain set dance routines: "Astaire in a solo, the two stars in a challenge dance, Astaire in a speciality dance, the two stars in a romantic duet, the two stars in a novelty dance incorporating them into a big production number on the Big White Set that tries to compete with Berkeley's style."[53] "So formulaic does the pattern become," Rick Altman observes of the numbers' sequencing, "that by *Top Hat* a routine is established which is rarely varied throughout the remainder of the series."[54] Dance-centric production numbers engender a different mode of production and reception, propelled by the display of the moving, on-screen body; and while the stationary, off-screen voice of the playback singer remains important in production numbers, it shares or even subsumes its primacy to the visual attractions of the dancing body. I suggest therefore that a process of *dance musicalization*—where a particular type of desired dance vocabulary precedes and influences the composition of the song—substitutes the process of song picturization in many Hindi film *production numbers*. In these instances, we may witness a displacement of "the priority of the song as a musical object, rather than as a visual object"[55] since the visual attraction of dance dictates the aural dimension of the song in many production numbers. In terms of reception as well, dance musicalization may offer an interpretive framework to understand why we remember certain numbers, such as "*Hoton pe aisi baat*" and the other dance numbers mentioned at the start of this chapter, as audiovisual composites rather than only as aural attractions. Dance influences the mode of production as the dancing star body authors, to a remarkable extent, the film's narrative as well as its making, and in turn the on-screen dancing body produces a mode of reception where, as spectators, we find ourselves compelled to move to the music, whether by tapping our feet, nodding our heads, getting onto a dance floor, joining a wedding *baraat* procession, or, in the case of reality television shows, competing to approximate the original choreographic composition. One of the functions of delineating a movement-centered taxonomy is indeed to point to this difference in the embodied spectatorship of song sequences and dance numbers, each producing its own spectatorial comportment and affective intensity.

Dance, Stardom, and Authorship

While leading actresses of the 1950s, such as Nargis, Meena Kumari, and Nutan, did have women-centric films especially designed to showcase their acting abilities, the dancer-actress wielded authorship of a different nature on account of her particular skills, which engendered a distinctive mode of performance, with altered relations between spectacle and narrative. Returning to producer-director J. Omprakash's assertion that working with a dancer-actress like Vyjayanthimala leads to an improvement in the film's music, we may presume that energetic, percussion-heavy, folk music–based songs like "*Bakad bam bam baaje damru*" ("The drum goes bakad bam bam") in *Kathputli* and "*Chad gayo paapi bichua*" ("A scorpion has climbed over me") in *Madhumati* (Bimal Roy, 1958) were composed to showcase the actress's spectacular dancing skills. In some cases, films come to exist only to celebrate the virtuosity of the dancer-actress. Lekh Tandon, director of *Amrapali* (1966), in which Vyjayanthimala plays the eponymous Hindu courtesan, admits, "I made Amrapali only because of Vyjayanthimala being such a great dancer and because of the choreographer Gopi Krishna. Without them, I wouldn't have made the film at all."[56] The film is marked with Vyjayanthimala's authorial stamp, featuring a series of dazzling production numbers designed to show off her classical dance skills, the raison d'être of the film (see color insert—image 2). Reviews, like this one of *Nagin* (Nandlal Jaswantlal, 1954), reiterate that the narratives in many Vyjayanthimala films are mere scaffolds for her resplendent dancing: "*Nagin*'s story seemed more like a flimsy excuse to string along a series of melodiously-composed Hemant Kumar [songs, performed] by a sinuous Vyjayanthimala. She had eight scintillating Lata solos to put across on screen—each was a hit."[57] Clearly, *Nagin*'s attractions seem to lie in its music and dance, with mention made only of the music composer, playback singer, and dancer-actress, suggesting as well a powerful connection between the workings of these three. Indeed, music and dance were so critical to the film that "the last four songs, two reels of musical climax, were [shot] in colour."[58] The presence of the dancer-actress in this instance produces an impetus for technological changes (only song-and-dance sequences being shot in color, for example), production innovations (cinematography, makeup and costume, sets and props, editing), the significance of certain industry personnel (music composers, playback singers, choreographers), and, through the concept of dance musicalization, I argue, the type of music composed for the film.

Erin Branningan notes of Rita Hayworth that she was one of the few female musical stars to take the lead in numbers that emphasized dance over song and that in the musicals following those she made with Astaire, she performs more solos than duets.[59] It is with a dancer-actress in particular that dance is rendered more important than song, and solos than duets, which changes the articulation of heterosexual coupling accordingly. Whereas, in a typical male-centered narrative, what Ravi Vasudevan terms "para-narrative units," such as song, dance, and comic sequences, create parallel pleasures to the central narrative,[60] in a female-centered dance film, the para-narrative unit of the song-and-dance sequence and, in particular, the production number that explicitly invites the spectatorial gaze upon the dancing body, deeply problematizes the work of the narrative. As noted earlier, the *Encyclopedia of Indian Cinema* describes *Kathputli* as a "Vyjayanthimala vehicle," consisting of loosely strung, expensively staged dance numbers.[61] The film's narrative construction is indeed in the service of Vyjayanthimala's scintillating production numbers, with only half-hearted attempts to resolve the miscommunication between her character, Pushpa, her husband, Shivraj, and the theater director, Loknath. A conventional "happy ending" is tagged on in the final minutes of the film. However, this remains a noticeably weak attempt to neutralize inadmissible conflicts and desires—especially those of Pushpa, for public performance and for Loknath—which entirely exceed this hasty resolution. The film, in its lack of dedication to the narrative demands of Indian domestic melodrama, including to heterosexual romance, reveals that its central investment is to put on display its leading lady's dancing abilities. Indeed, the film features only one romantic narrative number (*Manzil wahi hai pyaar ki*, discussed earlier), whose suggestions of a budding romance between Pushpa and Loknath are never pursued by the film. Thus, often in films starring dancer-actresses like Vyjayanthimala, the para-narrative unit of the dance number "floats free of the business of narrative,"[62] refusing to be integrated into the conventional exigencies of the male-centric plot, and opens up the popular cinematic narrative to other configurations of spectatorial and performative pleasures, including a markedly different aural landscape.

A Choreomusicological Approach to Song-and-Dance Sequences

Shammi Kapoor—the "swinging sensation," and one of the few dancing heroes of the 1960s—relates an anecdote about the recording of the song "*Tareef karoon kya uski*" ("How shall I praise her") in the film *Kashmir Ki Kali* (Shakti Samanta, 1964), where the playback singer, Mohammed Rafi, was worried about too many refrains that repeated the first line. Kapoor reminisces, "I showed Rafi-saab how I was going to sing the song, and I said that in my gestures, I would find a different way of singing the first line every time it came. And I told him to sing it the same way too."[63] Kapoor's anecdote points to the specialized knowledge of the body and of their personal gestural repertoire that dancer-actors possess. This somatic knowledge extends into a special engagement with sound and music in the song-and-dance sequence. Sherril Dodds and Susan C. Cook employ the phrase "bodies of sound" to theorize the intrinsic and mutually constitutive relationship between music and dance, bodies and sound: "The idea that neither the music nor the dance occupies a position in which one determines or dominates the other underpins our enquiry. Instead, we conceive a mobilization of meanings that come into play through the reciprocal exchange between popular music and dance."[64] Attention to the practices of moving and sounding bodies and to the linkages between the sensorial planes of sound and movement alerts us to how dancing bodies are instrumental in the creation, transmission, and reception of music.

Choreomusicology, a portmanteau word combining choreology and musicology, provides a useful theoretical framework to study the choreomusical relationships underpinning song-and-dance sequences. Rather than the old binary of parallelism and counterpoint, choreomusicologists recommend approaching music and dance as a composite form in which the two sensory planes are seen as being in a state of mutual implication or mutual possession.[65] Let us turn to the production number "*Bakad bam bam baaje damru*" ("The drum goes bakad bam bam") from *Kathputli* to ascertain what insights a choreomusicological analysis may provide (see Figure 1.3) (see ▶ video 01.09). In this number, Vyjayanthimala performs a dancing double role, as it were, playing up the *nrtta* or decorative gestural elements of a peacock heralding the rain, set to instrumental music, and showcasing expressive *nritya* and *natya* elements in her role as the dancing rural belle, lip-synching to the noted playback singer Lata Mangeshkar's voice. In the third shot of the sequence, featuring a long shot of Vyjayanthimala in the dancing peacock role, the instrumental music begins with two clangs to which she raises high one foot after another (in the manner of the *mayurigati* or peacock gait), followed by a musical shift to a more tinkling *santoor*-produced sound as she does a circular torso movement (a modified *bhramari*) and then leaps to a stop (*utplavana*) as the music also pauses.[66] This is followed by a horizontal neck movement (*sundari* or *attami* in the *Abhinaya Darpana*) to

Figure 1.3. Vyjayanthimala in *Kathputli* (Amiya Chakravarty, Nitin Bose, 1957).
Credit: Screen capture.

two percussive beats. In her discussion of choreomusicology, Stephanie Jordan discusses how, through somatic engagement, dance and the body can influence musical experience and thinking about music. "Rhythm is an immediate point of contact between the two art forms. As a phenomenon, it can, after all, enter through both the eye and ear," she remarks.[67] In "*Bakad bam bam baaje damru*," rhythm does enter aurally through the instrumentation (strings, drums, *santoor*) but equally, visually through Vyjayanthimala's leaping, swirling body, and staccato neck movements. Indeed, this entire opening section set to instrumental music serves to showcase her well-known facility with the *Bharatanatyam* movement vocabulary and especially foregrounds the desired components of *nrtta* exposition, which include *angasuddha* (clarity and firmness in the rendering of line), *tala suddha* (precision in relation to beat), *lasya* (grace), and *tandava* (vigor, strength, and speed of footwork and other gestures).

Tala suddha, or precision in relation to beat or to time, is especially key to considering rhythm choreomusically. Dancer-scholar Shobana Jeyasingh remarks, "through footwork it is possible to pattern time in such a minute and detailed way that on one level the dance is the percussive structure of the music".[68] Indeed, as "bodies of sound," dancing bodies produce music most explicitly when they engage in percussive footwork, clapping, leaps, and the like. In the ninth shot of "*Bakad bam bam baaje damru*," Vyjayanthimala makes her second entry—this time as the village belle—with a close-up of her feet. The music changes from the strings and percussion of the earlier section to a mellifluous flute-driven melody as we see the village belle's feet step forward delicately and then tap the ground four times, emphatically reinforcing the percussion (*damru*/drum) that joins the flute. The change in footwork is folded with the instrumentation, and indeed it is the tapping of the ground with the foot that accentuates or makes *audible* to us the *damru* that is referenced in the song. But dancers are not only music-makers with footwork and leaps; contact with a surface is not always necessary to produce sound. Gestures can also have their aural dimension, produced through an interaction with space. "Cine-choreographies" like sweeping camera movements or slow motion produce aural effects as well.[69] The next three shots in "*Bakad bam bam baaje damru*" are instructive on this point. Beginning with the close-up of the feet of the village belle, when the sonic *damru*/drum and visual foot taps are introduced, as if echoing the upbeat rhythm of the image and sound, the camera tilts up slowly to a high-angle long shot, taking in Vyjayanthimala's entire dancing body. The music, dance, and camera movement are braided together. As the flute-led melody develops (in a circular musical movement), Vyjayanthimala rotates her head sideways and circles her arms around her torso four times to the beat. Her circular dance movement appears to swivel the camera upward rhythmically as a third participant in this choreomusical *ménage à trois*. She changes the dance step only after the camera is stable and static at a high-angle position. Finally, as we arrive at the sung *mukhda*, or opening phrase, an uncharacteristically long one and a half minutes after the song has begun (underscoring this production number's purpose of putting on display Vyjayanthimala's *nrtta* skills), the imbrication of music, dance, and cinematography are in evidence again as, in a slightly low-angle shot, the village belle rises rhythmically to the beat of the "*bam bam bam*" of the song, and portrays through *mudras* or gestures the beating of the *damru* (drum) and the dance of the *mayur* or peacock. Onomatopoeic lyrics like "*bam bam bam*" and "*jhan jhanake ghunghroo*" (the sound of anklets) reflect the intertwined choreomusical foundation of dance numbers as they perform the function of the *nattuvangam* (metal cymbals) and *sollukattu*s in *Bharatanatyam*, which set the rhythm for the *nrtta* sections, or the spoken *bols* in *Kathak* to which rhythmic footwork, or *tatkar*, is performed. These onomatopoeic lyrics are of a piece with the process of dance musicalization as they point to the specificities of verbal composition as well for dance numbers.[70]

A choreomusicological analysis of "Bakad bam bam baaje damru" encourages us to think of music and dance as not just "call and response," but as deeply imbricated with each other and with the cinematic apparatus. The opening shots of this production number illustrate how dance moves reiterate key musical structures and elements such as pulse and rhythm, and how musical phrasing is accentuated through dance gestures. Adopting this choreomusicological approach, we may appropriate the term *song picturization* as reflecting dance's power to *visibilize* music. In many instances, this enables a reversal of the audiovisual terms of engagement so that we begin to *see* music and *hear* dance. "This is not music you can know alone, you have to know it with the dance," remarks dance practitioner-theorist Jade Power Sotomayor, regarding the Mexican Son Jarocho folk form.[71] Anyone who has taken Zumba classes or danced to Caribbean soca will recognize how the music is composed with the dancer in mind, speeding up, slowing down, and pausing in keeping with the leaping, sweating, gyrating body of the dancer who *activates* the music. Similar choreomusical synchrony is at work in the music for Indian "folk" dance forms like *Dappaankoothu, Bhangra, Lavani,* etc. In the embodied music-making of Hindi film production numbers and pure dance numbers, the visual attraction of dance often dictates the aural dimension of the song. We only have to *hear* a song without watching the accompanying picturization, or *watch* a dance without the accompanying music, to appreciate the effect of choreomusical synchrony in some numbers while recognizing that others don't lose from lacking the visuals (such as "*Jalte hain jiske liye*" for my father) or the music (for example, the innumerable soundless GIFs of Bollywood dance moves circulating on the internet).

Conclusion: The Choreomusicking Body

Matthew Rahaim, in his study of gestures and voice in Hindustani music, employs the term *musicking body* to understand the body that comes alive in the moment of musical performance. While his focus is on the gestural repertoire of the *Hindustani* vocalist or musician, in the realm of Hindi film music, where the voice and the body are split between the playback singer and the on-screen performer respectively, the on-screen dancing body provides the gestures that combine with the off-screen voice and instrumentation to embody melodic ideas. Rahaim aims to "highlight the consubstantiality of voice and body by transcribing bodily action, no less than vocal action, as music" and asserts that melodic action is made dynamic through "the immaterial curves" the musician's body traces in the air.[72] A choreomusicological approach to the Hindi film song-and-dance sequence advances the concept of a "choreomusicking body," composed of a conjoining of the playback singer's voice, the on-screen performers' gestural repertoire, the music director's composition, the choreography team, as well as the bodies of the often-nameless musicians who produce the instrumental soundtrack for the number, among many others.

This reconceptualization of the production of film music and dance through the multi-bodied choreomusicking body deepens our analysis of the ideological work of the musical number in popular Hindi cinema. One may push further, for example, the theorization of the "dual-star text" and the work of Lata Mangeshkar's voice in "managing" the potentially dangerous circulation of the actress's body in public spaces[73] by considering the difference in the reception of Mangeshkar's voice when she sings for a dancer-actress like Vyjayanthimala and for an actress like Nutan, who is not particularly known for her dancing abilities, and of whom it has been written: "She exudes very little physicality. The body does not seem to matter. No wonder it was rare to see Nutan dance on screen, despite being a trained Kathak dancer."[74] The Mangeshkar-Nutan star text is associated with song sequences featuring little to no dance movements (often set to S. D. Burman's slow, melodious compositions), while the Mangeshkar-Vyjayanthimala star text is best known for its vigorous production numbers (often set to C. Ramchandra's brisk and robust dance music). Using the choreomusicking body as an analytical framework helps us note how the heroine's on-screen comportment has the potential to alter the reception of a playback singer's voice, which in turn determines aesthetic judgments about the quality of acting and music. Nutan, hailed as a sensitive actress, was also Mangeshkar's favorite on-screen body for her voice.[75] The singer notes of Nutan: "her presentation of the song on the screen used to be very natural. The gestures and emotions that take place while singing a song used to be enacted by her to perfection,"[76] suggesting a closely imbricated "musicking" body, where Mangeshkar sees her voice as perfectly complemented by the composure of Nutan's non-dancing body. This consubstantiality of voice and body is not as evident in Mangeshkar's comments on Vyjayanthimala: "[she] performed most of the dance oriented roles in films and complemented the dance with her acting skills. . . . Her dancing skills and my songs in the movies *Kathputli, Nayi Dilli* and *Madhumati* were highly appreciated by the audience."[77] Mangeshkar's separation of her voice from Vyjayanthimala's dancing body and of dancing from acting (see Chapter 4 for a discussion of this binary that informed many reviews of Vyjayanthimala's films—is she a "serious actress" or merely a "dancing star"?)[78] prompts us to examine hierarchies of *musical* value between these categories of performance: Are song sequences and narrative numbers considered musically superior to production numbers? Such a hierarchy is familiar to us from the world of classical Indian music, where concert music is more highly regarded than music accompanying dance (similar to concert music vs. ballet music in the Western context).Consider here as well the higher status accorded by the industry to Mangeshkar's dulcet "narrative-number voice" over her sister, Asha Bhosle's flamboyant "production-number voice."

A choreomusical analysis allows us to tell the story differently. Shikha Jhingan notes how playback singing allowed on-screen stars the freedom "to work on their performance with a clear referent, the recorded song, using the disembodied voice of the singer to enhance their own performance, emoting according to the tonal and expressive registers of the pre-recorded voice."[79] A choreomusical approach proposes a reverse inquiry: Do playback singers base their singing upon on-screen bodies? How does the gestural repertoire of the on-screen performer impact the musical performance of the singer? Did the gloriously expressive body of Hindi cinema's favorite vamp, Helen, prompt the playback singer, Asha Bhosle, to include trilling laughter and whispered sighs in her vocalization of Helen's baroque production numbers? So far, this has been discussed as a cultural articulation of modes of femininity through the figures of the raunchy vamp, the demure heroine, and the pious playback singer.[80] However, a choreomusical analysis that accords equal importance to the "sounding body" of the dancer-actress and to the bodies that produce the music, illuminates, for instance, the skill, talent, competence, and range of motion in voice and body required to bring alive the otherwise-disparaged dancing vamp figure through trained dancing bodies, playback singers who specialize in rhythmic harmonies, and composers and musicians who render the song danceable.

The theorization of Hindi film song-and-dance sequences must take into consideration the *combinatoire* of expression produced through the choreomusical exchanges of music and dance, as well as playback singers and on-screen bodies, and recognize the singularity of dance as a means of picturization. Analyzing how gesture, voice, and music work together to embody melodic ideas allows for a proliferation of methodological approaches to the study of the song-and-dance sequence that may do justice to the manifold affective responses we have to listening to songs (without the video—on the radio or on our phones), watching song-and-dance sequences on their own, watching them as part of the film narrative, just listening to songs, or dancing to/with them. A combination of industry observations, spectatorial speculation, and choreomusicological approaches informs my proposal to include *dance musicalization* in our discussion of the song-and-dance sequence so that we may move beyond the unidirectional logic suggested by the process of song picturization and begin to understand the multiple logics mobilized in the assembly and reception of these spectacular attractions.

2

Choreographing Architectures of Public Intimacy

A Spatio-Corporeal Approach to Hindi Film Dance

The most memorable musical number in the 1971 film *Caravan* (Nasir Hussain) remains "*Piya tu ab toh aa ja.*" Winning Asha Bhosle the Filmfare award for best female playback singer, featuring an extravagant, multiplanar set, and celebrated as one of the dancer-actress Helen's most elaborately choreographed cabaret numbers, the cine-choreography of "*Piya tu ab toh aa ja*" attests to the skill and virtuosity of the choreomusicking body that creates production numbers (see ⓥ video 02.01). As Helen's character, Monika, hears her lover call, she rises from her slump, caressing her face and hair to the beat of the plush rhythm section of the musical score, the camera tracking back in sync with her as she sighs and heaves toward it. We then get three close-ups that showcase a "micro-choreography" of Helen's face, composed of small movements articulated across the intimate surfaces of her quivering lips and her eyes, glittering with blue-green eye shadow, registering corporeal excess all over her very mobile face and body.[1] With her elegantly splayed fingers, she then harnesses the camera into a crane shot that follows her as she traverses the space of the set, climbing stairs, sprinting into a gilded cage, gliding down a slide, and emerging in the next match-on-dancing-action shot before the ready, waiting camera to inaugurate the sung part of the song with her trademark sequin-encrusted shimmy (see color insert—image 3). The sensuous contact between the glistening, smooth surfaces of Helen's body and the improvised playground slide, a prop that produces a perpendicular axis between her and the camera, animates the spectacular, sensory logics of the cabaret experience. The next shot shows Helen mobilizing, with her side shimmy, an elaborate aerial crane shot along the hotel bar, a wallpaper of flamingos, and the slide that now offers a diagonal vector to the composition, as she strokes and slides up against it.

Within a few moments of the opening of the number, we see, hear, and *feel* the pulsating rhythm of the "cabaret assemblage" as the camera glides, swoops, and crawls on the ground, producing an intense, embodied intimacy with Helen's Monika, even as the playback singer Asha Bhosle's throaty sighing and heavy breathing, and music composer R. D. Burman's score's brisk tempo and high rhythmic density produce what we might call a "music of the body." Cinematographer Munir Khan, choreographer Suresh Bhatt, and art director Shanti Das, who each had four-decade-long careers, working on numerous films from the 1950s through the 1990s, contribute to this cine-choreography by producing planes of action via lighting, props, camera cranes, tracks, tilts, and pans, through which Helen's dancing body participates in multiple modes of engagement with the built space around her. While there has been extended discussion of the ideological production of femininity through the on-screen bifurcation between the Hindi film vamp and heroine, if we shift from a narrative to a spectacular logic, we uncover the production processes behind the fetishized space of the cabaret to examine how it is in fact a central location for Hindi cinema's generation of particular spatio-sensory pleasures. While popular Indian cinema has always negotiated sexual desire through musical numbers, certain spatio-corporeal formations like the cabaret and the cinematic *mujra* produce a specific geography of affects that might explain why they continue to inform the cine-choreography of production numbers in Bollywood today.[2] This chapter examines how production numbers serve as the impulse for a range of exceptional constructions of bodies, movements, and spaces, and how these might draw on classical and folk dance formations, while also producing their own spatio-corporeal architectures of public intimacy.

Reading Dance through a Body-Space-Movement Framework

Within the field of dance studies, there has been some investigation of the relationship between dance and space, where, through motion, dance is understood to use space as well as to *create* it, and to define the properties of the space it creates. The dancing body alters space in particular ways; in other non-dancing modes of being, such as sitting, standing, walking, sleeping, etc., bodies occupy space in a different way than when dancing. As performance theorist Peggy Phelan notes, "While it is true that bodies usually manage to move in time and space, dancing *consciously* performs the body's discovery of its temporal and spatial dimensions."³ While all actions are performative, dance gestures and movements configure spaces as markedly so. In the narrative number, for instance, the romantic couple does not merely walk through a field of tulips or mustard flowers (preferred spaces for romantic encounters in Hindi film song-and-dance sequences of the 1980s and 1990s), but their jaunty perambulations, their stroking of the flowers and of each other, or their running across the field from opposite directions to collapse in each other's arms bespeaks a different relationship to space, one that transforms the field into a space for the performance of romance. Similarly, a sequence featuring a group of colorfully dressed *Bhangra* folk dancers accompanying the principal protagonists in a seemingly spontaneous jig on a Punjabi plain mobilizes folk dance to transform the locale into a metaphor for the nation.⁴ The movement vocabulary of the performers' bodies changes the function of the space they mobilize. In these examples, the locations are marked as spaces of spectacle not only through their physical attributes (red tulips, golden mustard flowers, etc.), but just as much through the performers' bodies, costumes, and movements.

The intertwined relationship of dance and space, of movement and environment, is apparent in the spaces mobilized by Hindi cinema for the staging of dance. These include spaces for professional performance, such as the stage, princely courts, the *kotha* (the Islamicate *tawaif* or courtesan's performance space), the temple, and the cabaret, among others, and those for apparently spontaneous performances, such as wedding venues, discotheques, bedrooms, hilltops, and fields.⁵ A consideration of these spaces prompts a number of questions: How do these spaces affect the kinds of dance performed in them? At the same time, how are these cinematic spaces defined by these dance vocabularies? What is the relationship, in other words, between performer, movement vocabulary, and the space of performance?

In *The Production of Space*, Lefebvre develops the central argument that every society (and within it, every mode of production) constructs its own space. He outlines three categories in this analysis of space: spatial practice, representations of space, and representational spaces. While representations of space may be conceptualized by scientists, planners, social engineers, and the like as a system of verbal signs, representational spaces are directly *lived* through their associated images and symbols, and tend toward systems of nonverbal signs.⁶ More specifically about spaces of performance, he remarks that theatrical space implies both a representation of space in that the scenic space corresponds to a particular conception of space (he provides the examples of classical and Elizabethan drama) as well as the representational space established through the dramatic action itself.[7] Considering film dance as a mode of production that produces its own space and spatial practices through particular gestural regimes and rhythms of music, movement, editing, etc., we may understand the representation of this space as conceptualized by the film's director, choreographer, art director, costume designer, cinematographer, and editor, among others. The representational space, meanwhile, comes alive through the gestural vocabulary of the dancers, as well as the actions carried out by these various other inhabitants of the space. The cinematographer's tracking movement, the choreographer's off-camera demonstration of moves, the editor's fingers cutting a shot all harmonize into a spatial choreography generated through the labor of film dance production. While the studio floor or outdoor location conceptualized as the space for dance performance is designed as an "abstract space" by the film industry for profit, through its use by the dancing bodies of choreographers and performers, it also becomes a representational space that is lived in particular ways.[8]

Representational space, Lefebvre notes, "is alive: it speaks.... It embraces the loci of passion, of action and of lived situations."[9] If one considers the Hindi film song-and-dance sequence as a particular kind of representational space, its spatial logics and practices illuminate dynamic histories of representation in the Bombay film industry. For instance, the spatial codes of Hindi film dance with the leads (typically, the film's stars) in the foreground and the "extras" or backup dancers in the background create a hierarchy of bodies and spaces that determine where the spectatorial eye will rest, even as the ear picks out the lead melody from the undifferentiated chorus. The camera and lighting aid in producing these architectures of visibility and presence. Lefebvre reminds us that "[r]edolent with imaginary and symbolic elements," representational spaces "have their source in history—in the history of a people as well as in the history of each individual belonging to that people."[10] The following sections on classical dance and folk dance attempt to unpack the overlapping cultural histories that produce the spatial practices of the Hindi film dance number. As will become evident in the discussion of specific spaces of dance in Hindi cinema, it is not just the space of performance, but the spaces between performers—between the often-heterosexual dancing couple, as well as between the lead dancers and the background dancers—that gesture to the cultural, aesthetic, and industrial logics of Bombay cinema's construction of gendered and classed bodies. Studying the shifts in these spaces offers one way of narrating a corporeal history of popular Hindi cinema—a history of representations through a history of spaces, as it were. For Lefebvre, attention to space produces a new way of looking at history: "History would have to take in not only the genesis of these spaces but also, and especially, their interconnections, distortions, displacements, mutual interactions, and their links with the spatial practice of the particular society or mode of production under consideration."[11] The analysis, in the next section, of the production number "*Ek do teen*" (*Tezaab*, N. Chandra, 1988) demonstrates how one may plot changes in the figuration of ideal Indian femininity by attending to the architectural construction of the dancing stage, which, by featuring a ramp, produces an imbrication of heroine, vamp, and fashion model.

But first, to elaborate on how spatial practices undergird but are also constructed through particular uses of the body, let us consider the reciprocally productive relations between spaces, bodies, and movement. The body and its gestures are central to Lefebvre's theorization of space: "Each living body is space and has its space: it produces itself in space and it also produces that space."[12] While the contours of a space of dance influence the comportment of bodies dancing within it and their corporeal exertions, the space is reciprocally reinscribed by the body's gestures, which may mobilize a variety of objects for their articulation and marshal a set of sensory affects that lend *body* to the space. Thus, while space is "a dynamic field of forces acting on and through the body,"[13] equally, the bodies of certain performers determine the spaces that circulate in popular Hindi cinema.

The famed dancing bodies of stars like Sadhona Bose and Vyjayanthimala, for instance, give rise to particular narrative situations and cinematic spaces. Films like *Alibaba* (Modhu Bose, 1937), *Kumkum the Dancer* (Modhu Bose, 1940), and *Raj Nartaki* (Court Dancer, Modhu Bose, 1942), in which Bose had top billing, were conceived as dance-dramas, with a significant portion of the budget set aside for art direction, to highlight the central attraction of her dancing body. In *Alibaba*'s spectacular final dance number, Bose's complex, hybrid choreography necessitated the construction of an elaborate set that would frame her performance (see ▶ video 02.02). Five ornate arches form the backdrop to the performance space, leading to two sets of curving stairs that symmetrically frame the entry of the dancers, who then perform in front of a fountain, the spray of water visually pleating with their undulating moves (see Figure 2.1). The floor design is also composed with the

Figure 2.1. From the song booklet for *Alibaba* (Modhu Bose, 1937).
Credit: National Film Archives of India.

choreography in mind, with the alternating checked and circular tile pattern creating an engaging visual geometry, and the entire spatio-corporeal spectacle captured in multiple top-angle shots. In *Raj Nartaki*, the focal points of the film are Bose's temple and court dance sequences. To showcase its dancing star's training in the *Manipuri* form, the film required the construction of sets depicting a temple and a court, the traditional spaces for the performance of that dance form (see Figure 2.2).

Another dancing star, Vyjayanthimala, played the role of a professional dancer in multiple films, and as with Bose, the presence of the dancer-actress necessitated the production of spaces—such as the *kotha*, the princely court, and the professional stage—that emphasized the star's dancing skills.[14] The *Encyclopedia of Indian Cinema* notes of Vyjayanthimala's career that every film featuring her

> almost always has a mandatory dance sequence evoking "classical art" associations.... This pseudo-classical style... is a filmic equivalent of calendar art's version of Ajanta murals and Tanjore glass paintings, taking over the icon of the large-hipped full-bosomed beauty developed by Ravi Varma.[15]

Vyjayanthimala's training in the South Indian classical dance form of *Bharatanatyam* significantly influenced the film narratives and, in particular, her costumes and the mise-en-scène of dance numbers in her films. Her dancing body made routine in Hindi cinema South Indian visual motifs

Figure 2.2. From the song booklet for *Court Dancer* (Modhu Bose, 1941).
Credit: National Film Archives of India.

such as the *gopuram* (intricately carved entrance dome to temples), used as a backdrop for stage dances in films like *Ladki* (M. V. Raman, 1953) and *New Delhi* (Mohan Segal, 1956). The Ravi Varma–esque calendar art iconography led to the construction, in many of her costume dramas, of ornate statuary and plaster-of-Paris fluted columns, amidst which she executed her semi-classical dance movements, the cultural sources and their cinematic renditions folded in the promiscuous play of popular, commercial film.[16] These examples illustrate the force of dancing star bodies on the material construction of cinematic spaces in popular Hindi film, and more broadly the connections between bodies, cultural forms, and spaces as they echo each other's imbricated histories.

The Spatio-Corporeal Matrix of Film Dance

In her analysis of architecture as an inhabiting force within choreography, professional choreographer Carol Brown argues that "the materiality of the body coincides with the materiality of the space,"[17] which allows for a matrixial set of relationships between body, space, and architecture. Brown describes this spatio-corporeal field as "a transgressive threshold of co-emergence for the dancing subject and the unfolding spaces within choreography as encounter."[18] Reading choreography as a matrix of relationships between the body and the built, and performers and audience, we may analyze, for instance, new articulations of the dancing female body in 1990s Hindi cinema by examining the foldings of bodies and spaces, in particular the newly constructed dancing body of the star Madhuri Dixit ("made over" through Saroj Khan's choreography, as discussed in Chapter 5) and the space of the stage-ramp produced for the enormously popular production number "*Ek do teen*" from the 1988 film *Tezaab*. This dance number, commonly seen as signaling the collapse of the coy heroine and salacious vamp binaries of Hindi cinema, transformed the performing body of the heroine by mobilizing the erotic movement vocabulary of the vamp and by altering the space of performance. "*Ek do teen*" combines the more conventional production number space of the heroine—the stage—with a ramp that projects out of this stage and calls to mind the vamp's nightclub setting that often featured a bar-top, a walkway, or some other surface that allowed for tactile relationships with her spectators. Ranjani Mazumdar describes the performative space of the vamp: "At the center of the club is a ramplike stage for the dancer, designed to provide her easy access to the spectators. She moves from the stage to the customers at the table, blurring the intended separation from the stage."[19] The ramp in "*Ek do teen*" allows Dixit's character, Mohini, to sashay into the standing audience while remaining above them and out of their reach. Unlike the vamp, this newly forged heroine does not walk among the male spectators of her performance; they have to look up to her, thus marking her difference from the sexually available vamp. And yet, it is the ramp that facilitates low-angle shots of Mohini, and perpendicular access to her dancing body, modes of shooting earlier reserved for the vamp.

Dance theorists Alexandra Carter and Janet O'Shea, argue that interrelated theories of corporeality and architecture help us see "the space of the dance not just as a neutral void but also as 'performative,' as the interior spaces of the body become entwined with 'the external spaces of performance.'"[20] The ramp and Dixit's movement vocabulary embody the matrixial relations of location and action, for instance, through dance movements choreographed on a horizontal plane. Dixit crawls, writhes, and clambers forward and backward—all vampish moves quite unlike the earlier dance of the heroine, which was mostly vertically oriented, performed standing or sitting, but rarely lying down on the ground. The ramp acts as a conduit between the spaces of the stage and the nightclub, while Dixit's movement vocabulary embodies the threshold between the performance repertoire of the heroine and the vamp. In this dance number, the ramp also acts as a space for modeling clothes, a routine included in the choreography (see ⊚ video 02.03). Lefebvre remarks that "understandings of the body are radically affected by the history of spaces."[21] The ramp as fashion runway produces a figuration of the heroine as fashion model, signaling new attitudes to and of the body in the Indian cultural imaginary, even as the professional fashion industry was taking off in the country in the late 1980s. A similar spatially oriented reading of Aishwarya Rai's turn as an "item girl" in "*Kajra re*" from *Bunty aur Babli* (Shaad Ali, 2005) suggests how the performance of a *Kathak*-derived *mujra* in the space of a nightclub enfolds old and new figurations of the dancing woman as *tawaif* (courtesan), Bollywood item girl, and bar dancer.[22]

The performance space of "*Ek do teen*" opens up as well a consideration of time in relation to dance and space. Through the image of the tree trunk, Lefebvre theorizes the imbrication of space and time: "each place showed its age and, like a tree trunk, bore the mark of the years it had taken it to grow. Time was thus inscribed in space."[23] The stage-ramp bears the marks of the traditional performance spaces of various female bodies—the heroine's stage, the vamp's nightclub, and the fashion model's runway—which may be read as spatial and temporal markers of women's figurations in popular cinema and culture more broadly. The image of the tree trunk also prompts a reflection on the spaces of dance in terms of sedimentation and accumulation, where film dance spaces bear traces of gestures, movements, bodies, and music that tell a layered story of the production of spectacle in Indian cinema. As film sets are erected and dismantled, used and reused, they are traversed by multiple laboring bodies—of the workers who construct and paint the sets, the *dresswalas* or costume assistants who procure the costumes that will inhabit and produce the space of dance, the musicians who create the acoustic space (for space is constructed not only optically, but also through the sonorous, the haptic, and the sensorial), and not least, the dancers who make the space "come alive." The body-space-movement framework allows for imagining a wide range of networks and pathways—of production economies, film stock, mise-en-scène elements, music, body cultures, social discourses on respectability, and gender norms, among others—that contribute to the production of the representational regimes and affective intensities of film dance.

Drawing on Rudolf Laban's vision of dance as a "living architecture," where space acts as a precondition of movement and movement as a "visible aspect of space," Brown refers to "dance-architectures" as allowing for choreography to emerge "through an enfolding between somatic awareness and sceno-architecture."[24] The following sections will attend to the dance-architectures of the *kotha* and the cabaret nightclub to uncover the social relationships latent in spaces, so that through film dance, we may examine Bombay cinema's production of its social space and time. "Every social space has a history," as Lefebvre remarks;[25] society's script is deposited on it, and uncovering this history requires deconstructing the uncertain traces left on the space by social activities. For Lefebvre, "repetitious spaces" such as highways and airports are the outcome of repetitive gestures.[26] Hindi cinema's repetitious dancing spaces, such as the *kotha* and the cabaret, produce and are produced by the gestures of the Islamicate *tawaif* and the Westernized vamp, their bodies both agents and products, generative of and responsive to the spatio-corporeal logics of film dance.

Dance-Architectures of Public Intimacy: The *Kotha*

The history of spaces such as the *kotha* (salon) in courtesan films, or the nightclub-cabaret where vamps danced in erotic abandon from the 1950s to the late 1980s, tells us a lot about the kinds of bodies and movement vocabularies employed in Hindi cinema's regimes of representation. In her ethnography of *tawaif*s in Lucknow, Veena Talwar Oldenburg describes the *kotha* as a site of inhabitation, a household, and a seat of musical training and performance.[27] The cinematic *kotha* is often rendered as a brothel, and a culturally vibrant space of music, dance, and poetry in some courtesan films. Ira Bhaskar and Richard Allen describe the space of the courtesan thus:

> The space of the *mehfil* where the *mujra* takes place is central to the genre of the Courtesan film. It is at once an architectural environment, a social space and a performance space in which the spectacle of song and dance and the cinematic rendition of that spectacle cohere, and in which the entertainment offered to the spectator within the film interacts in complex ways with the entertainment of the film.[28]

The space of the *kotha* hosts the event of the *mehfil* where a paying audience (almost always composed of men) is seated on three sides of a room, the musicians on the fourth, and the female *tawaif* or courtesan dances in the middle.[29] The dancing body of the *tawaif*, her gestures, and movement vocabulary belong to and are indeed defined by the characteristics of this architectural environment and the arrangement of bodies within this space. The *tawaif* typically dances in a central square or rectangular space, performing in sitting, standing, and supine postures, directing her attention to each member of the male audience by turn through eye gestures, hand movements, and by dancing up to them (see color insert—image 4).

In *Pakeezah* (Kamal Amrohi, 1972), the preeminent example of the Muslim courtesan film, the dancer-protagonist, Sahibjaan (played by Meena Kumari), features in a series of production numbers set in the space of the *kotha*. Two of these—"*Thade rahiyo*" and "*Chalte chalte*"—take place in *Gulabi Mahal* (rose mansion), an opulent *kotha*, and are memorable instances of the intricate foldings of bodies, spaces, and movements (see color insert—image 5). In "*Thade rahiyo*," Sahibjaan, employs her *Kathak* movement vocabulary to delicately traverse the entire space of the *Gulabi Mahal*, from the grand fountains in the front to the recessed pools at the back (see ▶ video 02.04). The cine-choreography of the dance braids together the lavish spectacle of the Islamicate *tawaif*'s virtuosic dancing and the resplendent *kotha* with its curvilinear arches, ornate pillars, vibrant Persian carpets, and baroque crystal chandeliers. The cinematic *tawaif* is rarely ever shown dancing outside of this space, while this performative space within the *kotha* is rarely depicted except to house the *tawaif*'s dance. The body of the glamorous "public" woman and the feudal space of the *kotha* produce and exist only for each other. Indeed, none of *Pakeezah*'s narrative numbers takes place in the *kotha*, and Sahibjaan does not deploy the *Kathak* movement vocabulary in any of them. In the narrative number "*Mausam hai aashikaana*," for instance, instead of dancing in fine silks and elegant jewelry among the still pools and indoor spaces of the *kotha*, Sahibjaan wanders about in the forest ranger Salim's *lungi* (male sarong) and shirt by a tent pitched on the banks of a freely flowing river. This narrative number depicts the space and comportment of private romance, while the space of the *kotha* and the vocabulary of the *mujra* produce the *tawaif*'s public and sexually available body. The body-space-movement organization of the *tawaif-kotha-mujra* performance matrix involves particular modes of training and industrial practices in order to generate specific energies and intensities.

The publicness of the bodies, spaces, and movements of the *kotha* and, as we shall see in the next section, the cabaret, are reflected as well in the cinematography of production numbers located in these spaces. The organization of these spaces and the spatial practices of the dances performed in them call for and enable dynamic camera movement. The *mujra* and the cabaret number often feature horizontal pan shots of the audience, and zoom-ins or tracking shots on individual spectators, frequently the leering villain, and less frequently, a besotted hero. The moving camera and frequent cuts between performer and audience attest to their performative repertoires being overlaid on each other. Pan and tilt movements are also designed to capture the specific attributes of these spaces—the Islamicate splendor of the *kotha* or the magnificently florid excesses of the cabaret-nightclub, both created at considerable cost for the production number. The cine-choreographic practices of the *kotha* and the cabaret produce a particular collision of infrastructures, bodies, and spaces. These in turn render the mediated sensorium of the *kotha* and the cabaret as intensely experimental cinematic and performative spaces. The spatial, temporal, and expressive functions of camera movement, art direction, and dance choreography produce a mutual constitution of the corporeal and the architectural, enabling us to apprehend spatiality beyond the visual, and to understand the intricate networks of labor that produce the spatio-sensory affects of production numbers set in these spaces.

In relation to the dance form itself, the courtesan film and the cinematic *mujra* draw from a particular narrative about the history of *Kathak* and of its traditional exponents. In his discussion of *Kathak* history, Mohan Khokar contends that the foremost artists of the dance form until the twentieth century were men, who often danced in temples and in some of the courts of the various "native" states (by which one assumes he is referring to non-Mughal courts). Female dancers, on the other hand, were *nach-walis* or *nautch* girls, who performed a courtly and, according to him, bawdy version of *Kathak*:

> The tradition of this dance began with the Moghuls, when there was a wholesale importation of dancing-girls from Persia, for the entertainment of the pleasure-seeking rulers and their fawning toadies. . . . the girls began to perform a Kathak of their own—a style which, while retaining the basic graces of the art, divested itself of much of its dignity and directed itself towards sensualism. Eventually, the dance of the nautch girls came to be associated with voluptuousness and lasciviousness, and the dancers came to be categorized as women of easy virtue.[30]

In this narrative, the space of the temple and the Mughal court produce different kinds of dance and dancing bodies. With the anti-*nautch* movement launched in the late nineteenth century, the confiscation of *kothas* by the British following the Indian Mutiny of 1857, and the decline of the feudal order in the early twentieth century, many of the *kotha*s did turn into brothels, which in turn altered the *mujra* form as well. The most routine employment of the *Kathak* vocabulary in the popular Hindi film is in the courtesan melodrama, pointing to the constitutive braiding of the *tawaif*'s dancing body, the space of the *kotha*, and the generic form of the tragic melodrama that produces a particular history of the performance of *Kathak* by women. In the process of canonization of classical dance forms during the 1950s and 1960s, *Bharatanatyam* was constructed as a purely Hindu form in its lineage, while *Kathak* had a more checkered genealogy as a Hindu courtly and temple dance form "corrupted" by the importation of Persian dancing girls by the Mughals.[31] The acclaimed *Kathak* dancer Shovana Narayan laments the difference in popular Hindi cinema's representation of the two dance forms: "over the years, it became easy to portray licentiousness with a 'mujra' that was identified incorrectly as Kathak and anything religious with Bharatanatyam."[32] A spatio-corporeal framework reveals how popular Hindi cinema renders these received histories of performance cultures through interconnections, distortions, and displacements of dancing figures and spaces of dance.

Choreographing Public Intimacies through the Cabaret Assemblage

Similar to the *tawaif-kotha-mujra* matrix, the Hindi film vamp's "cabaret" performance evinces a close folding of performative bodies and spaces. From the 1950s to the 1980s, the cabaret functioned as one of Hindi cinema's stock locations *and* performative repertoires. "An illicit landscape of gambling, gangsters, and smugglers, and the excessive and dangerous display of female sexuality," as Ranjani Mazumdar describes it,[33] the cabaret was a virtual space that mainly existed in the cinematic imagination as the location for the vamp's dance—a provocative, Westernized floor-show, also referred to as the cabaret. The use of the same word to describe the space and the dance coded by this erotic movement vocabulary attests to their imbrication, and the difficulty in determining whether the space of the nightclub-cabaret was conceived first and a dancing body commensurate with its moral and aesthetic coding created later, or whether the movement vocabularies developed by vamps of the 1950s, such as Cuckoo and Helen, necessitated the

Figure 2.3. Cuckoo in *Awara* (Raj Kapoor, 1951).
Credit: Screen capture.

routine inclusion of a space that could accommodate this new erotic register of physical movement (see Figure 2.3). The space of the cabaret is influenced as well by Bombay cinema's film noir spaces, characterized by smoky dark cellars, deep shadows, and an atmosphere of intrigue, as well as by the sensuously undulating movement vocabulary of the femme-fatale in song-and-dance sequences such as *"Tadbeer se bigdi hui taqdeer bana le"* (*Baazi*, Guru Dutt, 1951), and *"Aaiye meherbaan"* (*Howrah Bridge*, Shakti Samanta, 1958). The body-space-movement matrix of the cabaret is acoustically produced by specific playback singers and a Western, often blues- and jazz-inspired soundtrack. The languorously seductive voices of Geeta Dutt and Asha Bhosle complement the languid movement vocabulary of the actresses Geeta Bali and Madhubala in *"Tadbeer se bigdi hui"* and *"Aaiye meherbaan,"* respectively. In the decades that followed, Asha Bhosle's husky and jaunty vocal timbre made her the de facto voice of the vamp.

Let's return to the Helen-Bhosle cabaret number "*Piya tu ab toh aaja*" to examine how cinematic processes are written through by a variety of choreographic operations. After the opening segment discussed at the start of this chapter, we learn that Helen is performing this cabaret number for a large audience of seated spectators, including the film's heroine, Sunita (played by actress Asha Parekh), who, it must be noted, sits *still*, quite literally *petrified*, throughout this number, the camera framing her in a static medium close-up. The moral "looseness," as it were, of the vamp, on the other hand, loosens the camera itself into delirious movement. In an interview with journalist Khalid Mohamed, Helen remarks, "Every girl should flirt with the man who's handling the camera, and not with the hero, producer or the director. If she makes the photographer feel wanted, he'll make her look gorgeous, giving her an edge over the leading lady."[34] This privileging of the relationship between the dancing vamp and the cinematographer is revelatory of the representational logics of the cabaret assemblage, as Helen routinely mobilizes spatio-cinematic infrastructures such as camera trolleys, color film stock, and sliding ramps through her libidinous dance moves. Marking the transition to the next stanza of the song, she leaps to the floor, drawing the camera close to the ground, toppling the vertical plane by performing her sinuous undulations in the horizontal dimension, in stark contrast to the (physically and morally) upright heroine. Through its radial geometries and multidimensional figuring of space, the cine-choreography of the cabaret assemblage produces in us a dizzying, voluptuous, and carnally dense response.[35] Indeed, this kind of floor work, a regular feature of the cabaret's grammar, displaces the distancing effects of the perspectival organization of the proscenium stage, and of other types of Hindi film song-and-dance sequences that emphasize the separation of audience and performer. The kinesthetic spaces of the cabaret allow for and indeed are produced by the vamp wrapping herself around architectural features, objects like tables and bar-tops, not to mention members of the audience, laying a hand on a man's thigh here, a sequin-stockinged leg on a table there (see Figure 2.4).

In the scintillating cabaret number from *Talaash* (O. P. Ralhan, 1969), "*Kar le pyaar*," Helen's ostrich-feathered, sequined-bikini-clad dancing body twirls amidst the audience, manipulating space as a pliable material of her dance (see ⊙ video 02.05). Stroking and caressing people, chairs, tables, pillars, and floors, Helen performs a spatial praxis through dance that generates the cabaret's matrixial relationship between bodies, space, and movement. Gesturing to the imbrication of dance and space implicit in the word *cabaret*,

Figure 2.4. Helen in *Smuggler* (Aspi Irani, 1966).
Credit: Screen capture.

Helen's movement vocabulary produces and is produced by the performative space of the cabaret nightclub with its rotating, reflective bar-tops, slides and ramps, arches and balustrades. Her dance demands a discontinuous space containing multiple dimensions that are then rendered cinematically contiguous through the deeply tactile, vibratory, and kinesthetic cine-choreography of the cabaret number. The Franco-Burmese Helen, who literally crossed militarized Indo-Burmese borders during World War II to enter the Bombay film industry in the 1940s, figuratively functions as a border-crossing provocateur who produces a vibrant commons through the cabaret, where otherwise regulated intimacies find expression.

Given the internal audience's active participation in the cabaret's geography of affects, with its own gestural repertoire in sync with the performer—whether nodding, toe-tapping, or sweating from the proximity of the vamp's corporeal excess—it becomes apparent that the cabaret's choreography generates a distinctive organization of physicality, for both the performer and the viewer. In the cabaret number "*Baithe hain kya uske paas*" from Vijay Anand's 1967 film, *Jewel Thief*, the space and the spatial practices of the cabaret allow for multisensory engagements between bodies—ocular, acoustic, haptic, and even gustatory with the ritual pouring of libations (see ⊙ video 02.06). In the mediated sensorium of the cabaret, audiences don't just watch a performance, but experience an entire gamut of affects. Like in the cinematic *kotha*, where performance and spectatorship are not strictly separated, in the cabaret, bodies fold upon each other, choreographing architectures of public intimacy. Helen and her dancing double are framed between each other's gyrating bodies, rubbing up against themselves and the people seated at the bar, who in turn, infected by the contagion of the two dancing women's movements, sway in and out of various same- and opposite-sexed couple formations. Through a spectacular regime of dance performance and reception, the cabaret constitutes a commons, as it were, for the expression of the libidinal energies of public intimacy. Lefebvre's discussion of leisure spaces like beach resorts as eroticized spaces of consumption specifically designated for sex, pleasure, and physical gratification comes to mind in relation to the cabaret, a space eroticized by the performative repertoires of both performing and spectating bodies.[36]

What of us, the external spectators, and our somatic response to the cine-choreography of the cabaret? Do we participate in the gestural exchange between performer and viewer that choreographs these architectures of public intimacy? In "*Piya tu ab toh aaja*," the cinematography is propelled by Helen's dance moves, participating in the production of the erotic charge of the vamp through camera placement and movement across the space of the cabaret. Does the camera produce kinesthetic sensations of movement in the external film spectator as well? In an essay on camera movements and the "problem of point of view," Daniel Morgan discusses internal and external spectators, and how, through camera movement, we inhabit multiple positions within the world of the film, seeing "imaginatively" not only from the position of an internal spectator, but also with the camera as it moves through this world.[37] In the Hindi film cabaret, there always are internal spectators, and the vamp is frequently framed through their gaze. Indeed, a key internal spectator in the cabaret assemblage is the hero and or the villain through whom we might gain access to this performative space. However, we rarely ever identify with the hero's distracted gaze, which is on a quest for the villain or some other plot-driven exigency. Rather, we might arrive at the cabaret with these male protagonists, but then float free in this realm of cine-choreographed desires, even as the camera breaks free of any character's point of view and occupies vantage points along ceilings and floors, on the underside of objects, producing a series of perceptual relationships that are critical to the affective force of the cabaret assemblage.

The cabaret further complicates the mobilization of our gaze because the vamp frequently employs a double regime of gazes—looking at the internal audience, but also directly addressing our gaze by looking straight into the camera. The camera is often in hectic motion during this direct address, executing 360-degree pans or simultaneous track and zoom shots that intensely dynamize our perceptual-affective reception. In his analysis of Sam Raimi's Spider-Man films, Scott Richmond posits that the elaborate choreography of camera movements in these films puts us "less in the position of Spider-Man/Peter and more in the position of a dance partner, in a kind of superhero pas de deux."[38] But, he continues, we are rendered as passive dance partners, not at all in control, flung around in unexpected ways, and very probably enjoying our disorientation.[39] Like in the Spider-Man and other superhero films, predicated on extraordinary abilities of movement, the cabaret assemblage—with its spectacularly mobile dancing woman and cinematography—effects a temporary unbounding of our ordinary perceptual and proprioceptive self-possession. In the mobility of the on-screen dancing body, the camera, and the "moved" spectator, we ascertain a tripartite production of what dance scholars have referred to as kinesthetic empathy, where perception is grounded not just in the eye but in the entire body.[40] Through a combination of bodies and technics, cabaret cine-choreography contributes to the epistemological fantasy of being in a place we cannot be, the fantastical Hindi film nightclub.

Chetan Anand, director of the 1954 noir film *Taxi Driver*, was criticized in a popular magazine for creating an unreal space, a cabaret for the seductive club dancer character Sylvie, "If there is one restaurant like that in the whole of India, we would like Chetan Anand to give us its address as we need the relaxation more than the taxi drivers of our city."[41] Mani Rabadi, Helen's personal designer, remarks, "I'd never seen a cabaret in my life—I used to produce out of my imagination."[42] The Hindi film cabaret is, in many ways, a virtual space, produced through a combination of real and imagined spaces (see Figure 2.5). To invoke Foucault's discussion of

CHOREOGRAPHING ARCHITECTURES OF PUBLIC INTIMACY 77

Figure 2.5. Helen in *Gumnaam* (Raja Nawathe, 1965).
Credit: Screen capture.

heterotopia through the metaphor of a mirror, which functions both as a utopia, reflecting an unreal virtual place that allows one to see oneself, but also a heterotopia, in that it is a real object,[43] we may posit the cabaret (with its ramps, swings, slides, and all that horizontal writhing), as a countersite, a heterotopia that mobilizes and dis-articulates the "real spaces" of the proscenium, the fashion ramp, the playground, the bedroom. No wonder, then, that when the 1960s Hindi film *heroine* stages a cabaret number, it resides in the bedroom-turned-cabaret, as seen in *"Buddha mil gaya"* from *Sangam* (Raj Kapoor, 1965). Elizabeth Grosz argues that "the limits of possible spaces are the limits of possible modes of corporeality."[44] Through her dancing body, the vamp (and Helen in particular) produces and inhabits the heterotopic space of the cabaret, which mobilizes otherwise incompatible spaces to produce these pulsating architectures of public intimacy in Hindi cinema.

Bodies, Spaces, and Movements in Indian Classical and Folk Dance

While it is a commonplace to describe Hindi film dance as a hybrid of Indian classical and folk dance forms, this section undertakes a closer examination of the influence of these dance cultures on Hindi film dance, the representation of these dance forms on screen, and the analytical tools that aesthetic treatises on dance can provide for the study of film dance. Rather than establish trajectories of origins and derivations between the categories of classical, folk, and film dance (themselves contentiously defined in the mid-twentieth century, as discussed in Chapters 3 and 4), a genealogical approach highlights strata of simultaneity so that one may link these categories through gestures, marks, and traces.

While Hindi film dance has different aesthetic and affective aims than classical Indian dance forms, the detailed documentation of the codifications of the dancing body in treatises like the *Natya Shastra* and *Abhinaya Darpana* provide useful methodological approaches for the study of movement vocabularies in Hindi cinema.[45] Rather than treat these texts as part of an unbroken, upper-caste, Sanskritized lineage, as indeed they were mobilized for the "revival" of Indian dance forms in the 1940s, and continue to be employed in upper-caste classical dance training and performance circuits today, I aim to excavate these texts' corporeal aesthetics through their embodied performance by *devadasis*, *tawaifs*, dancer-actresses, choreographers, backup dancers, and the like.[46] It is worth noting that in the *Natya Shastra* and *Abhinaya Darpana*, the word *natya* refers to acting and dancing, since both performative modes were combined in Sanskrit theater. The art historian A. K. Coomaraswamy, who translated the *Abhinaya Darpana* into English in 1917, notes in his introduction that while this treatise's principles may no longer apply entirely to contemporary, hybrid Indian theater, "authentic Indian acting . . . survives in the 'Nautch,' a form of dance which sets forth a given theme by means of song and gesture combined, [which] together with the sister art of music, must be regarded as representing the most perfect form of old Indian practical aesthetic culture now surviving."[47] Upper-caste nationalist reformers canonized *Bharatanatyam*, *Kathak* and other dance forms as classical by gentrifying this very *nautch* form and marginalizing its traditional creators and performers, who in fact provide a vital genealogy for dance and acting in popular Indian cinema. Through their forceful participation in various Indian film industries, members of hereditary performing communities, including *kalavant, devadasi, tawaif,* and *kalavantulu* artists, played a defining role in establishing the gestural language and performance repertoires of popular cinema.[48] By the 1940s and 1950s, these treatises were explicitly mobilized in the dance training of middle- and upper-class women, including dancer-actresses like Sadhona Bose, Vyjayanthimala, and Waheeda Rehman. These networks of training with traditional gurus and film choreographers, and the state's text-based canonization of classical dance forms also inform my turn to these treatises as inflecting Hindi cinema's attitudes toward dance and acting, albeit through winding, circuitous routes.

The terms *lokadharmi* and *natyadharmi*, described in the *Natya Shastra*, may be employed to consider differences in the aesthetic organization and spectatorial address of Hindi film dance and what comes to be canonized by the mid-twentieth century as Indian classical dance. As Khokar describes them, the *lokadharmi* form is "down-to-earth in its character and true-to-life in its manner, easier to follow, has a wide appeal" while the *natyadharmi* form is that which is "formal and contrived by rigid rules and principles, harder to follow, meant for those equipped to understand the art."[49] While these terms were originally used to differentiate between "classical" and "folk" dance traditions, or the dance practice of professionals in the temples and the courts and those of the "folk" marking festivals, season changes, and other events, they function as eloquent descriptors of contemporary *natyadharmi* classical Indian dance forms and the *lokadharmi* popular Hindi film dance style. Specifically, in terms of gestural vocabulary, Kapila Vatsyayan notes that in *natyadharmi* forms, the same dancer assumes different roles, without change of costume, and "the whole range of impersonal human situation and experiences [is] expressed through gestures."[50] A single dancer may essay the role of say, the mischievous baby god, Krishna, and his mother, Yashoda, as well as the young, flirtatious Krishna and his lover, Radha. The same dancer may also delineate through hand, eye, and other bodily gestures the entire locale in which a scene unfolds, such as the lapping of waves and blooming of lotuses in a lake, the swaying of plants on its bank, etc. Describing the renowned *Odissi* dancer Kelucharan Mahapatra's enactment of the role of Krishna through gestures of flute-playing and then his impersonation of Radha, through gestural descriptions of her body, Uttara Asha Coorlawala notes, "the same single performer represents empowerment and seduction, religion and sensuality, theatrical artifice and human emotions, male and female, dominant and subordinate positions."[51]

During a period—the 1950s—when establishing hierarchies of taste between classical and folk dance forms was of paramount importance to cultural institutions like the Sangeet Natak Akademi (which would canonize dance forms like *Odissi* only when they had demonstrated a long textual, Sanskritized lineage, and marginalized traditional *mahari* performers), dance historians like Vatsyayan frame this difference along gestural lines. She notes of *lokadharmi* conventions:

> While the classical dancers describe the animal or the bird through a series of movements and gestures, the folk dancers become the bird through one or two characteristic movements of the bird . . . the hands and the vast body of gesture language used in classical dance styles are practically absent in all tribal and folk dancing.[52]

Hindi film dance, flagrantly promiscuous in its borrowings and appropriations, equally mobilizes classical dance *mudras* (gestures) and folk dance and other movement vocabularies. For instance, in the "semi-classical" dance number, "*Bakad bam bam baaje damru*" from *Kathputli* (Amiya Chakrabarty, Nitin Bose, 1957), the *Bharatanatyam*-trained Vyjayanthimala dons two costumes—of a peacock and a village girl—to depict the two characters in the song, and appropriates gestural vocabularies from multiple sources (see ▶ video 01.09). This hybrid "semi-classical" style borrows movements and gestures from classical dance but renders them in a popular idiom by making them less strictly codified. In her dancing "double role" Vyjayanthimala, echoing Vatsyayan's description of folk dance vocabulary, depicts the peacock through simulations of the bird's actual movements, such as its forward-backward neck movement, the unfurling of the tail, and leaps and twirls in the air. The choreography blithely mashes this up with classical dance gestures such as the *mayura hasta mudra* (peacock hand gesture) and the *pralokitam drishti mudra* (eye gesture in which the eyeballs rapidly flit from side to side). Given the breadth of its address to a large constituency of viewers, Hindi cinema nimbly and ingeniously creates a seamless amalgam of various dance forms without adhering strictly to the conventions of any of these. So, while song-and-dance sequences often deploy classical dance gestures, especially when the dancer is a classical dance exponent within the diegesis, the rigorous correspondence between gestures and meaning that is mandated in post-revival Indian classical dance is not a feature of these hybrid film dance depictions. Rather, the style is recognized as "classical" through costume (often some variant of the *amrapali* costume),[53] makeup, and select body codifications such as the distensions of the neck typical of *Bharatanatyam*, or the *chakkars* or spins of the body from the *Kathak* lexicon. Film dance is thus characterized by style recognition (certain formations as "classical," others as "folk," etc.), rather than by strict adherence to the codes and conventions of the dance forms it borrows from.

Studying the stance adopted by the dancing body and the body's occupation of space in various dance forms is instructive for an analysis of Hindi film dance. Most classical Indian dance forms feature codified movements in space along straight lines, diagonals, figures of eight, and spirals. What is distinctive about post-revival, upper-caste, canonized *Bharatanatyam*, for example, is its definition of movement in space along straight lines or triangles. This in turn creates a movement vocabulary that is characterized by lateral movements of the head, lower limb movements along straight lines or marking two sides of an imaginary triangle, and upper limbs following the lower limbs or weaving circular patterns along the space covered by the lower limbs. *Kathak*, like Indian miniature painting, conceives of space only in straight lines, which leads to a front-back treatment of space in its movement vocabulary.[54] Movement patterns in *Odissi*, on the other hand, are decidedly circular, with the *minadandi* movement (literally, covering space like a fish) being the most common technique to cover space through semi-circular turns of the leg. Movements known as *gheras* cover space in circles, semi-circles, and concentric circles.[55]

The highly codified movement of feet, knees, torso, neck, head, arms, wrists, etc., in classical dance forms produces particular relationships to space and time, with the sculptural attitude of the classical dance body emerging from the dancer's effort to achieve the perfect pose that will convey a sense of timelessness. Vatsyayan observes that in Indian classical dance, "the human body has been conceived of as a mass which can be equally divided along a central median. Further movement is determined by the nature of deflections from this median."[56] In *Kathak*, for instance, torso movements are produced only through changes in the angle of the shoulder line, with the depressing of one shoulder and raising of the other creating the trademark *kasak masak* movement. In *Bharatanatyam*, "the dancer emerges from a stance of perfect balance to execute a series of abstract geometric movements in a given time cycle, and returns to a pose of perfect equilibrium."[57] In this dance form, the torso is never split into the upper or the lower torso through deflections of the waist. Choreographer Saroj Khan's comment on the *Bharatanatyam*-trained actress Hema Malini's dancing skills is revelatory of corporeal figurations that emerge from training in certain classical dance forms that rub up against the movement vocabularies of Hindi film dance at particular historical moments:

> I choreographed a *tandav* [a vigorous dance item] with Hemaji. She is a brilliant dancer but she is a stiff dancer, though now she has opened up. Before, she had that Bharat Natyam style so it would take time to loosen her body. One day I was assisting P. L. Raj in *Dharmatmaa* and we were shooting the song *Meri galiyon se logon ki yaari badh gayi*. She had to do a movement that she just couldn't do because of her Bharat Natyam training.[58]

This production number's choreography, with belly-dance influenced torso deflections and chest-heaving, demanded a comportment that Malini's *Bharatanatyam*-trained body found difficult to approximate.

Through its eclectic borrowings, Hindi film dance folds the spatiotemporal inhabitations of classical and folk dance forms, and also borrows freely from transnational forms such as cha-cha-cha, modern jazz, salsa, etc., where the emphasis is on the coverage of space—whether floor-space or space in the air—through leaps and jumps. Adopting freely from myriad movement vocabularies, Hindi film dance emerges as a vital space of experimentation, where different gestural systems are mixed through a mongrel logic to produce a choreography of great affective force. Rather than just throwing together different styles, film choreographers give considerable thought to the requirements of *bhava* (emotion) and *rasa* (affect), invoking the vocabularies of different dance styles to generate a particular *rasa*. In *Kathputli*, for instance, while the more routinely used movement vocabularies of *Kathak* and *Bharatanatyam* are employed in production numbers that showcase Vyjayanthimala's classical dance training, the dance form of *Kathakali*—with its spread-out hands and legs, fixed, strong torso, and dramatic, pulsating eye movements—is invoked for the fiery, impassioned expression of her character's agony in the final production number.[59]

The *Natya Shastra* and *Abhinaya Darpana* describe three performative categories of dance: *nrtta*, *nritya*, and *natya*. *Nrtta* refers to "pure" dance movements that are not intended to convey a particular meaning to the audience but rather to demonstrate the dancer's skills. *Nrtta* movements are defined by three essentials: a basic stance, ornamental hand gestures, and movement of the legs or feet. In contrast, *nritya*, or expository dance, is meant to convey a narrative or an idea to the onlooker, and includes *abhinaya* (expression), conveyed through the *mukhaja* or the face (involving movements of the eyebrows, eyelids, eyeballs, nose, lips, chin, and mouth), and *sarira* or the body (using the major limbs, and movements of the head, chest, waist, hips, thighs, hands, and feet). *Natya* is a broader theater-related category in which *nrtta* and *nritya* are both utilized, but in addition, the element of drama is introduced through the use of the spoken word and other conventions of the stage.[60] These categories help parse different types of dance in Hindi cinema as well, where some numbers expressly include passages to show off a dancer's movement skills while others demonstrate the performer's facility with facial expression. The *antara* and *mukhda* of a song are often dominated by *nritya* and *natya* formations, where dance movements are accompanied by facial expressions to convey the semantic import of the song.[61] The instrumental interludes that typically punctuate these sections frequently feature *nrtta* or pure dance, with an emphasis on physical movement. Additionally, production numbers are more focused on *nrtta* since the lyrical content of the song is not as important as the dance movements.[62] Narrative numbers, on the other hand, are more likely to feature elements of *nritya* and *natya* since they aim to further the narrative.

Body Zones and the Production of Affect

Different parts of the dancing body are deployed in the performative categories of *nrtta*, *nritya*, and *natya*. The *Natya Shastra* presents a dizzying variety of movements and expressions, constructed through various body units. It details as many as eighty face movements, produced by the head, eyes, nose, cheeks, mouth, lower lip, and chin. Eye movements are codified into thirty-six kinds of glances, which employ the eyebrows, eyelids, eyelashes, eyeballs, and pupils. Similarly, specific instructions are provided for the use of the hands, arms, breasts, sides, belly, waist, thighs, shanks, and feet to produce different kinds of gaits, leaps, jumps, and whirling movements of the body.[63] In the spirit of popular Hindi cinema's whimsical appropriations, I adapt this elaborate lexicon to deconstruct the dancing female body in Hindi cinema into three broad categories—the face, the torso, and the limbs. Each of these "body zones" is capable of a variety of addresses, depending on the deployment of their constituent parts, and the social connotations of those gestural articulations.

In his annotation of the *Abhinaya Darpana*'s description of the functions of the face in dance, Khokar notes, "The face of the dancer becomes the register of the flitting feelings and passions that well up in response to the words of the song and their emotionally charged musical release; the eyes, eyebrows, mouth, lips and cheeks all become potent instruments of suggestion and insinuation."[64] Vatsyayan remarks of the face and torso: "The movement of the minor limbs, particularly the *mukhaja* [facial] ones, like the eyebrows, eyeballs, eyelids, chin, nose, lips etc. relate to *abhinaya* [expression]. On the other hand, thighs, waist, side and chest movements are primarily discussed as *nritta* technique."[65] The face then is commonly considered to express and register feelings, while the limbs and torso define the body's relationship to space. The tripartite structure I have proposed—comprising the face, torso, and limbs—helps to analyze the ways in which the performing female body is constructed, and the relationship of film dance to other dance forms. In Hindi film dance, the facial features most employed are the eyes and the lips, while torso movements focus on the breasts, the waist, and the buttocks. As mentioned before, movements of the limbs or of individual fingers, for example, are not strictly codified as in classical dance forms, but create kinesthetic patterns and context-specific meanings in each instance of eclectic appropriation. Each of these body zones also interact with each other to produce varied affects, complementing or counteracting the insinuations of certain moves. In Chapter 5, for instance, I discuss how Madhuri Dixit's famously "innocent" smile attenuates the suggestive torso movements that she appropriates from the vamp. While the vamp's face is marked as bawdy on account of her lustful glances, her biting of the lip, etc., Dixit's smile conveys the appropriate attributes of the heroine—innocence, vulnerability, and a non-threatening sexuality. In one of the films discussed in Chapter 4, *Sadhna*, in which the *Bharatanatyam*-trained Vyjayanthimala plays a "coarse" courtesan, Champabai, the purportedly raunchy *mujra* dance number, "*Kaho ji tum kya kya khareedoge, yahan toh har cheez bikti hai*" ("Tell me sirs what would you like to buy, all sorts of things are for sale here") is rendered anodyne by the dancer-actress's energetic jumps and leaps that put her footwork on display but convey nothing of the courtesan's flirtatious coquetry, usually communicated through the raising of the eyebrows and sidelong glances. Dance critic and historian V. A. K. Ranga Rao, approves of the "toning down" of this production number through Vyjayanthimala's moves and the camera placement: "Considering that it was set in a bordello, it could have been a lascivious come-on. By the camera angle (no cleavage), movements (no bumps and heaves) and her expression, it was a straightforward invitation to come and have fun."[66] The emphasis on footwork rather than on the torso and the eschewal of traditional facial gestures employed for seduction ensure that a respectable dancer-actress like Vyjayanthimala can perform a *mujra* number without censure (rendering the number bland and barely remembered).

Adrienne McLean asks, in her discussion of Judy Garland, "Which parts of the body (are allowed to) speak and perform, and in what contexts? Which parts of the body repeat the discursive meaning already placed upon bodies by culture? What kinds of physical training and competence produce what effects?"[67] Dance is a crucial vector in popular Hindi cinema's representational logic, inflected by the categories of class, caste, gender, and regional identity. In *Raj Nartaki* (1942), discussed at length in Chapter 3, the dancer-protagonist's court dance includes a series of close-ups of her *hasta mudras* (hand gestures), rendered in the Manipuri lexicon. Indian theories of aesthetics and perception link *drishti* (looking) with *rupa* (form) and *nama* (naming).[68] While in a classical dance form, the dancer may employ eye movements to direct the audience's attention to an action or a part of the body, in this pure dance number, the camera adopts this focused gaze through the use of close-ups, leading the spectator to discern the form and name of each gesture. Through a focus on hand gestures, this sequence brings to the fore the film's pedagogical project of teaching film viewers about the gestural language of newly-gentrified dance forms.

McLean's reference to physical training and competence calls our attention to the labor of producing the perfect on-screen dancing body. Employing the "body zones" framework to deconstruct the dancing body affords insights into the assemblage of body parts that construct the dancing star body. In the Anglo-Indian background dancer Edwina Lyons's memoir, for instance, the author remarks that Edwina's sister Philomena's "legs were used for Madhubala's legs in a couple of films" and that the star "[came] to her personally and [thanked] her for it."[69] The Anglo-Indian backup dancer's legs speak and perform a certain cosmopolitan identity, and replace the legs of the perhaps-coy, perhaps-not-as-well-trained-in-dance female star, whose on-screen figuration emerges as a composite of variously trained, classed, and raced bodies. In *Pakeezah*'s final production number, "*Teer-E-Nazar Dekhenge*," the courtesan Sahibjaan dances on broken glass, leaving a trail of blood on the white cloth on which she performs her intricate *tatkar* (rhythmic footwork). This bloodied display of her dance skills is intended to communicate her despair at her lover marrying someone else, a respectable woman unlike herself. Significantly, Meena Kumari, the actress playing Sahibjaan, was not a trained *Kathak* dancer and found the footwork in this part of the number difficult to perform. Padma Khanna, a trained *Kathak* dancer, acted as the body double for the close-up shots of the footwork. The body double and the blood bespeak the materiality of dancing bodies, of the training, rehearsal, and special effects required to produce the spectacle of the production number.

Backup Dancers and Spatial Practices of the "Background"

The standard arrangement of dancing bodies in most Hindi film production numbers is characterized by one or more centrally-placed dancers (typically the heroine/vamp or the principal romantic couple) and a group of "background" or backup dancers. These background dancers usually wear identical costumes that are always differentiated, however, from the costume of the principal dancer(s). They also perform identical moves, sometimes in synchronization with the central performer(s), at other times, differentiated from the more spectacular moves of the central performer(s). Indeed, as the appellation suggests, the principal function of "background" dancers is to provide a *ground* against which the *figure* of the central dancer(s) stands out. This is similar to the figure-ground relation in music where the chorus serves to foreground the individual voice. In the Hindi film song-and-dance sequence, this relation is achieved by creating a uniform background of costume, gestures, and moves against which the main dancers are foregrounded. Since they function as an element of the spatial architecture of the dance number, background dancers are not morally coded like the principal performers are—as vamp or heroine, for example—but remain anonymous stewards of spectacle. Not surprisingly, then, we rarely see them in close-up shots; medium and long shots of their dancing bodies produce an abstract, dynamic background against which the drama of dancing protagonists is staged.

Group choreography of this type is influenced not only by Broadway and Hollywood traditions of uniformly lined-up chorus girls, but also by Indian classical and folk dance traditions. The *Natya Shastra*, for example, describes group formations such as *gulma* (a closed cluster made by dancers), *srinkhala* (a chain formed by dancers holding hands), *latabandha* (a creeper-like formation produced by dancers putting their hands around each other),[70] which are evidenced in numerous Hindi film song-and-dance sequences. While in production numbers performed on stage, background dancers function to augment the spectacle through synchronized movements, in many off-stage production numbers as well as narrative numbers, they often accompany and dance along with the romantic couple, all of them cycling, picnicking, partying, celebrating a wedding, etc. Here, in addition to the preceding roles, the background dancers create a sense of community, constituting networks of family and friends with whom the hero and heroine stage social dances. Through their collective presence, background dancers produce a sense of community and indeed of the folk in a diverse range of song-and-dance sequences.

In terms of dance, the arrangement, gestural vocabulary, and function of background dancers within the choreography are significantly influenced by folk dance conventions. The individual and collective figuration of the central performer(s) and the background dancers respectively is similar to that of the individuated classical dancer who occupies center stage to display virtuosic moves and that of folk dancers who typically perform identical moves in matching costumes. "In contrast to classical dancing," Vatsyayan notes that in folk dance, "the vocabulary of movements is restricted to a few mannered motor movements and does not allow for individual variations or improvisation. Improvisation may occur in the whole group in some rhythmic patterns but not through the evolution of new movements by a single dancer."[71] Similarly, in Hindi film dance configurations, the central performer(s) perform the most spectacular moves and often seem to improvise, while for the background dancers, the emphasis is on sameness and repetition. Additionally, just as "the whole system of *mukhaj abhinaya* (facial mime), so distinctive of classical forms, is minimum in the folk forms"[72] so too in film dance, the central dancer may display a range of facial expressions, but the background dancers predominantly perform only physical moves involving the torso and the limbs in order to construct a space out of their rhythmically synchronized movements. Accordingly, background dancers are mainly featured in the instrumental interludes of song-and-dance sequences while the focus is on the stars in the lyrical, sung sections, where the voice and body, song and dance are combined. Similar to the instrumental interlude's function of "filling out" a song, background dancers are employed to fill out the space of the dance number.

Production numbers staged in the spaces of the *kotha* and cabaret often foreground the musicians apparently performing the song, who are otherwise rendered invisible as behind-the-scenes labor in narrative numbers and song sequences. The visibility of the Hindustani musicians accompanying the *tawaif* and the Western band in the cabaret number renders these as public spaces and bodies committed to the production of musical entertainment. Indeed, as the experience of the backup dancer Edwina Lyons (see Figure 2.6) attests, only certain kinds of bodies attuned to particular spatial practices were sought for these spaces: "when films began to be influenced much more by Hollywood (gangster, criminal, urban), night club dance became an accessory. Apart from the main dancer, usually Helen or Bela Bose, they needed backup dancers who could do those kinds of dances. Edu and her family members fit right in!"[73] Women from Edwina's Anglo-Indian community of mixed British and Indian ancestry were among the first to join the urban workforce in the early twentieth century, and along with *baiji*s or performing women from the Muslim courtesan tradition, were also early

Figure 2.6. Edwina Lyons and Herman Benjamin in *Love Marriage* (Subodh Mukherjee, 1959).
Credit: Screen capture.

entrants into the film business, figuring them as "public" women during this period. Descriptions of their work in the Bombay film industry reveal the place of these bodies and their spatial practices in the popular Hindi film narrative: "they work in groups, get to know each other and typically do not need much rehearsal. The work is reasonably hard, very enjoyable for those who love dancing and pays well, roughly about 5–10 times a secretarial or low-level desk clerk job."[74] The mixed-race body, trained in waltz and swing, ragtime and jazz, even if considered part of the "background," has been central to producing, through these dance and musical practices, the spatio-corporeal architecture of the Hindi film cabaret.

Siegfried Kracauer, in an essay titled, "The Mass Ornament," discusses the Tiller Girls, an early twentieth-century dance troupe comprising chorus girls of identical height and weight, performing precisely matching steps. The Tiller Girls, argues Kracauer, do not appear as human beings, but as a mass ornament containing no individuals or organic energies, their performance the opposite of the communal dancing at village festivals and other events involving folk dance.[75] If we follow Kracauer's assertion that the mass ornament re-enacts the contemporary reality of capitalist production, the varying formations of Hindi film background dancers from the 1950s to the present Bollywood dispensation become an eloquent testament to the particular instantiations of capitalism in the Indian subcontinent. Until the 1990s, the arrangement of background dancers in Hindi film numbers was never as precise (in terms of coordinated movements, costume, or exactly identical bodies) as the Western chorus girl formations they were influenced by. Quite unlike the Tiller or Ziegfeld girls, for example, the ragtag team of typically working-class background dancers intimated the discontinuous assembling processes not only of Hindi cinema but of South Asian modernity itself. With the arrival of high-budget Bollywood films, buttressed by a triumphalist neoliberal discourse, however, the song-and-dance sequence changed radically. One reason ascribed for the newfound global appreciation of Bollywood dance numbers is their high production value and their "international" look. This has been achieved, in part, by replacing the working-class background dancers who proliferated in the 1970s and 1980s with Caucasian women (typically from Russia, Central Asia, and Eastern Europe), and with upper-class Indian college students trained at dance schools such as the Shiamak Davar Institute for the Performing Arts. Director-choreographer Farah Khan, among the first to introduce these changes in the background dancer formation, remarks:

> I insisted that people dancing in dance troupes should be fit. There is no point in forty-year-olds playing college students. So I brought young people into the troupe. Naturally, in comparison actresses had to look good as well. It is also to do with how India has changed. Many more people work out and go to the gym now.... It is nice to have bodies in shape.[76]

The perfectly coordinated movements of these lithe new dancing agents of "India Shining" accord serendipitously with Kracauer's observation that "[a] system oblivious to differences in form leads on its own to the blurring of national characteristics and to the production of worker masses that can be employed equally well at any point on the globe."[77] In the following chapters, we will encounter a range of background dancers—from the upper-caste *bhadramahila* dancers of Sadhona and Modhu Bose's theater group, "Calcutta Amateur Players," in the 1930s and 1940s, to Anglo-Indian background dancers like Edwina in the 1950s and the 1960s. The background dancers performing behind Madhuri Dixit in the 1980s and in the 1990s narrate radical shifts in India's economic policies during this period. While in 1988, a ragtag group of working-class junior artists dance in the shadows behind Dixit in "*Ek do teen*," by 1997, the dance numbers of *Dil toh Pagal Hai* (Yash Chopra) are populated with the uniformly lithe, leotard-clad, gym-trained students of the choreographer Shiamak Davar's institute of contemporary dance, among the first of its kind in India. A focus on the overshadowed "behind-the-star" bodies of background dancers thus illuminates transforming body cultures, changing economies of film production, and the shifting logics of capital.

3
Corporealizing Colonial Modernities

Azurie and Sadhona Bose as Co-Choreographers of New Mobilities in the 1930s and 1940s

Court Dancer (Modhu Bose, 1941) was hailed for being the "first Indian film with dialogue in English to be entirely produced in India with an all-Indian personnel."[1] Also released in Hindi and in Bengali—as *Raj Nartaki*—this extravagant, trilingual production was promoted as Wadia Movietone's most ambitious film to date (Figure 3.1). Through this "orientalised classical dance film for European audiences,"[2] studio founder J. B. H. Wadia sought to change the image of Wadia Movietone, which had until then mainly produced stunt films such as *Hunterwali* (Homi Wadia, 1935), *Miss Frontier Mail* (Homi Wadia, 1936), and *Diamond Queen* (Homi Wadia, 1940). These action films were extremely popular among the working-class "mass audience" but were almost entirely ignored by the press as lowbrow cultural products. *Court Dancer* was conceived to change all that with its high production values, its showcasing of Indian "classical dance," and its acclaimed Bengali dancer-actress, Sadhona Bose, a petite, classically trained dancer whose star text was seen to be in complete contrast to that of the muscular, Australian-born, British-Greek "Fearless Nadia," the rambunctious heroine of the Wadia stunt films. In 1941, as the nationalist reconstruction of Indian culture was hectically under way, it is no surprise that the culturally aspirational J. B. H. Wadia chose to showcase "classical" Indian dance in his prestige project. During a period when reformist discourses drew upon various cultural forms, the newly reconstructed classical dance idioms not only became respectable themselves, but also lent respectability to other domains of public performance such as the theater and cinema. The Bengali actress-director couple, Sadhona and Modhu Bose—who had already combined the generic syntaxes of social melodrama and orientalized classical dance in their "dance socials," *Abhinaya* (Modhu Bose, 1938) and *Kumkum the Dancer* (Modhu Bose, 1940)—brought to *Court Dancer* their intermedial expertise spanning film, theater, and dance. Sadhona Bose, in particular, brought to

Figure 3.1. From the song booklet for *Court Dancer* (Modhu Bose, 1941).
Credit: National Film Archives of India.

the film the cultural capital of classical dance and her upper-class, upper-caste *bhadramahila*[3] star text.

Examining why J. B. H. Wadia chose an orientalized dance film as his prestige project, with Sadhona Bose as the face of this big-budget, trilingual production, centered around a courtesan's doomed love for a prince, enables an exploration of the relationship between discourses on dance and cinema during the 1930s and 1940s. Bose is a striking example of a film actress of this period whose stardom owed in very great measure to her ability to dance.[4] Her oeuvre of twelve films, from *Alibaba* (Modhu Bose, 1937) to *Vikram Urvashi* (Modhu Bose, 1954), was conceived and designed around the display of her dancing skills, whether through oriental dance fantasies or a generic tendency I describe later in this chapter as the *dance social*.[5] As evident in her two extant films—*Alibaba* and *Court Dancer*—and in song booklets and promotional materials of her other films,[6] Bose was a dazzling performer of production numbers,[7] a trailblazing choreographer of group dances featuring a large number of background dancers, and an adventurous costume designer, whose creations reflect the same hybrid, "oriental," modern aesthetic encountered in her dance.[8] Bose's career as among the first and very few costume-designer-choreographer-dancer-actresses in Indian cinema produces a complex narrative of the embourgeoisement of dance and film cultures during this period. As the principal star of *Court Dancer* and other films, she emblematizes the cultural cachet that dance came to acquire by the early 1940s, albeit when performed by an upper-class, upper-caste woman from a "respectable" background. However, the vulnerability of her stardom also reveals continued contestations around women's participation in the public sphere, especially as dancers and film actresses.

A year after *Court Dancer*'s grand premiere, J. B. H Wadia's friend, the fantasy and stunt film director Kikubhai Desai, released his last film, *Sheikh Chilli* (1942). This film also featured a court dancer, but unlike Bose's prestige production that centrally mobilized her dancer-actress star text, this B-movie's court dancer was accorded no character name and no visual presence in the song booklet (the film itself, like many low-budget productions, does not survive). *Sheikh Chilli*'s court dancer was played by the German-Indian Azurie, who featured regularly as a "dancing girl" in Hindi cinema from 1935 to 1947, earning a latter-day description as "the first great item dancer of Hindi cinema" (see color insert—image 1).[9] Unlike upper-caste Hindu dancer-actresses like Sadhona Bose (and Sitara to some extent), Azurie's outsider status in terms of ethnicity, classical dance training, and her firm association with popular entertainment through the *bazaar* cinema[10] earned her a reputation as an itinerant dancing girl rather than a dancing heroine, someone who featured in dance numbers but not in the rest of the narrative. While few of her dance numbers survive, from song booklets, journalistic accounts, and production numbers like "*Jab Usne Gesu Bikhraye*" in *Shahjehan* (A. R. Kardar, 1946), one gathers that Azurie was a regular performer of "novelty dances," which the stunt film director Homi Wadia describes as "gypsy," Arabic, or Turkish dances, sometimes including belly-dancing and often credited as "Oriental Dances" (see ▶ video 03.01).[11] Even if Bose's cinematic presence is elusive, her authorship as a dancing *heroine* is amply evident in film publicity materials, especially in the design and logics of the song booklets for her films, making it possible to argue for her place as an artistic pioneer in Indian cinema. As an itinerant dancer who rarely appeared outside of song-and-dance sequences, Azurie is rendered even more invisible in the official archive. Including figures considered marginal to the history of South Asian cinemas—dancing girls like Azurie—opens up the history of film dance in the 1930s and 1940s beyond acclaimed stars, acknowledging the pivotal labor of shadow figures left out of cinematic narratives and official histories. As a mixed-race woman who emigrated from India to Pakistan, from screen to stage, dexterously managing her star text between being a sex symbol and an English-Bengali-Urdu magazine columnist, demanding respect and funding for Indian/Hindu and later Pakistani/Muslim dance forms, Azurie helps us advance new histories of the female body in South Asian film and dance, corporeal histories forged relationally across axes of caste, class, religion, and region.

The 1930s are a key moment for the study of film dance, when, as Madhuja Mukherjee notes, "the film-song became an autonomous spectacular 'song and dance' unit."[12] Scholars have examined how, by the mid-1930s, film music comes to have an independent existence through the radio and the gramophone.[13] The transition from the song sequence to the song-and-dance unit deserves further attention. A focus on dance reveals significant changes in actors' movement on-screen, the organization of spectacular attractions within film narratives, and emerging cine-choreographic practices that influence cinematography, art direction, choreography, and editing. With the introduction of playback singing in 1935, music and dance are slowly decoupled, allowing for greater on-screen mobility. As performers and choreographers of spectacular production numbers from the mid-1930s onward, Bose and Azurie are key figures in these cine-corporeal transformations, artistic pioneers who, through the conceptualization of space, movement vocabulary, costume, and the general "look" of popular film dance, contribute to a new cinematic and dance idiom and indeed to a newly emerging mass culture. Building on scholarship on actors and singing stars of this period, this chapter's attention to dancer-actresses brings the question of the mobility and visibility of the female body front and center. An analysis of movement and dance profoundly corporealizes social analyses of gender, including rhetoric about the public-private divide articulated during this period and earlier, highlighting the relationship between women, dance, and modernity, placing dance not at the margins of social developments in the 1930s, but at the very heart of the "women's question."[14] Using their few extant films, song booklets, posters, newspaper and magazine articles, print advertisements, and Bose's autobiography, *Shilpir Atmakatha* (Autobiography of an Artist), this chapter undertakes a study of the two dancing women's careers to examine female participation in cinema and dance during the period.[15]

The 1930s and 1940s are a critical period for studying discursive formations around dance as well, with the so-called revival of classical dance forms, which involved an appropriation of the cultural practices of traditional performers like *devadasi*s and *tawaif*s by upper-caste, upper-class performers.[16] While there is a rich body of scholarship on the canonization of performing arts during this period, which was marked by a spirit of intense political and cultural nationalism,[17] it is important to include in this conversation a discussion of how the nationalist appropriation of dance as a key cultural form translated to the screen. Considerations of gender, class, caste, and religion are imperative to understanding what kind of dancing was now sanctioned as respectable, which in turn determined the kinds of dancing bodies that could achieve cinematic stardom. Bose's elite social background and classical dance training, for instance, make her a part of the significant shift in female stardom in the 1930s and 1940s, as an emergent bourgeoisie and the demands of cultural nationalism decree as disreputable or not-Indian-enough the earlier film actresses, who were mainly drawn from the Muslim courtesan tradition or the Anglo-Indian community.[18] However, Bose's primary identification as a dancer inflects her stardom in very particular ways. By reading Bose and Azurie's performing bodies and careers alongside each other, I also aim to dislodge unitary accounts of the impulses and controversies around dance on film by a new class of urban performers. As dancer-choreographers composing and performing their own dances, and determining the aural and visual contexts in which these dances take place, both women redistribute and re-gender creative roles that had been typically dominated by men. With their performative energies proliferating across cinema, concert dance, and theater (through their ambitious dance-dramas), both women prevail as intermedial artists, engaged in a radical exploration of how dance can be mobilized across various old and new media platforms. Azurie and Bose acts as nodes for tracing multiple figurations that fold into the dancer-actress, and reading them alongside each other contests binary figurations of heroine and vamp, *bhadramahila* and sex siren, the "cultured lady" of social melodrama and the dancing girl of *bazaar* cinema, *devadasi* or *tawaif* and classical dancer, dancer and choreographer. Indeed, studying these once-famous, now-forgotten dancing stars excavates a dense, intersecting, global history of early twentieth-century discourses on dance and on dancing women that features oriental dancers like Ruth St. Denis, the prima ballerina Anna Pavlova, cultural reformers in the subcontinent Rabindranath Tagore, Uday Shankar, and Rukmini Devi Arundale, among many others. In their spirited and skillful production of and participation in a global circuit of entertainment economies, Azurie and Bose marshal dance to co-choreograph new mobilities in this late colonial period.

Orienting Dance to a New Class of Female Performers

Sadhona Bose (1914–1973) was born into a prosperous Bengali family in Calcutta. Her father, Saral Chandra Sen, a barrister, was the fourth son of the social reformer Keshab Chandra Sen, a member of the Brahmo Samaj, and later, the founder of the breakaway "Brahmo Samaj of India."[19] Her mother, Nirmala Sen, was the daughter of Burma's (now Myanmar) first Indian Administrator, General P. C. Sen. Two of her aunts were members of the royalty, queens of the princely states of Cooch Behar and Mayurbhanj, and her older and younger sisters married into the royal families of Chittagong and Kapurthala, respectively. In keeping with her Brahmo Samaj background, Bose was given a diverse education, attending the Loreto Convent school, and also learning music and dance at prestigious institutions such as the Sangeet Sangha and the Sangeet Sammilani. She took *Kathak* lessons from Tarakanath Bagchi, and learned *Manipuri* dance from Guru Senarik Rajkumar. She was a pupil of the famous *Thumri* exponent, Girijasankar Chakrabarti, and took piano lessons from T. Francopolo. Later, in the 1930s, she also learned music from the film music composer Sachin Dev Burman.[20] However, while Bose and her sister Nilina (who later became a renowned Thumri exponent by the name of Naina Devi) took Thumri lessons and learned dance, these were not meant to be professional pursuits. Naina Devi recollects, "Taking up dance or music as a profession however was out of the question. Even Mejdi (Sadhona), so as not to jeopardize my chances of finding a good match, did not become a professional actress until after I was married, and even then, my parents disapproved strongly of her decision."[21] Additionally, while the family generously patronized the arts, care was taken not to associate with traditional *female* performers of music and dance, the *tawaif*s or courtesans. Naina Devi reports, "The house was always full of music. My brothers would organize *mehfil*s of the leading male singers—Girija Babu (Girijasankar Chakrabarti), Enayet Khan and others, but none of the tawaifs."[22]

The attitude of Bose's family toward *tawaif*s or to the professional performance of music and especially dance by women was not uncommon at the time, and reflects the status of dance in public discourse in the early decades of the twentieth century. By the late nineteenth century, the split between body and voice was exacerbated as dance and music increasingly diverged. While singing (privately) would become a respectable activity for middle-class women, dance carried with it the unshakable association with courtesans who traditionally both sang and danced. Even within North Indian Hindustani musical traditions, certain forms were preferred over others. By the 1920s, music scholars like V. D. Paluskar and V. N. Bhatkande were textualizing orally transmitted Hindustani musical practices, but as Nita Kumar and Vidya Rao have argued, this process of textualization happened at the expense of musical forms like the *Thumri* and the *Kajri*, sung by the courtesans.[23] Bhatkande charged what he called "light classical" musical forms with lewdness, blaming "illiterate Muslim singers" and their ignorance of "spiritual" Sanskritic traditions for this.[24] Matthew Rahaim, in his study of gestures and voice in Hindustani music, notes that scholars such as Bhatkhande systematized and wrote about Hindustani music in a way that omitted gestural articulation altogether. Through this period of the severing of the voice from the body, male and female singers employed "smaller" gestures so as not to attract attention to the body.[25]

Beginning in 1882, the British government, with the support of many Indian reformists, launched the anti-*nautch* movement to abolish traditional dancing women such as the *tawaifs* and the *devadasis*, who performed publicly, and whose art was seen, by the anti-*nautch* campaigners, as a mere pretext for prostitution.[26] As Soneji explains, these social reform movements, starting from the mid-nineteenth century, were aimed at dislodging professional dancing women from their hereditary social, ritual, and aesthetic performance practices, seeking to criminalize their lifestyles on the basis of their nonconjugal sexuality.[27] An 1894 pamphlet, "Opinions on the Nautch Question," published by the "Punjab Purity Association" (one of many "social purity associations" sponsored by the Purity movement in England for the reform of public and private morals), demonstrates how the bourgeoisie sought to separate "the gem from the dirt," the song being the gem and dance, the dirt.[28] Significantly, this pamphlet includes the opinions of Sadhona Bose's social reformist grandfather, Keshab Chandra Sen, on the *nautch* as well:

> The nautch-girl is a hideous woman . . . hell in her eyes. In her breast is a vast ocean of poison. Round her comely waist dwell the furies of hell. Her hands are brandishing unseen daggers ever ready to strike unwary or wilful victims that fall in her way. Her blandishments are India's ruin. Alas! her smile is India's death.[29]

Given this contempt toward dance, how did Sen's grand-daughter come to be a celebrated public performer around forty years later? The *Court Dancer* song booklet describes Bose as "Young, Beautiful and Vivacious, of high birth and cultural and social attainments. . . . The progressive instincts of her famous grandfather have found fruitful echo in the versatile artistry of Sadhona." What were the shifts in discourse over this period that allowed a girl from Keshab Chandra Sen's own upper-class Bengali family to learn dance forms like *Kathak* and musical forms like the *Thumri* that were the domain of the *tawaif*s through the nineteenth century and until the early decades of the twentieth?

By the 1920s, cultural revivalists like E. Krishna Iyer started crusading against the anti-*nautch* movement and began to "rehabilitate" dance forms such as *Sadirattam* performed by the *devadasi*s in South India. For these dance forms to be deemed acceptable by bourgeois patrons, however, reformers like Iyer had to accede to part of the anti-*nautch* campaigners' demand—that the social customs and rituals associated with these forms be excised and only the "pure art" be retained. Iyer, a lawyer in Madras, tried to secure audiences for the hereditary *devadasi*s, but when that failed, he began studying Sadirattam himself, and in 1926, presented it as the dance form of *Bharatanatyam* before the cultural elite of Madras.[30] That same year, between January 8 and May 9, 1926, the Denishawn Dance Company, formed by Ruth St. Denis and Ted Shawn, performed over 100 dance concerts in India. St. Denis, celebrated as a pioneer of modern dance in the United States, performed a series of productions inspired by "Indian themes," such as *The Nautch, The Dance of the Black and Gold Sari, The Cobras, Yogi,* and *Radha*. As the titles suggest, these pieces presented India as a land of dancing girls, snake charmers, and spiritual mystique.[31] St. Denis's performances are reported to have rekindled in her bourgeois Indian audiences an interest and pride in their dance forms. The dance critic Walter Terry, for example, claimed that St. Denis's "non-authentic Indian dance helped reawaken the subcontinent's slumbering dance art and [was] at least partially responsible for the renascence of India's respect for its 2,000 year old heritage."[32] The circular, imperial logics of appropriation and gentrification become apparent when we consider Priya Srinivasan's research on how St. Denis's rise to fame as one of the "foremothers" of American modern dance and as an "Oriental dancer" is founded on her encounter with *nautch* dancers at a 1904 show, called the Durbar of Delhi, in Coney Island.[33] Two years later, she presented the piece *Radha,* her spiral turns and whirls haunted by the effaced labor of the *nautch* dancers. "Oriental dance," as Joan Erdman explains, was a term initially used by Europeans and Americans to describe balletic dances that were "eastern in theme, content, mood, costume, musical accompaniment, inspiration, or intent."[34] It is worth noting that dance is a key element of the fascination with the Orient, mobilizing as it does the prevailing interest in oriental fashion, textiles, and arts and crafts. Indeed, by the 1920s, "oriental dance conjured up expectations of exotic movements, glittering costumes, flowing lines, sublime dedication, and minor mode or strangely tuned music."[35]

The legendary Russian ballerina Anna Pavlova toured India a year later, in 1927. In the early 1920s, she had choreographed a production titled *Oriental Impressions* that included Indian-themed pieces such as *Krishna and Radha* and *A Hindu Wedding*. These pieces were co-choreographed and performed by a young Indian art student who would go on to become the global icon of modern Indian dance, Uday Shankar. In addition to influencing Shankar and introducing him to the world of dance in 1922, during her 1927 visit to India, Pavlova directly inspired two other key figures in Indian dance. She encouraged Rukmini Devi Arundale, the Brahmin wife of the British head of the Theosophical Society, to learn and perform *Bharatanatyam* in public, and also exhorted the socialite Leela Sokhey to study *Kathak*. Sokhey, under the stage name Madame Menaka, went on to popularize *Kathak* around the world.[36] Meanwhile, in 1930, the Madras legislative assembly passed a bill to "absolve" *devadasi*s of their service to the temples, which in reality deprived the temple dancers of their erstwhile prestige, financial independence, and rights to property inheritance. This dissociation of dance from the *devadasi* was intended to remove the stigma from public dancing and encouraged non-*devadasi* women from middle- and upper-class families to study dance. In a move similar to Bhatkande and Paluskar's mission to textualize Hindustani music, Arundale undertook the reconstruction of *Sadirattam*, reclaiming it as *Bharatanatyam*, "the purest and most 'authentic' traditional dance of the Natya Shastra, effectively shifting the focus of the dance from the living tradition to texts."[37]

Recognizing that there was no "classical" Indian music or dance outside the *nautch*, these reformers belonging to the Hindu bourgeoisie turned to ancient and medieval Sanskrit texts like the *Natya Shastra* to project an unbroken tradition of "respectable" national cultural forms, a process referred to as "Sanskritization" by later scholars.[38] In articulating the movement vocabulary of *Bharatanatyam*, for example, Arundale stripped Sadirattam of much of what was considered its objectionable *sringara* (erotic) elements, and emphasized the *bhakti* (devotional) elements of the form. Her aversion to the braiding of religious piety and sexual desire that characterized the *devadasi* dance idiom is evident in this interview:

> *Sringara* is not sensuality. It also means a love of a great kind, such as the love of Radha for Krishna as depicted in Gita Govindam.... So if it has been said that I am against *sringara*, I can only say that the inference is wrong. But there are certain types of *padams* [category of dance item] that I have objected to. From one *vidwan* [scholar] I learnt the old *padam* tamaraksha with a lot of sanchari bhavas of the languishing *nayika* separated from her lover.[39] She describes not only her love but the whole process of physical contact and in gestures at that! To depict such things is unthinkable for me. A famous man gave me a book on *sanchari bhava*. When I read it I just felt sick.[40]

The *devadasi* performative repertoire included elegant poetic exposition, elaborate metaphors, and a complex gestural vocabulary, including a set of over fifty *rati mudras* or hand gestures that depicted various kinds of sexual union.[41] Davesh Soneji, in his magisterial study of *devadasi*s, argues that the so-called dance revival of the mid-twentieth century should be understood in terms of new taste hierarchies, "the cultivation of specific taste habits among the elites of Madras"[42] that now declared the dance of the *devadasi* sexually explicit, casual, "unclassical," "aesthetically impoverished and morally dubious,"[43] in contrast with a newly constructed *Bharatanatyam*. As we shall see later in this chapter, these binaries inflected discourses on film dance and especially the star texts of Bose and Azurie that were enmeshed in dualisms of tradition and modernity, classical and erotic dance, and danseuse and dancing girl figurations.

A closer examination of the actual dancing women, their training, labor, and legacies, contests rigid historiographies and helps us engage more deeply with identities forged in particular historical circumstances. Avanti Meduri, for instance, cautions against a staging of the history of the dance revival "as a struggle between two women inscribed in two different caste and class backgrounds: "Brahmin Rukmini Devi and devadasi T. Balasasaraswati."[44] Instead, through a study of both pioneers' engagement with translocal, global modernities, she invites us to consider how the two women shouldered the burden of a reinvented tradition, "a burden emerging not from the stable core of the self, but from the contingency of the institutional and political context of Indian nationalism and international Orientalism in which they were speaking, writing, and dancing."[45] The inadequacies of a tradition-modernity model of social change in this period become considerably apparent when we consider the many, seemingly conflicting cultural negotiations at work in the embourgeoisement of dance. The transmutation of *Sadirattam* into *Bharatanatyam* by figures like Arundale, for example, was informed by nationalist, reformist, and global-Theosophical goals aiming for the construction of "a gendered middle-class respectability that is simultaneously upper caste, Brahminic, modern, and westernized in its sensibility."[46] Thus, while the Western ballet-trained Arundale sought to "cleanse" *Sadirattam* of its erotic elements, she also simultaneously "modernized" the *Bharatanatyam* costume, creating a leaner silhouette that would allow for greater freedom of movement. As Uttara Asha Coorlawala has argued, Sanskritizing a dance form involves not only relating it to older Sanskrit texts and rediscovering or reinventing its methodology, but also "refining" the dance form by adapting its costumes, repertory, and technique to urban sensibilities.[47] As Soneji demonstrates though, the *devadasi* repertoire was already undeniably modern in synthesizing heterogeneous dance and music genres such as the *nottusvaram* ("note" song) riffing on Irish marching-band tunes, Parsi theater, and, by the 1940s, popular Telugu film songs.[48] While their hybrid practices boldly produced and participated in an incipient cultural modernity, the potential for the emergence of the citizen-subject of modernity "could only be seized by middle-class women who mobilized the flexibility and 'modernity' of these forms by reworking them to nationalist ends, and not by *devadasis* who were framed by the state as archaic emblems of a degenerate, embarrassing past."[49] In keeping with the nationalist impetus behind cultural reform, the Sanskritization of many dance forms in the 1930s and the 1940s not only marginalized traditional female performers like the *devadasis* and *tawaifs*, but also led to an erasure in official and academic accounts of the influence of Western oriental dance. As Erdman argues, by mining ancient texts to theorize the dance of the present, Indian dancers and scholars "invented a new dance tradition based on claimed antiquity, asserted authenticity, well-intentioned chauvinism, and middle-class purity."[50] These values made classical dance training and performance a suitable domain for "proper" Indian women (up to the point of marriage). In 1936, Arundale instituted the Kalakshetra Foundation in Madras, where respectable young girls flocked to study dance for the first time.

Closer to Bose's home in Bengal, by the early 1920s, Rabindranath Tagore introduced dance in the curriculum of the Viswa-Bharati University he had established at Santiniketan. In 1919, on a trip to the region of Manipur in North East India, Tagore saw a performance of *Manipuri* dance and remarked that he "felt that there he had at last found the solution to the tragedy of India's dying dance."[51] He invited *Manipuri* dancers from Agartala to teach at Viswa-Bharati. However, to avoid criticism for introducing formal dance training in the curriculum, the university magazine expunged any mention of dance: "Two artistes have arrived at Shantiniketan from the court of the Maharaja of Tripura. The male students of the ashram are learning musical exercise to the rhythm of Manipuri Khol."[52] The replacement of dance with physical exercise and the emphasis on male students' training are revelatory of the censure attending dance training or performance, especially by women. However, by 1925, Tagore invited the *Manipuri* dancers Nabakumar Singha and Baikunthanath Singha to Viswa-Bharati to teach female students, as he considered the dance form apt for women. The classes, however, were not publicized so that the residents of the town of Shantiniketan would not find out about them.[53] Through the 1920s and 1930s, Tagore invited various folk and classical dance practitioners to Viswa-Bharati who introduced, for example, the "cymbal dance" from Saurashtra, *Garba* of Gujarat, *Kathakali*, *Kaikuttikali*, and *Kallammuli* from Kerala, the *Kandy* dance of Sri Lanka, Russian ballet, English ballroom dancing, and Bengali folk dances such as *Raye-Beshey* and Jaari.[54] This eclectic inclusion of dance forms in the university curriculum was in keeping with Tagore's desire to change the status of dance in India and reintroduce it to "respectable society": "Dance is a part of performing arts courses in every country, and is respected as a medium of expressing emotions. Just because it has disappeared from our respectable society, we have assumed that we don't have it anymore."[55] Increasingly, dance became an important element in his plays as well, moving as he did from *gitanatya* or musical drama to *Rabindra Nritya Natya* (Rabindra Dance-Drama)—plays including dance, songs, and instrumental music. *Rabindra Nritya*, the hybrid dance form in his dance-dramas, featured stylistic idioms drawn from several Indian and Southeast Asian dance traditions, such as *Kathakali*, *Manipuri*, Javanese and Balinese dance forms, and the Kandy dance of Sri Lanka.[56] The aim was to create a new dance style liberated from what he deemed the formulaic choreography and narratives of classical Indian dance and to encourage the performer to use dance gestures to interpret character and situation. Tagore's turn to dance, Esha Niyogi De argues, coincides with his critique of nationalist sexual politics. Between 1933 and 1939, Tagore wrote the famous dance-dramas, *Tasher Desh*, *Chitrangada*, *Chandalika*, and *Shyama*, that present women as autonomous agents of desire, significantly through a portrayal of the desiring body as a dancing body, "one that moves and self-expresses with dignity in full public view," breaching the "nationalist and patriarchal ideals of respectable (high caste/class) domesticity."[57] Tagore's initial appropriation of dance for "respectable society" and then his refashioning of it into an anti-imperialist expression of female desire points to the complex and contradictory impulses around the "revival" of classical dance forms and the fraught and precarious terrain of caste, class, and gender undergirding the politics of female visibility in early twentieth-century India.

Around the same time, in the 1930s, another Bengali, Uday Shankar, formed his dance repertory—the "Uday Shankar Company of Hindu Dancers and Musicians"—that extensively toured Europe and America. Shankar was hailed as the progenitor of modern Indian dance. His repertoire consisted of episodic "theme" dances that combined poses and gestures from classical and folk dance forms, as well as from temple paintings and sculpture seen on his travels in India. Given his mostly Western audience through the 1930s and 1940s, Shankar learned to present a variety of short items that he made accessible to this audience by avoiding complicated *hasta-mudras* or hand gestures that had very specific coded meanings in the movement vocabulary of many Indian dances.[58] He also replaced the complex footwork found in most dance forms with simple stepping and skipping foot movements.[59] Additionally, where Indian audiences familiar with local dance vocabularies would delight in the restatement of phrases and emotions with subtle changes, and dance performances would often take place over many long nights, Shankar held his European and American audiences' attention with brief, episodic dances featuring short, repeated dance movements. Because he took inspiration from sculpture and painting, his ballets were often characterized by static poses and tableaus (see Figure 3.2).

As with the oriental dances of St. Denis, Pavlova, and others, Shankar's international success was attributed in large part to his ability to "determine European audiences' span of attention to oriental dances, their reliance on elegant or exotic costuming and jewelry to accord with their own interest in fashion, their need for the exotic to fulfill expectations, and their keen interest in the sensual and the romantic."[60] His appropriations of various movement vocabularies and his reconstruction of these for an urban, Western audience

Figure 3.2. From the song booklet for *Kalpana* (Uday Shankar, 1948).
Credit: National Film Archives of India.

make Shankar a key figure in dance choreography for the Indian stage and screen in the late 1930s and through the 1940s. During his 1933 India tour, for example, when Shankar presented his repertoire to Indian audiences, spectators were reportedly enthralled by the production of this "stage dance" which they had witnessed until then only when foreign performers such as the Denishawn Company visited India.[61] While previously, dance performances were staged in royal courts, temples, or private salons, Shankar was among the first Indian performers to adapt these for the modern stage. Nilanjana Bhattacharjya, in her study of his hybrid innovations in music and dance, notes that "[t]he field of dance integrated Shankar's interests in visual art, set design, special effects and performance."[62] Just as, in the first two decades of the twentieth century, the new recording technology of the gramophone required a reformatting, as it were, of Indian musical forms, presenting dance on stage and screen significantly altered the duration and movement vocabulary of dance forms. We must not forget that the pioneers of popularizing these new musical formats and bringing them from the salon spaces of the *mehfil* and *mejuvani* private soiree contexts to a larger middle-class consuming public were *tawaif*s and *devadasi*s.[63] Similarly, we can trace multiple networks of influence on film dance, which often presents, like stage dance of this period, simplified dance techniques, shortened durations of three- to seven-minute pieces, and an attention to visual spectacle. Rather than constructing a history of pitched battles and abrupt innovations, when we consider how the categories of "oriental dancers," "classical dancers," and "traditional performers" are intertwined in complex genealogies, we notice how multiple instantiations of female presence in the public space are folding into each other during this and earlier periods. The diverse performance lineages that feed into Bose and Azurie's adventurous, hybrid movement vocabularies disrupt linear narratives of female public performance and deeply enrich histories of female labor and agency in articulating colonial modernity.

Dance Becomes Respectable for the *Bhadramahila*

This performance history of classical and oriental dance in India in the early decades of the twentieth century illustrates the easy hybridity among dance forms during this period, when performers appropriated with a great degree of freedom from Indian dance forms (to be classified a few years later into the categories of "classical" and "folk"), as well as oriental dance, to create performance idioms that were traditional and modern, cosmopolitan and nationalist at the same time. It also helps trace how dance is constructed as a national cultural heritage that slowly comes to be embodied in young, upper-caste, bourgeois women. While in South India, Arundale's Kalakshetra Foundation became a key training and research center for *Bharatanatyam*, in Bengal, Tagore's dance-dramas "were among the first ones to be choreographed and performed onstage with the participation of girls from 'good' families," and Shankar's dance company had a number of female dancers from "respectable" families as well.[64] One such aspiring *bhadramahila* (literally, polite or decent lady, but referring more broadly to bourgeois Bengali women) dancer was Sadhona Bose, a member of Keshab Chandra Sen's extremely respectable family.[65]

In 1927, Sadhona Bose's future husband, Modhu Bose, founded the theater group "Calcutta Amateur Players" (C.A.P.). In his autobiography, *Aamar Jeeban* (My Life), Bose remarks, "It was always my dream to create my own theatre group, where men and women from progressive, aristocratic, respectable families would perform."[66] This bourgeois class that Bose refers to were known in the Bengali vernacular as *bhadralok*, broadly referring to the educated elite. Modhu Bose, grandson of the famous historian R. C. Dutt, a student at Santiniketan and Bidyasagar College, and briefly, assistant cameraman in London and at the UFA Studio in Germany, was very much of *bhadralok* stock himself. Taking up acting as a profession, especially by the kind of *bhadramahila* women Bose wanted in his group, was still taboo during this period, as is reflected in the struggle over the naming of the group: "First I thought that our troupe would be named "Calcutta Art Players," but everyone suggested that it was important to mention the word "amateur" otherwise no parents would agree to allow their daughters to perform in our group."[67] To avoid controversy, C.A.P. initially promoted its plays as private charity shows performed by amateur players, given the deep prejudices against paid public performance by "respectable" women.[68] At the premiere of Bose's C.A.P. production of the play *Alibaba* in 1928, there was a *dharna* [protest] outside the hall against the mixed casting of men and women from respectable families.[69] Khirode Prasad Vidyavinode's 1897 adaptation into Bengali of the Alibaba story from the *Arabian Nights* was one of the most popular pre–World War I plays, advertised as a "magnificent Comic Opera" and a "genuine Fountain of Mirth and Merriment."[70] The reaction against this particular C.A.P. production was no doubt fueled by outrage at respectable, *bhadramahila* women performing in an oriental song-and-dance spectacular. Bose quotes a review of his play in the magazine *Nachghor* to highlight the gentrification undertaken by C.A.P. of such oriental plays:

> We apologize. We were not correct in what we expressed in our last issue about men and women from respectable families participating in "Alibaba" staged at Empire. Before watching the play last Sunday we had no idea how one can edit out the disreputable parts of a play like "Alibaba" such that even the feelings of the most orthodox individuals will not be hurt. The play has been portrayed in such an ugly manner in other contemporary playhouses.[71]

The inclusion of the *bhadralok* altered the very plots of these plays, removing erotically charged or bawdy elements that would offend the sensibilities of the actors in and the audiences for this newly sanitized entertainment. The cultural forms of theater in the 1920s and film in the 1930s were marked by a discourse of respectability where, spurred by a spirit of cultural nationalism, the *bhadralok* or English-educated urbanized Bengalis were urged to participate in and thereby improve these forms.[72] The emphasis was on expurgating the theater and the cinema of their "low-bred" personnel, including the *baijee* actresses from the Muslim courtesan tradition, as seen in this opinion piece in a magazine: "I hope that the educated, civilized society would try for the upliftment of this art form [cinema] with their taste and restrained and beautiful manners and behavior."[73] C.A.P. turned professional in 1936, nine years after its inception, and was finally named "Calcutta Art Players," as Modhu Bose had originally planned. Figure 3.3 features Sadhona Bose with C.A.P. performers in the filmed version of *Alibaba* released the next year.

Like many C.A.P. performers, Sadhona Sen (Sadhona Bose's name before marriage) was permitted to perform in amateur shows for public charities. She performed in Modhu Bose's 1930 play, *Daliya*, at the age of sixteen. They were married the same year. The couple worked as a team over the next two decades, producing plays, films, and dance-dramas. In her autobiography, Sadhona Bose remarks on the fraught social discourse around acting and dancing by women:

> It is not like theatre was an acceptable or reputed thing in society, unlike now. . . . As for bhadramahilas entering the theatre either professionally or as a hobby, it was strictly prohibited. . . . Amidst much disrespect, at the cost of losing our reputation, hearing lot of negative things from orthodox

Figure 3.3. Sadhona Bose with C.A.P. performers in *Alibaba* (Modhu Bose, 1937).
Credit: National Film Archives of India.

households and a major section of the local print media, we had to stay fixed on our decision to be on stage.[74]

Because Bose worked solely in her husband's plays and films (until 1943 when she starred in Chaturbhuj Doshi's film, *Shankar Parvati*, which was seen as a betrayal by Modhu Bose and precipitated a temporary separation between the couple), there was some deflection of the general disapproval attendant upon dancer-actresses at the time. This also had some reviewers ascribing her stardom entirely to Modhu Bose: "It is doubtful whether the young Sadhona Sen . . . would ever have turned out to be the great artist that she is today had not she met Modhu Bose. . . . Sadhona Sen would, in the normal course of events, have adorned the home of a leading politician or an official."[75] In choosing a career as a dancer-actress-choreographer-costume designer, Bose marks a shift in the construction of the *bhadramahila* from an educated woman, trained in cultural forms like music and dance, but destined for domesticity, to a professional, public performer who defined the evolution of film dance and of forms like the dance-drama.

In addition to her training in classical dance and music, and her work with Modhu Bose and C.A.P., Sadhona Bose's associations with Tagore, Shankar, and Pavlova establish her as being at the center of the movement to reinvent Indian dance forms, as is evident in her own performance and choreography. In 1930, Bose played the heroine in Aparesh Chandra Mukhopadhyay's dramatized version of Tagore's short story *Daliya*, directed by Modhu Bose. She mentions being under Tagore's tutelage: "During the course of rehearsing for this play, Rabindranath Tagore himself taught me acting. I would receive these lessons at his house in Jorasanko. . . . I am extremely lucky that Tagore was so pleased with my acting that he came and saw each and every run."[76] Early in her autobiography, Bose also talks about her meeting with Pavlova, who watched a performance of Bose's play *Alibaba* at the Empire theater and invited her to perform in her *Krishna and Radha* ballet. The performance never took place, which Bose refers to as her "greatest misfortune."[77] Bose also cites a review of her dance-drama *Omar Khaiyyam* in *The Statesman* that compares her with Pavlova: "Sadhona Bose's ballet now at Regal theatre is the most lovely that has been seen in Delhi since Pavlova visited us. In colour, composition, and movement it is the equal of Russian ballet at its best."[78]

Bose was close friends with Uday Shankar and his French dance partner, Madame Simkie, in Calcutta.[79] Earlier, Shankar had tried to persuade Bose's parents to allow her to join his troupe. But when they insisted that she be accompanied by a guardian, he refused as he was working on a tight budget and could not afford to include an extra person in his troupe. Bose describes this as the second biggest setback in her life after the cancellation of Pavlova's project.[80] Shankar's influence on Bose's films and dance-dramas was also felt through Timir Baran, an important musician in Shankar's troupe in the 1930s, the music composer for Modhu Bose's films *Kumkum the Dancer* and *Court Dancer*, and long-time collaborator with Sadhona Bose on her stage ballets. A disciple of the renowned *sarod*[81] player Ustad Allauddin Khan, Baran displayed in music the same eclecticism that Bose did in dance, improvising on Indian classical music, introducing the violin and guitar in his orchestra, and taking melodic inspiration from Middle Eastern musical forms. Baran retained Shankar's emphasis on dance-centered percussion-based rhythms in his film compositions, an early instance of dance musicalization, where Bose's dance vocabulary determined a certain musical score for her films. During a period—the 1930s and 1940s—when dance movements were not yet as strictly codified as they would be by the 1950s, in her film and stage choreography and costume design, Bose brought in elements of classical dance forms like *Manipuri*, but also freely borrowed from *Rabindra Nritya*, Western ballet, and Middle Eastern and Southeast Asian forms. Bose herself refers to her plays as "neo-classical ballets," which have their "base in tradition but are at par with the rhythm of the times."[82] She discusses how her neo-classical ballets offer a modern interpretation of traditional forms: "As I grew up, I added my own touches to traditional Indian dances and tried to give them a new look, which would have the potential to bring a fresh perspective to dance."[83] An admirer of Western ballet and ballroom dancing, she asserts, however, that Indian dancers should not blindly emulate Western dances but adhere to the tenets of traditional Indian dance.[84] This simultaneous appeal to tradition and modernity can be understood in the context of the contemporary nationalistic rhetoric in India that sought to create a picture of an ancient civilization with rich cultural forms, ready to embrace the ideals of modern nationhood.

The Initiation of the *Bhadramahila* into Cinema

Neepa Majumdar, Rosie Thomas, and Kaushik Bhowmick, among others, have delineated the history of female film stardom in Bombay cinema from the 1920s through the 1950s.[85] Considering the figure of Sadhona Bose within this history—of the transition of the Hindi film actress's lineage from the Muslim courtesan to the Anglo-Indian professional to the "cultured" Hindu lady—illuminates particular tensions related to dancing women on-screen. The report of the Indian Cinematograph Committee (ICC), formed in 1927 with the interlinked agendas of regulation, reform, and education, is revelatory of prevailing attitudes to Indian film actresses of the time, including remarks such as: "With a few exceptions (mostly in Bengal), the actors and actresses are not drawn from the cultured classes. The actresses are mainly recruited from the 'dancing girl' class. Indian women of the better class do not take up film-acting as a profession."[86] That a common discourse inflected film acting and dancing, specifically the popular *nautch* forms, is evident in the various pronouncements of the mostly bourgeois respondents in the ICC.[87] A member of the Punjab board of film censors, Diwan Bahadur Raja Narendranath, for example, observed that the cinema was replacing the *nautch* as entertainment for men.[88] Bhowmick discusses how it was easy to make this analogy between the cinema and the *nautch* in the context of the cosmopolitan *bazaar* cinema of the 1920s and early 1930s, which was a pastiche of Oriental fantasies, Parsi-Urdu theater-style romance plots, and Hollywood stunt film scenarios, highlighting the exotic charms of the heroine through her dancing.[89] The transition to the talkie film and the film industry's desire to create a more acceptable image for itself in a bourgeois-nationalist mode resulted in the emergence of the bourgeois "cultured lady" as "the touchstone by which cinema was to be brought to the attention of the cultural elite" and whose educational status was highlighted in order to align the film actress with the new public role of women in the national movement.[90]

The 1939 New Year issue of the Bengali magazine *Deepali* includes a photo feature captioned "India's four educated, aristocratic film stars" and lists the actresses featured in the image: Sadhona Bose, Devika Rani, Leela Desai, and Chhaya Debi (see color insert—image 6). The largest image in this feature is of Bose in a demurely wrapped sari and *bindi* (dot on the forehead), lending her a distinctly Hindu appearance, quite unlike her Arabic dancing girl look in her film debut *Alibaba* (Modhu Bose, 1937). The feature's emphasis on education and aristocracy makes evident the mapping of cinematic stardom along the axis of class as a new generation of privileged-class and -caste filmmakers and audiences sought to reform the cinema. In her study of the Indian "Modern Girl" in the 1920s and 1930s, Priti Ramamurthy discusses a 1939 series on film personalities in the *Illustrated Weekly of India* magazine that actively reconstructed actresses as *Bharatiya naris*, respectable icons of Indian womanhood. By this time, acting had been coded as acceptable professional work, "which 'trailblazing' upper-caste Hindu women had to be educated into and worked extremely hard at."[91] Tellingly, the photo series discussed by Ramamurthy also features Sadhona Bose and Devika Rani, both pictured reading a book. Bose's profile includes details of her well-known family and describes her as "having a well-won reputation as a danseuse."[92] This new avatar of the professional, public dancing woman—as danseuse, not a dancing girl—is at a respectable distance from the earlier figure of the professional courtesan; Bose is portrayed as drawing from the "Hindu" dance forms of *Manipuri*, *Kathakali*, and *Kathak* rather than from the *mujra* dance repertoire of the Muslim courtesan.

One of the major areas of reform of the cinema in the 1930s was on-screen dancing. While the early talkies were marketed as "all talking, singing, dancing" films, the increasingly dominant and intertwined discourses of respectability and social reform led to a regular condemnation of dancing (and of that other form of on-screen sensuality—kissing). In a magazine column, Vishwambhar Prasad ("Premi Visharad"), for example, opined that popular films of the times were unfit for women, children, and respectable society because of the dances and kissing.[93] The removal from exhibition circuits of *Zarina* (Ezra Mir, 1932)—a film that featured eighty-six kisses and what were deemed to be risqué dance sequences by Zubeida, one of the top stars of the silent era—precipitated a move toward self-censorship, with the film industry informally but effectively banning mouth-to-mouth kissing and ensuring that dance sequences were significantly denuded of their erotic connotations. However, the association of on-screen dancing with female eroticism was not so easy to shake, as is suggested by this 1935 editorial in *Moving Picture Monthly*: "The 'Purity' campaign which convulsed the American moving pictures did not cause any furor in India. Barring dance sequels [sic], Indian films possess no such 'Evil.'"[94] As the only "evil" in Indian films, dance conflicted with the nationalist and pedagogical aims of the film industry in the mid- to late 1930s. Relatedly, the new impulse to use cinema as a tool of moral self-improvement required that all signs of the Islamicate courtesan be eliminated from the film actress, which included changing the names of Muslim performers to Hindu ones.[95] Modhu Bose recounts his selection of the heroine for his first sound film, *Selima* (1935):

> After searching for a heroine for quite some time, we selected a girl from Faizabad.... I named her "Madhavi." Her mother was a nautch girl but she was brought up in a different environment at a relative's place. Her mother did not want her to follow her profession so Madhavi's gait, action, and movements were far from that of a nautch girl.[96]

After this film, Modhu Bose did not need to bother with renaming or remaking his actresses in the *bhadramahila* mode since his wife, Sadhona Bose, who would go on to play the female protagonist in most of the rest of his films, already fit the description. Sadhona Bose's plays and films were promoted as neo-classical ballets and film ballets, respectively, distancing them in name and idiom from any associations with the *nautch*. On account of her expertise in Indian dance forms and her upper-caste background, Bose was seen as symbolizing the essence of indigenous tradition, even though she freely appropriated from non-Indian dance forms and costuming traditions. Indeed, throughout her career, despite her bold experimentations with dance idioms, Bose was celebrated as upholding national traditions and thus was easily appropriated into the prevailing discourse of cultural nationalism. In parts of her autobiography, she projects herself as something of a social reformer through her dance and theater performances. Describing a pan-India dance tour with Madhu Bose and C.A.P., she says, "We stepped out of our home with the mission to serve Indian audiences with our dance dramas."[97] Where dance was seen as an excuse, in the popular film genres of the 1920s and early 1930s, for risqué erotic display, the "dance social" genre created by the Boses in the late 1930s and 1940s employed "classical" dance as a pedagogical tool to educate the masses about their cultural heritage and as a medium for socially useful entertainment.

Azurie, The Dancing Girl and Dance Columnist

In 1936, the Bengali film periodical *Chitrapanji* carried a series of articles on whether middle-class women should dance or not.[98] One reader responded, "if a woman moves her arms and legs at her will in her bedroom, that is not a problem since no one sees this. But, if the same woman dresses up and performs on stage before a group of men, then can't we men say a word [...] The ultimate aim of a woman's life is to be a wife and a mother; it would be a lie to suggest that she wants to be a dancer or an actor."[99] Earlier that year, the magazine published an article by a dancer-actress who had recently been featured in the Bengali film *Sonar Sansar* (Debaki Bose, 1936), Srimati Ajoorie. The article titled, "Why Is Dance Neglected," avers, "Dance is India's own treasure. . . . But alas, there is hardly any respect for dance in the heart of Indian citizens at present."[100] "To produce box-office hits, the producers are compromising on dance by catering to cheap taste. But sadly enough it is the dancers who have to suffer the blame on behalf of these producers," concludes the author.[101] Making her debut the previous year in the Bombay film industry as a dancer in multiple films—*Bhen ka Prem* (J. K. Nanda) (see Figure 3.4), *Katl-e-Aam* (Arolkar, Rele), *Judgment of Allah* (Mehboob), *Chandrasena* (V. Shantaram), and *Bal Hatiya* (Ram Daryani)—this columnist, variously named Miss Azoorie, Azurie, Srimati Ajoorie, and Madam Azoorie, takes us on a rather different but intersecting journey through dance in Indian cinema in the 1930s and 1940s. Anna Marie Gueizelor (1907/1916–1998), later named Azurie, was born in 1907 or 1916 (there is some debate about this) in Bangalore to a German-Jewish father and a Hindu Brahmin mother (her caste status was foregrounded in Azurie's accounts).

Figure 3.4. Azurie in the song booklet for *Bhen ka Prem* (J. K. Nanda, 1935).
Credit: National Film Archives of India.

Surgeon General Gueizelor, a strict disciplinarian, disapproved of "Eastern dancing." Anna was encouraged instead to learn ballet and play the piano. But her heart lay in the "Eastern" dances she watched on secret trips to the movies.[102] Upon their move to Bombay, the famous Muslim reformer and litterateur Atiya Fyzee-Rahamin encouraged the teenage Anna to learn Indian classical dance (the dance forms, *Bharatanatyam, Manipuri,* and *Kathak* are mentioned in some accounts).[103] Anna's identity as a dancer was fashioned further by a visitor to Fyzee-Rahamin's Three Arts Circle, the Turkish writer and political activist Khalida Adeeb Khanum, who renamed Anna as Azurie. Reportedly, when Khanum heard that Anna was known by the prefix of "some 'Devi'" she scowled and announced, "the name should be Butan-e-Auzrie rather than Devi!" referencing Amir Khusrau's allusion to the divine beauty of statues of goddesses carved by Azar, a mythical sculptor.[104]

While Hindu majoritarian pressures have been understood as influencing the name changes of Muslim, Jewish, and Anglo-Indian actors during this period, Azurie's pre-film-career renaming points to a different cultural matrix of Muslim cosmopolitanism.[105] The retention of this name by the Bombay film industry suggests that Anna's new Islamicate name was actually seen as appropriate for her status as a dancing girl, recalling the "exotic" dancing girls of the *bazaar* cinema of the 1920s and early 1930s.[106] Rosie Thomas notes of the period, "the subaltern bodies of the erotic arts—cabaret and *nautch*—provided many of the female stars of India's silent cinema."[107] In the 1930s and 1940s, a Hindu renaming was only required in the construction of the bourgeois, cultured leading lady, not a necessary accoutrement for a Eurasian dancing girl like Azurie. In the song booklet for *Katl-e-Aam* (Arolkar, Rele, 1935), for instance, as the dancing girl in the film, Azurie retains her name, whereas the heroine, the Jewish star Esther Victoria Abraham, appears under her Hindu screen name Pramila, reflecting the complex fashioning of female identities and performance registers on and off the screen. Figure 3.5 features an image from the song booklet for *Sonar Sansar*, directed by the acclaimed New Theaters filmmaker, Debaki Bose. It encapsulates the many complex constructions of cinematic femininity through Azurie's dancing girl figuration. In mimicking the Western ballet dancer on the poster behind her, Azurie crystallizes in this image her many figurations, the shock of her exposed legs under her nonchalantly lifted *ghagra* reminding us of her training in ballet, marking her mixed Eurasian heritage, and also the long history of the *bazaar* dancing girl. Even if the films are no longer available, the arrangement of limbs, costumes, and dance poses in these images is

Figure 3.5. From the song booklet for *Sonar Sansar* (Debaki Bose, 1936).
Credit: Jadavpur University Media Lab.

eloquently suggestive of the many transitions in which dancing women and actresses were involved during the period.

After being spotted on a film set and asked to "carry a pot and swing [her] hips for a scene,"[108] Azurie began to feature regularly as a dancing girl in the movies from 1935 to 1947. Her filmography on IMDb and *The Encyclopedia of Indian Cinema* registers a fraction of the fifty-odd films she is reported to have danced in. Some promotional materials and newspaper articles report a number as high as 200–300 films.[109] My reconstruction of Azurie's long career is deeply indebted to song booklets from the 1930s and 1940s, and to contemporary online fan blogs. I find this noteworthy, as both function as sites of fandom, motivated by a deep spectatorial desire to retain traces of the film long after its exhibition run. Indeed, fans are critical for the production of corporeal histories on account of their intense, somatically charged relationship with stars and celebrities. The impassioned obsession in some fan blogs over Azurie (and others, like the backup dancer from the 1950s, Edwina Lyons) sometimes produces the only archive for dancing women like her, otherwise marginalized by official accounts of female pioneers in the realm of popular entertainment. To recover the ephemeral corporeal histories of Indian cinema, we have to turn to the places where the dancing girl resides—and in fact, reigns: promotional materials that serve as visual archives for these icons of spectacle, and song-and-dance sequences that archive bodies not found in the rest of the film narrative.

The song booklet for *Bal Hatiya* (Ram Daryani, 1935) features Azurie as a nameless "temple dancer," but includes a full-page photographic still that gives me my first arresting glimpse of this dancer-actress-choreographer (Figure 3.6). My search for Azurie and her contributions to 1930s and 1940s Bombay cinema has been characterized by this simultaneous textual, narrative erasure and visual excess. In booklet after booklet, Azurie is listed as a generic dancer with no character name, and no mention in the film synopses, but she bursts into spectacular hypervisibility in the images. Even as most of her films from this period are lost, these song booklets make evident that the presence of the German-Indian, Jewish-Hindu Anna Marie Gueizelor resides in the spectacular imagination of the film, in its musical numbers, rather than its textual articulation of plot and character. Sadhona Bose, as an upper-caste, upper-class Hindu star, on the other hand, dominates both, and indeed makes the narrative pirouette around her dancing skills (see color insert—image 7). Through elaborate photo-illustration collages featuring extensive typographical flourishes, multiple booklet cover designs for the same film, all headlining her star value, and rich, full-color reproductions, these booklets present Bose as the central attraction and authoring presence across a range of narratives, with dance as the central element of that attraction.

Azurie is quite literally a shadow figure in one of her rare surviving song-and-dance sequences, from *Chandrasena* (V. Shantaram, 1935), featuring her silhouetted form dancing on a drum (see ▶ video 03.02). This musical number alternates between medium close-ups of the singer-actress Rajani's face to capture her vocal performance and long shots of Azurie and four backup dancers dancing on drums to the song. Through its separate singing and dancing women, the sequence produces aural and visual regimes of female spectacle. Azurie's silhouetted form emblematizes the simultaneously

Figure 3.6. Azurie in the song booklet for *Bal Hatiya* (Ram Daryani, 1935).
Credit: National Film Archives of India.

fetishized and invisibilized form of the dancing girl. The acclaimed director of the film, V. Shantaram, who employed a female silhouette as the emblem of his famed Prabhat Film Company, is reported to have said, "Give me a girl with a figure like Azurie's and I'll give you anything."[110]

The silhouetted lineaments of Azurie's dancing body enable her mythification as courtesan, celestial dancer, icon of spectacular femininity, while erasing specifics of her name, mixed-race origins, and acquisition of hybrid dance styles. The early conflation of the categories of dancing girl and sex symbol is apparent in the persistent eroticization of her star text. "Annette wore the most daring outfits and danced straight into the hearts of men—and women. Her body, her figure, became things that were discussed in every quarter, every circle," remarks one reporter.[111] Reportedly, one of her dances in *Parwana* (J. K. Nanda, 1947), to the song "Saiyaan Ne Unglee Maroree Re," was considered too vulgar and was excised from the film.[112]

Parallel to journalists' breathless reports on her body, clothing, and dance are Azurie's own newspaper and magazine columns, which articulate a feisty resistance on multiple fronts. Indeed, what makes Azurie particularly fascinating is that through the 1930s, she writes columns on dance, actively mediating what it means to be a female public performer in the fields of dance and film, and adroitly producing different personas through her dance, writing, and later stage career. In her 1935 column, "Dance, A Sacred Art," she makes a case for Indians to bestow upon dance the respect it deserves, echoing cultural revivalists like E. Krishna Iyer, Rukmini Devi Arundale, and others engaged in the effort to lend "respectability" to Indian dance. Following her entry into the Calcutta film industry in 1936 (she works on a film each with the highly regarded Debaki Bose and P. C. Barua), she writes a column in Bengali in *Chitrapanji*, as mentioned earlier. Azurie's negotiation of a new industry and cultural context is evident in her adoption of the honorific title of a married woman, "Srimati," for added respectability, the relatively anodyne images accompanying the article, and her disavowal of her own figuration as a Westernized screen dancer. She notes in the article, "These days many film producers are compromising on dance by importing western dances and often vulgarity to give cheap thrills. This insults our indigenous dance forms and results in loss of respect for the art of dance."[113] There is a telling disjuncture between Azurie's own columns, which reflect her self-fashioning as a respectable oriental dancer, and writings by others who construct a risqué dancing girl persona. In a 1943 article in *filmIndia*, titled "Baburao Patel Kicks Indian Dancers About!" the irascible, opinion-making editor describes Bose as an ideal, technically accomplished film dancer: "Sadhona is perhaps the only one who is so near my ideal. She knows enough technique to impress the average dance-lover, she has more than enough natural grace, she has sweet womanly looks, a suitably pleasant expression and in addition to all this just that little something which puts kick into her work and satisfies the spectator."[114] He goes on to exclaim about the more audacious Azurie:

> Oh, that girl! She is a League of Nations in whom every dance of the world is found with all the labels wrongly stuck. She can hardly be called a classical dancer representing any cultural school of the country. She specializes in mass entertainment and I wouldn't be surprised if she starts dancing on her head one day because people like it.[115]

Apparent here are the respective affiliations of authenticity and exoticism with high art (Bose's "dance socials") and popular entertainment (Azurie's dance numbers in low-budget films), but Patel's imperious pronouncements also call attention to the varying status of oriental dance on stage and screen in this transitional period of the 1930s and 1940s.

A 1937 photo-feature on dance in the Bengali magazine *Deepali* includes a photograph of Srimati Azurie alongside other well-known dancers like Uday Shankar, Nataraj Vashi, Madame Menaka, and Ram Gopal.[116] The range of postures, gestures, and costumes on display here reflects the variety of dance idioms circulating during this period that is marked not only by intense political and cultural nationalism, but also by a frenetic internationalism in the exchange of cultural forms, as is evident in the international locations mentioned in the photo-feature. As we shall see later, Azurie returned to the oriental dance circuit with a traveling troupe in the late 1940s. Of the celebrated oriental dancers here, the mixed-race Azurie is the only one to feature as an itinerant dancing girl in the movies, her multi-hyphenated identity a vehicle for border-crossing between the categories of stage and screen, oriental dance and *bazaar* cinema, Eurasian and Islamicate figurations. Her partner in the Radha Krishna dance featured earlier is a mixed-race Anglo-Indian dancer-choreographer, Tony, renamed Krishna Kumar, who was trained by Azurie. The dancing pair feature as well in musical numbers in multiple films in the 1940s, as dancing partners in *Naya Sansar* (N. R. Acharya, 1941), *Sanjog* (A. R. Kardar, 1943) and *Rattan* (M. Sadiq, 1944), and as co-choreographers in *Meri Duniya* (Mazhar Khan, 1942) and *Yaad* (Mazhar Khan, 1942). In the well-known production number from *Rattan*, "*O Jaanewale balamwa*," as Azurie and Krishna Kumar dance before the protagonist couple and their family, we observe two representational regimes at work—the private exchange of glances that articulates the principal couple, and a public vocalizing of their emotions by the professional dancing couple (see ▶ video 03.03). While the stars, Karan Dewan and Swaran Lata, get the close-ups in the song, and a place in Bombay film history, narrating a corporeal history of cinema through the dancing girl mobilizes our attention toward other aspects. We learn, for instance, that Azurie trained her vibrant dance partner, Krishna Kumar, and his brother, Robert (renamed Surya Kumar) in film dance and choreography, "picking them up from an orphanage and training them till they were perfect dancers."[117] The brothers went on to choreograph memorable dance numbers in *Awaara* (Raj Kapoor, 1951), *Pyaasa* (Guru Dutt, 1957), *Nau Do Gyarah* (Vijay Anand, 1957), etc., carrying Azurie's gestural legacy into big-budget films in the 1950s and beyond.[118] We also learn that two years prior to *Rattan*'s release, Azurie had introduced the film's music composer, Naushad Ali, to the producer-director A.R. Kardar, giving Naushad his first break as an independent music director in Kardar's *Nai Duniya* (1942). She recalls in an interview, "when Kardar wanted me to choreograph a dance for his film, I told him I wanted a new music director and suggested Naushad... he passed the test and Naushad was made."[119] While in official histories of Hindi cinema, Naushad's career is celebrated and Azurie's forgotten, reconstructing a corporeal history—founded on choreography, rhythm, the need for a new kind of music for new dance moves—excavates the contributions of these occluded figures in the production of Indian cinema's particular sonic and visual attractions. In such a history, Azurie emerges as an eloquent ambassador of this exciting period of flux in dance and the cinema through her mobility across cultural, regional, ethnic borders, quite literally mobilizing her dancing body across the stage, the screen, the written word, and from Bombay to Bengal to Tamilnadu, and, in 1947, to post-Partition Pakistan.[120] But let us return first to Sadhona Bose's corporeal maneuvers through the 1930s and 1940s.

Alibaba: Gentrifying the Oriental Spectacular

Sadhona Bose made her cinematic debut in Modhu Bose's Bengali film, *Alibaba* (1937). She had performed the same role—of the effervescent servant-girl Marjina—in the stage version in 1934. The stage and film versions both featured C.A.P. performers. Modhu Bose's *Alibaba* followed a long line of film adaptations in various Indian languages of the *Arabian Nights* tale of a woodcutter who chances upon a cave filled with stolen treasures.[121] However, in his version, the eponymous hero, Alibaba, is a minor character, while Sadhona Bose's Marjina is the central protagonist of the film. Even the song booklet for *Alibaba* is dominated by Bose's Marjina, with its only two color pages featuring her prominently (see color insert—image 8). Resplendent in an intricate silver crown inspired by Cambodian Khmer classical dance, her imposing profile framed by a silver wing-like epaulette, she dominates the concluding page of the *Alibaba* booklet, a luminous moon in the inky night that a diminutive Alibaba trudges through in the bottom right corner. Textually and visually, the booklet announces to audiences of 1937 the arrival of a new star. In most of her films that followed, Bose continued to be the central protagonist, with the narratives designed to showcase her facility with dancing and singing. In *Alibaba*, Bose performs in ten of the film's fourteen musical sequences, with two song sequences that put on display her vocal training, two "pure dance" numbers set to instrumental music, and the rest, narrative numbers that are integrated into the diegesis and extend it through song and dance.[122] In these, Bose dances as she sings, employing props like peacock-feathered brooms and decorative metal whips, and settings such as long, winding staircases that allow for extended dance movements. The first narrative number in the film is the famous Abdullah-Marjina sequence, "*Chhi Chhi Etta Janjal*" ("Oh! What a dreadful lot of rubbish") (see ▶ video 03.04). The *Encyclopedia of Indian Cinema* describes this particular sequence as one "that long set the standard for film musicals."[123] Where earlier song-and-dance sequences featured more static framing, producing frontal, tableau-like scenes, the variations in camera distance and the use of continuity editing techniques in this number ensure a more cinematically engrossing dance performance.

In a 1934 article for the Bengali magazine *Ruparekha*, titled "Rhythm in Screen," Modhu Bose remarks, "In all good motion pictures, even though the motion is of substanceless shadowgraphs and is only an illusion after all, the rhythmic flow should be felt muscularly and mentally to create in the audience the maximum of interest, pleasure and appeal."[124] Bose goes on to discuss the creation of cinematic rhythm through narrative modes such as comedy and tragedy, but in his films that feature Sadhona Bose, song-and-dance sequences emerge as the primary means of creating a "muscular" and "mental" rhythm in the audience. Reviews of *Alibaba* compare the staginess of the narrative with the dynamic treatment of space and movement in the song-and-dance sequences. According to the *Encyclopedia of Indian Cinema*, "The slow, mannered acting and the frontally framed tableau shots are enlivened by the dance scenes,"[125] indicating the differences in visual, aural, and performative registers between these two modes of cinematic presentation. The mention of dance in review after review of the film highlights the "muscular" rhythm added by the choreography, for example, in this review in *Bhagnadoot*:

> Direction and proper expression of the cinematic language have made *Alibaba* stand among the first class films. Such *Lasya* (grace) has never been expressed through cinematic dance. Among the actresses, Sadhona's acting comprising of her song-and-dance deserves maximum praise.[126]

The equal place accorded to dance attractions as to the narrative is reflected in the *Alibaba* booklet, where a number of pages feature one image from a key dance sequence and another from an important narrative event, indicating the primary attractions in the film. From her first film itself, then, Bose promoted dance as a key element of her star text.

Bose's contribution to popular Indian film dance derives not only from her own performative flair, which prompted the design of lavishly produced "pure dance" and production numbers for the dancer-actress, but also from her choreographic innovations such as orchestrating dances with many background dancers, articulating a syntax of cine-choreography that employs mise-en-scène elements such as costumes and architectural motifs, camera placement and movement, editing patterns, and the layering of performance spaces through central-background dancer relations to produce physically dynamic dance sequences. *Alibaba*'s two "pure dance" sequences set to instrumental music are the most spectacular of the song-and-dance sequences in the film and marshal architectural features, a large number of background dancers (from the C.A.P. troupe), elaborate costumes, and intricate dance moves by Bose to produce a new dance idiom in Indian cinema. In the first of these (seen in Figure 3.3), Marjina and a group of dancing girls in Alibaba's employ perform a dance to wake up their master. The group dance is framed by Islamicate arches and windows that convey the oriental setting of the story but also echo the movement vocabulary of the dancers as they rhythmically raise their arms in arch-like formations (see ▶ video 03.05). The most remarkable feature of Bose's costume in this number is the diaphanous wing-like prop attached at the hips to her slinky satin gown that sways provocatively as she executes belly dance-like moves to a percussive beat in this most "oriental" of the film's dances (evoking the imagined Orient of the *Arabian Nights*, in this case).[127] The next number is the climactic dance performance from the Arabian Nights tale, where Marjina does a dagger dance before Alibaba and the leader of the thieves, stabbing the leader and protecting her master at the end of the performance (see ⏵ video 03.06). The architectural design of the set for this number once again highlights Bose's complete vision for her choreography. A set of five ornate arches forms the background, from which two winding sets of stairs afford entry for the dancers, who then perform in front of a fountain (seen in Figure 2.1 in Chapter 2). Marjina wears a fantastically hybrid costume, composed of harem pants, a tunic with a dazzling geometric pattern, silver epaulettes, and an intricate crown (see Figure 3.7). Likewise, her movement vocabulary is influenced by Khmer and Sri Lankan *Kandy* dance. In a film dominated by Bose's singing and dancing attractions, this is a fittingly spectacular finale that combines the attractions of her distinctive movement vocabulary, hybrid costumes, and extravagant sets.

Figure 3.7. From the song booklet for *Alibaba* (Modhu Bose, 1937).
Credit: National Film Archives of India.

Borrowing from international oriental dance vocabulary, Urdu *qissa-dastaan* storytelling traditions, Parsi theater, newly emerging "classical" Indian dance forms, and Hollywood, the Boses participated in the cosmopolitan modernity that marked the orientalist Indian films of the 1920s and 1930s, but were resolutely highbrow and employed a discourse of classicism to signal their difference from the lower-brow oriental fantasy genre. Thomas notes, for example, that Modhu Bose's *Alibaba* "was widely celebrated and seen as more 'respectable' than the Wadia's Islamicate films, despite being more obviously derivative of Hollywood (and Western theatre) and less directly related to indigenous traditions."[128] According to a contemporary review of the film, "The dances that she [Bose] directed and danced had very little touches of Indian dance but we loved them."[129] Sadhona Bose's reputation as a classical dancer from a wealthy Brahmo family, Modhu Bose's standing as the director of C.A.P. with its *bhadralok* performers, and the general address of their plays and films to upper- and middle-class audiences established them as more authentically Indian than low-brow oriental dance and film practitioners. It was this "respectable orientalism" that prompted J. B. H. Wadia to invite the Boses to participate in his international prestige project, *Court Dancer*.

Court Dancer: Cultural Nationalism through the Oriental Dance Social

The first Indian film in English, distributed by Columbia Studios in the United States, *Court Dancer* was aimed at bringing respectability to the Indian film business. The film's three lavishly produced promotional booklets, one for each language the film was released in, are an early instance of publicity material generated to promote Indian films and culture in the West (see color insert—image 9). The English booklet includes J. B. H. Wadia's speech at the film's preview, in which he remarks that *Court Dancer* "will serve as India's messenger to the entire English-speaking world, because it will contribute its quota in eradicating the myth of the backwardness of this great country of ours."[130] Significantly, the booklets foreground Wadia's vision and Sadhona Bose's dancing credentials as foundational to this expensive project, with "life sketches" of the producer and the dancer-actress (described as "exceedingly well-read"), and a section titled "Dance Numbers in *The Court Dancer*" by K. A. Chidambaram featuring extended discussion of the film's three production numbers. Alongside extracts from the writings of Max Müller and other Indologists on Indian art and philosophy, the booklet includes photographs of cameras and film equipment as if to present the burgeoning Indian film industry as a part of that heritage, and showcasing dance as both a traditional and technological attraction. The film's central investment in dance is evidenced in the involvement of traditional dance gurus, Jayashankar from Kerala Kalamandalam (the Malayalam poet Vallathol's school of performing arts in South India) and Guru Senarik Rajkumar from Manipur,[131] and music composer Timir Baran transporting his musicians from Calcutta to Bombay, since according to Modhu Bose, the stunt-film-producing Wadia Movietone did not have an orchestra of its own.[132] *Court Dancer*'s mobilization of the English language, classical dance, and a glamorous *bhadramahila* star signals the film's aspirations toward a "modern" nationalism, where cultural forms like dance become the defining feature of national differentiation; *filmindia* editor Baburao Patel lauds the film as establishing India's stature in the world: "I know what it is to be an Indian in those arrogant foreign countries where every coloured man is taken for a barbarian. . . . as a cultural propaganda, "The Court Dancer" is a patriot's gift to the nation."[133]

The three production numbers in *Court Dancer* display a scintillating synthesis of reformist narratives, dance pedagogy, hybrid movement vocabularies, and innovative cine-choreography. It is significant that we first see Bose's courtesan character, Indrani, dancing the *Raas Lila* in the *Manipuri* style (Figure 3.8), establishing her "purity" and the spiritual function of dance (with its extra-diegetic resonance in the purported "cleansing" of

Figure 3.8. From the song booklet for *Court Dancer* (Modhu Bose, 1941).
Credit: National Film Archives of India.

traditional dance forms of their erotic elements to promote a *bhakti*-based classical dance idiom). The audience for this *Raas Lila* sequence includes the appreciative prince, Chandrakirti, and a group of holy men among whom the high priest of the kingdom sits unrecognized (see ⊙ video 03.07). The high priest, moved by Indrani's dance, is about to bless her, when the king intervenes and reveals that she is the court dancer, upon which the holy man retreats in horror. His reaction bespeaks the bifurcation of the chaste temple dancer and the morally corrupt court dancer, a distinction that animated the anti-*nautch* movement in the colonial period and which has been naturalized in contemporary accounts of most Indian classical dances, as for example, in this assertion by the celebrated Kalakshetra-trained *Bharatanatyam* dancer, Leela Samson:

> Until the early years of the 20th century, dance was still a vital part of temple ritual. . . . During British rule, however, a period of degeneration set in. *Devadasis* began to dance in the courts of princes and in the homes of rich landlords. The religious significance of dance was forgotten. . . . The temple dancer became a court dancer, often of ill repute.[134]

While there are extensive records of court dancers from well before the colonial period, placing the blame for the "degeneration" of dance forms entirely on the British points to the nationalist impulse—echoed in much of the dance scholarship through the twentieth century—to construct a continuous "Indian" tradition that was destroyed by British intervention.

Only later do we witness the more sensuous court dance, which she must perform as part of her professional obligation, unlike the *Raas Lila*, which is presented as an expression of her "true" spiritual self. In the spectacular court dance, unlike the communal space of the *Raas Lila* that is democratically occupied by many dancer-devotees, the architectural features of the court are employed to highlight Indrani's dancing body. In the opening shot of the sequence, her grand entry into the court is framed along a long flight of stairs between two intricately carved arches. The camera is placed at the foot of the stairs, the low-angle shot emphasizing the scale of the scene. The cine-choreographic production of these numbers and their centrality to the film's conception are apparent in Modhu Bose's autobiography, where he mentions that he and the editor first put together the dance sequences rather than the rest of the narrative, and that "while shooting the long dances, we always used two cameras, sometimes even three. For all the three [language] versions, we took each shot thrice."[135] In this court dance, Indrani is dressed in a more hybrid costume than the *Raas Lila*'s traditional *Manipuri* one. The highlight of this dance sequence is a series of close-ups of Indrani's hands, meant to highlight certain classical *hasta mudras* or hand gestures (see Figure 3.9, see ▶ video 03.08). In his autobiography, Modhu Bose remarks, "To understand India's classical dances, one needs to have thorough knowledge about the technique, 'mudra' etc. of each form. If the audience does not understand the meaning of the mudras and movements, they cannot obtain the complete pleasure that the performance can yield."[136] The Boses employ the series of close-ups as a pedagogical tool to educate the film's intended audience of foreign viewers and upper-class urban Indians at a time when Indian classical dance forms were being popularized precisely among these constituencies. In addition to formal innovations like this special-effects sequence and elaborate cine-choreography, the Boses undertook a pedagogical role as cinematic reformers of discourses around female dancing by forging a new genre that I refer to as the *dance social*.

Figure 3.9. Still from *Court Dancer* (Modhu Bose, 1941), showing the superimposition of stars over Indrani's fingers to explicate the meaning of the gesture.
Credit: Screen capture.

Choreographing the Dance Social

From the available information on Sadhona Bose's films, one gathers that she played the role of a dancer-actress in at least three films: *Abhinaya* (Modhu Bose, 1938), *Kumkum the Dancer* (Modhu Bose, 1940), and *Court Dancer* (Modhu Bose, 1941). While the very titles of these films (*abhinaya* translates from the Sanskrit as expression, especially through dance) proclaim dance as their principal attraction, the narratives and the generic tropes mobilized in these films point to the Boses' sustained engagement with issues surrounding the public performance of dance by women. As gleaned from the *Abhinaya* song booklet, Sadhona Bose plays Manisha Chowdhury, a "modern woman," winner of the "Miss Bengal" beauty contest, who, when she learns of her husband's love for another woman, leaves home and becomes a famous theater actress by the name of Debi Indrani. The film concludes with Manisha/Indrani giving up her husband so he can marry his pregnant lover. In *Kumkum the Dancer*, Bose plays the eponymous heroine, a village girl, who avenges her trade union father's incarceration by earning a precarious living as a dancer in a dramatic company. Bose goes on to play a sacrificing heroine in *Court Dancer*, too, which tells the tragic tale of ill-fated love between a prince and a court dancer, whose profession is not accorded the respect it deserves. *Court Dancer* concludes with Indrani swallowing poison and killing herself in order to protect her prince and the state of Manipur. In all three films, Bose's dancer protagonist is marked by a double figuration—as the housewife Manisha and the dancer-actress Debi Indrani in *Abhinaya*, as the poor village girl and the wealthy daughter-in-law who stages a play to avenge her father in *Kumkum*, and as the spiritual dancer of the *Raas Lilu* and the sensuous court dancer in *Court Dancer*.[137] This doubling bespeaks the tensions surrounding the construction of cinematic narratives around a female dancer, who needs to be recuperated from her profession by being depicted as forced to dance or as dancing for a higher purpose. The films purport to present dance more as a tool for personal and spiritual expression than as a medium for entertainment.

I detect a generic tendency in these films that I refer to as the *dance social* on account of the imbrication of spectacular dance sequences and a melodramatic narrative form that, through the figure of the dancing protagonist, articulates changing relationships between the social and the individual, the public and the private, and shifting configurations of the traditional and the modern. The "social," a generic mode particular to popular Indian cinema, is typically considered a reformist genre, with a focus on the representation of contemporary love, marriage, and family life. Its thematic focus is on the conflict between inherited, feudal values and forces of social change. As Richard Allen and Ira Bhaskar note, this conflict is "typically focused around the heroine as a figure of virtue in whom the value of tradition inheres, but also as a victim who is exploited by the very traditions she is required to uphold."[138] The Boses' recurrent figuration of the tragic dancer-actress as the noble, sympathetic victim of social orthodoxy is similar in form and intent to the female protagonists of 1930s socials such as *Kunku* (V. Shantaram, 1937) and *Aadmi* (V. Shantaram, 1939), who contest middle-class orthodoxy and inevitably meet with a tragic fate. As dancing protagonists, however, Sadhona Bose's characters bring to the fore both the attractions of female dancing and contemporary reformist debates around bourgeois women training in dance. Ravi Vasudevan notes that "a substantial vein of social films was devoted to making a critique of Indian society and setting up an agenda for change."[139] The *Court Dancer* song booklet includes the entreaty, "If the supreme sacrifice of the court dancer were to win for her even a little sympathy of our prejudice-ridden world, the message of this film will not have gone in vain." The recurrent figure of the court dancer in popular Hindi cinema from the 1930s through the 1960s must be read in the context of the anti-*nautch* and the dance "revival" movements, so that these historical or "period" films are seen as addressing very contemporary issues of women and public performance.

The self-reflexive address of many of Bose's films, where she plays a dancer-actress, also makes evident the new discourse around actresses that Hindi cinema of the late 1930s and 1940s wanted to propagate—of dancers and theater actresses and, by extension, film actresses, as cultured, misunderstood, tragic figures, persecuted by a barbaric society that does not accord them the dignity they deserve. It is no coincidence that these roles are played by a *bhadramahila* dancer-actress like Bose, whose star text simultaneously demands respect for public dancing by women and announces that the prostitute-actress is now a thing of the past. While the bazaar cinema of the 1920s and 1930s had its own share of dancing women, the focus was not on the subjective experiences or emotions of these characters, but rather on their external dancing bodies. By turning the gaze inward and narrativizing the lives of dancing women, Bose's films announce a new genre and a new kind of star. Where older genres like the stunt or adventure film (which often also featured a sequence of dances) were seen to be driven by external goals, Bose's dance films overtly elaborate the psychology of dancing protagonists through the tropes of realist tragedy and melodrama. This fit in with the bourgeoisie's preference for didactic, "serious" cinema, where even if there was no room for "serious philosophical" films, as one critic put it, the way out was to make films with "acute touching tragic plots or social deformities."[140] After the playful and light-hearted oriental fantasy *Alibaba*, most of Bose's later films are in the mode of serious or tragic melodrama, with the dancing protagonists beset by moral questions triggered by their status as dancer-actresses, reflecting thus upon Bose's own experiences in theater and in the cinema, as well as social discourses around dancing and acting. Employing the tropes of the social, which Vasudevan refers to as the genre of modernity,[141] and the one favored by the Indian middle class, the Boses articulate a modern-nationalist discourse of dance, not presented as a lure for the mass audience, but rather as a tool for social reform, especially concerning the figure of the dancer-actress. The melodramatic form enabled a combination of a radical social message with acute elevation of feeling,[142] which, when coupled with dazzlingly staged dance spectacle (see Figure 3.10), produced a deep sense of kinesthetic empathy for the dancing protagonist.[143] Anupama

Figure 3.10. Image of a spectacular production number in the song booklet for *Kumkum the Dancer* (Modhu Bose, 1940).
Credit: National Film Archives of India.

Figure 1. Azurie in the song booklet for *Bhen ka Prem* (J. K. Nanda, 1935).
Credit: National Film Archives of India.

Figure 2. Still from *Amrapali* (Lekh Tandon, 1966), featuring Vyjayanthimala.
Credit: Screen capture.

Figure 3. Still from *Caravan* (Nasir Hussain, 1971), featuring Helen.
Credit: Screen capture.

Figure 4. Still from *Pakeezah* (Kamal Amrohi, 1972).
Credit: Screen capture.

Figure 5. Still from *Pakeezah* (Kamal Amrohi, 1972).
Credit: Screen capture.

Figure 6. Photo from the 1939 New Year issue of the Bengali magazine *Deepali*, featuring Sadhona Bose, Devika Rani, Leela Desai, and Chhaya Debi.
Credit: Jadavpur University Media Lab.

Figure 7. Song booklet cover for *Kumkum the Dancer* (Modhu Bose, 1940).
Credit: National Film Archives of India.

Figure 8. From the song booklet for *Alibaba* (Modhu Bose, 1937).
Credit: National Film Archives of India.

Figure 9. Song booklet cover for *Court Dancer* (Modhu Bose, 1941).
Credit: National Film Archives of India.

Figure 10. Helen in Teesri Manzil (Vijay Anand, 1966).
Credit: Screen capture.

Figure 11. Vyjayanthimala in *Amrapali* (Lekh Tandon, 1966).
Credit: Screen capture.

Figure 12. Song booklet cover for *Kalpana* (Uday Shankar, 1948).
Credit: National Film Archives of India.

Figure 13. Waheeda Rehman in *Guide* (Vijay Anand, 1965).
Credit: Screen capture.

Figure 14. Still from *Tezaab* (N. Chandra, 1988).
Credit: Screen capture.

Figure 15. Still from *Beta* (Indra Kumar, 1992).
Credit: Screen capture.

Figure 16. Dixit and Khan rehearse dance moves on *Jhalak Dikhhla Jaa*.
Credit: Screen capture.

Kapse notes that the social was a "cinematic force-field, a modality that expressed shifts, modifications, and innovations that spurred melodrama to take root in a new cinematic environment."[144] The Boses' dance socials cannily combined the attractions of salon dance, sumptuous costume and set design, literary prestige, and social melodrama to reconfigure cinematic representations of dancing women, which would echo through courtesan and court dancer films for many decades to come.

Neepa Majumdar argues that the 1940s, especially in the period after World War II, were marked by the rise of the star system which led to a greater emphasis on the star as genre: "The story was subordinated to the star text, and the star text was not merely one among several heteronomous elements that went into the final film text, but rather, along with music, the overriding one that organized and structured everything else."[145] In authoring the genre syntax of the dance social with her dance-centric star text from the late 1930s, Sadhona Bose prefigured this shift. Her agency as a certain kind of dancing actress allowed her to shape the stories written for her. Indeed, the famous Bengali playwright Manmatha Ray is said to have written *Kumkum the Dancer* specifically for Bose,[146] and was also the author of the play *Rajnati*, performed by Bose and C.A.P. on stage, and adapted as *Raj Nartaki* and *Court Dancer*. Kathryn Hansen notes in her discussion of Parsi Theater's transition from "sensation dramas" to social dramas (*samsara khel* or *samajik natak* in Hindi and Gujarati) in the early twentieth century, "Important agents of the social's circulation were playwrights who went to work for film companies, adapting their stage works into screenplays."[147] These social dramas also "decisively placed female characters at the center, their titles often consisting of a woman's name,"[148] of which we see echoes in Bose's dance socials, including *Kumkum, Meenakshi* (Modhu Bose, 1942), and *Raj Nartaki*. The influence of Bose's dancing body on the narratives of her films is evident in these descriptions in the *Encyclopedia of Indian Cinema*: [*Kumkum the Dancer*:] "Dance film idealizing poverty made mainly to showcase Sadhona Bose's talents"[149]; [*Shankar Parvati*:] "A dance-based mythological [that] highlights Bose's dancing talents"[150]; [*Court Dancer*:] "Set in feudal Manipur, presumably to display Bose's abilities in the famous classical dance form of the region."[151] The suggestion that whether the film is a social, like *Kumkum*, a mythological, like *Shankar Parvati*, or a costume drama, like *Court Dancer*, the generic syntax is in service of Bose's overriding star quality of dance, is recurrent in most reviews of Bose's films, such as this one of *Kumkum the Dancer*:

> Sadhona Bose, probably the most alluring and fascinating personality that has ever thrilled an audience of Indian dance lovers, is the star, soul, substance and inspiration of the forthcoming Sagar Movietone release "Kumkum the Dancer".... The picture was made to provide a vehicle of expression for the beautiful art of this great and in her own way unique, Bengalee artiste whose dancing is really a miracle of exquisite grace and enchanting loveliness.[152]

Genres, narratives, locations, cinematic spaces, music, costume, and makeup become "vehicles" in Bose's films to drive her star attribute to the fore. As seen in the earlier discussion of dance musicalization, dancing stars substantially determined the musical compositions they would perform to. Sadhona Bose's collaborations with Timir Baran in plays, films, and her later dance-dramas attest to the influence of her dancing body on the aural-scape of her performance contexts. As author, the actor exerts a different kind of force than the director or other crew members. In the use of her or his particular body, gestural vocabulary, and range of expressions, the star produces certain narratives, cinematic spaces, and mythologies. While Modhu Bose was instrumental in creating the dance social genre as well, Sadhona Bose's physical skills as a dancer and her construction of a *bhadramahila* dancing body mobilize a particular cinematic assemblage in the 1930s and 1940s that skillfully blends the spectacular attractions of film dance with a discourse of cultural nationalism.

Cosmopolitan Mobilities of Dancing Women

Sadhona and Modhu Bose made three multilingual films—*Kumkum* and *Meenakshi* in Bengali and Hindi, and *Court Dancer* in those two Indian languages and in English—bringing their cosmopolitan construction of the dance social to varied audiences across the country. During the production of *Meenakshi* (1942), Sadhona Bose made a forceful assertion of her star power. The film, produced by the prestigious New Theatres, was originally supposed to feature the foremost male star of the times, K. L. Saigal. After *Court Dancer*, Sadhona Bose's contracts included a clause that in the title credits, her name would appear separately on a different title card. Saigal requested that his name be added on Bose's title card, even if in a smaller font size, but she refused. Modhu Bose reports:

She was hell bent that there will be no changes in the clauses of her contract. B. N. Sircar of New Theatres heard everything and said that "when Mrs. Bose has refused, I can't do anything. Work will progress according to the contract. If Saigal doesn't agree, we have to replace him." That is how Najmul Hossain came to play the role in the last minute.[153]

This incident gives us a sense of Bose's confidence in her stardom, especially after acting in the prestige production, *Court Dancer*. *Meenakshi* did not receive very favorable reviews, however, and this *filmindia* review may also suggest a transition in spectatorial tastes from dance films to social melodramas that would become the defining cinematic genre in India in just a few years: "The man who brought the first dancing girl to the screen, seems to have done the greatest harm to our industry. Because, if a dancer is cast in a picture, the director forgets to tell the story and keeps his girl dancing in his picture. To find illustrations in support of this statement, pictures featuring Sadhona Bose, Leela Desai and Sitara may be seen."[154] The waning, by the mid-1940s, of the careers of all three dancer-actresses mentioned in the review suggests the fading of the dance film in the wake of the rise of the omnibus social, which attempted to integrate song-and-dance sequences more seamlessly into the central narrative.[155] The dance film's unabashed celebration of its female leads' dancing skills produced a very different kind of star text, where dancing was not "merely an additional asset to the acting talents of these dancing heroines"[156] but the very foundation of their popularity and stardom.[157]

Bose's own star text underwent radical transformations during this period. In 1942, she signed her first film with a director other than Modhu Bose. Soon after the release of *Shankar Parvati* (Chaturbhuj Doshi) in 1943, she left Modhu Bose's apartment and moved into her own in the posh Marine Drive area of Bombay, precipitating a separation between them. Modhu Bose recounts that the apparent problem was that he had raised objections to the loud music and night-long parties that Sadhona Bose used to indulge in regularly.[158] A long concluding section of his autobiography dwells at length on this period and is revelatory of their relationship as husband and wife, director and star. He projects himself as the architect of her star text: "Since she was just 13, whatever success she achieved on stage and screen was all under my direction.... Maybe now Sadhana felt that whatever film she works on will be a hit only because of her,"[159] and proceeds to express his opinions on women acting in films in general:

The reasons [for female actors] losing balance between home and career are their rising ego and financial independence. . . . She [the female star] feels that taking anyone's advice will hurt her pride and belittle her. This spells doom for her. The once happy *sansar* [family/household] is broken. Waywardness becomes a way of life and she falls into the clutches of insanity. . . . From my years of experience I have come to the conclusion that those who want to take up acting—especially film acting—as a profession cannot maintain a *sansar*.[160]

Bose's transition to this attitude from his zealous mission in the 1920s to bring girls from respectable families into the theater and cinema speaks volumes about the anxieties of the *bhadralok* regarding the psychological and financial independence accrued to women from participating in the public sphere. While Sadhona and Modhu Bose were reconciled after a few years, and made two more films together (*Shesher Kabita* in 1953, and *Vikram Urvashi* in 1954), this episode exposes the sustained resentment around the *bhadramahila* wresting independence from her director-husband, and directs our attention toward the socio-historical contexts in which the voices of female pioneers in the realm of entertainment are produced and circulated. A consideration of Bose's personal life, including her early insistence on a career in dancing and acting, her marriage and then separation from Modhu Bose, rumors about extravagant parties and promiscuity, and later, about a life of penury and destitution, reveals her tenacious resistance to contemporary gender norms and also the particular imbrications between the personal lives of dancing women and their relationship to the public world of civil and political life.

In the mid-1940s, Sadhona Bose composed a stage ballet titled *Bhookh* (Hunger) on the Bengal famine, which broke fresh ground by being the first Indian dance ballet to deal with a contemporary theme.[161] *Bhookh* initiated a new trend in ballet composition, and through the 1940s and early 1950s, Bose composed and participated in dance ballets such as *Birth of Freedom, Whither Now, Divine Source, Samarpan,* and *Ajanta*.[162] Despite accounts of her alcoholism and general dissipation during these years, she was approached by new dance ballet groups such as the Indian Revival Group and New Age Dancers, pointing to the tenacity of her star text and professional image as a trailblazing dancer-choreographer.[163] During this same time, Azurie's career also evinces mobilities across media and regions. Around 1947, she is reported to have married a Muslim naval officer, and moved to Pakistan shortly after Partition. Inaugurating the debate about the place of dance in the newly formed Islamic state of Pakistan, she opened the first "Academy of Classical Dance" in Rawalpindi, despite violent opposition from the *maulvis* of the town.[164] In her columns in Pakistani newspapers in the 1950s, she negotiates newly forming cultural policies of the Islamic nation, where dance is a thorny issue as it raises the specter of continuities with an occluded Indic past.[165] Adroitly navigating attitudes toward dance and female participation in the public sphere, Azurie developed a post-Partition rhetoric of fashioning an exclusively Islamic dance lineage:

> It has taken me ten years studying the various tribes settled all over Pakistan. The best platform for basing the new dances is to take elements out of the various folk dances which bear the description and integrity of the Muslim race, and apply it to the present mood of our thinking. This will be the new dance of Pakistan. I have already termed [it] Pak Raks (pure dance).[166]

Soon Azurie became a founding member of the Pakistan-American Cultural Centre in Karachi, and a board member of the National Council of the Arts in Islamabad. The poet Faiz Ahmed Faiz is reported to have said to her, "your mourners will find even your grave empty as you'll come out of it to dance."[167] Her mobility calls attention to the relative porosity of new borders as she travels to Bombay and back in 1958 to dance in the Hindi film *Bahaana* (M. Kumar, 1960). Disappointed with the nascent Pakistani film industry, berating films of having "no storyline, no scenario, poor direction,"[168] she quit the movies and started touring internationally with her dance troupe, with well-received tours to Singapore, Malaysia, Australia, Africa, and the United Kingdom. In the Pakistani press, she claimed to "not be too fond of Bharat Natya dance which is a pure temple dance compared to Kathak which originated in the Muslim court of Wajid Ali Shah."[169] However, a program for her performance in London announces a recital of "the Seven Types of Dancing embodied in Three Techniques—Kathak, Manipuri, and Bharatanatyam."

Just as with Punjabi-Urdu cinema, whose lines of continuity Ravi Vasudevan reads as "a counterweight to the ruptures inflicted by the nation-state on the idealized integrity of a cultural geography,"[170] in Azurie's dance tours, this hybrid oriental dance blurs the divides wrought by Partition, recuperating dance forms as allowing for embodied modes of subcontinental belonging and kinship. In *Borders and Boundaries: Women in India's Partition*, Ritu Menon and Kamla Bhasin raise the important question, "do women have a country?"[171] Their feminist historiography of the Partition discusses how women were kept out as subjects of this history. In the case of a dancing woman like Azurie, the same question may prompt us to consider the visceral cosmopolitanism of Azurie's multi-hyphenated body that dances across and between borders, a corporeal repository of cultural practices that cannot be partitioned into neat national legacies. Through the mobility of dance forms in her repertoire as well as her physical mobility across borders, Azurie nimbly navigates questions of religious and national identity.

After General Zia-ul-Haq imposed martial law in 1977, disbanding the Arts Councils, banning dancing by women on stage as "un-Islamic," Azurie spent the last two decades of her life teaching dance at home and at the Station School in Rawalpindi. Across the border, in Calcutta, through the 1960s and early 1970s, Sadhona Bose held dance classes in her home as well, and just before her death in 1973, was appointed as dance trainer at Calcutta's Star Theatre. Students of both dancers report to have not known that their teachers were famous dancing stars. Like so many female pioneers in dance, music, and film, including Gauhar Jaan, Sulochana, Meena Shorey, and others, both women are reported to have lived out their last days in penury. However, as others have noted, these narratives of famed female performers dying penniless are strategically deployed as cautionary tales of moral instruction and obscure these artists' creative acts of self-fashioning and extraordinary resilience.[172] In the next chapter, we will find echoes of Bose and Azurie's narratives in both cautionary social reform films like *Sadhna* (B. R. Chopra, 1958) and in the protagonists of *Guide* (Vijay Anand, 1965) and *Teesri Kasam* (Basu Bhattacharya, 1966), who resolutely hold on to their dancing careers, reflecting the place of these pioneers in the realms of the social and the imaginary, of the dancing woman as both a discursive figure and a set of social practices. Described as the Pavlova of India at different points in their careers (just as Ram Gopal was called "the Nijinsky of India"), both Bose and Azurie employed their skills in dance performance and choreography, costume and set design, writing dance columns and an autobiography to assiduously fashion themselves as dancing women participating in a cosmopolitan, transnational dance network that intersected in significant ways with nationalist projects of modernity in the newly formed India and Pakistan.

Moving Legacies

Situating Azurie and Bose as co-choreographers of new mobilities in the 1930s and 1940s alerts us to the material histories of dancing bodies and intersecting narratives of labor, resistance, fame, and erasure. While histories of performing women in the Indian subcontinent in the nineteenth and twentieth centuries often draw a linear trajectory of prominence and eventual decline of various constituencies, including *devadasi*s and *tawaif*s, Anglo-Indian and other Eurasian actresses, and oriental dancers, Azurie and Bose's dancing bodies and figurations fold these performative repertoires upon each other in varied manifestations, producing a gestural genealogy that contains overt and subterranean traces of performing women before them. Azurie may be read, for instance, as a vestige of the Anglo-Indian, Eurasian heroine of the 1920s and early 1930s who disappeared with the arrival of the talkie. As a dancing woman featured only in production numbers, like other mixed-race dancing women who followed in the 1940s and 1950s—Cuckoo and Helen—she did not have significant speaking parts in films. But her dancing body was decidedly voluble, unleashing spectacular energies that altered the representational logics of Hindi cinema. If we trace the lineage of film dancers from Azurie (and Shehzadi Begum before her) to Cuckoo (whom Azurie trained) to Helen (trained by Cuckoo), we write a very different narrative of Bombay cinema and indeed of South Asian cultural modernities, a corporeal history produced through the interlinked network of these remarkable dancing girls.[173]

Similarly, while upper-caste Hindu actresses like Devika Rani and Bose were declared ambassadors of India, and their success with Indian films in English was seen as enhancing the "prestige of the Indian screen in the eyes of the foreigner,"[174] reading the brahmin Bose and Caucasian Fearless Nadia alongside each other mobilizes a corporeal analysis of modern Indian womanhood in the late colonial period. Both actresses were pitched as representing Homi and J. B. H. Wadia's conflicting visions of the nationalist project.[175] As an action heroine in the Wadia stunt films, Nadia became a popular nationalist icon, signifying Indian strength and power, while through her physical prowess in dance, Bose came to signify Indian "culture." As modes of mobility, dance and action sequences serve as central devices in constructing the iconicity of Bose and Nadia's star bodies as signifiers of national culture and power, respectively, allowing for contradictory and discontinuous relationships between gender, race, and nationalism to prevail.

Women's history, as Joan Kelly notes, has the dual goal of restoring women to history and restoring our history to women.[176] As the authors of significant changes in women's participation in the performing arts, Azurie and Bose had to continuously walk the line between respectability and censure. The construction of their careers at the intersection of the paradigms of modernity and national identity, cosmopolitanism and tradition, demonstrates the complex and dynamic interactions between the categories of gender, nation, and culture during this period.

Political shifts and the formation of the new nations of India and Pakistan significantly altered the performance landscape in the late 1940s and early 1950s. Ramamurthy notes that the cosmopolitan New Woman faded from Indian cinema by the end of the 1930s, as she was seen as "unfit for the all-important job of nurturing cultural nationalism."[177] Soneji observes that by the 1940s, "the aesthetics and politics of dance were already in the hands of non-devadasi women."[178] With the systematization and Sanskritized, textually grounded canonization of dance forms in the early 1950s, when the Indian government set up cultural institutions like the Sangeet Natak Akademi (The National Academy for Music, Dance and Drama), the oriental dance forms developed by Uday Shankar, Ram Gopal, and others were disparaged and came to be considered "semi-classical" at best, and inauthentic hybrids at worst. Even as, in the 1950s, Bose and Azurie moved from cinema to dance-dramas and international dance tours, where they were often promoted and received as oriental dancers, producing a hybrid of various dance styles, a new generation of dancer-actresses entered the Bombay film industry, trained in the recently canonized and more strictly codified dance forms of *Bharatanatyam* and *Kathak*. Film dance in the 1930s and 1940s remains a site of frenetic experimentation in music, set and costume design, and cine-choreographic innovations that aim to capture new mobilities on screen.

4

From the Cabaret Number to the Melodrama of Dance Reform

Folded Corporeal Histories of the Dancer-Actress in the 1950s and 1960s

The 1962 film *Dr. Vidya* (Rajendra Bhatia) is little known today, except for a scintillating dance-off between two of Hindi cinema's most celebrated dancers, Helen and Vyjayanthimala (see Figure 4.1). While the narrative leading up to the production number elaborates popular cinema's customary staging of the modernity-tradition conflict enshrined, in this case, in the bodies of the Franco-Burmese Helen and the Tamil brahmin Vyjayanthimala, once the women begin dancing, they emerge as collaborators and co-choreographers of this spectacle of movement. Helen gets on stage first, swinging and gyrating, and sings, "*Aye hai dilruba*" ("Oh my sweetheart"), addressing her competitor, who shortly joins her on stage (see ⊙ video 04.01). The two women's outfits alternate in tones, Helen's light-colored bodice and dark skirt contrasting with Vyjayanthimala's dark body suit and white tulle attachment. As the stand-in for tradition, Vyjayanthimala's character wears a modified, modernized *Bharatanatyam*-style head ornament, but rather than the routine dance-off between "Western" and state-sanctioned "Indian" dance styles, what we have here is Vyjayanthimala adopting Helen's movement vocabulary, with her splayed fingertips and legs, gyrating hips, and high leaps. Both performers get long instrumental sections to showcase their dance moves, as they leap in the air, sprawl on the floor, twist and swivel into 360-degree spins, mobilizing all the space on the floor beneath and in the air around them with their agile limbs and twirling torsos. A panoply of cine-choreographic devices—low-angle shots to capture the dancing duo together, high-angle shots to catch their floor moves, canted angles as we reach the virtuosic climax, frequent cuts to an appreciative audience, and play with stage lighting—is marshaled to portray their electrifying mobility as they annex space and delineate their performative terrain.

Figure 4.1. Helen and Vyjayanthimala in *Dr. Vidya* (Rajendra Bhatia, 1962).
Credit: Screen capture.

While the double framing could, on the surface, be read as reproducing the binary of female figurations in popular Hindi cinema along the raunchy vamp–demure heroine divide, the delight that the two women take in each other's skills and the equal distribution of screen space and time underscore their shared influence on the choreography of this production number. Seen through this oppositional gaze that foregrounds female labor, skill, and agency, the dance-off becomes a celebration of dancing women's mobility, rather than singularly located in conflict and difference. In her autobiography, *Bonding: A Memoir*, Vyjayanthimala expresses her respect for Helen: "how she performed for the camera was commendable . . . I'm saying that as a dancer since I have worked and danced with her. . . . We worked in a few films and bonded very well. She is one person with whom I really got along in the industry."[1] On a television show, Helen gushes about her dancing partner: "My favorite dancing actress is Vyjayanthimala. I'm lucky to have done three to four films with her."[2] The dance-off operates as a primary site for the bonding of dancing women as their intensely trained bodies join in an exultation of their singular capacities for movement. In a rare equalizing gesture, *Dr. Vidya*'s opening credits place both dancing women on the same title card that reads, "Vyjayanthimala, Manoj Kumar, AND Helen." Helen and Vyjayanthimala both made their debut in the Bombay film industry in 1951, with *Awara* (Raj Kapoor, 1951) and *Bahar* (M. V. Raman), respectively. Both women came from the outside—Helen from Rangoon, Vyjayanthimala from Madras—and brought to Bombay cinema movement vocabularies that would come to define Hindi film dance. In her first films, *Shabistan* (Bibhuti Mitra, 1951) and *Awara*, and for many years after, Helen was a backup dancer, often in the shadow of another Eurasian dancing woman, Cuckoo, who introduced her to the industry. From 1958, with the peppy production number, "*Mera naam Chin Chin Chu,*" (*Howrah Bridge*, Shakti Samanta), she rose to fame as the principal dancer-vamp for the next twenty-five years. Vyjayanthimala, trained in *Bharatanatyam*, was initially disparaged by the Hindi film industry as a dancer from the South with meager acting potential until her 1955 film, *Devdas* (Bimal Roy). Without erasing the unequal financial and representational hierarchies into which each performer was slotted based on caste-class privilege, what is common to both is that their primary identification as dancers required the Hindi film narrative and industry to make space for their dancing bodies. These were typically coded antipodally, but watching Helen and Vyjayanthimala dance together activates an alternate vision of Bombay cinema's logics and economies of production, one considerably driven by moving, dancing women. Their dancing bodies evince continuities in production economies across the vamp and heroine figuration, for instance, in costume design, a central aspect of the production of the film dancer. Two of costume designer Bhanu Athaiya's most notable designs of this period are her flamenco outfit for Helen in the production number "*O Haseena Zulfanwaali*" from *Teesri Manzil* (Vijay Anand, 1966), and her definitive *amrapali* costume for Vyjayanthimala's production number, "*Neel Gagan Ki Chhaon Mein,*" that same year in the extravagant courtesan film, *Amrapali* (Lekh Tandon, 1966) (see color insert—images 10 and 11).

As discussed in Chapter 1, reading the production number as the product of a multi-bodied "choreomusicking body" focuses our attention not only on the on-screen performers' gestural repertoire, but also on off-screen music production, cinematography, editing, and other industrial practices. Mohan Segal, producer of *Dr. Vidya*, and director earlier of *New Delhi*

(1956), which featured dazzling production numbers by Vyjayanthimala, studied dance at Uday Shankar's India Culture Centre in Almora, and worked at Prithviraj Kapoor's Prithvi Theatres as actor and choreographer. In his film, *New Delhi*, he had introduced a new, rather unusual costume designer, who was in charge of costumes on *Dr. Vidya* as well—Smt. Yadugiri Devi, Vyjayanthimala's grandmother, of whom the dancing star says, "She did what was right for me, guiding my career. She also designed my costumes in many of my early films. She understood what looked good on me."[3] A grandmother who always accompanied her granddaughter on film sets to protect her from the exploitative practices of the film industry also began to participate in the industry, designing costumes for three other films during the period: *Kath Putli* (Nitin Bose, Amiya Chakrabarty, 1957), *Madhumati* (Bimal Roy, 1958), and *Aas ka Panchhi* (Mohan Kumar, 1961). Mother to Vasundhara Devi, Vyjayanthimala's mother, who performed scintillating Carmen Miranda–inspired dances in the Tamil film *Mangama Sabatham* (T. G. Raghavanchari, 1943), Yadugiri Devi was a key figure in constructing Vyjayanthimala's star text as an indisputably respectable, upper-caste, *Bharatanatyam* dancer and actress, assiduously expunging any gossip about the actress's courtesan lineage and foregrounding her training under famed *nattuvanars* instead.[4] She not only designed Helen's flouncy skirt and Vyjayanthimala's form-fitted hybrid outfit in this dance-off, but was also responsible for introducing to the Bombay film industry the choreographer of this number, the dance director B. Sohanlal. Yadugiri Devi brought the *Kathak*-trained Sohanlal and his brother, B. Hiralal, to Bombay from Bangalore to train Vyjayanthimala in "North Indian dance" for *Nagin* (Nandlal Jaswantlal, 1954), the dancer-actress's first film outside the Madras studios. Vyjayanthimala reminisces, "My grandmother . . . said they are from Rajasthan and if they come to teach you it will be very authentic. They were very fine gestures, very fine movements, very graceful at the same time, not one flicker of the eye or jerk of the head was left out, everything was absolutely timed."[5] Hiralal and Sohanlal went on to become the most sought-after choreographers during these two decades, producing a hybrid of various classical and folk dance forms.[6] Vyjayanthimala (and Yadugiri Devi, quite literally a shadow figure that propelled and sustained her grand-daughter in the spotlight) introduced a new idiom of dance in Bombay cinema through her own training in *Bharatanatyam* and the introduction of these two choreographers into the industry.[7] Corporeal histories that account for the labor of numerous visible and unacknowledged bodies excavate deep, interlinked stories of industrial practices and networks. *Dr. Vidya* marked the debut of B. Sohanlal's dance assistant, Saroj Khan, who would make the figure of the choreographer rise to prominence nearly twenty-five years later, with her production number for Madhuri Dixit, "*Ek do teen*," in *Tezaab* (N. Chandra, 1988).[8] Khan recalls, "I became Master Sohanlal's assistant at a young age and the first lady I taught was Vyjayanthimala. It was a classical number, 'Pawan Diwani Na Maane.'"[9]

The choreomusicking body behind "*Aye hai dilruba*" is animated as well by the playback singers for the two dancing women, Geeta Dutt for Helen, and Asha Bhosle for Vyjayanthimala. The two voices, often designated as suited to on-screen dancing, typically by vamps, and on occasion by a dancing heroine, made aurally sensible the erotic, cosmopolitan energies of production numbers in the 1950s and 1960s. Tellingly, "*Aye hai dilruba*" was not included in the gramophone record of *Dr. Vidya*'s soundtrack, making apparent its status as a dance number, meant to be seen more than heard. The dance musicalization logics of many production numbers emphasize the joint pleasures of listening and viewing, the dancing bodies on-screen *activating* the sonic qualities of the song. A choreomusicological approach encourages us to exult then in the multisensory affects of the production number assemblage generated by these very many off- and on-screen bodies. In the only other production number in the film (the one with which a fourteen-year-old Saroj Khan started her choreographic career), "*Pawan Diwani Na Maane*," Vyjayanthimala performs a "traditional" Indian dance, a *Bharatanatyam*-hybrid, to Lata Mangeshkar's vocals. Mangeshkar—whose dulcet and decorous voice and carefully controlled star text was seen as "managing" the potentially dangerous circulation of the actress's body in public spaces[10]—also voices all of Vyjayanthimala's narrative numbers in *Dr. Vidya*, while Asha Bhosle sings Helen's other song in the film, a spirited *qawwali*.[11] A corporeal history, sensitive to these performers' lineages, however, upends easy binaries between the film's three female playback singers and foregrounds the strenuous labor that female performers expended not only on screen but behind the scene, in highlighting and obscuring aspects of their histories. The sisters, Lata Mangeshkar and Asha Bhosle, as Anjali Arondekar in her study of the Gomantak Maratha Samaj notes, hailed from a Goan *kalavant* lineage of hereditary, professional female entertainers, a "*devadasi* diaspora" that included the renowned Hindustani vocalists Mogubai Kurdikar, Kesarbai Kerkar, and Kishori Amonkar.[12] An analysis of the choreomusicking body that produces "*Aye hai dilruba*"—including Helen,

Vyjayanthimala, Yadugiri Devi, Sohanlal, Saroj Khan, Geeta Dutt, and Asha Bhosle, among many others—excavates the various performance legacies, of *devadasi*s, *tawaif*s, *nattuvanar*s, *Kathak gharana*s, and Eurasian dancers, that come to bear on popular Hindi film through these many performing bodies, *bonding* together their embodied gestural knowledges of music, dance, theater, and cinema.

Hindi cinema stages dance in multiple sites during the 1950s and 1960s. It is a time of tremendous development in the narrative number, infusing romantic solos and duets with great mobility as they often move to outdoor spaces. It is also a production-number-filled time of the cabaret and the *mujra*, the Islamicate courtesan film, the mythical Hindu court dancer film, and social melodramas with dancer protagonists. Indeed, films of this period pulsate with the question of what to do with dancing women, both fictional characters and the real-life actors who perform them. Across the vamp's cabaret number, whose vocabulary was formalized in the 1950s and which became a mandatory requirement of film distributors by the 1960s, the courtesan film, which "emerge[d] as a vehicle for the acting talents of women" and featured the top actresses of the time, and social melodramas with a preponderance of production numbers when the heroine in question was a dancer-actress, we witness a variety of negotiations around the figure of the dancing woman, a source of both danger and pleasure, revulsion and fascination.[13] This chapter considers how dancer-actresses of various caste, religious, and class configurations co-choreograph the dance-scape of Bombay cinema in the 1950s and 1960s.

The Sangeet Natak Akademi Seminars on Film and Dance

A 1966 *Filmfare* article titled "Dance in Cinema: Gimmick or Necessity," proclaims:

> Among the actresses who came to the fore in the fifties were some good classical dancers—Vyjayanthimala, Padmini and Waheeda Rehman. . . . One good resulted from this "elevation" of the dance from the vamp to the heroine—its quality improved and it began to be taken seriously. With a few exceptions, the dance in films is now less vulgar (as leading ladies perhaps are reluctant to perform provocative cabaret numbers).[14]

Through the 1950s and 1960s, the classical dance training of actresses like Vyjayanthimala, Padmini, Kamala Laxman, and a few others was routinely cited to highlight the gentrification of film dance by these early generations of upper-caste, non-*devadasi* women trained in *Bharatanatyam*. Hari Krishnan's nuanced account of the "celluloid classicism" of *Bharatanatyam* alerts us to how these actresses enabled Bharatanatyam to become a popular yet classical art form on stage and screen. He remarks, "The persistent signposts of [*Bharatanatyam*'s] classicism were created not only in the hermetic space of the imaginary of the nation's bourgeoisie, but also through its interface with the popular as it came into being in the age of celluloid."[15] M. S. S. Pandian argues that Tamil cultural elites engaged with the new medium of cinema in the 1930s by deploying binaries such as classical versus non-classical, contrasting *Bharatanatyam* and *Carnatic* music, which they authorized as high culture, against the low cultural forms of Company Drama and *Therukoothu* (folk street theater).[16] Pandian cites the cultural critic Muktha Seenivasan's praise for the upper-caste dancer-actresses of Tamil cinema of the 1950s and 1960s—Kumari Kamala, Vyjayanthimala, and the Travancore sisters (Padmini, Lalita, Ragini)—as ushering in "astonishing progress" into dance in Tamil cinema.[17] Like several other critics, Seenivasan erases the labor of the very many *devadasi* women at the vanguard of choreographing and performing dance in Tamil cinema. Davesh Soneji observes that while "almost all of the earliest female stars of Tamil cinema—T. R. Rajakumari, Sayi-Subbulakshmi, S. P. L. Dhanalakshmi, N. Rajalakshmi, Tiruvelveli Papa, and others—came from *devadasi* families," with the embourgeoisement of dance and cinema in the 1940s and 1950s, "women from *devadasi* families could simply no longer 'make it' in the world of cinema, just as they could not in the new world of dance."[18] Studying dance in Bombay cinema during this period demands an examination of cultural institutions set up by the post-colonial Indian state in the 1950s that concertedly erased the history of traditional performing women as the progenitors, preservers, and practitioners of performance arts, and reconstructed a Sanskritized "classical" tradition to bring dance into the realm of upper-class and -caste respectability.

In January 1953, the Union Ministry of Education instituted the Sangeet Natak Akademi, a national academy of dance, drama, and music (that included film until 1961).[19] According to the organization's inaugural annual report in 1953–1954,

The necessity of such an organization was all the more compelling in view of the fact that all of a sudden the erstwhile princely patronage to the arts had ceased to function or was fast ceasing. In the void thus created, the art traditions were faced with the grave risk of breaking down in an atmosphere of general decline in our cultural and artistic values.[20]

Princely states such as Awadh, Tanjavur, Hyderabad, etc., had fostered a cultural environment where *tawaif*s, *devadasi*s, and traditional musicians were accorded financial and social prestige and patronage. The Akademi represented the state's project to extricate these performing arts from their traditional milieus and transplant them onto the "secular" stage. The Akademi organized four seminars—film (1955), theater (1956), music (1957), and dance (1957)—to bring together knowledgeable elites in each field to engage in "stock-taking."[21] One of the principal functions of the Akademi was to codify and hierarchize dance practices. The 1958 Dance Seminar classified various dance forms by linguistic group, designating them along the binary of classical and folk. To be canonized as classical, dance forms had to claim antiquity through a textual tradition traced back to the *Natya Shastra* and other ancient and medieval treatises on performance. Declaring an initial canon of four classical dance forms—*Bharatanatyam*, *Kathakali*, *Manipuri*, and *Kathak*—the Akademi's "Expert Committee on Dance" decided through their annual awards which dances would be recognized as "authentic" classical forms, compiling technical terms and texts on music, dance, and drama, and organizing regular dance festivals.[22]

Meanwhile, as art historian Jyotindra Jain has argued, the Government of India's Republic Day parades (organized every January 26, since 1950, to honor the date on which the Constitution of India came into effect) enlisted various folk dance forms to "perform" the cultural diversity of the nation while emphasizing an abstracted, generalized notion of Indian tradition. Dance was one element in a range of symbols, performances, and spectacles—such as the national flag, the national anthem, and the national calendar—that was designed to unify several separatist tendencies.[23] Jawaharlal Nehru, the first prime minister of the nation, who institutionalized the Republic Day parade, with its folk dance performances, writes: "the procession would be a moving pageant of India in its rich diversity. . . . I would love to see in our procession people from various parts of India including our tribal people, the Nagas from the North East, the Bhils from Central India, the Santals and others showing that they are also full partners in this great enterprise of India going ahead."²⁴ Dance was harnessed as a means to corpo-realize national and regional identities. Significantly, despite the official mandate for "authenticity," the production of the nation and its communities frequently occurred through mixed or even invented traditions. Govind Vidyarthi, a technical officer at the Sangeet Natak Akademi, reveals the behind-the-scenes production of these Indian folk and tribal traditions:

> With more and more urban people presenting folk dances there has been an increasing tendency to include pretty college girls and even "extras" who dance for the films. Usually a Dance-Director-Choreographer accompanies them and one could see in the Talkatora Camp hectic rehearsals for the "creation" of a folk dance. These urban folk dancers are a feast for the camera and they hit the headlines in the press.²⁵

Jain notes that images of these dances came to form the basis for the canonization of folk dance forms through their use by dance historians like Kapila Vatsyayan and Mohan Khokar in their authoritative books, *Traditions of Indian Folk Dance* and *The Splendours of Indian Dance*, respectively.²⁶ The reference to film "extras" or backup dancers constructing folk dances highlights the circular relationships forged by this period between traditional performance, stage shows, and the cinema. Well-known film choreographers from this period, including Hiralal, Sohanlal, Gopi Krishna, and Lacchu Maharaj, designed and employed these performative stencils to produce on-screen folk dances that typically worked as shorthand to convey rural simplicity and a sense of community through seemingly spontaneous group dances involving no monetary transaction.²⁷ As Arundhathi Subramaniam notes, "the "folk dance" in Hindi cinema is, almost by definition, "exotic" and "folksy" because regional features have to be ironed out to make it seem like it could be performed in almost any hamlet in the country."²⁸

On-screen "classical" dance seemed to present more of a problem. The first of the Sangeet Natak Akademi's all-India seminars was the Film Seminar held in 1955, centered around discussions of how the cinema of the new nation could be recruited to promote "Indian culture." The seminar, whose directors were the thespians Devika Rani and Prithviraj Kapoor, included film directors, producers, actors, music composers, lyricists, etc., from across the country. Tensions between the Akademi's discourse of "authenticity" and popular cinema's unbridled hybridity became especially conspicuous in the discussions on film music and dance. Music composer Anil Biswas, for example, made a case for the composition of distinctively Indian film music: "When our music goes to a foreign country, that country should recognize it as something Indian and not a part of its own music.... I am a lover of Western music, but as *Western music*. I still maintain that our music must retain the character of being Indian."[29] While disparaging the inclusion of non-Indian music, Biswas celebrated hybridity within Indian musical forms, referring to popular film music as "the product of the beautiful marriage between folk and classical music ... which today has made the whole of India music-conscious."[30] He concludes his presentation with the declaration, "An ideal film-music, when it is in its true character, will be a beautiful amalgamation and take the new shape of the new music of new India."[31] Biswas's claim of national cultural status for film music is a forceful counteraction against the state's proscription of film music on All India Radio during this decade. Starting in 1952, the Minister of Information and Broadcasting, B. V. Keskar, banned film music on the state-owned radio station for its hybridity, and specifically its use of Western instruments that "challenged the aims of the national cultural policy."[32] Not unrelatedly, the government had also issued an edict in 1954 that banished from All India Radio any female performer "whose private life is a public scandal,"[33] designed to prevent any government patronage for traditional performers like *baijis*, *tawaifs*, and *devadasis*.

Through the period of the All India Radio ban, the film industry claimed as its cultural project the transmission of India's musical traditions to the common people. The Hindi and Marathi film actress Durga Khote made a similar claim for film dance at the Film Seminar:

> The consciousness of rhythm and dance in the homes of people inspired by films has given birth to scores of dance academies. Indeed, had it not been for the film actress, the Bharat Natyam, the Kathakali, the Manipuri and the Kathak dances would never have left the threshold of their provinces and become part of Indian culture. Through the medium of films, it is the film actress who has taken these arts to the homes of the people.[34]

Khote's claims for the pedagogical role played by film dance and the dancer-actress proved to be contentious, provoking disagreement from some others present at the seminar. The Bengali actress from Jean Renoir's *The River* (1951), Suprova Mookerji, for example, sharply countered Khote's claim:

> In taking the art to the masses, we have often debased their tastes because the examples set by the films on dancing and music have not always been

too healthy. Bharat Natyam, Kathakali, Manipuri and other forms of folk dances, I may be permitted to say, have survived and even made advances to their techniques in spite of the films. As a matter of fact, few would look to films for their correct interpretation.[35]

Even as classical dance forms were just beginning to be canonized, their movement vocabularies were hastily being ossified to separate traditional lower-caste performers from new upper-caste ones, screen from stage, and to sever dance forms from their hybrid, protean origins. Uday Shankar, innovator of his own composite modern Indian dance style, presented a trenchant criticism of popular film dance at the seminar:

> As regards the classical dances, it pains me to find that with the growing interest to introduce dance in motion pictures, a slow deterioration of classical dance is spreading its shadow over the art itself, and is bound to cause great harm to our classical dance, in course of a short time. I may even call it "motion picture classical dance," instead of recognizing it as representing the real one.[36]

Later criticized himself by classical puritans for "presenting oriental dance from Europe, not quite Indian and certainly not authentic,"[37] Shankar is a pivotal figure in understanding shifting constructions of cultural heritage to fit changing discourses of national modernity from the 1930s into the 1950s and 1960s. Predating Nehru's Republic Day parades, Shankar's 1948 film, *Kalpana*, attempts to create a sense of a varied but connected Indian nation through a hybrid of classical and folk dance forms imbued with nationalist intent (see color insert—image 12). Dance is central to the film's production of a folk possessing a varied but inclusive Indian cultural tradition. In a key segment of the film, the protagonist Udayan's cultural institute (modeled on the Uday Shankar India Culture Centre that Shankar set up in Almora in 1939) organizes the *Vasanta Utsav*, or "Spring Festival of India," where delegates from all over India and Asia are invited to present their dances. The festival, which takes up more than forty-five minutes of screen time, functions as a spectacular display of the nation through dance (see ▶ video 04.02). Nilanjana Bhattacharjya notes how, by the mid- to late 1950s, as the Sangeet Natak Akademi defined "authenticity" more rigidly, Shankar's "departure from recognized traditions was considered antithetical to the promotion of Indian traditional arts," and his "exclusion from the Akademi led to his virtual exclusion from the official narrative of Indian culture."[38]

The drive to fix cultural forms that would embody the aesthetic and ethical ideals of the new Indian nation set the bar for "authenticity" in film dance as well. Whereas dancer-actresses like Sadhona Bose and Azurie flaunted hybridity and innovation in their performance and choreographic vocabularies, leading dancer-actresses of the 1950s and 1960s, such as Vyjayanthimala, Padmini, and Waheeda Rehman, had to constantly emphasize their rigorous training with traditional *nattuvanars* as well as their middle-class respectability. Through the violent marginalization of traditional female performers, public dance performance by upper-class and -caste women had been destigmatized and even allowed for their promotion as ideal national-cultural bodies, as evidenced in Vyjayanthimala's prestigious *Bharatanatyam* recitals for dignitaries such as the Indian president S. Radhakrishnan, prime ministers Jawaharlal Nehru and Indira Gandhi, Queen Elizabeth II, and US president Dwight Eisenhower.[39] In fact, it may be argued that on-screen *Bharatanatyam* by upper-caste dancer-actresses played as significant a role in the gentrification of the dance form as Rukmini Devi Arundale's Kalakshetra Foundation did. Kamala Laxman's dance in *Nam Iruvar* (A. V. Meiyappan, 1947) was hailed as ushering in a cultural revolution. "Dance schools sprouted all over and Bharatanatyam acquired respectability," declares one review of the film.[40] Laxman's film dances were seen as spurring national awareness of *Bharatanatyam*,[41] with even orthodox arts magazines celebrating her vanguard role: "through her, the art of Bharatanatyam spread to every nook and corner of the country."[42] Krishnan provides an in-depth examination of how Laxman's cosmopolitan Brahmin identity and her apprenticeship under the *nattuvanar* Vazhuvoor Ramaiah Pillai defined the conventions for staged performances of *Bharatanatyam* in Madras. "It was her work, not that of Rukmini Arundale and Madras's intellectual elites, that persistently straddled the stage and cinema and brought Bharatanatyam to South India's middle class in the 1940s," he argues.[43] Among the first dance forms to be canonized as classical, *Bharatanatyam* acquired national status as a symbol of Indian heritage, employed to visualize the nation across stage, print, and screen. The processes of nationalism, state patronage, and upper-class and -caste sponsorship selectively legitimized certain regional artistic forms as "national" and therefore "classical."[44] However, the inclusion of a South Indian dance form into the so-called all-India Hindi-Urdu film produced altered figurations of the dancing female protagonist, exposing fissures in the discursive constructions of "national" versus "regional" cultures and bodies. I discuss elsewhere Vyjayanthimala's 1950s films in relation to the national and subnational politics of on-screen *Bharatanatyam*, the interactions between Madras and Bombay studios, and the developing hierarchies between film industries and their claims to producing national cultural products,[45] and consider here how Hindi cinema negotiated the *Bharatanatyam*-trained bodies of Vyjayanthimala and Waheeda Rehman.

Classical Dance and the Hindi Film Heroine

Vyjayanthimala learned *Bharatanatyam* from the age of eight under the tutelage of Guru Vazhuvoor Ramiah Pillai, who was also Kamala Laxman's teacher, and then Guru Dandayudapani Pillai, who taught at Arundale's Kalakshetra Foundation. It was at one of her *Bharatanatyam* recitals that A. V. Meiyappa Chettiar, founder of the Madras film studio, AVM Productions, and the film director M. V. Raman saw her and approached her for her first film role in *Vazhkai* (A. V. Meiyappa Chettiar, 1949).[46] Waheeda Rehman, daughter of a district commissioner, trained under Tiruchandoor Meenaxi Sundaram Pillai, who initially refused to teach her because she was Muslim. She quotes him as saying, "She won't be able to express our *varnams* [musical compositions]. How will she do *abhinaya* [expressions]?" and adds, "then he saw my horoscope and realized that I would be his last student."[47] Both dancer-actresses were trained by highly respected *nattuvanars*, male members of the *devadasi* community who had reinvented themselves as dance teachers to urban elites and as film choreographers. While the cultivation of new taste habits among the elites of Madras required that *devadasis* be rendered invisible on the stage and in the movies, the male members of these performing communities, who felt a "need to develop a 'closed' patrifocal tradition ... independent of their illustrious womenfolk,"[48] reinvented themselves as the *Isai Velalar* caste, or "cultivators of music." Producing this new caste designation in the early twentieth century enabled the men to develop a niche occupation as the hereditary keepers of music traditions and as "authentic" dance masters from the past.[49] In the 1940s, many *nattuvanars* transitioned into the movies from Company Drama and played a defining role in cementing music and dance as the central spectacular attractions of the Tamil film.[50] As choreographers, they remained off-screen shadow figures that propelled a new class of on-screen dancers, even as the women of their own community and their *Sadir* movement vocabularies were erased from the screen.

A number of Vyjayanthimala's *Bharatanatyam*-based dances in both Tamil and Hindi films were choreographed by *nattuvanar* gurus, including V. S. Muthuswami Pillai, Vazhuvoor Ramaiah Pillai, and Dandayudapani Pillai. Through the period just before and after independence from British rule, the Madras film studio, AVM Productions, included *Bharatanatyam*-influenced dance performances, set to patriotic songs, sung by acclaimed Carnatic vocalists. Swarnavel Eswaran Pillai discusses how studio head A. V. Meiyappan brought together in *Nam Iruvar* (A. V. Meiyappan, 1947) the social reformer Subramania Bharathiar's poetry, the legendary Carnatic vocalist D. K. Pattammal, choreography by the *nattuvanar* Vazhuvoor Ramaiah Pillai, and Kamala Laxman's athletic *Bharatanatyam* skills to capitalize on the nationalistic zeal for freedom in early 1947.[51] In Vyjayanthimala's first film, *Vazhkai*, released two years after *Nam Iruvar*, Meiyappan repeats this strategy in the dance number "*Bharata samuthayam vaazhgave*," composed by Bharathiar and sung by Pattamal. Variously attired in military-style riding breeches, a Tamil half-sari, and Indian National Congress–style *khadi* suit and Gandhi cap, a spirited thirteen-year-old Vyjayanthimala marches and dances in front of the stage backdrop of a map of undivided India, producing a simultaneously nationalist, modern, *Bharatanatyam*-trained movement vocabulary (see ▶ video 04.03). Earlier in the film, her character's wealthy father encourages her to attend dance performances: "in my days, *natyam* (dance) only happened in the *kovil* (temple). Nowadays, all girls are born with anklets on their feet." The house help enthusiastically agrees, "there isn't a house without dancing in it." Through the wealthy, modern girl who is trained in *Bharatanatyam*, alongside horse-riding and other physical sports, Vyjayanthimala's early films, like *Vazhkai* and *Penn* (M. V. Raman, 1953), negotiate the status of dance in the elite cultural imaginary, with a Sanskritized *Bharatanatyam* presented as a desirable accoutrement of the modern South Indian woman.[52] Significantly, the dance numbers in most of her Tamil and Hindi social films from the 1950s are staged at college festivals, *kala kendras* or cultural centers, and at women's organizations, marking the movement of *Bharatanatyam* to *sabha*s or concert stages from the *devadasis*' earlier salon and temple performances.

Vyjayanthimala's Tamil debut, *Vazhkai*, was remade and released in Hindi two years later as *Bahar* (M. V. Raman, 1951) (in addition to a simultaneous 1951 release of the Telugu version, *Jeevitham*). In various interviews and in her autobiography, Vyjayanthimala credits herself with the introduction of classical dance into Hindi cinema:

Bahar took the entire North by storm.... The audience here had not seen those kinds of gestures, expressions, *mudras* [hand and facial gestures], and graceful movements with classical or folk touch.... This film became a trendsetter paving the way for dance with a definitive form in Hindi cinema. Until then, by and large, it seemed to connote some westernized shake-shake, or wriggling of the hips.[53]

Through the 1930s and 1940s, dancer-actresses like Sadhona Bose, Sitara, Azurie, and others had included elements of *Kathak, Manipuri,* and *Rabindra Nritya* in their dance numbers. The nine-year-old Kumari Kamala (later, Kamala Laxman) performed *Bharatanatyam*-style dance items in the 1943 Hindi films *Kismet* (Gyan Mukherjee) and *Ram Rajya* (Vijay Bhatt). However, with Vyjayanthimala's rise as a heroine in Bombay cinema, which offered her access to national, "all-India" stardom, *Bharatanatyam* became a definitive part of the idiom of Hindi film dance. Described as the "southern sensation with twinkle toes,"[54] Vyjayanthimala remarks that after the success of *Bahar* and *Nagin,* "semi-classical dance became an integral part of every Hindi film heroine's credentials."[55]

Comparing Vyjayanthimala's *Bharatanatyam*-influenced dance routines in Tamil and in Hindi cinema makes evident the work that the Hindi film has to do to accommodate this South Indian dancing body, foregrounding as well differences in genre and in the spectacular imaginations of the two film industries. In Tamil costume dramas like *Marma Veeran* (T. R. Raghunath, 1956), *Vanjikottai Valiban* (S. S. Vasan, 1958), *Parthiban Kanavu* (D. Yoganand, 1960), and *Chittoor Rani Padmini* (Chitrapu Narayana Rao, 1963), Vyjayanthimala's *Bharatanatyam* skills are put on resplendent display as pure dance attractions, while in Hindi socials like *Pehli Jhalak* (M. V. Raman, 1955), *New Delhi* (Mohan Segal, 1956), *Aasha* (M. V. Raman, 1957) and others, the narrative has to be designed to *accommodate* the South Indian dance form. In *New Delhi,* for instance, she plays a Tamil character, Janaki Devi, teacher of music and dance at the cultural center, *Kalamandir,* and for good measure, daughter of the head of the "South Indian Cultural Association." This character sketch allows for her stage performance of the *allaripu* item from the *Bharatanatyam* repertoire, choreographed by the *nattuvanar* V. S. Muthuswami Pillai. The *allaripu* item, bearing all the signs of newly coded classicism, transitions quite inexplicably and unexpectedly to a *Kathak*-influenced hybrid film dance with background dancers, choreographed by the *Kathak*-trained dance master, Hiralal, to the Hindi song, "*Murali bairan bhayi*" (see ▶ video 04.04). The cohabitation of *Bharatanatyam* and *Kathak* and of the choreographic signatures of Muthuswami Pillai and Hiralal in the same number is testimony to the corporeal labor of Vyjayanthimala's dancing body in bringing together movement vocabularies with their representative costumes, set design, choreography, and personnel. To transcend her identity as a South Indian dancer-actress, she had to demonstrate her proficiency in dance forms other than *Bharatanatyam*, as well as her nondancing histrionic abilities. In the latter half of *New Delhi*, the Tamil Janaki Devi play-acts as Mohini, a girl from Punjab, who performs the folk dance form of *Gidda* to the song "*Tum sang preet lagai*." Before the electrifying dance performance, Mohini/Janaki tells her uncle, "you won't be able to tell it is a Tamilian dancing on stage." Vyjayanthimala's adept performance of both the classical, geometrical *alarippu* item and the Hiralal-choreographed vigorous folk dance moves of *Gidda* render her body as the ground for the reconciliation of classical and folk dance binaries, North and South cultural and linguistic divides, reinforcing the film's message of national integration, while extra-textually hailing her as a national Hindi film actress, not merely a regional South Indian one (see ▶ video 04.05).

Similarly, in *Pehli Jhalak* (M. V. Raman, 1955), Vyjayanthimala's character, Devi, performs a range of dance forms, from *Kathak* to the Maharashtrian folk dance form of *Lavani*. The production number "*Na maro najariya ke baan*," in which Vyjayanthimala performs the "dancing double role" of the celestial lovers, Radha and Krishna, ends with a montage of newspaper headlines that alliteratively announce, "Madras goes mad over Devi," "Calcutta goes crazy over Devi," "Agra applauses [*sic*] Devi," "Delhi is dazzled by Devi," projecting the national appeal of the dancing star, Vyjayanthimala, across cultural centers. Significantly, she came to be regarded as a "serious" Hindi film actress only with her role as a *Kathak*-dancing *tawaif* in *Devdas* and in *Sadhna* (B. R. Chopra, 1958), both films produced and directed by Bombay industry insiders, unlike her earlier South Indian productions. The Urdu-Hindi courtesan film, in presenting a typically tragic narrative of the *tawaif* seeking respectability through heterosexual matrimony, had a different moral trajectory and relationship to dance than the Tamil costume drama.[56] In the three films in which Vyjayanthimala plays a *Kathak*-dancing courtesan—*Devdas*, *Sadhna*, and *Sunghursh* (H. S. Rawail, 1968)—she is eventually "rescued" from a life of professional performance. In the Hindi-language but Madras studios–produced "light comedies" and in the Tamil costume dramas she stars in all through the 1950s, on the other hand, her characters do not have to give up dancing, pointing to generic differences between the Madras and Bombay film industries.

Also trained by *nattuvanars* in Tamilnadu, and making her debut as a dancer who only appears in a single production number in the Telugu film, *Rojulu Marayi* (Tapi Chanakya, 1955), the Tamil Muslim Waheeda Rehman faced a contrasting situation to Vyjayanthimala in the Bombay film industry—of the erasure of her identity as a South Indian, *Bharatanatyam*-trained dancer. She recollects the enduring impact of her role as the noble prostitute Gulabo in her second Hindi film, *Pyaasa* (Guru Dutt, 1957): "because *Pyaasa* was such a serious, dramatic role, people thought of me only as an actress and not a dancer and for a long time I didn't get dancing roles."[57] Indeed, not until the 1960s, well into her acting career, did Rehman play a dancer-protagonist in films like *Roop ki Rani Choron ka Raja* (H. S. Rawail, 1961), *Mujhe Jeene Do* (Moni Bhattacharjee, 1963), *Guide* (Vijay Anand, 1965), and *Teesri Kasam* (Basu Bhattacharya, 1966) (see Figure 4.2). Her initial career in the Hindi film industry was dominated by roles that featured

Figure 4.2. Waheeda Rehman in *Guide* (Vijay Anand, 1965).
Credit: Screen capture.

narrative rather than production numbers, with her *abhinaya*, or facial expressions, routinely praised. The director Guru Dutt, for instance, who introduced her to the Bombay film industry, commented on her performance in the song "*Jaane kya tune kahi*" in his film *Pyaasa* (1957): "She did the song well because she is a dancer. She knows how to give silent expressions."[58] Unlike Vyjayanthimala, whose *Bharatanatyam*-based production numbers in the 1950s were seen as "authentic" and were choreographed by *nattuvanar*s, Rehman mainly worked with film choreographers like Hiralal and Sohanlal, who developed a hybrid of *Bharatanatyam*, *Kathak*, and a mix of folk dance forms. Additionally, Vyjayanthimala continued a parallel professional career in *Bharatanatyam* performance, which distinctly influenced her cinematic star text, while Rehman's did not carry the same "classical" connotations. "Many people didn't know that I am a trained dancer because they felt I didn't behave like one," she remarks in an interview,[59] suggesting that the cultural iconicity of a *Bharatanatyam* dancer did not accommodate an actress of Muslim lineage, who spoke Urdu, and did not conform to the physical appearance of a Hindu goddess (the iconicity that Vyjayanthimala in turn was sedimented into). She recounts that when, as a fifteen-year-old, she and her sister Shaheeda performed a *Bharatanatyam* recital before the distinguished politician C. Rajagopalachari, he commented, "it's surprising how good your Bharatanatyam *abhinaya* [facial expression] is despite you being Muslim girls."[60] The corporeal and expressive requirements of femininity articulated by a newly Sanskritized *Bharatanatyam* and a Bombay film industry newly encountering South Indian actresses trained in this dance form generated these contestations and figurations of Vyjayanthimala as an accomplished dancer who needed to prove her acting abilities and Waheeda Rehman as a "natural" actress who did not fit the mold of a *Bharatanatyam* dancer.

If we read Waheeda Rehman's stardom through her production numbers, rather than her justly celebrated acting in films like *Pyaasa*, *Kaagaz ke Phool* (Guru Dutt, 1959), *Reshma aur Shera* (Sunil Dutt, 1971), and *Khamoshi* (Asit Sen, 1970), among many others, we produce a very different diagram of her performing body and her body of performance, as it were. Upon her father's demise, in order to help with family finances and the medical treatment of her ailing mother, seventeen-year-old Rehman finally accepted one of the many film offers presented to her, dancing to the hit song "*Yeruvaaka saagaaro ranno chinnanna*," in the Telugu film *Rojulu Marayi*.[61] The production number, celebrating a harvest, was added on as a spectacular attraction after the film had nearly been completed, and went on to become a massive hit (see ▶ video 04.06). The add-on song-and-dance spectacle has been an intermittent practice, presaging contemporary Bollywood's more obligatory item numbers. Rehman's description of this dance number's reception bespeaks her early figuration as a dancing attraction: "in those days, audiences were known to throw coins at the screen to show their appreciation and that's what people did when my dance started. We were told that when the film was over, people would ask the projectionist to run the song again."[62] "*Yeruvaaka saagaaro*" had been composed for an earlier film that was shelved and was supposed to be shot with the famously agile dancer Kamala Laxman.[63] The *Kuchipudi* dancer-choreographer, Vedantam Jagannatha Sarma, had noticed Waheeda Rehman during her dance performances with her sister Shaheeda and recommended her to the producer of *Rojulu Marayi*.[64] Guru Dutt, chief guest at the 100th day celebration of the film's success, approached the young dancer to sign her up for his next Hindi film, *C.I.D.* (Raj Khosla, 1956). Like Vyjayanthimala, dance had led Rehman to the movies, both stage and screen "no longer taboo" for women like them, as Rehman remarked to me in a personal interview, discussing her transition from stage *Bharatanatyam* to hybrid film dance: "training in classical dance gives your body basic training and makes it so much easier to pick up other dances."[65]

Rehman quickly mastered the grammar of the varied corporeal habitations that film acting required, and that same year, debuted as an actress in *Jayasimha* (D. Yoganand, 1955), a Telugu swashbuckling adventure. Her status as a dancer meant that her role was primarily conceived around multiple production numbers, including the *Bharatanatyam*-based "*Nadireyi gadichene*," the most "traditional" *Bharatanatyam* she would perform on screen during her career, choreographed by the *Kuchipudi* guru, Vempati Satyam (see ▶ video 04.07). In her next and final film in the South, Rehman once again featured only in a production number in the swashbuckling oriental spectacular *Alibabavum 40 Thirudargalum* (T. R. Sundaram, 1956), the first full-length Tamil color film, shot in Gevacolor (see ▶ video 04.08). Her orientalized, *Arabian Nights*–style hybrid dance to the song "*Salaam babu*" brings to mind Sadhona Bose's dance nineteen years prior in *Alibaba* (Modhu Bose, 1937), their dancing bodies producing an alternate lineage of cinematic spectacle.[66] As discussed in Chapter 3, the Alibaba story and the Arabian Nights more generally had a long history of being adapted to the screen in various Indian film industries, their oriental aesthetic (defined broadly through imagined Persianate-Islamicate splendor) the perfect site for a cinematic staging of techno-spectacle. These oriental spectaculars were employed to showcase new technologies, including color stock, special effects, in-camera and editing tricks, as well as the attraction of the oriental dancing girl. *Alibabavum 40 Thirudargalum* included another oriental dance, "*Naama aaduvadhum*," by the dancing duo, Sayi Subbulakshmi, as well as thrilling action sequences to display its Gevacolor stock. Vyjayanthimala's dance numbers were also a key location for filmmakers to show off expensive film stock in the 1950s. "My first colour sequence was in what was then called 'Geva Colour' for the dream sequence in *Nagin*," she reminisces.[67] Music and dance were so critical to *Nagin* that "the last four songs, two reels of musical climax, were [shot] in colour."[68] In Vyjayanthimala's 1957 film, *Aasha* (M. V. Raman), only the song-and-dance sequences were shot in Gevacolor and Technicolor. More broadly, the courtesan films and period films about court dancers, like *Amrapali* and *Chitralekha* (Kidar Sharma, 1964), were seen as exemplary showcases for new color stock, in addition to production innovations in cinematography, makeup and costume, sets and props, music, and editing. The dancer-actress—from Sadhona Bose in J. B. H. Wadia's extravagant dance film, *The Court Dancer* (1941), to Azurie in V. Shantaram's *Chandrasena* (1935), to Vyjayanthimala in *Nagin*, to Helen in innumerable cabaret sets especially constructed for her, such as in *Teesri Manzil* (Vijay Anand, 1966), and Waheeda Rehman in *Alibabavum 40 Thirudargalum*—is a pivotal figure in choreographing these changes and fashioning new regimes of techno-spectacle.

Rehman's initial three films, celebrating her versatility across folk dance, *Bharatanatyam*, and oriental dance, prod us to imagine what her career might have looked like if she had stayed in the South, working in the Telugu and Tamil film industries that espoused different logics of cinematic spectacle and the *Bharatanatyam*-trained performer's place in it. They remind us as well that the itinerant dancing girl and the heroine are never too far apart, and that dancer-actresses take deep pleasure in presenting their skills on screen. Vijay Anand, director of *Guide* (1965), which featured Rehman as a classical dancer and included elaborate production numbers, remarks, "Waheeda Rehman had a grace in her demeanor that only a dancer could have. But the world and she herself had forgotten that she was a dancer. I realized she needed the role of a dancer and hence *Guide*."[69] Rehman recalls, "when *Guide* came my way, I told Dev [Anand], that if you want to, you can chop my dialogues but don't cut my dance sequences."[70] What is evident here is Rehman's desire to reclaim her dancing past, one obscured by an intervening decade of male auteur-directed social melodramas filled with song sequences and narrative numbers. What had been forgotten was the training of her body and her South Indian ancestry as she was molded into a leading Hindi-Urdu actress. Her profound yearning to dance in *Guide* is mirrored in her character, Rosie, pining to return to a life of dance.

In the prestige Hindi film adaptation of R. K. Narayan's novel, Rosie's mother, a *devadasi* (depicted in the film more as a "madam" of a brothel), keeps her away from a professional career in dance, and to ensure her a life of respectability, marries her off to the archaeologist Marco (Kishore Sahu), who forbids her to dance. On a trip to Udaipur, Rosie beseeches the tour guide, Raju (Dev Anand) to take her to a snake charmers' colony where "*naag-nritya*" (snake dance) is performed. Cut to a *saperan* (female snake charmer) dancing to the *been*, a wind instrument played by snake charmers. In a series of frames bonding the two dancing women together, we see between the dancing *saperan*'s jingling anklets Rosie's entranced gaze. She is lured into the dance right away, and like in this chapter's opening example of "*Aye hai dilruba*," here as well, the two women have eyes only for each other, while Raju is forgotten in the background. Both clothed in flaming red, Rosie and the *saperan* swing and slither in a dance as dangerous and exciting as the cobra's raised hood that they gesture toward.[71] They spin deliriously in a whirling frisson of folk and classical movements, blurring lines between the ritual folk dancer (the *saperan*), the banned *devadasi* (Rosie), and the *Bharatanatyam*-trained actress thirsting to dance (Rehman). This "pure dance" sequence with another dancing woman is Rosie's most eloquent moment of self-expression, exulting in her freedom to move, unencumbered by sung lyrics charged with furthering the heterosexual romantic arc of the film's narrative (see color insert—image 13).[72] It is a conversation only between the dancers and their dance, and the palpable excess of this sweaty, pulsating, enigmatic dance number is indeed emblematic of the excess of the dancing woman in popular Hindi cinema, marking a site of escape from the normative constraints of the narrative, as well as a dancer-shunning society more generally (see ⊙ video 04.09).

The sequence features an intricate soundscape built by a range of percussive, string, and wind instruments, moving between moods and tempos to showcase dance moves that alternate between gentle and soft *lasya* (grace) and strong, warrior-like *tandava* (vigor and strength). As the music and choreography showcase Rosie's skills and passion as a dancer, the sequence bears poignant and defiant testimony to what we lose when we ban the *devadasi*

(Rosie) or the dance-trained actress (Rehman) from dancing. As the audience watches agape, Rosie's dance takes on a life of its own. Her dancing partner, the *saperan*, retreats, noticing the searing intensity of this woman's desire to dance. Rosie sways, giddy and sweating, spurning assistance from Raju, and launches into a staggering, dizzying whirl that the camera accompanies with 360-degree pans. The dancing woman's harnessing of cinematic technologies to capture her moving body renders the dance number a site of maximal formal innovation, a techno-spectacle. Rehman recalls the elaborate camera setup for this whirling climax:

> In those days, we didn't have crab trolleys and the cameras were bulky and heavy. In the middle of the set at Mehboob Studio, they built a raised platform on which the camera and circular tracks were placed. . . . Fali Mistry, his assistant, and Goldie [Vijay Anand] sat there with the camera tilted down for the top shot. I danced round and round and the camera followed me on the circular tracks. . . . There was a camera assistant who ran alongside the tracks, holding all the cables—we both went round and round—it must have looked like a jalebi being fried.[73]

From Rehman's insistence on retaining all her dance numbers in the film and having Hiralal and Sohanlal as choreographers, to her character Rosie steadfastly holding on to her career as a professional dancer, we may read *Guide* as driven centrally by the affective energies of the dancing woman. Soon after this reawakening of her dancing body, Rosie buys anklets in the market and sings with wild abandon, "*Kaanton se kheench ke yeh aanchal, todke bandhan baandhoon payal, koi na roko dil ki udaan ko, dil woh chala. Aaj phir jeene ki tamanna hai*" ("I pulled my sari from thorns, I broke all my ties and tied dancer's anklets around my feet. Don't stop the flight of my heart, I want to live again!") reiterating that her primary relationship is to her dance, which she remains wedded to, even as Raju dies at the end of the film.

Citing the snake dance as her favorite number in the film because it highlights her "pure dance" skills, Rehman compares the labor involved in its production with the ease of featuring in narrative numbers (for example, "*Gaata rahe mera dil*" in *Guide*): "In a love song the couple would usually hold hands, or run through fields. So no dance steps were required."[74] On the other hand, the sweat and heavy breathing in the snake dance are revelatory of the labor expended by Rehman and her dancing partner, and off-screen by the camera crew and the many other bodies involved in the production of this production number. Rehman recalls the strenuous rehearsals she went through:

> Hiralal broke my bones. We rehearsed in a sound studio in Dadar between five and eight in the morning. Then I'd come home, have a bath and go to another studio to shoot some dialogue scenes. Straight from there I went back to the dance rehearsal and we'd work till 10 or 11 in the night. My God! It killed me. I couldn't walk for days . . . because all my muscles were aching so much.[75]

It is noteworthy that Rehman's dancing partner, Sheela, was assistant choreographer to Hiralal. Vijay Anand remarks that she was so supple and graceful that he told Rehman to watch her for inspiration.[76] While we rarely have accounts from technical crew members in the Bombay film industry, one can imagine how much labor Sheela might have expended on the snake dance, assisting Hiralal with the conceptualization of the dance, standing in for Rehman while she was away on other sets shooting "dialogue scenes," rehearsing her own part in the dance, training backup dancers for the other opulent production numbers in the film, among many other tasks. Rehman recalls that Sheela "was very good and graceful. I told her to become a solo dancer. But she had her own logic and said: 'I won't get many solo dances, but as an assistant I can work on ten pictures.'"[77] Saroj Khan, assistant to Hiralal's brother, Sohanlal, might have had similar reasons to move from being a backup dancer to assistant choreographer. In the same year of *Guide*'s release, Sheela worked as assistant choreographer and dancer on the considerably lower-budget *Tarzan Comes to Delhi* (Kedar Kapoor, 1965), which featured the wrestler-turned-actor Dara Singh and, in keeping with the unabashed dance-and-action attractions of B movies, a multitude of dancing women, including Bela Bose, Laxmi Chaaya, Helen, and Mumtaz. The careers of women like Sheela makes apparent the many histories yet to be written about the dancing woman in Hindi cinema across genres and production economies, not to mention the many off-screen bodies laboring to stage dance spectacle. *Guide*'s snake dance reveals the labor undertaken by the extensive choreomusicking body at work on production numbers, which centrally speak as well to the performative desires of the dancing women they feature.

Two years after *Guide*, Vijay Anand, considered "an expert at song picturization"[78] directed another spectacular production number in *Jewel Thief* (1967), "*Hothon mein aisi baat*" (see ⊛ video 04.10). With entire stanzas shot in one continuous take, this elaborate dance number was a cine-choreographic feat, featuring constant movement by a throng of backup dancers, a drum-beating hero (Dev Anand), a constantly moving camera, and at the center of it all, a dazzling dancing woman, Vyjayanthimala, who describes the shoot in her autobiography: "My god, it was so electrifying given the length of the footage. It was very fulfilling, since in one shot, I had to cover so much and that needed a lot of *dum* (stamina). Being a trained dancer, I didn't go out of breath."[79] Saroj Khan recalls Vyjayanthimala's performance in this production number: "She danced on a moving trolley. She gave seventeen difficult shots without complaining."[80] Crediting Sohanlal for the complex choreography around circular tracks, Vyjayanthimala also attributes her film dance performance to her classical dance training and a long career of performing to a live audience. Her description of her daily routine reveals the labor of keeping parallel careers going in film and dance:

> I would leave home around nine in the morning and be at the studios till six-seven in the evening. When I returned home, I'd barely have time for a hot drink, before I began my dance practice.... Vadyar Dandayuthapani was kind enough to come to Bombay every now and then to teach me more items.... the practice went on past midnight and Yagamma [Vyjayanthimala's grandmother] would put rosewater into my hands to splash on my face, so that I wouldn't fall asleep. I would even practice in my make-up room in-between shots and Vadyar was kind enough to come to the studio.[81]

Rehman and Vyjayanthimala's discussion of classical dance as a form of physical training and of the intensive work involved in rehearsing dance moves over days (often requiring significantly more time than rehearsals for narrative segments, or "dialogue scenes," as Rehman refers to them), not to mention conferring with choreographers, musicians, directors, cinematographers, costume designers, etc., alerts us to the extensive labor of constructing the affective architecture of dance numbers and to the dance-trained actress's central role in demanding and designing these spectacles.

Towards a Kinesics of Film Acting

In examining the role of dance in the construction of the stardom of dancer-actresses like Vyjayanthimala and Rehman, I encountered the routine binarization of the categories of acting and dancing (not unfamiliar to Hollywood and other film industries as well), with more somber, static, seemingly inward-looking performers hailed as proper thespians, the kind Rehman was fashioned into, and more mobile, seemingly outward-directed, dancing performers disparaged as mannered or theatrical. In her early "dance films," for instance, Vyjayanthimala was "shrugged off casually as a 'dancing star.'"[82] Studying how dance training influences acting repertoires trains our gaze toward movement, gesture, and bodily comportment. Shifting our attention to dance-related discourses of performance can alter our understanding of labor, virtuosity, and technique, even in non-dancing sequences. Through a focus on the dancer-actress Vyjayanthimala, this section proposes larger critical consequences for theorizations of acting when we read dancing and acting alongside rather than against each other, reconfiguring in the process, standards for acting that are predominantly founded on rubrics of psychological realism, transparency, and face-centered emoting.

Vyjayanthimala had, through the early 1950s, acted in dance-centric films, which earned her a reputation as mainly a dancer with meager acting abilities. In her memoir, she reminisces, "Till *Devdas* [Bimal Roy, 1955] happened, the critics kept harping that I was a dancer, not an actress. But after its release, I received terrific reviews . . . I earned my reputation and got accepted in the mainstream."[83] She ascribes this "metamorphosis from a dancer to an emoting actress" to the famed auteur Bimal Roy's ability to discern the "*bhavas* [moods] that flit across a dancer's face during those myriad *mudras* [gestures]."[84] Rather than replicate the discursive division between dancing and acting, moving and emoting, I suggest here that when we shift the dominant focus from realist, speech-driven, face-centric emoting, when we take seriously performance that is located not only in the face—that most celebrated expressive field for evaluating "good acting"—but across the body, in dancing legs, gesturing fingers, gyrating torsos, emoting necks and heads, we are able to locate the density and fluidity of performance in the physics of movement and gesture, sensitizing our evaluative criteria to the performing body's ability to produce and express meaning through movement. Dance scholar Sally Ness asserts, "When I think of dancers, I think of their bodies," elaborating that, "[i]n dance, the mind's 'I' can become variable, and may inhabit the person in an infinite number of ways, investing the authority of the first person in different body parts, or in the whole body simultaneously in any number of spatio-temporal relationships."[85] When we turn to dance to theorize film acting, we may similarly proclaim: "When I think of actors, I think of their bodies."

In *Reframing Screen Performance*, Cynthia Baron and Sharon Marie Carnicke note that "performances that lay bare an actor's physical control can illuminate the discipline that is the foundation of acting,"[86] which I extrapolate to consider how dancer-actresses who train to produce fully expressive bodies reveal the corporeal foundations of film acting. Baron and Carnicke also discuss how "characterizations that require actors to play more than one role especially highlight the skill behind the selection and combination of performance choices within a single production."[87] In popular Hindi cinema, dancer-actresses routinely play more than one role on account of the dual registers of performance that their dancing bodies engender, balancing more realist narrative segments that call for "transparent" acting (which maintains the illusion of characterization and does not call overt attention to the actor's skill), and dazzling production numbers in which their opacity as dancing stars becomes evident because of the extraordinary skill on display, produced through rigorous physical training.[88] The hyphenated identity of dancer-actresses bespeaks the dual regimes of performance written upon their bodies, which in turn they rewrite. When trained in certain modes of dance and theater, where verisimilitude plays a secondary role, screen actors bring to the cinema an embodied habitus of non-naturalistic performance. On the particular mode of performance in popular Indian cinema, Corey Creekmur notes that it is "frequently self-aware and explicitly acknowledged, rather than driven by the realist goal of a performer's full immersion into a role and narrative that typically earns the praise of western filmgoers when evaluating actors."[89] While this has been held as a commonplace, theories of dance are centrally important for understanding why these acting traditions developed in the popular Hindi film, which, with its exceptionally syncretic combination of the narrative and performance codes of melodrama, realism, the epic, music, and dance, requires actors to move through a vast range of performance modalities: naturalistic and non-naturalistic, transparent and opaque, individuated and mythic.

While the heterogeneous, omnibus form of the popular Indian film has been the subject of significant scholarship in the past two decades and has been traced to earlier theatrical traditions like *nautanki*, *jatra*, the Parsi Theater, etc., to understand the modes of acting required by this variegated form, we need to turn as well to theorizations of embodiment, of which I will focus on dance- and theater-centered ones here. "Every time an actor performs, he or she implicitly enacts a 'theory' of acting," observes Phillip Zarrilli, an actor-director trained in *Kalarippayattu*, a South Indian martial art form, elaborating that this theory is informed by "culture-specific assumptions about the body-mind relationship, the nature of the 'self,' emotions/feelings, and performance context . . . locatable within a set of historical, socio-cultural, and aesthetic/dramaturgical circumstances."[90] In her detailed account of training practices in Indian classical dance, scholar-practitioner Ananya Chatterjea notes, "the [Indian] dancer never learns to think in terms of muscularity, weight shift, energy manipulation, or finding her or his center,"[91] but instead, imbibes these principles through *angasuddhi* (purity of limb) and *saustabha* (purity of body line), among other principles, as delineated in performance treatises like the *Natya Shastra* and the *Abhinaya Darpana*.[92] As discussed in Chapters 3 and 4, the adoption of this textual tradition has had a complicated history through the colonial and post-colonial period in the Indian subcontinent. However, these texts are instructive here for their hermeneutic potential to reveal certain lineages of performance, particularly in the case of upper-caste and -class performers like Vyjayanthimala and Rehman, who were trained in recently textualized classical dance forms.[93] Vyjayanthimala marshals the language of this dance training in describing her own experience with film acting, underscoring the relationship of film performance to other corporeal practices: "It was my dance that lifted me and propelled me to reach the top. There were no dramatics; I never had any training in theater. . . . Dance has been the most crucial component in my evolving as an actress. Dancing is so much of *bhava* (mood) and *abhinaya* (expression of the emotion)."[94]

The *Abhinaya Darpana* charts the "course of the dance" (*natya-krama*) thus:

> The song should be sustained in the throat; its meaning must be shown by the hands; the mood (*bhava*) must be shown by the glances; rhythm (*tala*) is marked by the feet. For wherever the hand moves, there the glances follow; where the glances go, the mind follows; where the mind goes, the mood follows; where the mood goes, there is the flavour (*rasa*).[95]

This delineation of the production of affect (also described as *sāttvikabhāva*s [psychophysical responses] in the *Natya Shastra*) through a series of physical actions is at the heart of the corporeally grounded conventions of performance and reception that inform, however tangentially, the practices of classical-dance-trained actors in Indian cinema. When dancer-actresses bring to film these conventions of representation from codified styles of dance, they deeply alter the melodramatic-realist mode of acting in popular Hindi film and indeed the very structuring of the film's narrative architecture. Thus, when Vyjayanthimala stars as Pushpa, an actress-in-the-making in *Kathputli* (Amiya Chakrabarty, Nitin Bose, 1957), the film's climax must be articulated through an elaborate production number. In "*Bol ri kathputli dori*," the dancer-actress expertly shifts from a melodramatic-realist register of performance (tears and speech) to a non-realist, epic dimension wrought through dance. Employing the vocabulary of the classical South Indian dance form, *Kathakali*, traditionally performed by men,[96] Vyjayanthimala's strong swivels and grounded leaps testify to impressive strength and virtuosity, and generate variously the *rasas*, or affects, of *raudra* (anger), *veera* (courage), *bhayanaka* (terror), and *karuna* (pathos).[97] The movement vocabulary of *Kathakali*, with its heavy and muscular footwork, large, expansive movements of the limbs that allow the dancer to forcefully annex space, a fixed, strong torso, and dramatic, pulsating eye movements, enables Pushpa to eloquently express her agony and rage at the injustice meted to her (see ▶ video 01.05). As Pushpa spins in anguish and resentment, the camera too comes off its axis and sways in canted angles to the music as if it has all become too much to bear, until she collapses onto the floor to rousing applause from the audience. All that the film can do after this dizzyingly virtuosic climax is tag on a few minutes of hasty and feeble narrative closure that reconciles Pushpa with her husband. It is the danced finale that effects a complex, multilayered staging of the melodrama of female suffering under a patriarchal regime that limits women's movement (whether in terms of bodily comportment or moving out of the space of domesticity). This construction of the affective architecture of a film through dance helps explain why dancer-actresses (including other Hindi film actors like Sadhona Bose, Waheeda Rehman, Padmini, Madhuri Dixit, Sridevi, among others) perforce have a different performative repertoire than actors who do not dance or are not trained in dance. This opens up the assessment of acting beyond the criteria of naturalism and realism (employed by many Hindi film critics) to entirely different approaches to acting and embodying characters and their emotions.

As discussed in Chapter 2, the gestural systems of many Indian classical dance forms enable the individual dancer to assume different roles, so that a "whole range of impersonal human situations and experiences [is] expressed through gestures."[98] The same classical dancer may represent "empowerment and seduction, religion and sensuality, theatrical artifice and human emotions, male and female, dominant and subordinate positions."[99] Actors trained in dance fundamentally alter the representational logics of popular Hindi cinema by bringing to it this multiplication of personas through their ability to gesturally embody manifold singularities. In every one of her "dance films" in the 1950s, Vyjayanthimala plays multiple dancing roles, often dressed in drag to play both male and female parts.[100] She recalls how dance provided the training for impersonating a range of characters, "Perhaps that is why acting came naturally to me, for in my solo Bharatanatyam performances I portrayed different characters in quick succession. So, I did not have any problem emoting."[101] In a figuration that would become typical of her production numbers throughout her career, in "*Mere watan se accha koi watan nahi hai*" from *Ladki* (M. V. Raman, 1953), the seventeen-year-old Vyjayanthimala's dancing body proliferates in multiple roles on stage. She plays a male drummer and a female dancer from North-East India performing alongside each other, dancing women from different parts of the country, and in addition, the song includes multiple superimpositions of her dancing body and facial gestures. In another dance number from the same film, "*Na maro najariya ke baan*," Vyjayanthimala performs the "dancing double role" of the celestial lovers, Radha and Krishna. As she plays both the coy Radha and the amorous Krishna, her remarkable gestural repertoire is amplified once again across the screen.[102] These instances of dancing masquerade, all too common in Vyjayanthimala's production numbers, not only put on display her performative versatility, but also evacuate the dance numbers of male presence, producing radically altered figurations, in turn, of female protagonists in her films—as women who do not necessarily sing and dance to convey internal emotions centered around heterosexual romance, but as trained, professional dancers flaunting their magnificent artistry. Significantly, in later "serious" films that highlight her "acting" abilities over her trademark, flamboyant dance numbers, Vyjayanthimala's authorial control over the narrative is diminished, as her performative repertoire is subsumed and domesticated into the conventional trajectory of male-centered narratives.[103] She is never quite as luminously in charge once she transitions from the "histrionics" of the dance films of the 1950s (which sometimes function similarly to the Hollywood backstage musical)[104] to the verisimilar register of the social melodrama, where the ecstatic excess of her dancing body is circumscribed by more "integrated" narratives driven by the hero's goals.[105]

Theorizing acting through dancing bodies illuminates how certain movement vocabularies engender specific types of cinematic narratives, genres, and industries. This may be expanded to a broader corporeal theory of screen performance that attends to movement vocabularies, physical training, performers' idiogests, the shifting registers in bodily comportment when actors move through different narrative segments, and the relationship of cinema to other performance traditions.[106] When Vyjayanthimala employs *abhinaya* to enact a range of human and non-human subjectivities—rain, rivers, peacocks, snakes, thunder, lightning, flowers, gods and goddesses, and persecuted performing women like Pushpa in *Kathputli*—her actor's body is imbued with the capacity to embody multiscalar modalities, ranging from personal experiences to cosmic inhabitations. Even as narrative exigencies frame Pushpa as a puppet dancing to other people's tunes, allegorizing female subjection in a realist-melodramatic idiom, when this is articulated through dance, what erupts out of the narrative frame is Vyjayanthimala's dexterous choreography of multiple performance modes. In the body of a dancer-actress, the puppet turns into the adroit, commanding puppet master. This is why when we think of dancer-actresses, there is no way to not think of their bodies.

The Melodrama of Dance Reform

As evident in their filmographies, Vyjayanthimala and Waheeda Rehman's dancing bodies were particularly foregrounded in two types of films: unabashed dance films (Rehman's early dancing-girl roles in the South, and Vyjayanthimala's "light entertainments" in the 1950s), and what I describe as melodramas of dance reform. Unlike itinerant dancing girls—Cuckoo, Helen, Laxmi Chaaya, and others—when dancing heroines like Vyjayanthimala, Waheeda Rehman, and Padmini emerged as A-list actresses in Bombay cinema, narratives of reform were inevitably written around their dancing bodies. Significantly, through the 1950s, Vyjayanthimala and Padmini had flourishing parallel careers in the Madras film industry, dancing away in mythologicals and period dramas that proliferated in popular Tamil and Telugu cinema, unencumbered by the narrative scaffolding of reform. The greater prestige that social melodramas had accrued in Bombay cinema from the mid-1940s was related to their reform-driven narratives and their gentrified personnel, as signaled by Modhu and Sadhona Boses' "dance socials," discussed in Chapter 3. Melodramas of dance reform during the 1950s and 1960s attempted to combine the dance spectacular with the "social problem" film that articulated "respectable" citizenship in the emergent nation, producing in the process cinematic figurations riven with aspirations and anxieties around female sexuality, bodily movement, and economic independence. Dancing women continued to be a thorn in the side of the national-cinematic project of defining ideal citizens and institutions, their formidable physical and economic power threatening the financial and emotional economy of the normative household within and outside the films they featured in. In her study of female stardom in Indian cinema from the 1930s to the 1950s, Neepa Majumdar observes that "the connotations of public performance and, thus, of visual availability, shared by the female star, the stage actress, and the courtesan, make them all occupy an analogous space in the public imagination, a space that is morally defined in opposition to the domestic space of the wife."[107] The dancer-actress, whether playing the role of heroine or vamp, excelled in production numbers, which were typically staged as public spectacles, unlike the private expression of emotions in the narrative number or the song sequence. The movement vocabulary and public staging of the production number occupied an uneasy place within the domestic melodrama since it made much more apparent the visual availability of the female protagonist. The dance-trained bodies of the actresses who played these parts demanded the scripting of roles that would put on display their spectacular ability for movement, which in turn meant that their characters often exceeded the standard role of romantic lover, wife, and mother, women whose performative repertoire was meant to be circumscribed to song sequences and narrative numbers. These melodramas of dance reform may be read as commentaries on female film stardom in diegetic and extra-diegetic ways. Diegetically, the films narrativize female stardom by featuring protagonists who are acclaimed stage actresses, celebrated classical dancers, and famed courtesans.[108] The extra-diegetic engagement of these films with the contemporary industrial-economic structures of female stardom may be understood through their function as a "showcase" or "vehicle" for famous dancer-actresses like Vyjayanthimala, Waheeda Rehman, Padmini, Ragini, and others who, through their dancing, authored the spaces, actions, and narrative trajectories of the dance films they featured in. Through their spectacular production numbers, these dancing heroines often displaced the hero as the agent of action, exerting a strong authorial force that subverted the goals of the state and of the cinematic form of the "social." The variance between the economic and cultural agency of the dancer-actress and the diegetic narratives that portray her dance as performed in tragic circumstances of enforced labor, sexual oppression, and social ostracization produces the particular tensions of the melodrama of dance reform.

During this period, the association of public, professional dancing with traditional dancing women such as *tawaifs* and *devadasis* had not been completely severed, which evinced in many melodramas of dance reform enfoldments between the categories of professional dancer, courtesan, and prostitute, all figured as women of the *bazaar* rather than women of the home. Various historians and film scholars have related the discourse on Indian modernity in the nineteenth and twentieth centuries to the construction of a model of ideal womanhood. Most famously, Partha Chatterjee in the essay, "The Nationalist Resolution of the Women's Question," argues that the discourse of Indian nationalism was driven by the need to protect the spiritual essence of the nation, enshrined in the figure of the woman and the home. "The home was the principal site for expressing the spiritual quality of the national culture, and women must take the main responsibility of protecting and nurturing this quality."[109] A system of gendered dichotomies structured around inner/outer, *ghar/bahir* (home/world), woman/man, and spiritual/material thus shaped the nationalist project. To become the idealized repository of national values, the woman had to be recast and constantly reinvented through a pedagogical regime that combined tutelage in traditional (Hindu) customs as well as a modern education. The anxiety around the definition of Indian womanhood was fundamentally predicated on the private/public divide, separating the ideal Hindu woman not only from the English *memsahib*, but also from lower-class "public" women, chief among them the prostitute, the dancing girl, the courtesan.[110] Ranjani Mazumdar describes how the double location of this construction of the woman in both colonial ideology and middle-class nationalism's engagement with colonialism reproduces the Western metaphor of the streetwalker as the only possible public woman.[111]

Films featuring Vyjayanthimala and Rehman, such as *Devdas, Kathputli, Sadhna, Sunghursh, Roop Ki Rani Choron Ka Raja, Mujhe Jeene Do, Teesri Kasam,* and *Guide*, represent variations of the national-bourgeois project to transform the professional dancer (whether *tawaif, devadasi*, or *nautanki* performer)[112] into a non-dancing wife. In engaging with dance as *work*, these films deploy the dichotomies of *ghar* and *bazaar* (home and the public space of the bazaar with its dancing women and other vices), private and public, to narrativize the transition (or the impossibility thereof) of the dancing protagonist from *bai* to *devi* (courtesan to wife, woman of the bazaar to respectable woman of the home), addressing the newly independent nation's cultural mandate to recuperate traditional dance forms while marginalizing or gentrifying their original female performers. The central conflict of these films' narratives, produced through a split between two professions, that of the public dancer and the home-bound housewife, is evident at formal and narrative levels. The anxiety around this figuration is evident in the organization of production numbers and narrative numbers, public and private spaces (*kotha*/home, stage/bedroom, etc.), styles of costuming, makeup, and movement vocabulary, and indeed, even in the frequently doubled names of the dancing female protagonists, for example, Rosie/Nalini (*Guide*), Rajni/Champabai (*Sadhna*), Kamla/Kaminidevi (*Payal*, Joseph Taliath, 1957), Munni/Laila-e-Aasman (*Sunghursh*), Pakeezah/Sahibjan (*Pakeezah*, Kamal Amrohi, 1972), Jyoti/Jugni (*Namkeen*, Gulzar, 1982), etc. The contrast between the private name of the home and the public, professional name of the *kotha* or of the stage points to the doubled figuration of innocence and corruption that these narratives are obliged to devise when the female protagonist is a professional dancer.[113] The melodrama of dance reform's drive toward the social and psychic transformation of the dancing woman involves a process of renaming—from the Christian Rosie to the Hindu Nalini, the venal Champabai to the devout Rajni, Hira Bai to Hira Devi (*Teesri Kasam*). During this period, professional classical singers and dancers also remade their public personas through renaming or adding "devi" to their names. As Coorlawala notes, "in tandem with Rukmini Devi Arundale, *dasi* (servant) metamorphosed into *devi* (goddess), as several dancers of that period took on the appellation 'Devi.'"[114]

Sadhna, B. R. Chopra's 1958 "social problem" film, exemplifies a particularly didactic strain of the melodrama of dance reform, positing *tawaif*/courtesan culture as a social evil and proposing reform through marriage and monogamy. Sumita Chakravarty notes that "socials" like *Sadhna* and, earlier, *Aadmi* (V. Shantaram, 1939) "portrayed the trajectory of the prostitute from that of fallen woman to one restored to social respectability through marriage. The 'rescue' scenario, wherein the unfortunate woman trapped in a life of moral degradation is rescued by a good man, dominated these films."[115] In *Sadhna*, Vyjayanthimala plays a popular and prosperous *tawaif*, Champabai, who takes on the guise of a virtuous middle-class girl, Rajni, to earn some extra money from the masquerade. The deception is required by a young Sanskrit professor, Mohan, whose ailing mother wants to see him married before she dies. Early in the film, when she first meets Mohan and his mother, the Islamicate *tawaif*, Champabai, takes Mohan's leave with an inadvertent *aadab* (a Muslim form of greeting, common as well to cinematic *tawaifs*) that she quickly changes into a *namaste* (a common, typically Hindu gesture).[116] This gestural transformation prefigures the steady Sanskritization of Champabai into Rajni by the Sanskrit professor hero, and his pious mother who schools her in *sanskriti* (tradition). Through its movement from the opening *mujra* production numbers in the *kotha* (salon) to the concluding religious *bhajan* (devotional song) in the sacred space of the home, *Sadhna* produces a schematic narrative for the establishment of the normative upper-caste Hindu household with its ideal, home-bound, non-dancing daughter-in-law. Thresholds and doors spatialize the movement of the *bai* into the realm of the *devi*. Once she steps on the path to self-improvement, Champabai retreats from the volatile, sexually charged public space of the *kotha* and its coquettish production numbers into the private space of the conjugal home and of plaintive song sequences. The film's climax takes place, tellingly, at the threshold of the home, with Champabai's pimp on one side and Mohan's mother on the other, marking the dividing line between the Islamicate world of the *bazaar* and the sanctified space of the Hindu household that has no place for dance. Significantly, Champabai does not belong to a hereditary performing tradition (unlike Rosie in *Guide* or Hirabai in *Teesri Kasam*) and is forced into dancing when orphaned at a young age, which makes her recuperation as a proper subject of the normative Hindu family ideologically easier both for Mohan's modern humanitarian outlook and his mother's Hinduized reform agenda. *Sadhna*'s narrative of reform may be traced to the discourse of dance reform through the first half of the twentieth century. Janaki Nair observes that a central element of the new nationalist patriarchy's modernizing impulse was to formulate the resolution of the "problem" of the *devadasi*s within the framework of marriage.[117] Soneji parses out the legal and bureaucratic regulation of *devadasi* sexuality and attendant promises of a restructuring of the self, based on middle-class sexual ethics,[118] by examining how twentieth-century reform movements promised *devadasi*s "full participation as citizens in the emergent nation-state only if they were able to 'reform' themselves through marriage."[119]

Despite being a courtesan film, a genre typically marked by lavishly produced song-and-dance numbers, and especially one starring Vyjayanthimala, a dancer-actress whose very presence in a film signaled a conspicuous investment in dance numbers, *Sadhna* features only two production numbers in a total of six musical sequences. In keeping with the film's social reform agenda, even the two *mujra* dance numbers are self-reflexively critical of *tawaif* culture. The first, "*Kaho ji tum kya kya khareedoge, yahan toh har cheez bikti hai*" ("Tell me sirs what would you like to buy, all sorts of things are sold here") has Champabai gleefully listing the pecuniary transactions she excels in, while in the second, "*Aise waise thikanon pe jaana bura hai*" ("Frequenting places—like the *kotha*—is harmful"), she recites a litany of the financial, marital, and other woes that will befall the man who visits the *kotha*. The relative unpopularity of the two production numbers (compared to Vyjayanthimala's other dance numbers from the 1950s and 1960s) may be ascribed to their sanctimonious articulation of the perils, rather than the pleasures, of the *kotha*. The social problem film's intention is all too clear and devoid of the mix of danger and desire that otherwise pervades the cinematic *kotha*. Significantly, in recognition of her acting abilities, Vyjayanthimala won her first Filmfare Award for Best Actress for this film, buttressing the film's status as a serious-minded social drama that proved its leading actress's abilities beyond her famed proficiency in dancing. That it does not remain as well-remembered as her more dance-centered films, however, suggests that spectatorial tastes do not necessarily accord with the reform narrative, and that the pleasures of dance melodramas map onto narrative-spectacle relations in very complex ways.

In *Kathputli*, released a year before *Sadhna*, Vyjayanthimala's dancer-actress character, Pushpa, declares, "*Main stage ki mallika ke bajai ghar ki rani banoongi*" ("I will be queen of the home rather than empress of the stage"). However, the film hardly follows on this premise and showcases the dancing star in a series of scintillating production numbers (discussed in multiple chapters across this book), earning a description as "a Vyjayanthimala vehicle" consisting of "expensively staged dance sequences loosely strung together"[120] in the manner of the Hollywood backstage musical dedicated to putting on a show. *Kathputli*'s dispersed attractions may be read as a counterpoint to *Sadhna*'s didacticism, providing us with another model of the melodrama of dance reform, which, in not subsuming the pleasures of dance, produces a different diagram of female virtue and virtuosity. In an essay on the melodramatic mode in popular Hindi cinema of the 1950s, Ravi Vasudevan outlines the function of the female protagonist as fulfilling the various needs of the male subject, ranging from sexual gratification to the restoration of the moral order.[121] According to Vasudevan, the narrative and its agent, the hero, typically generate simple nurturing female figures, and sometimes more "active" ones like Chandramukhi, the *tawaif* (played by Vyjayanthimala) in *Devdas*, or Gulabo, the prostitute (played by Rehman) in *Pyaasa*. However, these latter figures are transformed from impure denizens of the *bazaar* to pure-hearted caretakers through the influence of the hero (and related agents of domesticity, such as his mother or family). Within this scheme, the woman's function is to restore identities and normalize family relations. However, when the plot is organized around *female* desire, the inherent instability in the popular cinema's process of meaning-making becomes singularly pronounced. "The transgression opened up is intolerable, and the pressure to see incommunication resolved and normalcy restored is given priority."[122] *Kathputli* features three models of femininity—Pushpa, who takes on the labor of professional dancing, her younger sister whom Pushpa labors to send to college and grooms for the bourgeois marriage market, and a third woman, played by the legendary *Bharatanatyam* dancer Kamala Laxman, whose character resembles the older model of the professional dancing woman. Kamala Laxman's character is an early instance of the item dancer—her production number is purely seductive and spectacular and not charged with the emotional registers of Pushpa's *melodramatic* dance numbers (like the final production number, "*Bol ri kathputli*," discussed in the previous section). Many courtesan films and melodramas of dance reform dramatize the transition, and the profound trauma associated with it, from the matrifocal households of traditional performers to the newly articulated heteropatriarchal space of the nuclear or conjugal family. The drama of *Kathputli* draws its force from the female protagonist's commitments to home and stage, and revolves around questions of physical and emotional labor. Pushpa dances to support her sister, husband, and director-mentor, and between dazzling dance numbers, nurtures, with song sequences, her daughter and her mentor's son. The film displays a striking lack of dedication to the narrative demands of securing and nurturing heterosexual romance, with conspicuously half-hearted attempts to resolve the miscommunication between Pushpa, her husband, Shivraj, and her director-mentor, Loknath. A conventional resolution is tacked on in the final minutes of the film, when Shivraj returns with their daughter to embrace Pushpa back into the familial fold. However, this remains a noticeably weak attempt to neutralize inadmissible conflicts and desires, centrally those of Pushpa for public performance and for Loknath, desires that remain palpable well beyond this hasty resolution. In films starring dancer-actresses like Vyjayanthimala and Rehman, not only does the para-narrative unit of the dance number "float free of the business of narrative,"[123] refusing to be integrated into the conventional exigencies of the male-centric plot, but the very presence and staging of these production numbers produces a different kind of narrative, a melodrama of the labor of performance, of dance as work, and of dancing women as a very particular category of melodramatic heroines.

In her account of *tawaif*s in Lucknow, Veena Talwar Oldenburg observes that "it is the 'normal' woman's social and sexual regimen that courtesans-in-the making must unlearn and supplant" by adopting a lifestyle that "gives them the liberation they desire, without jerking the reflexive muscle of a repressive system."[124] She likens *tawaifs* to male ascetics, rebelling against the housewifely stage, implicitly mandated for all women in both Hindu and Islamic cultural systems.[125] Waheeda Rehman conveys the complexity of the dancing woman as melodramatic heroine in *Guide* and *Teesri Kasam*, where the heroine (Rosie and Hirabai, respectively) remains an ambivalent figure on account of her sustained transgression, which takes the form of rejecting marriage and domesticity for a continued career in dance and/or theater. The male subjects in the two films (Raju and Hiraman, respectively) are left in a state of profound confusion and disillusionment because the female subjects will not transition into the position marked for them by the narrative, from *bai* to *devi* through marriage, signaling the impossibility of romantic heterosexual union. In *Teesri Kasam*, the third promise of the film's title refers to Hiraman's resolve not to transport a *bai* from a *nautanki* company ever again in his bullock-cart, while the first two resolutions are to not cart smuggled commodities and illegal bamboo, all these goods figured as illicit and corrupting of the innocent naïf. While *Sadhna*'s project of social reform is in line with the ideology of a benevolent nationalism that seeks to incorporate the margins into the mainstream,[126] through her refusal to be assimilated, Hirabai imperils the emotional economy of the innocent villager with his traditional scheme of domesticity, just as trade in smuggled goods threatens the national economy and its development-oriented five-year plans. In *Guide*, Raju, the agent of national modernity, the enabler figure who encourages Rosie to pursue a career in dance, regrets his abdication of the traditional role of the male subject: "I should have married you, but instead of making you goddess of my home, I decided to first make you queen of the world." Even as the film charts the national-cultural narrative of the transition of professional dancers from the *devadasi* community to the classical dance podium,[127] Raju's misgivings echo, for instance, those of Modhu Bose, discussed in Chapter 3, when he concludes at the end of his directorial career that the film actress (his wife, Sadhona Bose, in this instance) can never commit herself to a life of domesticity. These dancing melodramatic heroines reflect thus a range of anxieties associated with female performers, on- and off-screen, that extend into the 1950s and 1960s Majumdar's assertion that the ambivalence toward the cultural status of cinema in the 1930s rendered "stardom as feminized in relation to production studios," generating "implicit equivalences . . . between cinema, stardom, femininity, and nation."[128]

Conclusion: Enfolded Histories of the *Bai* and the *Devi*

An analysis of dance films and dancer-actresses in the 1950s and 1960s reveals the sustained and constantly reworked tensions between public performance and constructions of ideal femininity. While melodramas of dance reform articulate continuing anxieties about the participation of dancing women in the public sphere, the star texts of dancer-actresses like Vyjayanthimala and Waheeda Rehman serve to cleanse the image of the dancing woman, and, by extension, of the female film star. Discourses of respectability in relation to public performance by women, which defined much of the conversation around dancing and film acting through the first half of the twentieth century, are narrativized through dancing women in films of this period, figured through recurrent oscillations between disrepute and esteem, censure and veneration. The female public performer is a vital figure in the analysis of socio-cinematic figurations because her foregrounding of the enactment of the conventional female roles of seductress and domestic goddess, her all-too apparent masquerade, rips open the illusion of the cohesion and fixity of these roles and in fact their binary construction.[129] The repeated splitting of female characters can be read as part of the struggle to restrain what had come to be seen as the terrifying slippage between these roles—of the dancer, the *bai*, and the good wife, the *devi*, which remain in a complicated relationship marked by reciprocal anxiety and desire.

While the reform and revival impetus of the anti-*nautch* movement strove to starkly contrast the upper-caste wife and the *devadasi*, Amrit Srinivasan traces earlier parallelisms between the *sumangali* or married woman and the *nityasumangali* or the *devadasi* (who, wedded to the local deity, could never be widowed) as well as the coexistence, in Tamil theological doctrine and ritual service, of two goddesses, the *svakiyanayika* (inner or domestic) and the *parakiyanayika* (outer or public). While, as she notes, the Victorian ideals of the anti-*nautch* agitation could not digest this conceptual equivalence, "in regional Tamil understandings, being a private housewife or a professional god's wife were both parallel and legitimate life-possibilities for sect women, even though the second was a more restricted and difficult path, offering in compensation the chance of an education, artistic accomplishment, wealth and fame."[130] In *Teesri Kasam*, when dithering over Hiraman's proposal of marriage, which would mean leaving the *nautanki* stage, Hirabai ponders, "*Kahin aisa na ho ki Hira devi ko koi chahnewala na ho aur Hirabai ko koi dekhnewala na ho*" ("What if there is no one to love Hira Devi [the wife] and no one to look at Hira Bai [the stage actress]?"), articulating a complex range of desires for fame, domesticity, respectability, and a continued professional life as a publicly desired actress (which she chooses in the end). Even if *Sadhna*'s climax has Vyjayanthimala's Champabai cross the threshold into the normative Hindu household, the shadow of the Islamicate *tawaif* falls across this threshold. The *bazaar* is just a step away from the home, always ready to house the dancing woman once again. Oldenburg meets, in the course of her ethnographic fieldwork in Lucknow, a number of married women who ran away from oppressive husbands and households to become *tawaifs*.[131] Just as the housewives, the *devis*, in the split figuration of dancing protagonists in these films of the 1950s and 1960s, carry past histories of the *bai* in their names and their gestural repertoires, it is only when we consider longer lineages of dancing women that it becomes apparent that the *baijis* and the *devadasis*, the *tawaifs* and the *nautanki* actresses are constant shadow figures in corporeal histories not just of the Hindi film vamp, but also of its dancing heroine. When Helen and Vyjayanthimala jointly stage the spectacle of "*Aye hai dilruba*" in 1962, they bring to bear these intertwined, folded histories of training and labor that produce the dancer-actress in popular Hindi cinema.

5

Stardom *Ke Peeche Kya Hai* (What Is behind the Stardom)?

Saroj Khan and Madhuri Dixit as Co-Choreographers of 1990s Bollywood Femininity

The acclaimed photographer Dayanita Singh has a little-known set of photographs titled "Masterji Series" (1994) that uncovers the labor of Hindi film choreographer Saroj Khan and her team. Singh, who convinced the *Independent Magazine* to feature a series on Bollywood beyond its stars, recalls, "It was an exciting time. Madhuri Dixit had just taken over the mantle from Sridevi and was blossoming. Khan worked a lot with her; and usually did three shifts a day. While she had a large crew of assistants to do her bidding, I was always struck by her light-footedness when she demonstrated a move herself."[1] The one image in the series that features Dixit and Khan is from the sets of the dance number "*Jungle mein sher*" in *Prem Granth* (Rajiv Kapoor, 1996) (see Figure 5.1). Shot three years before the release of the film, Singh's photograph captures the labor of creating the dance number, holding still a moment—in tasteful monochrome—from the film's floridly multicolored production number (see ▶ video 05.01). As Kapoor, the film's director, walks away on the right side of the frame, Singh's camera centers the star-choreographer combination of Dixit and Khan, with a group of female backup dancers in a casual circle behind them. This is the space of dancing women, foregrounding the female star, her choreographer-mentor, backup dancers chatting among themselves, a woman in the background cupping her face, possibly a film extra, biding her time until called upon to play the part of a diegetic spectator. Dixit, in a rustic *ghagra-choli* (skirt and blouse), sensuously gazes down her arm, rehearsing a gesture of one hand delicately stroking the other, while Khan seems to already be enacting the next move, her left arm cocked at her waist, her right palm forming a seductive gesture at her pouting mouth, her eyes imperiously beckoning the camera. While, as a choreographer, she

Figure 5.1. Dixit and Khan on the sets of *Prem Granth* in Dayanita Singh's "Masterji Series."
Credit: Dayanita Singh.

remains off-screen in the final dance number, the creative authorship and labor of this Masterji (as Khan is known in the industry) are amply evident in the signature moves—referred to in the popular press as *jhatkas* and *matkas* (breast pulses, hip and waist undulations)—expertly performed by her star pupil, Madhuri Dixit.

Singh notes of the series, "I knew the photographs were too 'voluptuous,' too easy to like, if you will, and I've always struggled with how to exhibit them."[2] The images cannot shake off their pop-culture voluptuousness, amplified by the steamy, sexy movement vocabulary of Khan's choreography. The series captures Khan demonstrating dance moves and romantic poses with her female assistants, their bodies draped around each other, chests heaving, generating a charged homoerotic frisson between these laboring bodies. In this world mostly divested of men—of male directors, actors, and crew members—the labor of the choreographer, her assistants, backup dancers, and actresses is magnified. As they rehearse poses and attitudes to perform on-screen femininity, what becomes visible are the processes of training, rehearsal, embodied knowledge, performativity, and collaboration. It is in this spirit that I read the 1990s through Khan and Dixit's co-choreography of a new style of movement that produces corporeal formations and transformations between and across the bodies of dancer-actresses, choreographers, and spectators. The two dancing women's shared corpus of twenty-one films across more than three decades bears corporeal marks of their virtuosity in dance and their sustained labor in constructing a new gestural vocabulary for the Hindi film heroine, which erupts beyond their famed production numbers to render their entire oeuvre of films as choreographic phenomena.[3]

Moving Intimacies between Performing Women

While I have analyzed the role of dance in the production of Dixit's star text and its impact on the narratives woven around her dancing body elsewhere, here I foreground the processes of co-choreographing cinematic bodies, spaces, and movements.[4] A corporeal history of Hindi film dance cannot be written only through stars. Choreographers, dance masters, *nattuvanars*, *Kathak* gurus, and Anglo-Indian social dancing were all central to producing the corporeal habitations of the dancing body. Starting as a child actor (named Shyama) in *Parchhaiyan* (V. Shantaram, 1952), featuring as a ten-year-old backup dancer in *Howrah Bridge* (Shakti Samanta, 1958) among many other films (see Figure 5.2), becoming assistant choreographer to Sohanlal at the young age of fourteen in *Dr. Vidya* (Rajendra Bhatia, 1962), launching her career as an independent choreographer with *Geeta Mera Naam* (Sadhana Shivdasani, 1974), prompting the institution of the first Filmfare Award for choreography in 1989, and now established as a celebrity choreographer who features in televised dance shows, Saroj Khan has traversed Bombay's media history from black and white celluloid to color and digital technologies, from big to small screens. Her six-decade-long career in the Bombay film industry has left its choreographic signature on dancing women from Vyjayanthimala to Hema Malini, Sridevi, Madhuri Dixit, and Kareena Kapoor, among scores of others. Indeed, her choreography, a dynamic repository of different gestural regimes and movement vocabularies, acts as a corporeal archive of Hindi cinema's industrial practices and representational systems. Many of the dancer-actresses who performed her moves are carriers of her gestural stamp, especially those who, based on their own training and skill, are able to translate it fully on screen. In evidence here is a network of creative energies between the choreographer and the on-screen

Figure 5.2. Saroj Khan as backup dancer in *Howrah Bridge* (1958).
Credit: Screen capture.

dancer, between assistant choreographers and backup dancers, all creating meaning through movement.

Khan, along with the two most acclaimed dancer-actresses of the late 1980s and the 1990s, Madhuri Dixit and Sridevi, redefined choreographic styles, altering the spaces in which song-and-dance numbers were staged, and introducing radical changes in the costume and makeup of the dancing heroine.[5] They mobilized the erstwhile vamp's salacious movement vocabulary to generate a new kind of corporeal presence for the heroine, quivering with sensuousness, boldly libidinous. Every filmic space that brought in Dixit or Sridevi for a production number was transformed by the power of their dancing and Khan's choreography. Empty barns became sensationally activated by Sridevi and Dixit in dance numbers like "*I love you*" (*Mr. India*, Shekhar Kapur, 1987) (⊙ video 05.02) and "*Dhak dhak karne laga*" (*Beta*, Indra Kumar, 1992) (⊙ video 05.03), respectively. The hero was rendered a side show, a stunned, mute spectator to their danced expressions of sexual appetite. Instead, these production numbers may be read as intimate dialogues between choreographer and the dancing heroine, who had conceived and rehearsed the moves over days, figuring out which steps worked best, what fabric most effectively accentuated their undulating bodies, or what kind of bodice would show off their heaving chests to greatest advantage while protecting them from the censor board's moral policing. They walked, with great dexterity, the thin line between sensuous and censored female movement, between A and B movie status, U (Universal) and A (Adult) ratings. This era's codifications of feminine performance were choreographed by the labor of these three dancing women. Between them, they produced a diagram of femininity that continues to define the iconography of on-screen dancing women in Bollywood, including in item numbers, eroticized narrative numbers, and big-budget *mujra*s. The mise-en-scène and movement vocabulary of Sridevi's baroque production numbers in *Himmatwala* (K. Raghavendra Rao, 1983) now inspire part-parody, part-homage renditions in *The Dirty Picture* (Milan Luthria, 2011) and *Aiyyaa* (Sachin Kundalkar, 2012), while Dixit playfully participates in the very phenomenon she helped create, the item number.[6] This chapter's focus on training, rehearsal, and collaboration foregrounds the creative processes in Dixit and Khan's co-choreography that produced new corporeal figurations, which both dancing women continue to build on through richly intermedial careers in film, reality TV dance shows, and on web platforms.

"*Ek do teen*" as a Film Dance Classroom

Madhuri Dixit's fame as a dancer-actress owes much to a series of production numbers she performed early in her career. Although she made her acting debut in *Abodh* (Hiren Nag, 1984), it was the production number "*Ek do teen*" in *Tezaab* that launched her as a major A-list star. A review in the film magazine *Star and Style* signals the immense popularity of this dance number:

> The "ek do teen char" song has done it. Crowds are thronging to see Tezaab as if they're seeing a film after ages. In Bombay, and more generally, in the whole of Maharashtra, the song ... became a veritable rage in the Ganpati and Navratri festivals. ... Tezaab got an opening at the cinemas which no other Anil Kapoor-starrer must've ever got. The dances of Dixit and Anil Kapoor on this song are making the cine-goers dance, whistle, shower coins, yell, scream, and shout with joy. (*Star and Style*, December 2–15, 1988, 70)

The attribution of a film's success to a Dixit production number would become commonplace throughout the actress's career. Monika Mehta remarks on the effect of Dixit's dancing: "Through her spectacular dance performances, Dixit commandeered screen space in a way that seriously challenged the position of the male hero. People frequently entered theaters to watch her dance routines and left when the story started."[7] Examining the processes of training and rehearsal for her first such staggeringly successful production number reveals the networks of labor and collaboration behind Hindi film dance.

In my interview with her, Dixit recalled that, despite her classical dance training in *Kathak* and stage performances since the age of eight, she had floundered with film dance routines in the first few years of her career. "Then Saroj-ji came along. She said I'll have to do a lot of rehearsals for *Tezaab*. I had that 'Aha!' moment while shooting '*Ek do teen*.' It was like a classroom for me. I learned how to dance for the camera with this song."[8] When they had worked together on *Uttar Dakshin* (Prabhat Khanna, 1987), Khan had instructed Dixit to learn the performance practices of Bollywood dance for their next film, *Tezaab*, explaining that unlike Dixit's frontally presented *Kathak* performances on stage, in film dance, she needed to be constantly conscious of camera placement and movement, look into the camera confidently, and move from one floor mark to the next.[9] "That song helped me understand what film dance is all about. I never thought this kind of dance could be so difficult," remarks Dixit.[10] In Nidhi Tuli's documentary, *The Saroj Khan Story* (2012), *Tezaab*'s director, N. Chandra, recalls that he described to Khan and her team how he wanted a "wild dance" that would make the diegetic audience "tear their clothes with excitement."[11] Khan choreographed the dance and invited Chandra to finalize it before Dixit began to rehearse. "When I saw the signature movement itself I was convinced that she has hit the right note," exults Chandra.[12]

It took sixteen days of laborious rehearsal and seven days of shooting, including a final continuous twenty-four-hour shoot to produce the dance spectacle of "*Ek do teen*" (see color insert—image 14).[13] Khan had been working in the industry for decades, and Dixit had had a lackluster acting career for four years, until this production number, with its peppy tune and sprightly, vigorous moves, catapulted them to choreographer and actress stardom, respectively. It was seen to mark such a significant shift in Hindi film dance choreography that the popular Filmfare Awards instituted an award for best choreography in 1989 to recognize Khan's genius, while dance became a signature element of Dixit's stardom. She recalls that "*Ek do teen*" turned the tables for her: "Every producer wanted me to do a dance number in his or her film.... We were shooting a song for *Tridev*. There were three actresses. Sonam was a bigger star and so, she was made to stand in the centre. But as soon as *Ek Do Teen* became a hit, the producer changed our positions. I was in the centre."[14] Dixit would remain at the center of 1990s female stardom and would co-choreograph with Khan an entirely new repertoire of corporeal comportment for the Hindi film heroine.

Rehearsal and Training as Techniques of the Dancing Body

Examining processes of training and rehearsal unearths the labor, otherwise obscured, in discourses of skill and talent that inform discussions of Dixit and Khan's combined success over the next half-decade. These processes also illuminate the central role of the choreographer in producing the movement vocabulary of popular Hindi cinema over different periods, which is otherwise assumed to be generated through a series of idiosyncratic star gestures and the individual skills of actors. The discussion, in Chapter 4, of Waheeda Rehman's performance in the snake dance from *Guide* (Vijay Anand, 1965) demonstrates how the entire choreomusicking body, composed of the choreography and music teams, makeup artists, director, cinematographer, editor, and others, labors to produce the on-screen dancing body. Similar to Vijay Anand's instruction to Rehman to watch the assistant choreographer, Sheela, for inspiration, was the director Subhash Ghai's advice to the emerging star, Dixit: "I told Madhuri, when you don't understand what to do, just observe Saroj [Khan] carefully and copy her as well as you can. If you can do even 70% of what she does, you are going to be a very big star. And she was beautiful and had a great face. That was her great advantage. Otherwise Saroj Khan was a better dancer any day."[15] This figuration of the successful on-screen dancer as an expert mimic of the off-screen choreographer is repeated in many accounts of Khan and Dixit in particular. N. Chandra recollects how Madhuri rehearsed incessantly, "perfecting not just her hip-swinging hook step but also her expressions, a different one for every day of the month, as demonstrated by Saroj ji."[16] Khan herself recalls of the dancer-actress who would become her most famous protégé, "Madhuri

Dixit was like my shadow. She came to me when she was a kid. We became friends and after that we worked together in almost all of her films."[17]

Rather than posit the off-screen choreographer as the shadow figure to the on-screen dancing star, these accounts foreground the expertise of the choreographer, who is front and center in the processes of composition, training, rehearsal, and, increasingly, direction of the song-and-dance sequence. Dance rehearsals (just like rehearsals for action sequences) constitute a separate space within the film set, with different production logics, an independent head of production (the film's choreographer rather than director), and a group of workers (backup dancers, costume designers, art directors, etc.) who participate in the production of a specific attraction, the song-and-dance sequence. It is thus a prime location for the writing of corporeal histories of Bombay cinema that get left out of star- and director-driven accounts. Dayanita Singh's "Masterji" series captures precisely the thick corporeality of laboring bodies and the extended time of pre-shoot rehearsals that go on to produce the polished, condensed gestures of on-screen performance. Khan praises Dixit for her untiring desire to rehearse dance moves until she gets them right: "I don't think I'll ever find another Madhuri. Nowadays, actresses make a face at rehearsal, but Madhuri would go that extra mile."[18] She remembers the shooting of their popular production number, "*Chane ke khet mein*" from *Anjaam* (Rahul Rawail, 1994), when a complex movement that had to be shot in a single sequence proved difficult to execute, even after fifteen takes. "Madhuri got a bit frustrated, tired rather, and went into her van. We all were waiting outside expecting a response from her like . . . 'let's split the sequence in two halves' or 'give me some easy steps' etc. But this girl, Madhuri, comes out looking all fresh and says let's do it and the shot got OK in the first take," remarks Khan, noting that her favorite pupil would not let down her guruji (teacher).[19]

In an era before the widespread emergence of Bollywood dance classes and studios that today's aspiring actors train in, and in which Dixit and Khan themselves have commercial interests now, Dixit, as a newcomer to the industry, got her film dance training from her choreographer-mentor.[20] Figuring their collaboration along the lines of the traditional *guru* (teacher) and *shishya* (pupil), Khan and Dixit frame film dance training as cultural education, which they are both now seen as bestowing on numerous television and online platforms. Examining dance training is imperative for a corporeal history of Bombay cinema, as it is central to developing techniques of the body, the performance of gender, and the articulation of the romantic-erotic energies of the song-and-dance sequence. As in classical dance training, a tradition in which many film actors (including *baijis*, *devadasis*, and newly trained bourgeois women like Sadhona Bose, Vyjayanthimala, Waheeda Rehman, and many others) and dance masters (*nattuvanars* and other dance gurus) were trained, film dance may also be seen to follow an oral tradition, similar to the *sampradaya* or handing down of a classical dance repertoire through rigorous imitation of the teacher. Indeed, like traditional performing communities, many Hindi film choreographers often come from dance master lineages, with Saroj Khan training under and then marrying Sohanlal, her son Raju Khan joining the family trade, Chinni Prakash training with his grand-uncle, Hiralal (Sohanlal's brother), and Vaibhavi Merchant, Hiralal's grand-daughter, beginning her career as Chinni Prakash's assistant. In describing her classical dance training with Sohanlal, Khan recollects how he would make her hold a pose for three hours on end and not let her move an eyeball even as she cried.[21]

Ananya Chatterjea describes the process of classical dance training, where through repeated practice, "dance styles and repertoire were passed down from generation to generation, stored in the bodies of students who then became recognized performers."[22] Like the traditional guru, the film choreographer is off-screen, her training and dance composition made visible through the on-screen star-pupil. In a video uploaded to YouTube, titled "Madhuri Dixit's Dance Rehearsal with Saroj Khan from Movie Sahibaan," we see Dixit first practice an *Odissi*-based routine, and then see her and Khan rehearsing disco-inflected Bollywood moves (see ▶ video 05.04). Khan moves fluidly and confidently, tossing her head, calling out step numbers. Dixit watches carefully and moves tentatively alongside her as she learns the steps from her choreographer-mentor. As she begins to perform the routine herself, we see Khan's hand and then torso enter the frame, directing her, correcting her moves. Dixit performs the steps again, looking alternately at the camera and at her mentor, asking Khan if she is getting the moves right. We see her face focused and grimacing as she rehearses the steps again. Cut to a more polished performance where she looks confidently into the camera, turns on the famed Dixit smile, and perfectly executes the moves she has rehearsed with Khan. This three-minute video encapsulates the dance rehearsal process and highlights the labor of both dancing women in producing the final production number.

The frequent mention of Khan and Dixit together bespeaks their joint authorship of a new movement vocabulary for the 1990s heroine. Rather than think of Khan as the shadow figure to Dixit, or Dixit as executing skilled approximations of her choreographer's moves, these co-choreographers encourage us to think of techniques circulating *between* bodies, rather than transmitted from one to the other. Such circuits of creative labor between actor and choreographer undergird this book's aim to emphasize relational networks and to argue for the collaborative labor of dancing women in producing new forms of mobility, on- and off-screen. Neepa Majumdar delineates the framework of the "dual-star text" produced by the combination of the on-screen actress's body and the offscreen voice of the playback singer.[23] Given the pervasive role of Khan's choreography in the construction of the Dixit star text, one could conceive of a dual-star text in this instance, combining the choreographic prowess of Khan with the performance skills of Dixit. Dixit's body was the perfect vehicle for Khan's choreographic vision; together, the dancing heroine and the choreographer, who achieved stardom with "*Ek do teen*," conceptualized a new female movement vocabulary in popular Hindi cinema. Highlighting the choreomusicking logics of film dance and music composition, Khan notes of her work with Dixit, "she is a choreographer's delight. I always keep a music piece for her in every song, where she dances solo and the camera frame is kept steady, no trolley or zoom or anything. This is to show people how good this girl dances, without a break in shot" (see ▶ video 05.05).[24] The playback singer Alka Yagnik, who voiced a majority of Dixit's song-and-dance sequences, including "*Ek do teen*" and "*Choli ke peeche*" (*Khal Nayak*, Subhash Ghai, 1993), remarks of the actress's on-screen performance of her voice, "She just adds so much expression that I always felt that all the expressions I had put in the song were justified. In fact, she used to better it. I loved to see my songs enacted by her."[25] A combination of Yagnik's vocal innovations (starting with her breakout song, "*Ek do teen*"), Khan's training of and cine-choreographic attention to Dixit's movement vocabulary, and the actress's own skills and labor produce a new figuration of the dancing heroine, collaboratively constructed through the voice and bodies of multiple performing women.

Sculpting the Body through Choreography

Following "*Ek do teen*," the collaboration between Dixit and Khan produced many hits, including production numbers like "*Humko aaj kal hai intezaar*" (*Sailaab*, Deepak Balraj Vij, 1990), "*Dhak dhak karne laga*" (*Beta*, Indra

Kumar, 1992), and "*Choli ke peeche*" that were definitive of their co-created movement vocabulary, marked by hook steps built around the heaving of the chest, pelvic thrusts, and swaying of the hips. What made the authorship of the Khan-Dixit combination so immediately apparent was their technique of developing hook steps around a particular body zone in each song.[26] The body-space-movement framework, developed in Chapter 2, alerts us to how Khan and Dixit developed new moves in new spaces with the stage-ramp in "*Ek do teen*," the revamping of the traditional *Koli* folk dance with sinuous hip and waist undulations in "*Humko aaj kal hai intezaar*," the breast pulses that marked "*Dhak dhak*" and "*Choli ke peeche*," and the shoulder twist in "*Chane ke khet mein*" (see ▶ video 05.06). In each of their production numbers, a particular physiognomic aspect of Dixit's dancing body is the central piece of the choreography. With her aptitude for torso articulations, complex footwork, defined hand gestures, and nuanced facial expression, Dixit offered Khan a pliant dancing body for producing a corporeal vocabulary located in particular body zones. A few years following Saroj Khan, the choreographer Farah Khan did something similar for Hindi film heroes, isolating their bodies from the distributed gaze of the narrative number into the particularly engaged gaze of the production number.[27]

Khan notes of Dixit: "Of the many actors I have choreographed, she is the only one with whom I could experiment. I have given her so many weird dance steps, but she did them with ease and without complaints."[28] When Dixit worked with male choreographers like Chinni Prakash, Shiamak Davar, or Prabhudeva, on the other hand, her dances were never as salacious or her movement vocabulary split along body zones as with Khan. In films like *Pukar* (Rajkumar Santoshi, 2000) and *Dil Toh Pagal Hai* (Yash Chopra, 1997), among others, the focus is on her capacity for virtuosic movement, her *Kathak*-trained grace, her radiant smile. These comparatively tepid numbers are not where the Dixit star text is concentrated. Indeed, if she had not developed with Khan their particular erotic choreography in the 1990s, she would have featured in similar narrative and production numbers as her contemporaries, Juhi Chawla or Manisha Koirala, among many others. The articulation of particular body zones through Khan's hook steps is what differentiates her movement vocabulary as well from bold predecessors like Zeenat Aman and Parveen Babi, who had already introduced a new diagram of femininity in popular Hindi cinema in the 1970s with their disco-inflected dance moves, often performed to the singer Nazia Hassan's sultry voice, their risqué costumes, and physical self-confidence from earlier careers in fashion modeling. While in the case of Aman and Babi, sexiness was distributed across their performing bodies, with Dixit, the audience's gaze was drawn to particular body parts through the dance moves she and Khan developed. "I'd make moves simple so that they would have recall," notes Khan.[29] The repeatability of hook steps prompted a spectatorial culture of dancing fans replicating Khan-Dixit moves at weddings, in discotheques, and, for the past decade and a half, on immensely popular television dance competitions. By developing a movement vocabulary around particular body zones, the two women not only choreographed a new articulation of particular body parts, but also fundamentally altered spectatorship into a participatory mode grounded in mimicry of these very moves.

In my interview with her, Dixit remarks, "There were times when Sarojji would suggest a movement and I'd say we've done this before, let's try something else. We tried not to repeat steps, we tried to give something new with every song we did. For example, '*Ek do teen*' is very different from '*Choli ke peeche*' from '*Chane ki khet mein*.'"[30] Khan and Dixit's articulation of their choreographic process prompts a theorization of choreography as sculpting the body, where certain movements carve out a new kind of body and new spaces for it to move in. By locating their choreographic signature in particular body zones, Khan and Dixit produced a new map of the Hindi film heroine's body that plotted the corporeal terrain of on-screen femininity along certain danced pathways. This informed the iconography of Dixit's body in M. F. Husain's *Gaja Gamini* (2000), in an homage film like *Main Madhuri Dixit Banna Chahti Hoon!* (Chandan Arora, 2003), and in popular culture more broadly. The charge of Dixit's body zones activated in Khan-choreographed production numbers far exceeded the corporeal matrix of the film, often staying with viewers as their most viscerally experienced and remembered moments from the film. To re-enact the moves of a Dixit-Khan production number required fans (enacting a new mode of participatory fandom) to engage with precise body parts, to learn, to sculpt out of their own bodies, the breast pulses and the hip swaying that were immediately identifiable signatures of this choreographer-star combine.

Khan, Dixit, and Sridevi (who also brought complex bodily habitations from the Tamil and Telugu film industries), through a new language of movement, carved a new inhabitation for the Hindi film heroine. Kareem Khubchandani notes that "the heights of both actresses' careers herald and overlap with the rise of the choreographer within the film industry."[31] Indeed, it was with Khan's choreography of Sridevi's spectacular production numbers, "*I love you*" and "*Hawa Hawai*" in *Mr. India*, "*Main teri dushman*" in *Nagina* (Harmesh Malhotra 1986), and Dixit's "*Ek do teen*" that her choreographic signature became conspicuous. With eight Filmfare Choreography Awards and three National Film Awards for Best Choreography, her imprint on popular Hindi film dance is unmistakable. Her first award for "*Ek do teen*" shifted the description of choreographic labor from the appellation of "dance master" to "choreographer." Before Khan and other Bollywood choreographers gained visibility for their signature movement vocabularies, the dance master was an entirely behind-the-scenes figure, with a fleeting mention in film credits. Dance masters trained star bodies that took their place in the limelight. While the designation of "dance master" indicates a crew member who trains actors in mastering their moves, "choreographer" suggests a broader scope, of imagining and conceiving the dance, often directing it, and in keeping with the dance musicalization argument advanced in Chapter 1, collaborating with the music and directorial team to conceptualize the music of the film as well. With Khan, choreography came to be recognized as carving out dance performance as a separate modality of movement that redefined the contours of the star and the fan body.

New Diagrams of Femininity in the 1990s

Khan's authorship of Dixit's dance repertoire and of the entire design of the production number produced new diagrams of femininity in the late 1980s and early 1990s, a moment much discussed as marking India's entry into an era of economic regulation and globalization. Rupal Oza delineates how the "contentious debates over India's identity" sparked by globalization were particularly inscribed on women's bodies.[32] The period was perceived as producing a new image of femininity, marked by sexual openness, which sparked a number of controversies about women's representation, starting with a petition filed in 1993 in the Delhi High Court demanding the deletion of the Dixit-Khan production number "*Choli ke peeche kya hai?*" from the film *Khal Nayak*, followed by similar censorship attempts against other songs with double entendres. Oza cites as well petitions filed against satellite and cable television companies in 1994 by, among others, the National Commission for Women; the protests, in 1996, surrounding the Miss World Pageant hosted in Bangalore; the criminal complaints filed by the Hindu Right in 1997 against M. F. Hussain's painting of a nude goddess Saraswati; and in 1998, the raids on

Mumbai's dance bar nightclubs, and a state prohibition on female bar dancers working after 8:30 p.m.[33] The virulence of the outrage against film actresses for posing "semi-nude" in magazines, the furor over Hollywood actor Richard Gere kissing the Hindi film actress Shilpa Shetty at a fundraiser, and, most visibly, the long censorship battle waged against "*Choli ke peeche kya hai*" reflect the deep disturbance caused by these new images of femininity circulating in an increasingly mediated public sphere.

Dixit's reminiscence of her performance in "*Ek do teen*" is part of the discourse of "shedding inhibitions" that dominated contemporary choreographers' and female stars' defense against charges of having developed a scandalous new dance vocabulary: "*Tezaab* was an important film for me in terms of shedding inhibitions. . . . I knew I was a good dancer, but whenever I watched myself on screen I always felt I wasn't giving my best. I was holding back. . . . Saroj-ji introduced me to the language of cinema—how to sway and smile during a step."[34] Dixit's costumes and dance vocabulary in "*Ek do teen*" were seen as provocative at the time, and the number has been generally viewed as the marker of a new kind of performance aesthetic for the Hindi film heroine. Sangita Gopal observes that "Dixit's *jhatkas* and *matkas* (convulsive heaves and swings of the body) in this and subsequent dance numbers, definitively completed the blurring of the distinction between heroine (Indian) and vamp (Western) that had been in progress since the 1970s."[35] In "*Ek do teen*," unlike the dances of the erstwhile upright Hindi film heroine, Dixit's dance movements are often choreographed on a horizontal plane in relation to the stage she is dancing on; she crawls, writhes, and clambers forward and backward on the stage floor. In an instrumental interlude, low-angle shots capture Dixit on her knees, bent backward, and playing a saxophone in a short, spangled skirt—the cinematography, costuming, and arrangement of torso and limbs unmistakably borrowing from the representational history of the vamp (see ⓥ video 02.03). The particular moves—the heaving of the bosom and swaying of the hips—choreographed by Khan and performed by Dixit became markers of a new dance idiom for female stars of the period.

Oza observes that the response to the emergence of new figurations of womanhood in the 1990s was to create a media image of the Indian woman who can straddle tradition and modernity, who is an active consumer with a global outlook, but possesses values "that would make her grandma proud."[36] Madhuri Dixit's balancing act between her salacious production numbers and her image as a middle-class, upper-caste Maharashtrian outsider to the film industry provided Hindi cinema its perfect icon to valorize "[t]he modernization of the Indian woman . . . as a painless, non-conflictual, even harmonious process."[37] In her role as the feisty yet obedient daughter in *Hum Aapke Hain Kaun* (Sooraj Barjatya, 1994), a film that cemented the affluent and consumerist Hindu joint family as the preeminent social configuration of the Bollywood film, Dixit recuperates middle-class values right after being at the center of the *"Choli ke peeche"* controversy the year before. In *Beta* (1992), while she may writhe on the floor and rhythmically heave her breasts in the risqué production number *"Dhak dhak karne laga,"* in the rest of the narrative she is a duty-bound and demurely dressed daughter-in-law. Nandana Bose examines how Dixit expended considerable labor on producing a star text that foregrounded her middle-class, outsider status in the Bombay film industry.[38] The anxiety over recuperating the image of middle-class female respectability is fundamentally generated by the movement vocabulary of the Khan-Dixit production numbers, which the actress has to labor to balance with a counter-narrative: "I followed my own path. I got married, I settled, I'm happy. I was in this business and yet never in any controversy or scandal. So, I wasn't like your typical movie actress. I did sensuous dance numbers like *"Choli ke peeche kya hai"* and yet I maintained my reputation and my integrity."[39] Mirroring the strain of the "and yet" in Dixit's account, films featuring Dixit-Khan production numbers are especially riven with this tension and hence constitute critical texts for analyzing changing configurations of gender and sexuality in India during this period.

Co-authoring New Geographies of Desire

"By the nineties," observes Ranjani Mazumdar, citing Dixit's provocative dance numbers, "the earlier binary oppositions, so dear to the nationalist imaginary, had ceased to hold. The heroine now occupied the space of the vamp through a process marked by a public display of desire and an entirely new discourse of sexuality that threatened the old boundaries."[40] Considering how Hindi cinema of the 1990s labors to contain the subversive potential of the new heroine figuration, of which Dixit is emblematic, sheds light on the battles fought over the female body and its on-screen representations during this period. One of the key representational strategies, especially in Dixit's case, is to enlist two separate regimes of performance for the face and body. In her production numbers, torso movements are focused on the breasts, buttocks, and the waist, while eyes and lips primarily mark facial expression. Comments like this one from Rajendra Kumar, a Hindi film star of the 1970s, are commonplace in responses to Dixit's movement vocabulary: "there is no cheapness in her dance. She has a lot of grace."[41] This quality of grace was attributed to her training in *Kathak*, and her skill with *abhinaya* through facial expression. Another Hindi film star, Rishi Kapoor, remarks, "she combines her skill with steps with great expressions. She knows when she smiles that she's winning hearts."[42] Indeed, special mention must be made of Dixit's smile, which is seen as one of the highlights of her star body. In an interview, Saroj Khan says of the actress, "Madhuri Dixit is one actress who gets all the moves right, she moves right, she smiles at the right time."[43] Whereas the vamp's facial expressions are marked by suggestive glances and lip biting, Dixit and Khan ensure that Dixit smiles innocently, "at the right time," so that her famed smile attenuates her employment of the torso movements of the vamp.

In an article on Hindi film music and dance, film journalist Partha Chatterjee, otherwise quite stridently censorious of the song-and-dance sequences of the 1990s, notes of Dixit, "Madhuri's innocence, vulnerability, and girlish sexuality all come out as she slides, writhes, slithers, and shakes to the inane lyrics of 'Ek do teen.'"[44] While all the movements listed by Chatterjee refer to the torso and limb movements of the vamp, it is Dixit's smile that communicates to him the appropriate attributes of the heroine—innocence, vulnerability, and a non-threatening girlish sexuality. The other element that distinguishes Dixit's production numbers are her comic facial expressions. Even as she sways and glides voluptuously in "*Ek do teen*," she makes funny faces and winks comically at the audience. Dixit's sense of comic timing marks her performance, even within raunchy production numbers, as natural and spontaneous. In my interview with her, Dixit remarked, "Sarojji has the knack for combining body movements with lovely facial expressions. For the song, '*Akhiyan milaon*,' she insisted on a close-up of my facial expressions, which were funny and cute. When the camera comes this close and you are emoting, you make a connection with the audience, you hook them. After that, they're yours."[45] Dixit's face tempers the sinuous insinuations of her torso, her innocent smile replacing the knowing smirk of the vamp.

Narratively, her films of the period emphasize the female protagonist's reluctance to dance in a production number. *Tezaab*, for instance, presents Dixit's Mohini as an unwilling public performer. In three films in which Dixit plays the part of a professional dancer—*Tezaab*, *Sangeet* (K. Vishwanath,

1992), and *Devdas* (Sanjay Leela Bhansali, 2002)—dancing for a paying public is portrayed as reprehensible and something her character needs to be delivered from. The other condition in which the heroine performs the production number is out of a sense of duty. In *Khal Nayak*, for example, Ganga (Dixit) stages the production number "*Choli ke peeche kya hai?*" in order to nab the villain, Ballu, and save her fiancé Ram's reputation.[46] While, to ensure the film's popularity and success, significant portions of the budget and shooting schedule are devoted to Khan-Dixit production numbers, the screenplays tag on skimpy motivations for the heroine's bawdy dancing. Altering the spaces in which dance is staged is another strategy to accommodate the salacious production number of the 1990s. Staging a sexually explicit dance performance in a private space, as for example, the bedroom, enshrines it within the discourse of conjugal sexuality, quite unlike the public distribution of the vamp's performing body to a paying, viewing audience. The vamp is kept out of domestic spaces, but Dixit freely performs production numbers like "*Chane ke khet mein*" (*Anjaam*) at family gatherings.

Alternately, sexually brazen production numbers may be performed on stage, ensuring a clear-cut separation between narrative and performance spaces.[47] This separation of spaces retains the opposition between virtuous femininity and dangerous sexuality enacted through the heroine/vamp divide. Another space in which the heroine employs the vamp's movement vocabulary is in the hero or villain's fantasies.[48] This strategy, very common in the 1990s song-and-dance repertoire, displaces forbidden desires onto the space of male fantasy, relieving the heroine of moral approbation.[49] However, this erotic performance cannot escape its grounding in the dense materiality of the heroine's movement vocabulary and specific bodily comportment. Significantly, while Dixit won the best actress Filmfare award for *Beta*, the film's place in popular cultural memory and in her star text is secured by the "*Dhak dhak karne laga*" dance number. *Sangeet* flopped at the box office, but Dixit's bawdy dance number, "*Main tumhari hoon*," was hugely popular, highlighting the frequent failure of the 1990s Hindi film narrative's attempts to contain Dixit's dancing body. This also explains why production numbers were at the center of censorship battles in the 1990s. Petitioners were keenly aware of the narrative's inability to contain the energy of the dancing woman's body, which circulated with dangerous, infectious speed through new media such as cable television and, later, the internet.

While the power of Dixit's dance-driven stardom has been discussed in some of the scholarship on 1990s Hindi cinema,[50] what is less explored is

Saroj Khan's role in choreographing these new mobilities that exceed and disrupt the film narrative's exigencies. As a choreographer who designed the film's song-and-dance sequences, Khan was not involved with the rest of the narrative, which tries to recuperate the chaste, upright figuration of the heroine. The multiple authors of the heterogeneous Hindi film text produce fascinatingly fractured diagrams of femininity, creating an open text with anarchically dispersed meanings. Additionally, since the 1990s, dance numbers have been voraciously consumed separately from the film—on cable networks devoted to song-and-dance sequences, and eventually on the internet—and thus the separation of the production number's Dixit from the narrative's Dixit was more dramatic than in the case of earlier dancing heroines. As the author of the production numbers that redefine the heroine's figuration in Hindi cinema, Khan had a different vision for the films she worked on, one that ensured maximum popularity of the dance numbers, a creative showcasing of dance moves, and not necessarily a deep integration with the narrative. As her authorial presence grew stronger during this decade, the production numbers exerted more pressure on the narrative, erupting out of it in spectacular abandon, just as Dixit's body erupts out of its customary costume and comportment within the narrative to heave and grind in these provocative production numbers.

In *The Saroj Khan Story*, Khan narrates an anecdote of being summoned by the censor board to discuss excising the breast pulses from the *mukhda* (the opening and repeated stanza) of "*Dhak dhak karne laga*" (see color insert—image 15). When a censor board member complains of her choreographed moves, "you're shaking deliberately, we don't like that," Khan retorts that the heroine sings, "dhak dhak," and "from where will that sound come except from the heart? And where is my heart? Near my bustline. I can't show it through the bum."[51] Not only did the choreography remain unchanged, but Khan won a Filmfare award for best choreography for the dance number, just as she had in 1991 for the scintillatingly sensuous "*Humko aaj kal hai intezaar*" and in 1994 for the controversial "*Choli ke peeche kya hai*." The simultaneous censure and celebration of Khan's choreography is revelatory of the many negotiations and excitements around new corporeal articulations and desires in 1990s India. Dayanita Singh's "Masterji" series makes amply evident Khan's self-assured authorship of these new corporeal attitudes. As she shows Sanjay Dutt how to curl his arms and show off his pumped biceps, heaves her chest up to her assistant's rising bosom, or embraces an assistant in bed, resting her cheek on her chest while the star Rekha, dressed in drag, watches intently so she may replicate these gestures of coital intimacy in a musical number, Khan, the Masterji, is at the center of the action, directing stars and backup dancers, directors, and crew members on the production of a new language of the body in popular Hindi cinema. Sanjay Leela Bhansali notes of her choreography in his big-budget film featuring Dixit as a courtesan, *Devdas*, "the first time [Saroj ji] went on the floor and did that "*Maar dala*" step, I whistled and clapped. Look at those change-overs within a shot, every "*maar dala*" is different.... Actors have a hard time catching her nuances. She was like a school to me, like an institution of how to shoot a dance song."[52] Training Dixit in the articulation of every "*maar dala*" in this *Kathak*-based production number, and teaching Bhansali to dynamize space by experimenting with foreground-background relations between dancers and the camera in the film's other spectacular production number, "*Dola re dola*," Khan emphatically authors the corporeal, gestural, cine-choreographic histories of popular Hindi cinema during this period. In a shooting still from *Khal Nayak*, we see Dixit rehearsing a move from "*Choli ke peeche*" with Khan right behind, directing her, and the film's director, Subhash Ghai, standing respectfully behind Khan, watching her choreograph the complex moves of this central attraction of his film. Through her choreography, Khan is a central authoring force, a sculptor of bodies and spaces, creating the conditions for choreographers to direct song-and-dance sequences and indeed entire films now.

Shifting the focus from the censorship controversy over "*Choli ke peeche*," Dixit remarks that it is her favorite dance number with Khan: "It had all these folk dance moves and moves like the turning of the foot in the *lehenga* [skirt]. I would tell her, open your closet and get all these moves out. These are the things she has learned from the *maharathi*s [masters] of Indian dancing. She has this treasure of moves" (see ⊙ video 05.07).[53] Adrienne McLean remarks of screen dance, "There is often a sense of professional pride and display of ability in the dance performances, not just an external manifestation of internal feelings exclusive to heterosexual romance."[54] Thus, despite this and other production numbers' fetishistic display of Dixit's body, the sheer energy and virtuosity of her performance complicate the "to-be-looked-at-ness" of the female body.[55] Focusing on the physicality of movement that dance entails allows for a reading of Khan-Dixit production numbers as enabling the heroine and the female star to exceed narrative repression and to emerge as an active communicating subject. Mehta observes in her analysis of "*Choli ke peeche kya hai*?" that although the song "is a visual feast and invites a voyeuristic gaze, this spectacle works with rather than against the narrative's agenda (i.e., capturing the criminal); in fact, it is pivotal to the story."[56] While calling attention to the diegetic function of the song-and-dance sequence is important for complicating the theory of the gaze in film spectatorship, I suggest that even in production numbers that seem to have no evident diegetic value, the very act of dancing can complicate Mulvey's argument about passive and fetishized showgirls that are reassuring objects of the male gaze.[57] Mehta suggests interrogating the reduction of female characters' relationship to the image to the process of fetishization by paying attention to "the female body's ability to speak through gesture and movement."[58] McLean argues that dancing in particular can never be fully recuperated by narrative closure, as the very presence of a dancer on screen betrays "the essential duality, the distance between, narrative and spectacle," since "dance cannot be a fictional treatment of itself in performance. To dance, one has to be able to do it, not merely to suggest it."[59] On screen then, dance is a mode of performance that can reveal in a flash the distance between the real-life authority of a virtuoso performer like Dixit and the narrative-bound fictional characters she plays, thus preventing a reduction of the leaping, swinging, shimmying Dixit to a mere fetishistic image.

In discussing the body as archive, André Lepecki describes choreography as a dynamic system of transmission and transformation, an archival-corporeal system that turns statements into corporeal events and kinetic things.[60] When we read social shifts in the 1990s through the bodies of two dancing women, Khan and Dixit, we turn statements about economic deregulation and globalization into thickly corporeal events marked by new gestural vocabularies and the mobilization of new body zones (see color insert—image 16). Lepecki notes that dance is to be understood as that "which passes around (between and across bodies of dancers, viewers, choreographers) and as that which also, always, comes back around. Dance is the passing around and the coming around of corporeal formations and transformations."[61] In moving from production numbers to item numbers to reality TV shows and online dance platforms, Khan and Dixit distribute corporeal inhabitations that pass from their composing and trained bodies through those of participatory fans who train and perform these very gestures back to them, producing a moving cinematic and social history of the past three decades through their dancing bodies.

Epilogue
An Intermedial History of Hindi Film, Dance, and Music

In *Don: The Chase Begins Again* (Farhan Akhtar, 2006), a remake of the 1978 film *Don* (Chandra Barot), the A-list actress Kareena Kapoor makes a "special appearance" in the production number "*Yeh mera dil pyaar ka deewana*," shimmying sexily to seduce the eponymous don and avenge the murder of her fiancé at his hands (see ⓥ video 06.01). In the original 1978 film, this voluptuous production number is performed by the leading vamp of Hindi cinema, Helen. In both films, the character, Kamini, is killed by the don right after the production number, and the role is thus restricted to this dance number. The replacement of the vamp by a top Bollywood actress signals changes in the intervening twenty-eight years between the two films, specifically in terms of the production and reception of Hindi film dance and of female stardom. While the hero of both versions of the film is played by the most popular actor of that generation—Amitabh Bachchan in 1978 and Shah Rukh Khan in 2006—it is in the figuration of the contemporary Bollywood actress that we detect a significant shift. Madhuri Dixit's bold production numbers marked the bridging of the heroine-vamp divide in the 1990s, but as demonstrated in Chapter 5, this was not an easy transition and provoked a variety of battles over the display of the female body on screen. By the first decade of the new millennium, however, the dance vocabulary employed in the heroine's production numbers had altered so radically that the heroine-vamp divide and its concomitant moral binaries appeared to cease to be of much concern in public discourse around the cinema. *Don: The Chase Begins Again* also illustrates contemporary Bollywood cinema's investment in celebrating popular Hindi cinema of the past through remakes and intertextual references to older song-and-dance numbers. Indeed, dance routines are all-important to the Bollywood idiom, and globally, Hindi cinema is now primarily associated with dance and dance-related expressions of fandom.[1] In this Epilogue, to extend this book's examination of dance and female stardom up to the present, and to point to further areas of exploration that a focus on film dance opens up, I briefly discuss the changing role of the heroine as the "item girl," Bollywood intertextuality through dance, new modes of participatory fandom evidenced in reality dance shows, and how this book's sustained engagement with film dance produces an intermedial history of film, dance, and music.

From the Production Number to the Item Number

One of the principal markers differentiating contemporary Bollywood cinema from earlier modes of popular Hindi cinema is the item number. Popularly held to be inaugurated by the song-and-dance sequence "*Chaiyya chaiyya*" in *Dil Se* (Mani Ratnam, 1998), the item number is a production number that is blatantly unrelated to the film narrative and primarily intended to showcase raunchy dance moves and skimpily clad bodies, usually of women, of "item girls." Drawing on popular theatrical traditions such as *Tamasha, Nautanki*, as well as the urban "bar dancing" culture, the item number is often constructed like a music video.[2] Remarking on the separation of the item number from the rest of narrative, Nasreen Rehman notes, "The body and the item number circulate disembedded from celluloid, as autonomous goods on sale, in conflated fantasies of sexual desire and consumption."[3] Signaling a new economy of dance in Hindi cinema, the item number is a stand-alone attraction featuring bodies, spaces, movement vocabularies, and technical flourishes that are unconnected to the rest of the narrative.[4] The "item girl," the female performer at the heart of the item number, for example, rarely features in the rest of the narrative. Unlike the vamp, who was typically associated with the villain, and whose cabarets and production numbers were sometimes integrated into the narrative and helped move the plot forward, the item girl is purely an agent of spectacle, devoid of narrative purpose. Hence, the moral binaries that defined the vamp-heroine dyad do not apply to the item girl and the contemporary Bollywood heroine. This separation of the dancing body from moral codes points toward Bollywood cinema's economy of spectacle, where the body—often reconstructed through plastic surgery or extreme fitness regimens before the shooting of an item number, and through sets, costumes, cinematography, and editing—is presented as a commodity that materializes new patterns of consumption.

The difference between the older production number and the contemporary item number is evidenced in the cinematic construction of dance in these two forms. The item number, focused not as much on the dancing skills of the item girl as on her "sex appeal," engenders a movement vocabulary defined by the striking of sensuous poses, and a central focus on the gyrating torso. In a cinematic culture where dance has become a prerequisite for female and male stardom, the spectacle of the dancing Bollywood body is manufactured through a multiplicity of means rather than just through the performer's skills. Shyama, an actress from the 1940s and 1950s, remarks on the difference between the filming of dance in that period and today: "We used to dance the entire *mukhda* and *antara* in one take. Nowadays, actors do one move and cut, just a small move of the head, and cut."[5] Shyama's observation underscores the difference between figural dancing, where the dance is primarily produced through the body of the dancing figure, and the mechanical construction of dance through cinematography, editing, and special effects. Saroj Khan, the celebrated choreographer of the 1990s, notes of contemporary choreography: "The entire raw stock is brought to the editing table and the song put together there. We used to put camera angles according to the movement; now you can choose whichever angle you want. There's nothing much for the dance master to do."[6]

Initially, the item girl, like the vamp, was drawn from what was considered a lower rung of performers; "starlets" like Isha Koppikar, Amrita Arora, Rakhi Sawant, Koena Mitra, Negar Khan, etc., either featured as item girls in big-budget films or as heroines in low-budget multi-starrers. The 2005 film *Bunty aur Babli* (Shaad Ali), in which a top Bollywood actress, Aishwarya Rai, performed the item number "*Kajra re*," heralded the participation of A-list actresses in item numbers. Kapoor's reprise of Helen's cabaret number in *Don* is part of this phenomenon. In recent times, top male actors such as Shah Rukh Khan, Hritik Roshan, and John Abraham have also featured in item numbers. The participation of A-list actors and actresses in item numbers points to new configurations of stardom, where the star *body* rather than expressive attributes elicited in acting sequences becomes the defining feature of the star, and dance becomes the primary tool to showcase this ideal body.[7] The economies of stardom remain in place, as these top actors and actresses are paid exorbitant fees to put on display the spectacle of their dancing bodies. Thus, while Kapoor may adopt the movement vocabulary of the vamp in *Don*, the vamp-heroine binary is sustained in a different form in the price attached to gazing upon her shimmying star body versus that of Helen.

Citations of the Cinematic Past through Dance

Kapoor's recreation of Helen's dance in "*Yeh mera dil*" is one mode of Bollywood's commemoration of the past—through remakes of films and reproductions of older song-and-dance sequences. Another form of intertextuality with the past is through song-and-dance sequences composed of a collage of earlier styles of dance, music, choreography, and mise-en-scène. The song-and-dance sequence "*Woh ladki hai kahan*" from *Dil Chahta Hai* (Farhan Akhtar, 2001), for example, deploys a series of gestures, costumes, and locations associated with popular film dance to define and periodize popular Hindi cinema (see ⊙ video 06.02). The sequence alludes to cinematic eras through movement vocabularies that transition from jazz-inspired moves in the 1950s, to group "picnic dances" of the 1970s, to the synchronized gyrations of Madhuri Dixit's 1980s and 1990s numbers. Dance becomes the foremost attribute of popular Hindi cinema that is mobilized to recreate the history of this film industry and culture.

Similarly, the production number "*Dhoom tana*" (*Om Shanti Om*, Farah Khan, 2007) quotes from four dance numbers of the 1960s and 1970s. The film's protagonists are transposed into the corpo-realized spaces of popular Hindi cinema, where dance is the principal tool for the expression of desire. In the production number "*Phir milenge chalte chalte*" from *Rab Ne Bana Di Jodi* (Aditya Chopra, 2008), the male protagonist Raj, played by Bollywood's poster boy, Shah Rukh Khan, takes on the dancing personas of various stars from earlier eras of popular Hindi cinema, including Raj Kapoor from the 1950s, Dev Anand and Shammi Kapoor from the 1960s, Rajesh Khanna from the 1970s, and Rishi Kapoor from the 1980s. In this fantasy world, Raj dances alongside actresses from contemporary Bollywood, masquerading as heroines from the past. Dance, once again, becomes Bollywood's favored mode of articulating stardom and the unique characteristics of famous stars. In the extravagant production number "*Deewangi deewangi*" in *Om Shanti Om*, thirty-one stars from the Hindi film industry, who have no role otherwise in the film, make a "special appearance" for this song. Each of these stars displays his or her trademark dancing styles and gestures, so that every *body* comes to be a signpost for a certain phase in the history of the industry. Actresses such as Urmila Matondkar, Shilpa Shetty, and Priyanka Chopra, for example, re-enact their sensuous moves from *Rangeela* (Ram Gopal Varma, 1995), *Shool* (E. Nivas, 1999), and *Bluffmaster* (Rohan Sippy, 2005) (see ▶ video 06.03). Certain dance moves stand in for a star's whole career, and indeed for entire periods of popular Hindi cinema. Significantly, in the three intertextual song sequences discussed in the preceding section, none of the contemporary stars actually bears a resemblance to stars of the past (e.g., Bipasha Basu as Nutan, Kajol as Nargis, Sonali Kulkarni as Madhuri Dixit, etc.), but through dance, costume, and makeup, a resemblance is constructed. Through a re-enactment of dance moves, Bollywood commemorates the techno-spectacle of past production numbers to form a link to its own participation in and celebration of spectacle, as not an embarrassment anymore but a self-assured assertion of identity. Through dance, what is celebrated is a corporeal cinematic history of dress, gesture, dance moves, sets, and props.

New Choreographies of Stardom and Fandom

Through song-and-dance intertextuality, Bollywood aims to create a somatic nostalgia, where a repertoire of familiar gestures triggers a physical memory of past cultural rituals (such as dancing in the aisles, copying the trademark moves of your favorite stars, etc.). Dance is a key element in the film industry's construction of stardom as well as fandom, where the history of Hindi cinema is reconstructed through a remembering of epochal dance moves. Bollywood has spawned a veritable industry around dance across various old and new media platforms. In addition to dancing in their films, stars perform on television shows, online "dance academies," at award ceremonies, on "world tours" that draw huge expatriate and local crowds, and at weddings and private events of the wealthy. Majumdar discusses how in the 1930s, "the star's identity was primarily constructed in terms of the voice rather than the body" and hence "histrionic ability in all major actors was understood to include musical ability."[8] While, in the decades that followed, cinematic stardom was split between the off-screen voice of the playback singer and the on-screen body of the actor (not necessarily always dancing in the musical numbers), since the mid-1990s, when dance-heavy production numbers became de rigueur in most popular Hindi films, the ability to dance has become a key factor in an actor's ascent to stardom. In an industry where dancing skills constitute a significant part of a star's identity, any aspiring actor today needs to have dance training, often acquired at the numerous "Bollywood dance" schools that have sprung up in various parts of the country and the world.

The primacy of dance in the Bollywood aesthetic has also resulted in the increased visibility of the choreographer. Before the late 1980s, quite unlike music composers, the choreographer or dance master was a little-known figure among Hindi film viewers, with few exceptions like the Kathak-trained Hiralal, Sohanlal, and Gopi Krishna. The spectacular production number "*Ek do teen*," featuring Madhuri Dixit and choreographed by Saroj Khan, redefined film dance to such an extent that Hindi film choreographers such as Khan, Chinni Prakash, Shiamak Davar, Farah Khan, and others became household names from the 1990s onward. As discussed in Chapter 5, the spirited, rambunctious, uninhibited dance vocabulary of "*Ek do teen*" defined new performance paradigms for the Hindi film heroine, made the choreographer a key figure in the heterogeneous mode of production, and ensured that dance-centric production numbers became a mainstay of popular Hindi cinema. Today, the director, choreographer, and music composer work together on the processes of song picturization and dance musicalization. Given Bollywood's investment in staging spectacle, and the signal role of the song-and-dance sequence in this project, the choreographer is a vital crew member who often not only arranges dance moves, but also directs the entire song-and-dance sequence, making sure that the mise-en-scène, cinematography, and editing all contribute to the production of Bollywood's big-budget song-and-dance extravaganzas. One of Bollywood's most successful choreographers and directors, Farah Khan, describes the process of choreographing a song-and-dance sequence:

> When I choreograph, that entire piece is mine. First, I try to understand how the song fits into the film situation or an item. I discuss it with the director. Yes, and keep the actor in mind. There is no point in expecting the actor or actress to do things they cannot do. . . . Then, I work with the set designers, costumes. And I direct that piece. It is like a four to five minute short film within the film . . . in the middle of their film, they [the directors] can take four to five days off, as I direct the whole sequence.[9]

Khan's collaboration with set and costume designers and other film crew reminds us of the labor of the choreomusicking body and of how film dance is part of a larger complex of affects generated by particular types of bodies, movements, and spaces that, in Bollywood, serve to foreground the transnational aspirations and address of this cinema.

Concurrently, contemporary Indian fandom is increasingly enacted through song-and-dance competitions on television. There are innumerable reality shows designed around participatory fandom, such as *Boogie Woogie* (Sony Entertainment), *Dance India Dance* (Zee TV), *Nach Baliye* (Star TV), and *Jhalak Dikhhla Jaa* (Colors), that feature the entire spectrum of the country's youth—from urban hipsters to rural aspirants—competing for the closest approximation of a particular star's dancing style or enacting the trademark dance moves of a particular production number. In dialogue with these danced performances of fandom, Bollywood dance numbers routinely feature hook steps, which are then communally replicated on these TV shows, in discotheques, at weddings, and most recently, on video-sharing social networks like TikTok. Contemporary film fandom is increasingly enacted through mimicry based on a performative knowledge of the cinema. Whereas earlier expressions of fan culture centered around collecting film memorabilia, dressing like a star, or taking on his/her mannerisms, these private acts of embodiment have been eclipsed by the emergence of an industry devoted to fandom as embodiment. With an address to urban, cosmopolitan, and rural audiences, this new media-generated appropriative fan culture is linked to larger economies of aspiration and mobility. Participants are required to be somewhat familiar with Indian classical and folk dance forms, as well as hip-hop, contact improvisation, salsa, capoeira, etc., and to create hybrid vocabularies under the watchful eyes of celebrity judges from Bollywood, including dancing stars like Dixit and Mithun Chakraborty, as well as celebrity choreographers such as Saroj Khan, Farah Khan, Vaibhavi Merchant, and others. In a mediatized fan culture where dance forms are validated through TRPs (Target Rating Points that measure the viewership for a show) and audience polls, and dances are performed under broad rubrics such as "village dance," "festival dance," and "regional dance," the hybridity of popular Hindi film dance is foregrounded and celebrated more than ever before as these competing dancing bodies are implicated in new transnational circuits of reception and consumption.[10]

Intermedial Histories of South Asian Cinema, Music, and Dance

Historical and theoretical accounts of South Asian cinema have been attentive to the relationship between film and visual art in terms of representational logics, organization of the spectatorial gaze, and address to a mass audience.[11] Similarly, film production and performance practices have mainly been traced back to theater, with the heterogeneous, omnibus form of the popular Indian film as well as its personnel (actors, directors, producers, etc.) seen as drawing from earlier theatrical traditions like *nautanki, jatra,* and the Parsi Theater, among others.[12] *Dancing Women* demonstrates how dance- and music-centered histories and theoretical frameworks expand our analysis of cinematic performance, spatial organization, and labor networks. I summarize here how the book's focus on dance and music produces a corporeal, richly intermedial history of film in India in which performing women play a defining role.

When we consider that *devadasis, tawaifs,* and *baijis* were the earliest film actresses, we relate the labor histories of these founding film personnel with the histories of Sanskritization of musical and dance forms, the caste politics of the anti-*nautch* movement, and the marginalization of these performing women on the newly designated "classical" music and dance stage. They bring to the cinema, from the 1920s through the 1950s, and into the present through their descendants and disciples, these performance histories and bodily training. The hereditary practices of these performing women and their communities carry over to the film industries they participate in, prompting us to examine gendered labor in cinema, with its male musicians and dance masters and female singers and dancers, often descended from matrifocal *tawaif* and *devadasi* communities. We thus trace the textured genealogy of the male *nattuvanars*, who move from their role as dance teachers and musicians in temples, courts, and private salons to become the early, defining music composers and dance masters in Tamil and Telugu cinema. Likewise, we reconnect the careers of the acclaimed Hindi film playback singers, Lata Mangeshkar and Asha Bhosle, to their Goan *kalavant* lineage of hereditary, professional female entertainers. Locating them within this "*devadasi* diaspora" that includes the renowned Hindustani vocalists Mogubai Kurdikar, Kesarbai Kerkar, and Kishori Amonkar muddles categories of the classical and the popular, inviting us to pay closer attention to contexts of training, performance, and migration.[13]

Tracing the lineage of film personnel to older performing communities prompts us to examine the idioms they bring to cinema, including singing styles, movement vocabularies, *guru-shishya* traditions (that carry over, in the case of Vyjayanthimala, Padmini, and others, from classical dance classes to film studios with the same *nattuvanar* gurus), *riyaaz* or training practices, and how they encounter and fashion film-production practices, including rehearsal, collaboration, improvisation, new cultures of "professionalization" that draw on and rub up against earlier professional cultures. Corporeal histories that account for labor, training, and collaboration excavate deep, interlinked records of film industrial practices and networks emerging from multiple performance and visual cultures.

Reading film's history alongside histories of music and dance shifts our signposts for tradition-modernity arguments constructed around cinema, as for instance, when we trace the complex cultural negotiations already at work in music and dance repertoires in eighteenth- and nineteenth-century courts and salons that syncretize Hindu, Islamic, and British and other colonial presences and influences. The *devadasi* repertoire in this period synthesized heterogeneous dance and music genres such as the *nottusvaram* ("note" song) riffing on Irish marching-band tunes, Parsi Theater, and by the 1940s, popular Telugu film songs.[14] When the studios in the South produce their first talkies, these are the repertoires they draw on. Similarly, studying the influence of Western oriental dancers, such as Ruth St. Denis, Anna Pavlova, Madame Simkie, Ragini Devi, La Meri, Stella Bloch, and others, on Indian film choreography, costume, and makeup would vastly enrich intermedial histories of film and dance, as many of these dancing women develop stage dance repertoires in relation with the movie camera in the early twentieth century.

Most obviously, when we focus on song-and-dance numbers, it becomes imperative to study the transformations in music and dance wrought by changing performance contexts in the late nineteenth and early twentieth centuries, including the abbreviation of songs for the gramophone, alterations in vocal performance for the microphone, and the shortening and simplification of dance movements for Euro-American and bourgeois Indian audiences. Such intermedial attunement produces a richer, thicker history of how music and dance engage with and produce the language of the newly emerging mass cultural form of the cinema. Shifting attention from the ideological work performed by the bifurcation of narrative and spectacle in popular film grammar (which has dominated the study of Hollywood and popular

Indian cinema), studying the industrial practices and personnel required for "attractions" such as dance, action, horror, etc., produces a different history and theorization of labor, materiality, and economies of production.

When considered as part of a history of performance traditions, cinema's figurations, technologies, and practices reveal their rich intermedial connections, producing corporeal, gestural, visceral histories. Through a material history of the labor of producing on-screen dance, theoretical frameworks that emphasize collaboration such as the *choreomusicking body* and *dance musicalization*, aesthetic approaches to embodiment drawing on treatises like the *Natya Shastra* and the *Abhinaya Darpana*, and formal analyses of dance-driven "techno-spectacles," *Dancing Women: Choreographing Corporeal Histories of Hindi Cinema* offers a variegated, textured history of cinema, dance, and music. This intermedial account, relating film to other performance cultures, folds in aesthetics, material practices, and technologies to narrate histories of gesture and movement that reveal in turn the gestures and movements of social history. Cinema is part of a larger complex of corporeal practices, and the dancing women that populate this book foreground the labor, skill, and virtuosity of the many on- and off-screen bodies that produce the processes and pleasures of popular Hindi cinema.

Notes

Introduction

1. Carnatic music is one of two primary categories of Indian classical music, and is commonly associated with South India (the other being the North Indian *Hindustani* music). The *mridangam* is a percussion instrument that provides rhythmic accompaniment in a Carnatic music ensemble.
2. *Bharatanatyam* is a South Indian classical dance form, among the first to be canonized as "classical" by the Sangeet Natak Akademi (The National Academy for Music, Dance and Drama). In addition to a vast gestural vocabulary, *Bharatanatyam* is characterized by the *araimandi* (half-squat) stance, and the execution of geometric movements in a given time cycle.
3. From the 1950s through the 1980s, the Hindi film split female presence between the chaste heroine and the publicly dancing vamp. The distribution of virtue and vice between heroine and vamp, which also marked the moral binaries of East/West, tradition/modernity, wife/whore, is signaled through the names of the characters, their costuming, the spaces they inhabit, and above all through their dance movements. The heroine typically displays a restrained and modest movement vocabulary, while the vamp performs raunchy cabaret dance numbers in bars and nightclubs.
4. Jane C. Desmond, "Embodying Difference: Issues in Dance and Cultural Studies," *Cultural Critique* 26 (1993): 59.
5. Henri Lefebvre, *The Production of Space*, trans. Donald Nicholson-Smith (Oxford: Blackwell, 1991), 215.
6. *Kathak* is a North Indian classical dance form, one of the eight dance forms canonized as "classical" by the Sangeet Natak Akademi (The National Academy for Music, Dance and Drama). The Muslim courtesan film features a courtesan in an Islamicate setting. See Ira Bhaskar and Richard Allen, *Islamicate Cultures of Bombay Cinema* (Delhi: Tulika Books, 2009) for a discussion of various types of courtesan films in Bombay cinema.
7. For more on Kapoor's self-fashioning as India's Elvis, see Amit Rai, "An American Raj in Filmistan: Images of Elvis in Indian Films," *Screen* 35, no. 1 (1994): 51–77.
8. Adrienne McLean, "Feeling and the Filmed Body: Judy Garland and the Kinesics of Suffering," *Film Quarterly* 55, no. 3 (2002): 13.
9. For an analysis of how some of these binaries are figured in popular Indian cinema, see Rosie Thomas, "Melodrama and the Negotiation of Morality," in *Consuming Modernity: Public Culture in a South Asian World*, ed. Arjun Appadurai and Carol Breckenridge (Minneapolis: University of Minnesota Press, 1995), 157–182. For a description of *Bharatanatyam*, *Kathak*, and *Kathakali*, see Glossary.

10. In an interview, Helen asserts her authorship: "you can say that I am the one who introduced the cabaret and the belly dance in Indian films," as well as a certain coyness that feeds into the respectability discourse around costuming in dance numbers: "[f]or many years, I would wear a body stocking under the skimpy costumes" (http://in.movies.yahoo.com/interview-detail/151/5126/An-interview-Helen.html).
11. Vyjayanthimala's hybrid, red *Bharatanatyam* costume in "*Muqabla humse na karo*" may be read as a citational reference to her outfit in the dance number "*Neel gagan ki chaon mein*" from *Amrapali*.
12. Vyjayanthimala Bali and Jyoti Sabharwal, *Bonding . . . : A Memoir* (New Delhi: Stellar, 2007), 57.
13. P. L. Raj–Helen dance numbers include "*O Haseena Zulfonwali*" (*Teesri Manzil*, Vijay Anand, 1966), "*Mungda*" (*Inkaar*, Raj Sippy, 1977), "*Aa Jaane Jaan*" (*Intaquam*, R. K. Nayyar, 1969), "*Mehbooba Mehbooba*" (*Sholay*, Ramesh Sippy, 1975), and "*Yeh Mera Dil*" (*Don*, Chandra Barot, 1978). Raj choreographed Shammi Kapoor's dances in films like *Junglee* (Subodh Mukherjee, 1961), *Professor* (Lekh Tandon, 1962), *Bluff Master* (Manmohan Desai, 1963), *Teesri Manzil*, and *An Evening in Paris* (Shakti Samanta, 1967).
14. Bali and Sabharwal, *Bonding*, 76.
15. Erin Brannigan, *Dancefilm: Choreography and the Moving Image* (New York: Oxford University Press, 2011), 72.
16. In his discussion of the "cinema of attractions" framework that develops around early cinema's fascination with movement and rhythm, Tom Gunning draws on, among other kinds of early films, Loie Fuller's serpentine dances, of which about thirty films were made between 1894 and 1910. For more on attractions, see Tom Gunning, "The Cinema of Attractions," in *Early Cinema: Space, Frame, Narrative*, ed. Thomas Elsaesser (London: BFI, 1990), 50–62; Tom Gunning, "Loïe Fuller and the Art of Motion: Body, Light, Electricity, and the Origins of Cinema," in *Camera Obscura, Camera Lucida: Essays in Honor of Annette Michelson*, ed. Richard Allen and Malcolm Turvey (Amsterdam: Amsterdam University Press, 2003), 75–90; Nell Andrew, "The Medium Is a Muscle: Abstraction in Early Film, Dance, Painting," in *Film, Art, New Media*, ed. Angela Dalle Vacche (London: Palgrave Macmillan, 2012), 57–77. For a discussion of popular Indian film song-and-dance sequences as "attractions" and "interruptions," see Lalitha Gopalan, *Cinema of Interruptions: Action Genres in Contemporary Indian Cinema* (London: BFI, 2002); Sangita Gopal and Sujata Moorti, "Introduction," *Global Bollywood: Travels of Hindi Song and Dance* (Minneapolis: University of Minnesota Press, 2008), 1–60.
17. From the 1940s to the 1990s, a handful of male actors, such as Master Bhagwan, Shammi Kapoor, Amitabh Bachchan, and Jeetendra, danced in films, and even then, mostly in coupled dance numbers. Mithun Chakraborty, the disco-dancing sensation of the 1980s, is among the rare male actors whose dancing body was spectacularized in a manner similar to that of actresses, which has become more commonplace since the late 1990s, particularly with Bollywood stars like Hrithik Roshan, Shahid Kapoor, etc. I discuss male dancers in "A Genealogy of Gestures: Comic Male Dancing from

Bhagwan to Bachchan," in *The Blackwell Companion to Indian Cinema*, ed. Neepa Majumdar, Ranjani Mazumdar (Wiley-Blackwell), forthcoming.
18. Chapters 3 and 4 will examine how the dancing woman figures in nationalist discourses through the twentieth century, engaging in particular with the gendered dichotomies of *ghar/bahir* (home/world), inner/outer, and spiritual/material discussed, among others, by Partha Chatterjee, "The Nationalist Resolution of the Women's Question," in *Recasting Women, Essays in Colonial History*, ed. Kumkum Sangari and Sudesh Vaid (New Delhi: Kali for Women), 233–253.
19. Sadhona Bose was trained in the East-Indian classical dance form, *Manipuri*, and the North Indian form, *Kathak*, while the South Indian actresses Vyjayanthimala and Waheeda Rehman were schooled in *Bharatanatyam*. Madhuri Dixit was trained in *Kathak*. In each chapter, I discuss the significance of their classical dance training in the construction of the star texts of these dancer-actresses. Azurie, Saroj Khan, and Helen were trained in Bharatanatyam and Kathak by the film choreographers with whom they worked.
20. *Devadasis*, predominantly in southern India, and *tawaifs*, mainly in North India, were courtesans who performed in various spaces and contexts, including temples, courts, and private salons. Soneji notes that the term *devadasi* "is used to index a vast number of communities of women who are generally glossed by English phrases such as 'sacred prostitute' or 'temple dancer,' describing them instead as 'professional artists in a shifting colonial sexual economy,'" Davesh Soneji, *Unfinished Gestures: Devadasis, Memory, and Modernity in South India* (Chicago: University of Chicago Press, 2012), 6.
21. Surjit Singh, *Edwina: An Unsung Bollywood Dancer of the Golden Era* (n.p.: Professor Toofaani, 2015), 57.
22. Brannigan, *Dancefilm: Choreography and the Moving Image*, 7.
23. Brannigan, *Dancefilm: Choreography and the Moving Image*, 142.
24. Sally Ann Ness, *Body, Movement, and Culture: Kinesthetic and Visual Symbolism in a Philippine Community* (Philadelphia: University of Pennsylvania Press, 1992), 6.
25. Nandikesvara, *The Mirror of Gesture: Being the Abhinaya Darpana of Nandikesvara* (Cambridge, MA: Harvard University Press, 1917). Nandikesvara's late Sanskrit text is dated between the tenth and thirteenth centuries CE. The *Natya Shastra* is dated between 200 BCE and 200 CE. Authorship is attributed to the sage Bharata, but scholars consider it to be a synthesis of collective knowledge of production practices current at the time. The *Natya Shastra* is an encyclopedic treatise on performative modes in ancient Sanskrit theater, which included spoken parts, music, and dance. It examines in detail aspects related to acting, singing, and dancing, including the ideal playhouse, metrics, diction, intonation, character types, costumes and makeup, the representation of sentiments and emotions, the movements of every limb, conventions of time and place, and even canons of criticism and assessment.
26. Bali and Sabharwal, *Bonding*, 45.
27. Nasreen Munni Kabir, *Conversations with Waheeda Rehman* (New Delhi: Penguin Books India, 2014), 38.

28. A less-common discussion of the particularity of dance numbers and performers in Hindi cinema may be found in Paromita Vohra, "Bodily Fluid: The Movement of Bollywood Dance from Body to Body," in *Tilt Pause Shift: Dance Ecologies in India*, ed. Anita E. Cherian (New Delhi: Tulika Books and Gati Dance Forum, 2016), 183–195.
29. Laurent Guido, "Rhythmic Bodies/Movies: Dance as Attraction in Early Film Culture," in *The Cinema of Attractions Reloaded*, ed. Wanda Strauven (Amsterdam: Amsterdam University Press, 2006), 143.
30. Guido, "Rhythmic Bodies/Movies: Dance as Attraction in Early Film Culture," 139.
31. Douglas Rosenberg, *Screendance: Inscribing the Ephemeral Image* (New York: Oxford University Press, 2012), 39.
32. Rosenberg, *Screendance*, 41.
33. Andrew, "The Medium Is a Muscle: Abstraction in Early Film, Dance, Painting," 58.
34. Sangita Gopal and Sujata Moorti, eds., *Global Bollywood: Travels of Hindi Song and Dance* (Minneapolis: University of Minnesota Press, 2008), 25.
35. Anupama Kapse, "Melodrama as Method," *Framework* 54, no. 2 (Fall 2013): 149.
36. Suresh Chabria, *Light of Asia: Indian Silent Cinema 1912–1934* (New Delhi: Niyogi Books; Pune: National Film Archive of India, 2013), 49.
37. *Filmland*, June 1931, 15.
38. Gopal and Moorti, eds., *Global Bollywood: Travels of Hindi Song and Dance*, 19; Pallabi Chakravorty, *Bells of Change: Kathak Dance, Women and Modernity in India* (Calcutta: Seagull Books, 2008), 110; Booth, "Synchronicity and Continuity of Sound and Image in Early Indian Cinema," *South Asian Popular Culture* 15, no. 2–3 (2017): 109–122.
39. Shashikant Kinikar, ed., *Notes of Naushad* (Mumbai: English Edition, 2004), 56.
40. Booth, "Synchronicity and Continuity of Sound and Image in Early Indian Cinema," 115.
41. Shikha Jhingan notes that multiple claims have been made about the origin of the use of playback singing in Indian cinema. The music composer Saraswati Devi claims to have introduced playback singing in *Jawani ki Hawa* (1934), when the actress Chandraprabha could not sing due to a bad throat: "I asked Chandraprabha to move her lips while I kept the mike in front of me." The composer R. C. Boral, on the other hand, claims to have introduced the technique in *Dhoop Chaon* (1935). Shikha Jhingan, "The Singer, the Star and the Chorus," *India-Seminar*, 2009, doi: http://www.indiaseminar.com/2009/598/598_shikha_jhingan.html.
42. Gopal and Moorti, eds., *Global Bollywood*, 25.
43. McLean, "Feeling and the Filmed Body," 7.
44. Neepa Majumdar, *Wanted Cultured Ladies Only!: Female Stardom and Cinema in India, 1930s–1950s* (Urbana: University of Illinois Press, 2009), 173.
45. Jhingan, "The Singer, the Star and the Chorus."
46. Jhingan, "The Singer, the Star and the Chorus."
47. Gopal and Moorti, eds., *Global Bollywood*; Wimal Dissanayake and K. Moti Gokulsing, *Popular Culture in a Globalised India* (London; New York: Routledge, 2009); Yatindra Mishra, "The Bai and the Dawn of Hindi Film Music (1925–45)," *The Book Review* xxxiii, no. 2 (February 2009): 46–47.

48. Following Madhava Prasad ("This Thing Called Bollywood," *Seminar* 525 [May 2003]: 17–20) and Ashish Rajadhyaksha's descriptions of the term, "Bollywood" in this book stands for a specific mode of popular Hindi cinema that developed from the 1990s, characterized by, among other things, family melodramas, big-budget, spectacular song-and-dance sequences, characters who often live outside of India, a conscious display of multinational brand names, and an unmistakable address to a diasporic audience. Following closely on the heels of economic deregulation in India in 1991, Bollywood proceeded to trigger a larger entertainment complex that now includes television, music, advertising, fashion, and new media.
49. Krishna E. Iyer, "Film and the Traditional Arts," *Indian Talkies 1931–1956* (Mumbai: Silver Jubilee Souvenir, Film Federation of India, 1956), 12.
50. Sitara Devi, "Kathak-The Dance of Gods," *Indian Talkies 1931–1956* (Mumbai: Silver Jubilee Souvenir, Film Federation of India, 1956), 112.
51. Ranjan, "The Film Dance" *Filmfare*, April 26, 1957, 11.
52. Satyavaty, "Dance Forms of West Corrupt Our Films," *Filmfare*, April 18, 1952, 10.
53. Mohan Khokar, *Traditions of Indian Classical Dance* (Delhi: Clarion Books, 1984), 228.
54. Ranjan, "The Film Dance," 9.
55. Vijay N. Shankar, "Dance in Cinema: Gimmick or Necessity," *Filmfare*, April 15, 1966, 23. It is worth noting that the "serious" Indian art cinema typically regarded dance as a non-realistic interruption and indeed marked its difference from mainstream popular cinema through its eshewal of song-and-dance sequences. When included, the numbers would be rendered diegetic and realistic, as for example in *Bhumika* (Shyam Benegal, 1977), a biopic of a popular film dancer-actress, or in *Jait Re Jait* (Jabbar Patel, 1977), which participates in the parallel cinema's "developmental realist" project of depicting the subaltern subject and includes "tribal" dances in its narrative.

Chapter 1

1. In the Bombay film industry, the playback singer sings the song, which is then lip-synched by on-screen actors. Commercially available film song compilations may be categorized by playback singer, on-screen star, music composer, decades, or themes (for example, "Romantic hits of the 70s," "Haunting Melodies of Lata Mangeshkar," etc.).
2. Neepa Majumdar, *Wanted Cultured Ladies Only!: Female Stardom and Cinema in India, 1930s–1950s* (Urbana: University of Illinois Press, 2009), 191.
3. See Gregory Booth, "Religion, Gossip, Narrative Conventions and the Construction of Meaning in Hindi Film Songs," *Popular Music* 19 (2000): 125–146; Richard Dyer, *In the Space of a Song: The Uses of Song in Film* (Abingdon, UK; New York: Routledge, 2012); Majumdar, *Wanted Cultured Ladies Only!: Female Stardom and Cinema in India, 1930s–1950s*.
4. See Rick Altman, *The American Film Musical* (Bloomington: Indiana University Press, 1987); Steven Cohan, "'Feminizing' the Song-And-Dance Man: Fred

Astaire and the Spectacle of Masculinity in the Hollywood Musical," in *Screening the Male: Exploring Masculinities in the Hollywood Cinema*, ed. Steven Cohan and Ina Rae Hark (New York: Routledge, 1993), 46–69; Jane Feuer, *The Hollywood Musical* (Bloomington: Indiana University Press, 1993); Barry Langford, *Film Genre: Hollywood and Beyond* (Edinburgh: Edinburgh University Press, 2005).

5. See Rick Altman, *The American Film Musical* (Bloomington: Indiana University Press, 1987); Steven Cohan, "'Feminizing' the Song-and-Dance Man: Fred Astaire and the Spectacle of Masculinity in the Hollywood Musical," in *Screening the Male: Exploring Masculinities in the Hollywood Cinema*, ed. Steven Cohan and Ina Rae Hark (New York: Routledge, 1993), 46–69; Jane Feuer, *The Hollywood Musical* (Bloomington: Indiana University Press, 1993); Barry Langford, *Film Genre: Hollywood and Beyond* (Edinburgh: Edinburgh University Press, 2005).
6. Sangita Gopal, *Conjugations: Marriage and Form in New Bollywood Cinema* (Chicago: University of Chicago Press, 2011); Lalitha Gopalan, *Cinema of Interruptions: Action Genres in Contemporary Indian Cinema* (London: BFI, 2002); Anna Morcom, "Film Songs and the Cultural Synergies of Bollywood in and beyond South Asia," in *Beyond the Boundaries of Bollywood: The Many Forms of Hindi Cinema*, ed. Rachel Dwyer and Jerry Pinto (New Delhi; New York: Oxford University Press, 2011).
7. Morcom, "Film Songs and the Cultural Synergies," 162.
8. Gopalan, *Cinema of Interruptions*, 129–135.
9. Gopal, *Conjugations*, 39.
10. Gopal, *Conjugations*, 39.
11. Sangita Gopal and Biswarup Sen, "Inside and Out: Song and Dance in Bollywood Cinema," *The Bollywood Reader*, ed. Rajinder Dudrah and Jigna Desai (Maidenhead, Berkshire, UK; New York: McGraw-Hill: Open University Press, 2008), 147.
12. Most studies of the song sequence, for example by Arnold, Booth, Chandavarkar, Dutta, Morcom, Mukherjee, and Ranade, are focused on music.
13. One has only to consider the beefy Salman Khan signalling his star body with chest-baring gestures in action sequences, or the Bharatanatyam-trained dancer-actress Vyjayanthimala, to recognize the importance of these body-centered sequences in constructing particular types of star texts and cinematic narratives.
14. "Item girl" is a journalistic term for a female performer in a more recent Bollywood dance sub-genre known as the "item number," which bears no relation to the narrative but is inserted purely as a spectacular attraction.
15. Nasreen Munni Kabir, *Conversations with Waheeda Rehman* (New Delhi: Penguin Books India, 2014), 153.
16. Ravi Vasudevan, "The Melodramatic Mode and the Commercial Hindi Cinema: Notes on Film History, Narrative, and Performance," *Screen* 30, no. 3 (1989): 45.
17. Other examples of the narrative number include Chandralekha (T. R. Rajakumari) swaying by a tree to the song "*Saanjh savera*" ("At dusk and dawn") after her first encounter with the prince-hero in *Chandralekha* (S. S. Vasan, 1948); Amit (Amitabh Bachchan) and Chandni (Rekha) walking along tulip fields and singing "*Dekha ek khwaab toh yeh silsile hue*" ("These events as I saw in a dream," *Silsila*, Yash Chopra,

1981); and Ganga (Madhuri Dixit) berating her lover in "*Der se aana*" ("Your coming late") (*Khalnayak*/Villain, Subhash Ghai, 1993).
18. Cohan, "'Feminizing' the Song-and-Dance Man," 48.
19. Patricia Mellencamp, "Sexual Economics: Gold Diggers of 1933," in *Hollywood Musicals, The Film Reader*, ed. Steven Cohan (London; New York: Routledge, 2002), 72.
20. *Kathakali* is a South Indian classical dance form that originated in the region that is now designated as the state of Kerala, and is among the eight canonized classical dance forms. It is predominantly performed by men, whose face paint and costumes indicate the mythic or epic characters they represent.
21. Thomas Schatz, *Hollywood Genres: Formulas, Filmmaking, and the Studio System* (New York: Random House, 1981), 217.
22. Ashish Rajadhyaksha and Paul Willemen, *Encyclopedia of Indian Cinema* (London: British Film Institute, 1999), 350.
23. The Vyjayanthimala-Kishore Kumar dance comedies include *Ladki* (M.V. Raman, 1953), *Miss Mala* (Jayant Desai, 1954), *Pehli Jhalak* (M.V. Raman, 1955), *Aasha* (M.V. Raman, 1957), and *New Delhi* (Mohan Segal, 1956). "Devdas" came films like "Naya Daur," "Sadhana," "Madhumati."
24. Gopal and Sen, "Inside and Out," 152.
25. Gopal and Sen, "Inside and Out," 152.
26. In her study of the Hollywood musical, Jane Feuer discusses the prop dance, a set piece of many musicals that she refers to as the "bricolage" or "tinkering" solo, where a performer such as Astaire or Kelly makes props out of ordinary things at hand in the setting, creating an impression of spontaneity despite the number's carefully planned choreography or its special effects; see Feuer, *The Hollywood Musical*, 5–6.
27. In the textual tradition, drawing from treatises like the *Natya Shastra* and the *Abhinaya Darpana*, and employed since the 1940s by cultural nationalists and dance teachers and choreographers, *nrtta* refers to "pure dance" movements that are not intended to convey a particular meaning to the audience but rather to demonstrate the dancer's skills. *Nritya* is expository dance meant to convey a narrative or an idea to the onlooker through *abhinaya* or expression. In *natya*, *nrtta* and *nritya* are both utilized, but in addition, the element of drama is introduced through the use of the spoken word and other conventions of the stage (Khokar 1984, 58).
28. Kalpana Ram, "Being 'Rasikas': The Affective Pleasures of Music and Dance Spectatorship and Nationhood in Indian Middle-Class Modernity," *Journal of the Royal Anthropological Institute* 17, no. s1 (2011): 164.
29. *Manipuri* dance is a canonized classical dance form from the northeastern state of Manipur that predominantly depicts religious themes, especially the Raas Lila or the dance of Krishna and Radha.
30. In some song-and-dance sequences, the *nrtta* or "pure dance" segment can be employed to convey emotions and further the narrative as well. For example, when Sahibjaan (Meena Kumari) dances on a shattered glass lamp in the final song-and-dance sequence of *Pakeezah*, "*Teer-E-Nazar*," her intricate footwork, or *tatkar* in the Kathak lexicon, becomes a deeply expressive indicator of her emotions, while also

marking the mutilation of one of the most important parts of the body for the dance of the *tawaif*, her feet.

31. From the 1940s to the 1990s, a handful of male actors such as Master Bhagwan, Gopi Krishna (a classical dancer who acted in a few dance films), Shammi Kapoor, Amitabh Bachchan, and Jeetendra danced in films, and even then, mostly in coupled production numbers. On the other hand, most actresses during, before, and after this period have performed solo production numbers of varying types, displaying a range of dancing skills and expertise. Mithun Chakraborty, the disco-dancing sensation of the 1980s, is among the rare male actors whose dancing body was spectacularized in a manner similar to that of actresses. The current Bollywood dispensation has seen a change in that production numbers are now also choreographed for male stars like Hrithik Roshan, Shah Rukh Khan, and others. However, even now, while there is a proliferation of item girls, the corresponding equivalent for male performers, i.e., "item boys," are not a regular feature of Bollywood films.

32. Laura Mulvey, "Visual Pleasure and Narrative Cinema," in *Film Theory and Criticism: Introductory Readings*, ed. Leo Braudy and Marshall Cohen (New York: Oxford University Press, 1999), 837.

33. The absence of male actors in Hindi film production numbers, especially in the 1950s and 1960s, is underscored by the frequent presence of a female dancer dressed *en travestie* and performing as the male companion in the heterosexual dance pairing of the number. Examples of this include Sitara Devi's turn as a sprightly male folk dancer in *Mother India* (Mehboob Khan, 1957), Minoo Mumtaz's performance as a man dancing the Punjabi folk dance form *Bhangra* in *Naya Daur* (B. R. Chopra, 1957), and Cuckoo's *nautanki* performance in *Mujhe Jeene Do* (Moni Bhattacharjee, 1963).

34. Partha Chatterjee, "A Bit of Song and Dance," in *Frames of Mind*, ed. Aruna Vasudev (New Delhi: UBS, 1995), 197.

35. For an examination of male dancing in popular Hindi cinema, see Usha Iyer, "A Genealogy of Gestures: Comic Male Dancing from Bhagwan to Bachchan," in *The Blackwell Companion to Indian Cinema*, ed. Neepa Majumdar, Ranjani Mazumdar (Wiley-Blackwell, forthcoming).

36. This pattern of gendered entry begins to change in the late 1980s, when for example, the star Aamir Khan makes his debut entry with a song sequence, "*Papa kehte hain*" ("Father says") in *Qayamat se Qayamat Tak* (From Resurrection to Resurrection, Mansoor Khan, 1988). Released in the same year as *Tezaab*, this film is commonly seen to mark a return to the song-and-dance-filled love story after nearly a decade-and-a-half of action-oriented vigilante films. In this new dispensation, male actors start dancing much more than their predecessors, but the production number continues to be dominated by female performers.

37. Marc O'Day, "Beauty in Motion: Gender, Spectacle and Action Babe Cinema" in *Action and Adventure Cinema*, edited by Yvonne Tasker (Oxon: Routledge, 2004), 212.

38. Add Gopalan 19 here. Waheeda Rehman quotes the director Guru Dutt as saying, "In our business, we call a song the audience finds boring a 'cigarette song'—that's the moment when people leave the theater and go out for a smoke" (Kabir, *Conversations with Waheeda Rehman*, 47).

39. Many of Hindi cinema's attractions or interruptions are marked by their specific employment of the performing body. While I've discussed how the body changes in a dance sequence, comic sequences often derive their humor from bodily elements such as comic gestures, e.g., Keshto Mukherjee's drunken winking or Johnny Lever's farcical facial and bodily contortions. Dance sequences, comic interludes, and action sequences are all body-centric modes of performance set apart from the performative regime of the narrative.

40. Semi-classical dance is intermediate in style and gestural articulation between classical and popular dance. It borrows movements and gestures from classical dance but renders them in a popular idiom by making them simpler and less strictly codified. *Bharatanatyam* "dance ballets" and *Rabindra Nritya* (a dance form conceived by Rabindranath Tagore in the 1930s) are examples of semi-classical dance, as are the "classical dance" sequences in Hindi cinema that typically feature actresses trained in classical dance, such as Sadhona Bose, Vyjayantimala, Waheeda Rehman, Hema Malini, Jayaprada, and others.

41. Madhava Prasad employs the phrase "heterogeneous form of manufacture" to explain that, unlike the serial form of production in Hollywood, in the Hindi film industry, the various elements of the film are produced by specialists and then assembled; Prasad, *Ideology of the Hindi Film: A Historical Construction* (New Delhi: Oxford University Press, 1998), 42–45. The song-and-dance sequence is often produced separately by specialists, including the music director and the music crew, and the dance choreographer with her/his crew.

42. Vivian Sobchack, *Carnal Thoughts: Embodiment and Moving Image Culture* (Berkeley: University of California Press, 2004), 60, 68.

43. Susan Foster, *Choreographing Empathy: Kinesthesia in Performance* (New York: Routledge, 2010), 123.

44. Janet Adshead-Lansdale, *Dancing Texts Intertextuality in Interpretation* (London: Dance Books, 1999), 21.

45. Booth, "Religion, Gossip, Narrative Conventions and the Construction of Meaning in Hindi Film Songs," 143.

46. Majumdar, *Wanted Cultured Ladies Only!: Female Stardom and Cinema in India, 1930s–1950s*, 180.

47. Dyer, *In the Space of a Song*, 43.

48. Rick Altman, *The American Film Musical* (Bloomington: Indiana University Press, 1987), 230.

49. Sangita Gopal, "The Audible Past, or What Remains of the Song-Sequence in New Bollywood Cinema," *New Literary History* 46, no. 4 (2015): 809.

50. Adrienne L. McLean, "'It's Only That I Do What I Love and Love What I Do': 'Film Noir' and the Musical Woman," *Cinema Journal* 33, no. 1 (1993): 5.

51. Jason Beaster-Jones and Natalie Sarrazin, eds., *Music in Contemporary Indian Film: Memory, Voice, Identity* (London: Taylor & Francis, 2016), 8.

52. *Baaje Payal*, episode on Vyjayanthimala (Doordarshan, 2002). Television.

53. Cohan, "'Feminizing' the Song-and-Dance Man," 9.

54. Altman, *The American Film Musical*, 164.

55. Booth, "Religion, Gossip, Narrative Conventions and the Construction of Meaning in Hindi Film Songs," 143.
56. *Baaje Payal*, episode on Vyjayanthimala (Doordarshan, 2002). Television.
57. Dinesh Raheja, "Vyjayanthimala: Bollywood's Dancing Queen," rediff.com, 2002. May 15, 2013, https://www.rediff.com/movies/2002/may/06dinesh.htm.
58. V. A. K. Ranga Rao, "She Brought Lustre to the Silver Screen," *Sruti* 314 (November 2010): 32.
59. Erin Brannigan, *Dancefilm: Choreography and the Moving Image* (New York: Oxford University Press, 2011), 150.
60. Vasudevan, "The Melodramatic Mode and the Commercial Hindi Cinema," 50.
61. Rajadhyaksha and Willemen, *Encyclopedia of Indian Cinema*, 350.
62. Vasudevan, "The Melodramatic Mode and the Commercial Hindi Cinema," 50.
63. Ashish Rajadhyaksha, *The Sad and the Glad of Kishore Kumar* (Mumbai: Research for Cinema Studies, 1988), 59.
64. Susan C. Cook and Sherril Dodds, eds., *Bodies of Sound: Studies across Popular Music and Dance* (London: Routledge, 2016), 1.
65. Stephanie Jordan, *Moving Music: Dialogues with Music in Twentieth-Century Ballet* (London: Dance Books, 2000), 47.
66. These Sanskrit terms describing dance movements are taken from the classical dance lexicon codified in the twentieth century, which draws from the *Natya Shastra*, the *Abhinaya Darpana*, and other performance treatises.
67. Jordan, *Moving Music*, 52.
68. Shobana Jeyasingh, "Getting Off the Orient Express," in *The Routledge Dance Studies Reader*, ed. Alexandra Carter and Janet O'Shea (London: Routledge, 2010), 186.
69. Erin Brannigan uses the term "cine-choreography" to analyze how cinematic techniques produce new forms of choreographic practice: "The variety of movements featured in dancefilm are produced through the cinematic process and can be of any nature: the movement of a body part, crowd, object or graphic detail, and may be animated by outside forces such as natural elements or technological manipulation. It is these movements that create the *cine-choreographies* that constitute filmic performance in dancefilm" (ix).
70. Onomatopoeic phrases like "*payal ki chan chan*" (the clinking of anklets), "*kangne ki khan khan*" (the clinking of bracelets), and "*dola re dola*" (swaying of the body) proliferate in the Hindi film song-and-dance number.
71. Jade Power Sotomayor. "The Fandango Fronterizo: Moving Borders and Son Jarocho's Speaking and Space-Making Bodies." Lecture at the Stanford Colloquium on Dance Studies, 2016.
72. Matthew Rahaim, *Musicking Bodies: Gesture and Voice in Hindustani Music* (Middletown, CT: Wesleyan University Press, 2012), xi.
73. See Majumdar, *Wanted Cultured Ladies Only!: Female Stardom and Cinema in India, 1930s–1950s*; Sanjay Srivastava, "Voice, Gender and Space in Time of Five-Year Plans: The Idea of Lata Mangeshkar," *Economic and Political Weekly* (2004): 2019–2028.

74. Namrata Joshi, "Nutan," in *Women in Indian Film*, ed. Nasreen Munni Kabir (Delhi: Zubaan Books, 2008), 14.
75. Namrata Joshi, "Nutan," in *Women in Indian Film*, ed. Nasreen Munni Kabir (Delhi: Zubaan Books, 2008), 14.
76. "PIX: Lata Mangeshkar on Nutan, Mumtaz, Madhuri," Rediff.com, December 31, 2012, https://www.rediff.com/movies/report/slide-show-1-lata-mangeshkar-on-nutan-mumtaz-madhuri/20121231.htm (accessed August 22, 2015).
77. "PIX: Lata Mangeshkar on Nutan, Mumtaz, Madhuri," Rediff.com, December 31, 2012, https://www.rediff.com/movies/report/slide-show-1-lata-mangeshkar-on-nutan-mumtaz-madhuri/20121231.htm (accessed August 22, 2015).
78. A *Star and Style* feature on the actress's career reflects this prejudice: "In the wake of 'Devdas' came films like 'Naya Daur,' 'Sadhana,' 'Madhumati' and 'Paigham' rounding out Portrait No. 2 as the heroine who could no longer be shrugged off casually as a 'dancing star'" ("Vyjayanthimala," in *Star and Style*, June 15, 1966, 5).
79. Shikha Jhingan, "The Singer, the Star and the Chorus," India-Seminar, 2009, doi: http://www.indiaseminar.com/2009/598/598_shikha_jhingan.html.
80. For discussions of aural and on-screen femininity and how this was negotiated through the offscreen persona of Lata Mangeshkar, see See Majumdar, *Wanted Cultured Ladies Only!* (2009); Ranjani Mazumdar, *Bombay Cinema: An Archive of the City* (University of Minnesota Press, 2007); Monika Mehta, *Censorship and Sexuality in Bombay Cinema* (University of Texas Press, 2012); Anustup Basu, "The Face that Launched a Thousand Ships": Helen and Public Femininity in Hindi Film," *Figurations in Indian Film* (Palgrave Macmillan, 2013); Ajay Gehlawat, *Twenty-first Century Bollywood* (Routledge, 2015).

Chapter 2

1. For a discussion of microchoreographies, see Erin Brannigan, *Dancefilm: Choreography and the Moving Image* (New York: Oxford University Press, 2011), 39–61.
2. The *mujra* is traditionally a dance performance by *tawaifs*/courtesans in the *Kathak* style. It is a common production number modality in Hindi cinema.
3. Peggy Phelan, "Dance and the History of Hysteria," in *Corporealities: Body, Knowledge, Culture, Power*, ed. Susan Leigh Foster (London: Routledge, 1996), 92.
4. *Bhangra* is a vigorous Punjabi folk dance performed mainly by men.
5. In his essay on the *tawaif*, Mukul Kesavan coins the term "Islamicate" to "refer not directly to the religion, Islam, itself, but to the social and cultural complex historically associated with Islam and the Muslims, both among Muslims themselves and even when found among non-Muslims" (246). Mukul Kesavan, "Urdu, Awadh and the Tawaif: the Islamicate Roots of Hindi Cinema," in *Forging Identities: Gender, Communities and the State*, ed. Faisal Fatehali Devji and Zoya Hasan (New Delhi: Kali for Women, 1994).

6. Henri Lefebvre, *The Production of Space*, trans. Donald Nicholson-Smith (Oxford: Blackwell, 1991), 38.
7. Lefebvre, *The Production of Space*, 188.
8. For a magisterial theorization of filmed space in Indian cinema and a framework for a spatial film historiography, see Priya Jaikumar, *Where Histories Reside: India as Filmed Space* (Durham, NC: Duke University Press, 2019).
9. Lefebvre, *The Production of Space*, 42.
10. Lefebvre, *The Production of Space*, 41.
11. Lefebvre, *The Production of Space*, 42.
12. Lefebvre, *The Production of Space*, 170.
13. Carol Brown, "Making Space, Speaking Spaces," in *The Routledge Dance Studies Reader*, ed. Alexandra Carter and Janet O'Shea (Oxford; New York: Routledge, 2010), 59.
14. Films in which Vyjayanthimala plays the role of a professional dancer include *Devdas* (Bimal Roy, 1955), *New Delhi* (Mohan Segal, 1956), *Kathputli* (Amiya Chakrabarty, Nitin Bose, 1957), *Sadhna* (B. R. Chopra, 1958), *Amrapali* (Lekh Tandon, 1966), and *Jewel Thief* (Vijay Anand, 1967).
15. Ashish Rajadhyaksha and Paul Willemen, *Encyclopedia of Indian Cinema* (London: British Film Institute, 1999), 238.
16. Semi-classical dance, typical of Hindi film dance's representation of "classical dance," is intermediate in style and gestural articulation between classical and popular dance. It borrows movements and gestures from classical dance, but renders them in a popular idiom by making them less strictly codified and easier to perform.
17. Brown, "Making Space, Speaking Spaces," 70.
18. Brown, "Making Space, Speaking Spaces," 59.
19. Ranjani Mazumdar, *Bombay Cinema: Archive of the City* (Delhi: Permanent Black, 2007), 88.
20. Alexandra Carter and Janet O'Shea, eds., *The Routledge Dance Studies Reader* (Oxford; New York: Routledge, 2010), 19.
21. Lefebvre, *The Production of Space*, 59.
22. For a discussion of bar dancers and dance bars in Mumbai, see Anna Morcom, *Illicit Worlds of Indian Dance: Cultures of Exclusion* (London: C. Hurst, 2013), 142–170.
23. Lefebvre, *The Production of Space*, 95.
24. Brown, "Making Space, Speaking Spaces," 58, 65.
25. Lefebvre, *The Production of Space*, 110.
26. Lefebvre, *The Production of Space*, 75.
27. Veena Talwar Oldenburg, "Lifestyle as Resistance: The Case of the Courtesans of Lucknow," in *Contesting Power: Resistance and Everyday Social Relations in South Asia*, ed. Douglas E. Haynes and Gyan Prakash (Berkeley: University of California Press, 1991), 48.
28. Richard Allen and Ira Bhaskar, *Islamicate Cultures of Bombay Cinema* (Delhi: Tulika, 2009), 49.
29. The only other female presence in this space is often an older *tawaif*, now the owner or "madam" of the *kotha*. This older woman may be read as the choreographer of the

younger *tawaif*'s performance, a representative of the long history of the *mujra* and the repository of its knowledge.

30. Ashish Mohan Khokar, *Traditions of Indian Classical Dance* (Delhi: Clarion Books, 1984), 134.
31. Khokar, *Traditions of Indian Classical Dance*, 134.
32. Shovana Narayan, "Kathak: An Imperial Legacy of Theater and Rhythm," *Qrius*, June 20, 2016, doi: https://qrius.com/kathak-hindi-cinema/.
33. Mazumdar, *Bombay Cinema*, 86.
34. Khalid Mohamed, "Looking Back at the Life of Cabaret Queen Helen, as She Turns 77," *The Quint*, November 20, 2015, doi: https://www.thequint.com/voices/blogs/looking-back-at-the-life-of-cabaret-queen-helen-as-she-turns-77.
35. Scott Richmond analyses similar affects produced by camera movement in Sam Raimi's Spider-Man films. See Scott C. Richmond, "The Exorbitant Lightness of Bodies, or How to Look at Superheroes: Ilinx, Identification, and Spider-Man," *Discourse* 34, no. 1 (2012): 130.
36. Lefebvre, *The Production of Space*, 58.
37. Daniel Morgan, "Where Are We?: Camera Movements and the Problem of Point of View," *New Review of Film and Television Studies* 14, no. 2 (2016): 238.
38. Scott C. Richmond, "The Exorbitant Lightness of Bodies, or How to Look at Superheroes: Ilinx, Identification, and Spider-Man," *Discourse* 34, no. 1 (2012): 130.
39. Richmond, "The Exorbitant Lightness of Bodies," 130.
40. Susan Foster, *Choreographing Empathy: Kinesthesia in Performance* (New York: Routledge, 2010). "The viewer, watching a dance, is literally dancing along," notes Foster, as she proceeds to examine the potential of this kinesthetic empathy (Foster, *Choreographing Empathy*, 123).
41. *filmindia*, May 1954, 81.
42. Clare M. Wilkinson-Weber, *Fashioning Bollywood: The Making and Meaning of Hindi Film Costume* (London: A&C Black, 2013), 93.
43. Michel Foucault, "Of Other Spaces," trans. Jay Miskowiec, *Diacritics* 16, no. 1 (Spring 1986): 26.
44. Elizabeth Grosz, *Architecture from the Outside: Essays on Virtual and Real Space* (Cambridge, MA: MIT Press, 2001), 33.
45. The *Natya Shastra* is dated between 200 BCE and 200 CE. Authorship is attributed to the sage Bharata, but scholars consider it to be a synthesis of collective knowledge of production practices current at the time. Nandikesvara's late Sanskrit text is dated between 1000 and 1300 CE.
46. As discussed in detail in Chapter 3, in the late nineteenth and early twentieth centuries, upper-caste social reformers belonging to the Hindu bourgeoisie turned to ancient and medieval Sanskrit texts and commentaries to project an unbroken tradition of "respectable" national cultural forms, a process referred to as "Sanskritization" by later scholars. For more on the anti-*nautch* movement, the marginalization of traditional performers like *tawaifs* and *devadasis*, and the resuscitation of texts like the *Natya Shastra* and *Abhinaya Darpana*, see Davesh Soneji, *Unfinished Gestures: Devadasis, Memory, and Modernity in South India* (Chicago: University of Chicago Press, 2011)

and Avanti Meduri, *Woman, Nation, Representation: The Sutured History of the Devadasi and her Dance* (PhD dissertation, New York University, 1996).
47. Ananda Coomaraswamy, "Introduction," in *The Mirror of Gesture: Being the Abhinaya Darpana of Nandikesvara* (Cambridge, MA: Harvard University Press, 1917), 7.
48. See Hari Krishnan, *Celluloid Classicism: Early Tamil Cinema and the Making of Modern Bharatanatyam* (Middletown: Wesleyan University Press, 2019); Ruth Vanita, *Dancing with the Nation: Courtesans in Bombay Cinema* (USA: Bloomsbury Publishing, 2018); Davesh Soneji, *Unfinished Gestures: Devadasis, Memory, and Modernity in South India* (Chicago: University of Chicago Press, 2012); Anjali Arondekar, "In the Absence of Reliable Ghosts: Sexuality, Historiography, South Asia," *Differences* 25, no. 3 (2014).
49. Khokar, *Traditions of Indian Classical Dance*, 59.
50. Kapila Vatsyayan, *Indian Classical Dance* (New Delhi: Publications Division, Ministry of Information and Broadcasting, Govt. of India, 1974), 18.
51. Uttara Asha Coorlawala, "Darshan and Abhinaya: An Alternative to the Male Gaze," *Dance Research Journal* 28, no. 1 (1996): 24.
52. Kapila Vatsyayan, *Traditions of Indian Folk Dance* (Delhi: Clarion Books, 1987), 374.
53. The *amrapali* costume was named after Vyjayanthimala's costume in the film *Amrapali* (Lekh Tandon, 1966) in which she plays the eponymous Hindu courtesan. It became the default *Bharatanatyam* or sometimes even "classical dance" costume in Hindi film dance. The costume includes a short, tight blouse, a diaphanous sari wound tight around the legs, and does away with the *pallo* or the piece of cloth/section of the sari covering the blouse and the waist. This costume is much more revealing of the lines of the dancing body than the contemporary "traditional" *Bharatanatyam* costume.
54. Vatsyayan, *Indian Classical Dance*, 88.
55. Vatsyayan, *Indian Classical Dance*, 61.
56. Vatsyayan, *Indian Classical Dance*, 24.
57. Krishna Sahai, *The Story of a Dance: Bharatanatyam* (New Delhi: Indialog, 2003), 155.
58. Patsy Nair, "Saroj Khan: Actresses Now Don't Like to Work with Me," Rediff.com, March 29, 2012, https://www.rediff.com/movies/slide-show/slide-show-1-interview-with-choreographer-saroj-khan/20120329.htm.
59. See Chapter 4 for a detailed discussion of this production number, and through it, an examination of dance and acting.
60. Khokar, *Traditions of Indian Classical Dance*, 58.
61. In Hindi film songs, the opening stanza is referred to as the *mukhda*. It is the introductory and principal phrase of the composition that, like the chorus in Western music, is repeated after every following stanza. Each of these stanzas that form the body of the song is known as the *antara*. The *mukhda* and *antara* are sung by one or more characters, and are often interspersed with instrumental sections.
62. Production numbers like "*Bakad bam bam baaje damru*," "*Ek do teen*," and "*Dard-e-Disco*," for example, are dominated by a rhythmic quality rather than lyrical complexity.
63. Khokar, *Traditions of Indian Classical Dance*, 61.
64. Khokar, *Traditions of Indian Classical Dance*, 78.

65. Vatsyayan, *Indian Classical Dance*, 15.
66. V. A. K. Ranga Rao, "She Brought Lustre to the Silver Screen," *Sruti* 314 (November 2010), 34.
67. Adrienne McLean, "Feeling and the Filmed Body: Judy Garland and the Kinesics of Suffering," *Film Quarterly* 55, no. 3 (2002): 13.
68. Coorlawala, "Darshan and Abhinaya," 19.
69. Surjit Singh, *Edwina: An Unsung Bollywood Dancer of the Golden Era* (n.p.: Professor Toofaani, 2015), 57.
70. Vatsyayan, *Indian Classical Dance*, 17.
71. Vatsyayan, *Traditions of Indian Folk Dance*, 374.
72. Vatsyayan, *Traditions of Indian Folk Dance*, 374.
73. Singh, *Edwina*, 21.
74. Singh, *Edwina*, 21.
75. Siegfried Kracauer, "The Mass Ornament," in *The Mass Ornament: Weimar Essays* (Cambridge, MA; London: Harvard University Press, 1995), 76–78.
76. Nasreen Rehman with Farah Khan, "Dance in Bombay Cinema," *Marg* 64, no. 4 (June 2013): 76.
77. Kracauer, "The Mass Ornament," 78. "India Shining" was the marketing slogan meant to encapsulate a sense of economic optimism, adopted by the Hindu-right political party, the Bharatiya Janata Party, in 2004.

Chapter 3

1. Text from the film's opening credits, also emphasized in publicity materials like advertisements, song booklets, interviews.
2. Rosie Thomas, "Not Quite (Pearl) White: Fearless Nadia, Queen of the Stunts," in *Bollywood: Popular Indian Cinema through a Transnational Lens*, ed. Kaur Reminder and Ajay J. Sinha (London: Sage, 2005), 49.
3. The Bengali term for respectable, bourgeois women.
4. Leela Desai and Sitara are other well-known dancer-actresses during this period. I focus on Sadhona Bose here because her star text is deeply inflected by dance in that all her films are dance-centric, press reviews primarily focus on her dancing, and she has a parallel stage career as a professional dancer and choreographer.
5. Bose's filmography includes *Alibaba* (Modhu Bose, 1937), *Abhinaya* (Modhu Bose, 1938), *Kumkum the Dancer* (Modhu Bose, 1940), *Court Dancer* (Modhu Bose, 1941), *Meenakshi* (Modhu Bose, 1942), *Shankar Parvati* (Chaturbhuj Doshi, 1943), *Paigam* (Gyan Dutt, 1943), *Vish-Kanya* (Kidar Sharma, 1943), *Bhola Shankar* (Vishram Bedekar, 1951), *Shin Shinaki Boobla Boo* (P. L. Santoshi, 1952), *Shesher Kabita* (Modhu Bose, 1953), and *Vikram Urvashi* (Modhu Bose, 1954).
6. Since very few films from this period survive, I use paratextual materials like song booklets and press advertisements to produce these corporeal histories of film dance and female participation in it. Song booklets, cheaply produced and extremely popular during this period, were a key tool for film publicity. They included plot

synopses, cast and crew credits, song lyrics, production stills, and advertisements for upcoming films.

7. For a description of the *production number*, see the taxonomy of song-and-dance sequences detailed in Chapter 1.
8. From film credits and the autobiographies of Sadhona and Modhu Bose, it is clear that Sadhona Bose was responsible for choreography and costume design in at least four films—*Alibaba* (Modhu Bose, 1937), *Abhinaya* (Modhu Bose, 1938), *Kumkum the Dancer* (Modhu Bose, 1940), and *Court Dancer*—though it is likely that her influence on choreography, costume design, and art direction extended to most of her films.
9. S. Richard, "Azurie," *Dances on the Footpath* (blog), May 24, 2013, https://roughinhere.wordpress.com/2013/05/24/azurie/.
10. Kaushik Bhowmick, "The Emergence of the Bombay Film Industry, 1913–1936" (D. Phil. thesis, Oxford University, 2001).
11. Rosie Thomas, "Still Magic: An Aladdin's Cave of 1950s B-Movie Fantasy," *Tasveer Ghar* (website), ed. Christiane Brosius, Sumathi Ramaswamy, and Yousuf Saeed, http://www.tasveergharindia.net/essay/still-magic-aladdin-movie-fantasy.html.
12. Madhuja Mukherjee, ed., *Aural Films, Oral Cultures: Essays on Cinema from the Early Sound Era* (Kolkata: Jadavpur University Press, 2012), 49.
13. Alison Arnold, "Popular Film Song in India: A Case of Mass-Market Musical Eclecticism," *Popular Music* 7, no. 2 (1988): 177–188; Mukherjee, ed., *Aural Films, Oral Cultures: Essays on Cinema from the Early Sound Era*; Peter Manuel, *Cassette Culture: Popular Music and Technology in North India* (Chicago: University of Chicago Press, 1993).
14. In his famous essay, "The Nationalist Resolution of the Women's Question," historian Partha Chatterjee discusses the role of women's issues in the debates over social reform in nineteenth-century Bengal and the relationship of the social position of women to the politics of nationalism in India. See Partha Chatterjee, "The Nationalist Resolution of the Women's Question," in *Recasting Women: Essays in Indian Colonial History*, ed. Kumkum Sangari and Suresh Vaid (New Brunswick, NJ: Rutgers University Press, 1990), 233–253.
15. The difference in the titles of the autobiographies of Modhu and Sadhona Bose is noteworthy for the gender reversal it suggests: while Modhu Bose's *Aamar Jeeban* (My Life) implies a personal memoir, Sadhona Bose's title in the third person, *Shilpir Atmakatha* (Autobiography of an Artist) asserts the importance of her professional life and work as an artist. Significantly, she writes her autobiography in English, he in Bengali.
16. *Devadasis*, predominantly in South India, and *tawaifs*, mainly in North India, were courtesans who performed in various spaces and contexts, including temples, courts, and private salons. Soneji notes that the term *devadasi* "is used to index a vast number of communities of women who are generally glossed by English phrases such as 'sacred prostitute' or 'temple dancer,' describing them instead as 'professional artists in a shifting colonial sexual economy'"; Davesh Soneji, *Unfinished Gestures: Devadasis, Memory, and Modernity in South India* (Chicago: University of Chicago Press, 2012), 6.

17. For studies of the canonization of musical and dance forms during this period, see Soneji 2012; Amanda J. Weidman, *Singing the Classical, Voicing the Modern: The Postcolonial Politics of Music in South India* (Durham, NC: Duke University Press, 2006); Hari Krishnan, *Celluloid Classicism: Early Tamil Cinema and the Making of Modern Bharatanatyam* (Middletown, CT: Wesleyan University Press, 2019), Pallabi Chakravorty, *Bells of Change: Kathak Dance, Women and Modernity in India* (Calcutta: Seagull Books, 2008); Anne-Marie Gaston, *Bharata Natyam: From Temple to Theatre* (New Delhi: Manohar Publishers, 1996); Avanti Meduri, *Woman, Nation, Representation: The Sutured History of the Devadasi and her Dance* (PhD dissertation, New York University, 1996); Janet O'shea, *At Home in the World: Bharata Natyam on the Global Stage* (Middletown, CT: Wesleyan University Press, 2007); A. Srinivasan 1984; Maciszewski 2007; Veena Talwar Oldenburg, "Lifestyle as Resistance: The Case of the Courtesans of Lucknow," in *Contesting Power: Resistance and Everyday Social Relations in South Asia*, ed. Douglas E. Haynes and Gyan Prakash (Berkeley: University of California Press, 1991); Vidya Rao, "Thumri and Thumri Singers: Changes in Style and Lifestyle," in *Cultural Reorientation in Modern India*, ed. Indu Banga and Jaidev (Simla: Indian Institute of Advanced Study, 1996), among many others.
18. Neepa Majumdar, *Wanted Cultured Ladies Only!: Female Stardom and Cinema in India, 1930s–1950s* (Urbana: University of Illinois Press, 2009); Thomas, "Not Quite (Pearl) White: Fearless Nadia, Queen of the Stunts," 35–69.
19. The Brahmo Samaj, founded in 1828 by Raja Ram Mohan Roy and Debendranath Tagore, initiated social and religious reform, focusing on the emancipation of women through education, and the abolition of the dowry system. It also campaigned for the abolition of the caste system. In its proposal for the reform of Hinduism, Keshab Chandra Sen's "Brahmo Samaj of India" included aspects of Christianity, while its social campaigns focused on women's education and protests against child marriage.
20. Sadhana Bose, *Shilpir Atmakatha* (Calcutta: Pratibhas, 2012), 10–35.
21. Vidya Rao, *Heart to Heart: Remembering Naina Devi* (New Delhi: Harper Collins, 2011), 38.
22. Rao, *Heart to Heart: Remembering Naina Devi*, 39.
23. Nita Kumar, *The Artisans of Banaras: Popular Culture and Identity, 1896–1980* (Princeton, NJ: Princeton University Press, 1988), 149; Rao, "Thumri and Thumri Singers: Changes in Style and Lifestyle," 301.
24. Rao, "Thumri and Thumri Singers: Changes in Style and Lifestyle," 301.
25. Matthew Rahaim, *Musicking Bodies: Gesture and Voice in Hindustani Music* (Middletown, CT: Wesleyan University Press, 2012), 28–29.
26. *Nautch* is an Anglicized pronunciation and transliteration of the Hindustani word for dance, *naach*. Nautch had a pejorative intent and was especially used to designate the dance of the *tawaif*s and the *devadasi*s.
27. Soneji, *Unfinished Gestures*, 3.
28. Kaushik Bhowmick, "'Separating the Gem from the Dirt': Sexuality, Religion and Stardom in Early Bombay Cinema" (presentation, University of Warwick, 2011).

29. Pran Nevile, *Nautch Girls of India: Dancers, Singers, Playmates* (Delhi: Ravi Kumar, 1996), 168. During the same period, Soneji notes that figures such as Raghupati Venkataratnam Naidu solicited "purity pledges" from elite South Indian men, promising to refrain from watching or sponsoring "nautch" performances (Soneji, *Unfinished Gestures*, 120), while Sachdeva Jha documents the prohibition of *tawaif*-led performances by North Indian reformist caste associations and purity societies; Shweta Sachdeva Jha, "Frames of Cinematic History: The Tawa'if in Umrao Jan and Pakeezah," in *Narratives of Indian Cinema*, ed. Manju Jain (Delhi: Primus Books, 2009), 326–336.
30. Uttara Asha Coorlawala, "The Sanskritized Body," *Dance Research Journal* 36, no. 2 (2004): 52.
31. Pallabi Chakravorty, *Bells of Change: Kathak Dance, Women and Modernity in India* (Chicago: Chicago University Press, 2008), 110.
32. Uttara Asha Coorlawala, "Ruth St Denis and India's Dance Renaissance," *Dance Chronicle* 15, no. 2 (1992): 123.
33. Priya Srinivasan, "The bodies Beneath the Smoke, or What's behind the Cigarette Poster: Unearthing Kinesthetic Connections in U.S. Modern Dance," *Discourses in Dance* 4, no. 1 (2007): 7–8.
34. Joan L. Erdman, "Dance Discourses: Rethinking the History of the 'Oriental Dance,'" in *Moving Words—Rewriting Dance*, ed. Gay Morris (London: Routledge, 1996), 288.
35. Erdman, "Dance Discourses: Rethinking the History of the 'Oriental Dance,'" 288.
36. Coorlawala, "Ruth St Denis and India's Dance Renaissance," 134.
37. Coorlawala, "Ruth St Denis and India's Dance Renaissance," 134.
38. Urmimala Sarkar Munsi, "Another Time, Another Space," in *Dance Matters: Performing in India*, ed. Pallabi Chakravorty and Nilanjana Gupta (London: Dance Books, 2009), 62; Uttara Asha Coorlawala, "Classical and Contemporary Indian Dance: Overview, Criteria and Choreographic Analysis" (PhD dissertation, New York University, 1994), 57.
39. The *Natya Shastra* describes three categories of *bhavas* or emotional states, eight *sthayee* or dominant emotions (such as love, sorrow, anger, etc.), thirty-three *sanchari* or temporary/transitory emotions that contribute to the constitution of the *sthayee bhavas* (for example, doubt, bashfulness, lust, envy), and innumerable *sattvika bhavas* or physical expressions of feelings (through sweat, tears, etc.). Anupa Pande, *A Historical and Cultural Study of the Natyasastra of Bharat* (Jodhpur: Kusumanjali Prakashan, 1996), 313. In the context of Arundale's account, it is apparent that she is objecting to sexually explicit *sanchari bhavas*.
40. Gowri Ramnarayan, "Rukmini Devi: A Quest for Beauty—A Profile," *Sruti* 8 (1984): 23.
41. Soneji, *Unfinished Gestures*, 105.
42. Soneji, *Unfinished Gestures*, 24.
43. Soneji, *Unfinished Gestures*, 25.
44. Avanti Meduri, "Bharatanatyam as a Global Dance: Some Issues in Research, Teaching, and Practice," *Dance Research Journal* 36, no. 2 (Winter 2004): 23.
45. Meduri, "Bharatanatyam as a Global Dance," 21.

46. Kalpana Ram, "Dancing Off-stage: Nationalism and its 'Minor Practices' in Tamil Nadu," in *Dance Matters*, eds. Pallabi Chakravorty and Nilanjana Gupta (Routledge India, 2012), 5.
47. Coorlawala, *Classical and Contemporary Indian Dance*, 59.
48. Soneji, *Unfinished Gestures*, 11.
49. Soneji, *Unfinished Gestures*, 187.
50. Erdman, "Dance Discourses," 293.
51. Quoted in Kimiko Ohtani, "'Bharata Nāṭyam', Rebirth of Dance in India," *Studia Musicologica Academiae Scientiarum Hungaricae* 33, no. 1/4 (1991): 302.
52. The *Khol* is a double-headed wooden drum. Shantideb Ghosh, *Gurudeb Rabindranath o Adhunik Bharatiya Nritya* (Kolkata: Ananda, 2000), 41–42.
53. Ghosh, *Gurudeb Rabindranath o Adhunik Bharatiya Nritya*, 20.
54. Ghosh, *Gurudeb Rabindranath o Adhunik Bharatiya Nritya*, 11, 16–17, 44–45.
55. Ghosh, *Gurudeb Rabindranath o Adhunik Bharatiya Nritya*, 4.
56. Mandakranta Bose, "Indian Modernity and Tagore's Dance," *University of Toronto Quarterly* 77, no. 4 (2008): 1087.
57. Esha Niyogi De, "Empire, Vision, and the Dancing Touch," in *The Oxford Handbook of Screendance Studies*, ed. Douglas Rosenberg (June 2016), 447, https://www.oxfordhandbooks.com/view/10.1093/oxfordhb/9780199981601.001.0001/oxfordhb-9780199981601-e-21.
58. Fernau Hall, "Honoring Uday Shankar," *Dance Chronicle* 7, no. 3 (1984–1985): 331.
59. Hall, "Honoring Uday Shankar," 343.
60. Joan L. Erdman, "Performance as Translation: Uday Shankar in the West," *The Drama Review* 31, no. 1 (Spring 1987): 76.
61. Joan L. Erdman, "Who Remembers Uday Shankar?" (September 2011), https://mm-gold.azureedge.net/new_site/mukto-mona/Articles/jaffor/uday_shanka2.html.
62. Nilanjana Bhattacharjya, "A Productive Distance from the Nation: Uday Shankar and the Defining of Indian Modern Dance," *South Asian History and Culture* 2, no. 4 (2011): 486.
63. Shweta Sachdeva Jha, "Eurasian Women as Tawa'if Singers and Recording Artists: Entertainment and Identity-Making in Colonial India," *African and Asian Studies* 8, no. 3 (2009): 281; Amlan Das Gupta, "Women and Music: The Case of North India," in *Women of India: Colonial and Post-Colonial Periods*, ed. Bharti Ray (Delhi and London: Sage Publications, 2005): 467; Weidman, *Singing the Classical, Voicing the Modern*, 123.
64. Urmimala Sarkar Munsi, "Another Time, Another Space," 28.
65. It should be noted that not all Brahmo families were considered "respectable" or part of the *bhadralok* (the educated elite). In fact, through their affiliation with the Brahmo Samaj, they faced the ire of non-Brahmo following, upper-class Bengalis for radically violating traditional norms. Sen's family was part of the social and financial elite in Calcutta and hence exercised *bhadralok* privilege. The *bhadralok* class was by no means homogenous, and was marked rather by complex class-caste tensions. Not all *bhadralok* Bengalis, for example, considered dance to be a respectable profession.
66. Modhu Bose, *Aamar Jeeban* (Calcutta: Pratibhas, 2012), 110.

67. Bose, *Aamar Jeeban*, 110.
68. One notes a similar tension between amateur and professional status with respect to women's labor in the film industry in the 1930s, foregrounded only when "cultured ladies" take up acting as a profession. Nalini Tarkhud, film actress and columnist, remarks in a magazine column from 1933 titled "Cultured Girls and Cinema Acting:" "I am at a loss to understand why respectable girls are not expected to take up film acting as a profession. In the present economic depression this will be a means of support to many a cultured girl. We must not forget that not everybody in this world has a fat bank balance to work as an amateur and it is very narrow minded to expect honorary labour from the cultured ladies when the producer himself eagerly looks to making millions." Nalini Tarkhud, "Cultured Girls and Cinema Acting," *The Cinema Annual* (1933): 47. Honorary labor and pursuing acting as a hobby was an assured way for the "cultured" actress to distance herself from the paid, professional, working-class actress.
69. Bose, *Aamar Jeeban*, 111.
70. Rosie Thomas, *Bombay before Bollywood: Film City Fantasies* (Delhi: Orient Blackswan, 2014), 10; Ashish Rajadhyaksha and Paul Willemen, *Encyclopedia of Indian Cinema* (London: British Film Institute, 1999), 270.
71. Bose, *Aamar Jeeban*, 112.
72. Bhowmick, "The Emergence of the Bombay Film Industry, 1913–1936," 16; Mukherjee, *Aural Films, Oral Cultures*, 19, 27, 35.
73. R. M Ray, ed., *Indian Cinema in Retrospect* (New Delhi: Sangeet Natak Akademi, 2009), 290–291. In her book *Bengal Divided: Hindu Communalism and Partition, 1932–1947*, Joya Chatterji discusses how the period under consideration is characterized by a bourgeois discourse constructing Muslims as *chhotolok* (literally small people, referring here to caste, class, and educational differences from the *bhadralok*) while Hindus were urged to become *bhadralok*. Shweta Sachdeva Shah notes that the *Ashraf* class of Muslims, upper-class elites like the *bhadralok*, also considered lowbrow forms of popular entertainment such as *nautanki* and *nautch* obscene and immoral; Joya Chatterji, *Bengal Divided: Hindu Communalism and Partition, 1932–1947* (Cambridge: Cambridge University Press, 1994), 273.
74. Bose, *Shilpir Atmakatha*, 19.
75. "Sadhona Bose. A Thumbnail Sketch," *The Mirror* 3, no. 45 (March 1940).
76. Bose, *Shilpir Atmakatha*, 27. Over the next two decades, Sadhona and Modhu Bose would return to Tagore's works, with Sadhona Bose performing in a ballet version of the Tagore poem *Abhisar* (published in 1900 and performed in 1948 by the Indian Revival Group), and Modhu Bose directing a film *Sesher Kabita* (1953), based on Tagore's 1929 novel.
77. Sadhana Bose, *Shilpir Atmakatha*, 20.
78. "Review of Omar Khaiyyam," *The Statesman*, October 9, 1937.
79. Bose, *Aamar Jeeban*: 158–159.
80. Bose, *Shilpir Atmakatha*: 21–22.
81. The *sarod* is a stringed instrument, similar to a lute, used in North Indian classical music.

82. Bose, *Shilpir Atmakatha*, 64. The term, "neo-classical" has multiple valences in Indian dance scholarship. While Bose uses it to denote a "modern," hybrid form of classical dance, a new classical dance as it were, dance scholars like Vatsyayan refer to Indian classical dances in general as "neo-classical" rather than as "classical" to account for the appropriations and restructuring of these forms in the twentieth century. In this view, the term "neo-classical" acknowledges that these forms have all been "restructured or reconstructed in order to fit a model . . . to cater to a group of norms built to fit western performative models as well as Sanskritic aesthetic requirements"; Sarkar Munsi, "Another Time, Another Space," 34.
83. Bose, *Shilpir Atmakatha*, 15.
84. Bose, *Shilpir Atmakatha*, 68.
85. Majumdar, *Wanted Cultured Ladies Only!: Female Stardom and Cinema in India, 1930s–1950s*; Thomas, *Bombay before Bollywood: Film City Fantasies*; Bhowmick, "The Emergence of the Bombay Film Industry, 1913–1936."
86. Indian Cinematograph Committee, *Report of the Indian Cinematograph Committee 1927-28* (Calcutta: Government of India Central Publication Branch, 1928), 33. In Bengal, as discussed earlier, there was a move to encourage the participation of the Bengali *bhadralok* in semi-professional theater groups (such as Modhu Bose's C.A.P.), many of which would go on to produce cinematic adaptations of literary works in the sound period. Bhowmick notes, "Almost all the directors and actors entering Bengali cinema in this period came from the amateur stage specializing in realist theatre"; Bhowmick, "The Emergence of the Bombay Film Industry, 1913–1936," 126.
87. For more on the ICC and its attitude toward film actresses, see Priya Jaikumar, *Cinema at the End of Empire: A Politics of Transition in Britain and India* (Durham, NC: Duke University Press, 2006); and Babli Sinha, "Entertaining the Raj: Cinema and the Cultural Intersections of Britain, the United States, and India in the Early Twentieth Century" (PhD dissertation, University of Chicago, 2006).
88. Indian Cinematograph Committee, *Indian Cinematograph Committee 1927-1928: Evidence*, Volumes I and II (Calcutta: Government of India Central Publication Branch, 1928), 139.
89. Bhowmick, "'Separating the Gem from the Dirt': Sexuality, Religion and Stardom in Early Bombay Cinema," 6.
90. Majumdar, *Wanted Cultured Ladies Only!: Female Stardom and Cinema in India, 1930s–1950s*, 9–10.
91. Priti Ramamurthy, "All-Consuming Nationalism: The Indian Modern Girl in the 1920s and 1930s," in *The Modern Girl Around the World: Consumption, Modernity, and Globalization*, ed. Alys Eve Weinbaum et al. (Durham, NC: Duke University Press, 2008), 168.
92. Ramamurthy, "All-Consuming Nationalism: The Indian Modern Girl in the 1920s and 1930s," 168.
93. Vishwanbhar Prasad, "Savaak Chitrapaton mein Gayan ka Chunao," *Chitrapat* 11 (September 1932), 7.

94. Sruti Bandopadhyay, "Tradition and Change: Dance Dramas of Bengal," in *Time and Space in Asian Context: Contemporary Dance in Asia*, ed. Urmimala Sarkar Munsi (World Dance Alliance, 2005), 28.
95. In his essay on the *tawaif*/courtesan, Mukul Kesavan coins the term "Islamicate" to refer not directly to the Islamic religion itself, but to "the social and cultural complex historically associated with Islam and the Muslims, both among Muslims themselves and even when found among non-Muslims"; Mukul Kesavan, "Urdu, Awadh and the Tawaif: The Islamicate Roots of Hindi Cinema," in *Forging Identities: Gender, Communities and the State in India*, ed. Zoya Hasan (Boulder, CO: Westview, 1994), 246. I use the term here as many North Indian courtesans (for example, Malka Jan and her daughter Gauhar Jan) took on Muslim names to reinvent themselves as *tawaifs*; Jha, "Eurasian Women as Tawa'if Singers and Recording Artists: Entertainment and Identity-Making in Colonial India." See also Rosie Thomas's discussion of the term in relation to Indian film adaptations of the *Arabian Nights*. The term "Islamicate" refers here to "stereotyped conventions that construct an exotic fantasy of an historical cultural complex associated with Islam" (Thomas, *Bombay before Bollywood: Film City Fantasies*, 59).
96. Bose, *Aamar Jeeban*, 215.
97. Bose, *Shilpir Atmakatha*, 36.
98. *Chitrapanji* 10 (5), 1936.
99. *Chitrapanji* 11, no. 5 (1936): 535; quoted in Mukherjee, *Wide Screen*, 21. Madhuja Mukherjee, "When Was the 'Studio Era' in Bengal: Transition, Transformations and Configurations during the 1930s," *Wide Screen* 8, no. 1 (2019).
100. Srimati Ajoorie, "Why Is Dance Neglected," *Chitrapanji* 6, no. 6 (1936). All translations from the Bengali to English have been done by Pritha Chakrabarti.
101. Ajoorie, "Why Is Dance Neglected."
102. Marjorie Husain, "Madame Auzrie's Decades of Dancing," in *Madame Auzrie: An Album of the Dancing Queen*, ed. Kishvar Nāhīd (Karachi: Pakistan National Council of the Arts, 1995), 25–28.
103. Nāhīd, *Madame Auzrie: An Album of the Dancing Queen*, 30.
104. Azmat Ansari, "Tribute to a Great Dancer," in *Madame Auzrie: An Album of the Dancing Queen*, 32–33.
105. For the renaming of actors, see Sarkar Munsi "Another Time, Another Space," 77; Ravi Vasudevan, "Shifting Codes, Dissolving Identities: The Hindi Social Film of the 1950s as Popular Culture," *Journal of Arts & Ideas* 23–24 (1993): 109.
106. See Sachdeva Jha, "Eurasian Women as Tawa'if Singers and Recording Artists," for a discussion of how two Eurasian women entertainers, Malka Jan and her daughter Gauhar Jan, changed their names, religion, and lifestyles to reinvent themselves as celebrity entertainers, fashioning successful careers using new identities as *tawaif* singers and actors in the late nineteenth and early twentieth centuries. Azurie may be read as part of this genealogy of identity-making by mixed-race women in this period of colonial modernity, marked by new patterns of urban consumption.
107. Thomas, *Bombay before Bollywood: Film City Fantasies*, 162.
108. Ali Peter John, "Azurie Danced as if Possessed," *Screen* (February 29, 1980), 17.

109. In addition to dancing in numerous films, many of which did not include an official credit for dancers, Azurie is credited as choreographer on *Naya Sansar* (N. R. Acharya, 1941), *Meri Duniya* (Mazhar Khan, 1942), *Yaad* (Mazhar Khan, 1942), *Pannadai* (Ram Daryani, 1945), and *Parwana* (J. K. Nanda, 1947).
110. John, "Azurie Danced as if Possessed," 17.
111. John, "Azurie Danced as if Possessed," 17.
112. Surjit Singh, *Edwina: An Unsung Bollywood Dancer of the Golden Era* (n.p.: Professor Toofaani, 2015), 16.
113. *Chitrapanji* 6, no. 9 (1936).
114. Sushila Rani, "Baburao Patel Kicks Indian Dancers About!" *filmIndia* (May 1943): 37.
115. Rani, "Baburao Patel Kicks Indian Dancers About!" 37.
116. *Deepali*, Saradiya Puja Special Issue (September–October 1938), 200. Madame Menaka, among the first non-*tawaif* practitioners of *Kathak*, was considered an instrumental figure in the transformation of the maligned *nautch* dance into the respectable classical dance form, *Kathak*, in the 1930s. Ram Gopal was a famed modern Indian dancer and choreographer, who, like Uday Shankar, combined classical Indian dance with balletic choreography.
117. John, "Azurie Danced as if Possessed," 17; Singh, *Edwina: An Unsung Bollywood Dancer of the Golden Era*, 50.
118. Krishna Kumar, Surya Kumar, and Uday Shankar's erstwhile dance partner, Simkie, choreographed *Awara*'s song-and-dance sequences, including the extravagant dream sequence, pointing to how this network of oriental dancers brought their energies from stage to screen and left their traces across Bombay cinema through the 1950s and beyond.
119. John, "Azurie Danced as if Possessed," 17.
120. The one mention I could locate of Azurie's dancing in Tamil cinema is in Swarnavel Eswaran's discussion of the writer Kalki's film criticism. Eswaran mentions that in his review of the Tamil film, *Bhakta Kuselar* (K. Subramaniam, 1936), Kalki praises "the *Kathakali*-like Nepali dance of Miss. Azurie, but criticizes its context, as it seems the character of Balaramar has been thrust into the story for creating the (unnecessary) situation for the dance." Qtd in Swarnavel Eswaran, "Kalki alias Karnatakam: Tamil Cinema's First Critic," *Aran International e-Journal of Tamil Research*, January 23, 2020, https://www.aranejournal.com/article/5875.
121. Indian film adaptations of the Alibaba story include: *Ali Baba and the Forty Thieves* (Hiralal Sen, 1903–1904), *Alibaba Chalis Chor* (Alibaba and Forty Thieves, B. P. Mishra, 1927), *Ali Baba and Forty Thieves* (J. J. Madan, 1932), *Ali Baba* (Mehboob Khan, 1940), *Alibaba and the Forty Thieves* (Homi Wadia, 1954), *Marjina Abdulla* (Dinen Gupta, 1973), and *Alibaba aur 40 Chor* (Alibaba and Forty Thieves, Latif Faiziyev and Umesh Mehra, 1980).
122. For details on the differences between song sequences, narrative numbers, production numbers, and pure dance numbers, see the taxonomy of song-and-dance sequences in Chapter 1.
123. Rajadhyaksha and Willemen, *Encyclopedia of Indian Cinema*, 270.

124. Samik Bandyopadhyay, ed., *Indian Cinema: Contemporary Perceptions from the Thirties* (Jamshedpur: Celluloid Chapter, 1993), 76.
125. Rajadhyaksha and Willemen, *Encyclopedia of Indian Cinema*, 270.
126. Bose, *Aamar Jeeban*, 226.
127. See Thomas, *Bombay before Bollywood: Film City Fantasies*, 31–65, for an in-depth discussion of adaptations of *Arabian Nights* stories in early Indian cinema and the many inflections of the Orient in these.
128. Thomas, *Bombay before Bollywood: Film City Fantasies*, 64.
129. "Review of Alibaba," *Desh* 20 (February 1937), 5.
130. Song booklet for *Court Dancer* (1941).
131. Bose, *Shilpir Atmakatha*, 46.
132. Bose, *Aamar Jeeban*, 49.
133. "Review of Court Dancer," *filmindia* (October 1941), 18. Significantly, even though *Court Dancer* barely managed to recover its costs in the three language versions, it succeeded in gaining entry into the pages of film magazines, in contrast to the lack of attention to the financially successful Wadia stunt films (Majumdar, *Wanted: Cultured Ladies Only*, 107).
134. Leela Samson, *Rhythm in Joy: Classical Indian Dance* (New Delhi: Lustre Press, 1987), 30.
135. Bose, *Aamar Jeeban*, 50.
136. Bose, *Aamar Jeeban*, 312.
137. The *Raas Lila* is a devotional dance item in various classical and folk dance idioms depicting the dance of the god Krishna, his lover, Radha, and the *Gopis* (cowherdesses) of Vrindavan, where Krishna was raised. In *Court Dancer*, Bose performs the *Raas Lila* in the classical *Manipuri* style, where statues of Krishna and Radha are brought out of their rooms in the temple and placed in the center of the *rasamandali* (the circular area where the dance is performed).
138. Richard Allen and Ira Bhaskar, *Islamicate Cultures of Bombay Cinema* (Delhi: Tulika, 2009), 65.
139. Ravi Vasudevan, *The Melodramatic Public: Film Form and Spectatorship in Indian Cinema* (Ranikhet: Permanent Black, 2010), 103.
140. *Filmland* (May 13, 1933), 19.
141. Vasudevan, *The Melodramatic Public*, 141.
142. Kathryn Hansen, "Mapping Melodrama: Global Theatrical Circuits, Parsi Theater, and the Rise of the Social," *BioScope: South Asian Screen Studies* 7, no. 1 (2016): 66. Hansen, in her discussion of Parsi theater, mentions Betab's 1901 play, *Qatl-e-Nazir*, based on the murder of a courtesan in Lahore. Clearly, the courtesan was a critical figure for the discussion of social and moral reform but also for the production of "sensation dramas"; Hansen, "Mapping Melodrama," 65.
143. Susan Foster, *Choreographing Empathy: Kinesthesia in Performance* (New York: Routledge, 2010). "The viewer, watching a dance, is literally dancing along," notes Foster, as she proceeds to examine the potential of this kinesthetic empathy (123).

144. Anupama Kapse, "Dance Social: Melodrama as Method," *Framework* 54, no. 2 (Fall 2013): 150.
145. Majumdar, *Wanted Cultured Ladies Only!: Female Stardom and Cinema in India, 1930s–1950s*, 131.
146. "Bewitching Sadhona Bose Stars . . ." *The Mirror* 3, no. 40 (February 25, 1940).
147. Hansen, "Mapping Melodrama: Global Theatrical Circuits, Parsi Theater, and the Rise of the Social," 65.
148. Hansen, "Mapping Melodrama: Global Theatrical Circuits, Parsi Theater, and the Rise of the Social," 64.
149. Rajadhyaksha and Willemen, *Encyclopedia of Indian Cinema*, 266.
150. Rajadhyaksha and Willemen, *Encyclopedia of Indian Cinema*, 280.
151. Rajadhyaksha and Willemen, *Encyclopedia of Indian Cinema*, 272.
152. "Bewitching Sadhona Bose Stars . . . ."
153. Bose, *Aamar Jeeban*, 292.
154. "New Theatres' Disappointing Meenakshi," *filmIndia* (January 1943): 79.
155. Leela Desai played the role of a *devadasi* in *Bidyapati* (Debaki Bose, 1937) and of a courtesan, Roopkumari, in *Nartaki* (Debaki Bose, 1940). Her last film was *Nagad Narayan* (Vishram Bedekar, 1943). While Sitara played bit roles in a few films after the 1950s, the dominant phase of her film career as a dancer-actress in Bombay cinema ended with *Phool* (K. Asif) in 1944 and *Badi Maa* (Master Vinayak) in 1945.
156. "New Theatres' Disappointing Meenakshi," *filmIndia* (January 1943): 79.
157. The song booklets for Bose's later films—*Meenakshi* (Modhu Bose, 1942), *Paigam* (Surendra Desai, 1943), *Shesher Kabita* (Modhu Bose, 1953)—reveal transformations in Bose's star text. As she moves into what seem like more conventional social melodramas, the lack of dance poses in the production stills, of dance-themed illustrations, or a markedly decorative aesthetic suggests that these films might adhere more narrowly to the structure of the woman's melodrama, rather than cutting loose into the spectacular attractions of the dance social.
158. Bose, *Aamar Jeeban*, 300.
159. Bose, *Aamar Jeeban*, 301.
160. Bose, *Aamar Jeeban*, 318.
161. Ashish Mohan Khokar, "Yog Sunder: A True Prince of Dance," Narthaki.com, March 31, 2009, https://narthaki.com/info/tdhc/tdhc7.html; Sruti Bandopadhyay, "Tradition and Change: Dance Dramas of Bengal," in *Time and Space in Asian Context: Contemporary Dance in Asia*, ed. Urmimala Sarkar Munsi (Kolkata: World Dance Alliance, 2005), 131.
162. Khokar, *Classical and Folk Dances of India*, 223.
163. Mohan Khokar, "Yog Sunder: A True Prince of Dance."
164. *Maulvis* are teachers of the Quran in mosques. Saleem Asmi, "Memories of a Dancing Queen," in *Madame Auzrie: An Album of the Dancing Queen*, 42.
165. Feriyal Amal Aslam, "Choreographing [in] Pakistan: Indu Mitha, Dancing Occluded Histories in 'The Land of the Pure'" (PhD dissertation, University of California, Los Angeles, 2012), 99.

166. Azurie, "Dancing: Old and New," published in "The Civil and Military Gazette," January 11, 1959, reprinted in *Madame Azurie: An Album of the Dancing Queen*, 20.
167. Ansari, "Tribute to a Great Dancer," 31.
168. Husain, "Madame Auzrie's Decades of Dancing," 28.
169. Ansari, "Tribute to a Great Dancer," 34.
170. Ravi S. Vasudevan, "Geographies of the Cinematic Public: Notes on Regional National and Global Histories of Indian Cinema," *Journal of the Moving Image*, no. 9 (2010): 107.
171. Ritu Menon and Kamla Bhasin, *Borders and Boundaries: Women in India's Partition* (New Brunswick, NJ: Rutgers University Press, 1998), 251.
172. Soneji, *Unfinished Gestures*, 224–225; Amelia Maciszewski, "Texts, Tunes, and Talking Heads: Discourses about Socially Marginal North Indian Musicians," *Twentieth-Century Music* 3, no. 1 (2007): 132–133; Sachdeva Jha, "Eurasian Women as Tawa'if Singers and Recording Artists," 284; Salma Siddique, "Meena Shorey: The Droll Queen of Partition," *Bioscope: South Asian Screen Studies* 6, no. 1 (2015): 48.
173. Shehzadi Begum was the daughter of silent film director, producer, and actress Fatma Begum, sister of the film star Zubeida, and was credited as "dancer" in many films from *Abul Hasan* (1931) to *Adhar* (1945).
174. Ramamurthy, "All-Consuming Nationalism: The Indian Modern Girl in the 1920s and 1930s," 168.
175. Thomas, "Not Quite (Pearl) White: Fearless Nadia, Queen of the Stunts," 49–50.
176. Joan Kelly-Gadol, "The Social Relation of the Sexes: Methodological Implications of Women's History," *Signs: Journal of Women in Culture and Society* 1, no. 4 (1976): 809.
177. Ramamurthy, "All-Consuming Nationalism: The Indian Modern Girl in the 1920s and 1930s," 166.
178. Soneji, *Unfinished Gestures*, 72.

Chapter 4

1. Vyjayanthimala Bali and Jyoti Sabharwal, *Bonding... : A Memoir* (New Delhi: Stellar, 2007), 102.
2. *Baaje Payal*, "Baaje Payal: Episode on Vyjayanthimala." Doordarshan, New Delhi, 1998.
3. K. Pradeep, "Dance and Vyjayantimala" (November 2011), https://www.thehindu.com/features/metroplus/dance-and-vyjayantimala/article2591559.ece.
4. *Nattuvanars* were hereditary male musicians and choreographers in the *Sadirattam* tradition, who reinvented themselves as *Bharatanatyam* gurus in the revival period. In her autobiography, Vyjayanthimala labors to emphasize that Yadugiri Devi was the primary influence on her life, rather her mother, who abandoned the family for a lover when Vyjayanthimala was a young teenager (Bali and Sabharwal, *Bonding*, 31–32). In her research on dance in Telugu cinema, Rumya Putcha discusses the erased courtesan backgrounds of many dancer-actresses, including Vyjayanthimala. She

relates an interview with the Telugu dancer-actress, L. Vijayalakshmi/Vijji: "I mentioned, at one point, that it was significant to many scholars of dance, myself included, that film dancers such as Vyjayanthimala and Rajasulochana were born into hereditary performance—their mothers were courtesans. Without missing a beat, Vijji corrected me, "but it wasn't the training they received from their mothers or grandmothers that earned them prestige or film roles. These women trained rigorously with *gurus*, for years, in many different styles of music and dance, and that has nothing to do with whether or not they could trace their lineage to courtesan communities." This demonstrates larger industrial shifts as dancer-actresses sought to erase courtesan family histories and foreground training lineages under famed *nattuvanars* instead. (Rumya Putcha, "Cinematic Modernities and Cosmopolitan Citizenships: Affective Economies in Post-Independence Indian Cinema," *Paper presented at the Annual Conference on South Asia*, University of Wisconsin at Madison, October 12, 2018.)

5. *Baaje Payal*. "Baaje Payal: Episode on Vyjayanthimala." Doordarshan, New Delhi, 1998.
6. Hiralal's grand-daughter, Vaibhavi Merchant, is a well-known contemporary choreographer.
7. For more on Vyjayanthimala and other Madras industry personnel's contributions to Bombay cinema, see Iyer, "Bringing *Bharatanatyam* to Bombay Cinema—Vyjayanthimala and Tamil-Hindi Film Industry Interactions in the 1950s," in *Industrial Networks and Cinemas of India: Shooting Stars, Shifting Geographies, and Multiplying Media*, ed. Madhuja Mukherjee and Monika Mehta (New York: Routledge, forthcoming).
8. See Chapter 5 for an extended discussion of Saroj Khan.
9. Nidhi Tuli, *The Saroj Khan Story*, DVD (New Delhi: PBST and Films Division of India, 2012).
10. See Neepa Majumdar, *Wanted Cultured Ladies Only!: Female Stardom and Cinema in India, 1930s–1950s* (Urbana: University of Illinois Press, 2009); and Sanjay Srivastava, "Voice, Gender and Space in Time of Five-Year Plans: The Idea of Lata Mangeshkar," *Economic and Political Weekly* 39, no. 20 (2004): 2019–2028.
11. From the 1950s through the 1990s, a majority of heroine songs were voiced by Lata Mangeshkar, while her sultry-voiced sister, Asha Bhosle, often sang for the vamp.
12. Anjali Arondekar, "In the Absence of Reliable Ghosts: Sexuality, Historiography, South Asia," *Differences* 25, no. 3 (2014): 100.
13. Chakravarty notes of the courtesan film, one of the principal dance film sub-genres for showcasing an actress's dancing and acting skills, that it "emerges as a vehicle for the acting talents of women. Nargis, Meena Kumari, Vyjayanthimala, Suchitra Sen, and Sharmila Tagore, all top-rated actresses, took these roles at the height of their careers" (Sumita Chakravarty, *National Identity in Indian Popular Cinema (1947–1987)* (Austin: University of Texas, 1993), 275.
14. Vijay N. Shankar, "Dance in Cinema: Gimmick or Necessity," *Filmfare* 15 (April 1966): 23–24.

15. Hari Krishnan, *Celluloid Classicism: Early Tamil Cinema and the Making of Modern Bharatanatyam* (Middletown, CT: Wesleyan University Press, 2019), 159.
16. M. S. S. Pandian, "Tamil Cultural Elites and Cinema: Outline of an Argument," *Economic and Political Weekly* 31, no. 15 (1996): 950.
17. Pandian, "Tamil Cultural Elites and Cinema," 954.
18. Davesh Soneji, *Unfinished Gestures: Devadasis, Memory, and Modernity in South India* (Chicago: University of Chicago Press, 2011), 22.
19. The two other academies inaugurated the same year to "promote the cultural unity of the country" were the Sahitya Akademi (Literature) and the Lalit Kala Akademi (Fine Arts including Visual Arts); *Sangeet Natak Akademi Report 1958–59* (New Delhi: Sangeet Natak Akademi, 1959), 1–2.
20. *Sangeet Natak Akademi Report 1953–54* (New Delhi: Sangeet Natak Akademi, 1954), 1.
21. *Sangeet Natak Akademi Report 1958–59* (New Delhi: Sangeet Natak Akademi, 1959), 2.
22. *Sangeet Natak Akademi Report 1958–59*, 12–15.
23. Jyotindra Jain, "India's Republic Day Parade: Restoring Identities, Construction the Nation," *Marg, A Magazine of the Arts* 59, no. 2 (December 2007): 52.
24. Jain, "India's Republic Day Parade: Restoring Identities, Construction the Nation," 53.
25. Govind Vidyarthi, "Republic Day Folk Dance Festival," *Sangeet Natak* (April–June 1969): 82.
26. Kapila Vatsyayan, *Traditions of Indian Folk Dance* (Delhi: Clarion Books, 1987); Mohan Khokar, *The Splendours of Indian Dance* (New Delhi: Himalayan Books, 1985).
27. Examples may be found in *Mother India* (Mehboob Khan, 1957), *Naya Daur* (B. R. Chopra, 1957), *Madhumati* (Bimal Roy, 1958), and *Ganga Jamna* (Nitin Bose, 1961), among many other films of the period.
28. Arundhathi Subramaniam, "Dance in Films," in *New Directions in Indian Dance*, ed. Sunil Kothari (Mumbai: Marg Publications, 2003), 135.
29. R. M. Ray, ed., *Indian Cinema in Retrospect* (New Delhi: Sangeet Natak Akademi, 2009), 169.
30. Ray, *Indian Cinema in Retrospect*, 170.
31. Ray, *Indian Cinema in Retrospect*, 180.
32. Shikha Jhingan, "Re-embodying the "Classical": The Bombay Film Song in the 1950s," *BioScope* 2, no. 2 (2011): 159.
33. Qureshi, Regula Burckhardt. "Female Agency and Patrilineal Constraints: Situating Courtesans in Twentieth-century India." *The Courtesan's Arts: Cross-cultural Perspectives* (2006): 312.
34. Ray, *Indian Cinema in Retrospect*, 183.
35. Ray, *Indian Cinema in Retrospect*, 185.
36. Ray, *Indian Cinema in Retrospect*, 238.
37. Joan L. Erdman, "Dance Discourses: Rethinking the History of the 'Oriental Dance,'" in *Moving Words—Rewriting Dance*, ed. Gay Morris (London: Routledge, 1996), 295.
38. Nilanjana Bhattacharjya, "A Productive Distance from the Nation: Uday Shankar and the Defining of Indian Modern Dance," *South Asian History and Culture* 2, no. 4 (October 2011): 491.

39. "A Life Dedicated to Dance . . . Vyjayanthimala Bali," *Samudhra* 8, no. 6 (April 2010): 5.
40. Randor Guy, "She Danced Her Way to Stardom," *The Hindu*, January 7, 2002. Web https://web.archive.org/web/20071105220853/http://hinduonnet.com/mp/2002/01/07/stories/2002010700100200.htm (accessed May 15, 2013).
41. Uttara Asha Coorlawala, "The Sanskritized Body," *Dance Research Journal* 36, no. 2 (2004): 57.
42. "Kamala on the Silver Screen," *Sruti* 48 (1988): 32.
43. Krishnan, *Celluloid Classicism*, 139.
44. Purnima Shah, "Where They Danced: Patrons, Institutions, Spaces: State Patronage in India: Appropriation of the 'Regional' and 'National,'" *Dance Chronicle* 25, no. 1 (2002): 125–141.
45. Iyer, "Bringing *Bharatanatyam* to Bombay Cinema."
46. Krishnan, *Celluloid Classicism*, 155.
47. *Baaje Payal*, "Baaje Payal: Episode on Waheeda Rehman." Doordarshan. New Delhi, 1998.
48. Amrit Srinivasan, "Temple 'Prostitution' and Community Reform: An Examination of the Ethnographic, Historical and Textual Context of the Devadasi of Tamil Nadu, South India" (Doctoral dissertation, Cambridge University, 1984), 201.
49. Soneji, *Unfinished Gestures: Devadasis, Memory, and Modernity in South India*, 143.
50. Theodore S. Baskaran, *The Eye of the Serpent: An Introduction to Tamil Cinema* (Chennai: Westland, 2013), 39.
51. Swarnavel Eswaran Pillai, *Madras Studios: Narrative, Genre, and Ideology in Tamil Cinema* (New Delhi: SAGE Publications India, 2015), 112.
52. See Krishnan, *Celluloid Classicism*, 155–157, for a discussion of Vyjayanthimala's place in *Bharatanatyam*'s refiguration in South India, and Chapter 3 of his book for an extended discussion of *Bharatanatyam* and bourgeois nationalism.
53. Bali and Sabharwal, *Bonding*, 45.
54. S. Janaki, "Vyjayantimala Bali: A Many-Splendoured Voyage of Self-Discovery," *Sruti* 311 (August 2010): 10.
55. Bali and Sabharwal, *Bonding*, 45. Semi-classical dance is intermediate in style and gestural articulation between classical and popular dance. It borrows movements and gestures from classical dance but renders them in a popular idiom by making them less strictly codified and easier to perform.
56. In "courtesan films," the courtesan is the protagonist and focalizer of the narrative. *Pakeezah* (Kamal Amrohi, 1972) and *Umrao Jaan* (Muzaffar Ali, 1981) are famous examples of this genre.
57. *Baaje Payal*, "Baaje Payal: Episode on Waheeda Rehman."
58. Nasreen Munni Kabir, *Conversations with Waheeda Rehman* (New Delhi: Penguin Books India, 2014), 38.
59. Anuj Kumar, "Queen of Hearts," *The Hindu*, July 28, 2012, https://www.thehindu.com/features/cinema/queen-of-hearts/article3692441.ece (accessed March 25, 2013).
60. *Baaje Payal*, "Baaje Payal: Episode on Waheeda Rehman."

61. Kabir, *Conversations with Waheeda Rehman*, 1–4.
62. Kabir, *Conversations with Waheeda Rehman*, 2.
63. M. L. Narasimham, "Rojulu Maaraayi (1955)," *The Hindu*, July 31, 2014, https://www.thehindu.com/features/friday-review/rojulu-maaraayi-1955/article6268472.ece.
64. Kuchipudi is a South Indian classical dance form that is believed to have originated in a village named Kuchipudi in what is today the Indian state of Andhra Pradesh.
65. Waheeda Rehman, interview by Usha Iyer, Mumbai, India, June 15, 2013.
66. For more on Bose, see Chapter 3.
67. Shakti Salgaokar and Blessy Chettiar, "Why Vyjayanthimala has 'nothing to say' about today's heroines," *DNA*, September 26, 2011, https://www.dnaindia.com/entertainment/report-why-vyjayanthimala-has-nothing-to-say-about-today-s-heroines-1591825.
68. V. A. K. Ranga Rao, "She Brought Lustre to the Silver Screen," *Sruti* 314 (November 2010): 32.
69. *Baaje Payal*, "Baaje Payal: Episode on Waheeda Rehman." Doordarshan. New Delhi, 1998.
70. Waheeda Rehman, interview by Usha Iyer, Mumbai, India, June 15, 2013.
71. In her interview with me, Rehman commented on how much interest the film's costume designer, Bhanu Athaiya, took especially with costumes for dance sequences.
72. See Chapter 1 for a taxonomy of song-and-dance sequences.
73. Kabir, *Conversations with Waheeda Rehman*, 150–151.
74. Kabir, *Conversations with Waheeda Rehman*, 153.
75. Kabir, *Conversations with Waheeda Rehman*, 149.
76. *Baaje Payal*, "Baaje Payal: Episode on Waheeda Rehman." See Chapter 5 for an extended discussion of the choreographer-dancer relationship.
77. Kabir, *Conversations with Waheeda Rehman*, 150.
78. Waheeda Rehman, interview by Usha Iyer, Mumbai, India, June 15, 2013.
79. Bali and Sabharwal, *Bonding*, 101.
80. Rajul Hegde, "Picking Bollywood's Favourite Dancing Queens," *rediff Movies*, November 17, 2010, https://www.rediff.com/movies/slide-show/slide-show-1-saroj-khan-on-her-favourite-bollywood-dancers/20101117.htm#5.
81. Bali and Sabharwal, *Bonding*, 67.
82. "Vyjayanthimala," *Star and Style*, June 15, 1966, 5.
83. Bali and Sabharwal, *Bonding*, 77.
84. Bali and Sabharwal, *Bonding*, 72.
85. Sally Ann Ness, *Body, Movement, and Culture: Kinesthetic and Visual Symbolism in a Philippine Community* (Philadelphia: University of Pennsylvania Press, 1992), 6.
86. Cynthia Baron and Sharon Marie Carnicke, *Reframing Screen Performance* (Ann Arbor: University of Michigan Press, 2008), 185.
87. Baron and Carnicke, *Reframing Screen Performance*, 185.
88. Baron and Carnicke differentiate between transparent and opaque performance elements, noting that contemporary forms of realism and naturalism in Euro-American performance conventions call for transparent acting where "the opaque

body and voice of the actor becomes the vehicle for the virtual realm of the story." See Baron and Carnicke, *Reframing Screen Performance*, 182–183.
89. Corey Creekmur, "Madhubala in *Mughal-e-Azam*," in *Close-Up: Great Cinematic Performances*, Volume 2: *International*, ed. Kyle Stevens and Murray Pomerance (Edinburgh: Edinburgh University Press, 2018), 163.
90. Phillip B. Zarrilli, ed., *Acting (Re)considered: A Theoretical and Practical Guide* (New York: Routledge, 2005), 3.
91. Ananya Chatterjea, "Training in Indian Classical Dance: A Case Study," *Asian Theatre Journal* 13, no. 1 (1996): 75.
92. The *Natya Shastra* is dated between 200 BCE and 200 CE. Authorship is attributed to the sage Bharata, but scholars consider it to be a synthesis of collective knowledge of production practices current at the time.
93. See Chapter 3 for a discussion of "Sanskritization" of dance forms and the resuscitation of texts like the *Natya Shastra* and *Abhinaya Darpana*. By the 1940s and 1950s, these treatises were explicitly cited in the dance training of middle- and upper-class women, including dancer-actresses like Vyjayanthimala, Waheeda Rehman, etc., and hence their relevance here.
94. Bali and Sabharwal, *Bonding*, 45.
95. Nandikesvara. *The Mirror of Gesture, Being the Abhinaya Darpana of Nandikesvara*, trans. Ananda Coomaraswamy and Gopala Kristnayya Duggirala (New Delhi: Munshiram Manoharlal, 1970), 17.
96. *Kathakali* is one of the eight canonized Indian classical dance forms. It is predominantly performed by men, whose face paint and costume indicate the mythic or epic characters they represent.
97. In Indian aesthetic theories of performance, *rasa* (quite literally, taste or flavor) refers to the unified emotional core of a play. A preeminent treatise, the *Natya Shastra*, describes eight *rasas* that can be communicated in performance—desire, amusement, grief, anger, determination, fear, revulsion, and amazement. For more, see Sheldon Pollock, *A Rasa Reader: Classical Indian Aesthetics* (New York: Columbia University Press, 2016).
98. Kapila Vatsyayan, *Indian Classical Dance* (New Delhi: Publications Division, Ministry of Information and Broadcasting, Govt. of India, 1974), 18.
99. Coorlawala, "Darshan and Abhinaya," 24.
100. These include *Bahar* (M. V. Raman, 1951), *Ladki* (M. V. Raman, 1953), *Pehli Jhalak* (M. V. Raman, 1955), *New Delhi* (Mohan Segal, 1956), *Kathputli*, and *Aasha* (M. V. Raman, 1957).
101. Bali and Sabharwal, *Bonding*, 45.
102. This doubling of dance performance is in evidence in the case of other contemporary dancer-actresses like Sandhya and Padmini as well. In the production number "*Arre ja re hat natkhat*" ("Go away, you mischief-maker") celebrating the colorful festival of Holi in *Navrang* (Nine Colors, V. Shantaram, 1959), Sandhya performs a "dancing double role" presenting a female dancer frontally with a male dancer's costume on her back, literally turning back and forth between the two personas. The Bharatanatyam-trained Padmini plays the male and female lovers in "*Piya milan ko

chali radhika" ("Radhika goes to meet her lover") from *Payal* (Joseph Thaliath Jr., 1957), both sequences demonstrating the dancer-actresses' facility with incarnating different roles.

103. Some of these films include *Sadhna* (B. R. Chopra, 1958), *Gunga Jumna* (Nitin Bose, 1962), and *Sangam* (Union, Raj Kapoor, 1965) for which she won major acting awards.

104. Vyjayanthimala's dance-centered comedies included *Bahar* (M. V. Raman, 1951), *Ladki* (M. V. Raman, 1953), *Miss Mala* (Jayant Desai, 1954), *Pehli Jhalak* (M. V. Raman, 1955), *Aasha* (M. V. Raman, 1957), and *New Delhi* (Mohan Segal, 1956).

105. Lesley Stern describes performers who delight in the exhibition of virtuosity as histrionic. She traces histrionic performances to earlier traditions that used "stylised conventional gestures with a limited lexicon of pre-established meanings" and histrionic cinema to encounters with theater and opera (282–283). Lesley Stern, "Acting Out of Character: *The King of Comedy* as a Histrionic Text," in *Falling for You: Essays on Cinema and Performance*, ed. Lesley Stern and George Kouvaros (Champaign: University of Illinois Press, 1999).

106. Erin Brannigan describes a performer's idiogest as their gestural idiolect, their corporeal specificity that defines the gestural parameters not just of that performer but the overall character of the films in which they appear. See Brannigan, *Dancefilm: Choreography and the Moving Image*, 142.

107. Majumdar, *Wanted Cultured Ladies Only!: Female Stardom and Cinema in India, 1930s–1950s*, 14.

108. Significantly, unlike the audiovisual spectacle of dance, of which the woman is constructed as the primary agent, *aural* stardom tended to be narrativized through male protagonists. There were a slew of films on classical vocalists, always male, in the 1950s and 1960s, including *Baiju Bawra* (Vijay Bhatt, 1952), *Basant Bahar* (Raja Nawathe, 1956), *Kohinoor* (S. U. Sunny, 1960), and *Sangeet Samrat Tansen* (S. N. Tripathi, 1962). V. Shantaram's *Jhanak Jhanak Payal Baje* (Tinkling of the Anklets, 1955), featuring the classically trained dancer and choreographer Gopi Krishna, is one of the rare films from the period that focuses on a male dancer.

109. Partha Chatterjee, "The Nationalist Resolution of the Women's Question 1989," in *Recasting Women, Essays in Colonial History*, ed. Kumkum Sangari and Sudesh Vaid (New Delhi: Kali for Women, 1989), 243.

110. In the context of Indian classical dances associated with the temples of India, which were seen as "intense repositories of the inner spiritual core," Kalpana Ram employs Chatterjee's argument to note the "peculiarly prominent role played by women from the middle class in the maintenance and elaboration of these kinds of dance traditions" by cleansing the dance of its erotic elements and marginalizing the traditional dancers; Kalpana Ram, "Phantom Limbs: South Indian Dance and Immigrant Reifications of the Female Body," *Journal of Intercultural Studies* 26, no. 1–2 (2005): 130–131).

111. Ranjani Mazumdar, *Bombay Cinema: Archive of the City* (Delhi: Permanent Black, 2007), 82. Shweta Sachdeva Jha discusses the demarcation of private and public spaces in colonial India according to codes of sociability, where "decent women did

not interact with men who were not related to them. . . . Only prostitutes socialized with men in public. Thus the tawa'if was a 'public' woman, as she entertained men who were unrelated to her in a public space"; Shweta Sachdeva Jha, "Frames of Cinematic History: The Tawa'if in Umrao Jan and Pakeezah," in *Narratives of Indian Cinema*, ed. Manju Jain (Delhi: Primus Books, 2009), 177. Anna Morcom similarly notes that public female dancing was incompatible with marriage and respectability because these dancers associated with men outside the traditional patriarchal circle of the father and the husband; Anna Morcom, *Illicit Worlds of Indian Dance: Cultures of Exclusion* (London: C. Hurst, 2013), 14.
112. *Nautanki* is a North Indian folk dance and theater performance tradition. Often in Hindi cinema, *nautanki* is reduced to a generic folk dance performance, frequently of a raunchy nature.
113. A narrative variation on this split is the double role, where an actress plays out the good girl/bad girl binary through two roles. For example, in *Anhonee* (K. A. Abbas, 1952), Nargis plays the courtesan, Mohini, and her good sister, Roop (the names signifying "seductress" and "beauty," respectively), while in *Raat aur Din* (Satyen Bose, 1967), she plays the schizophrenic housewife Varuna, whose alter ego, Peggy, is a bar dancer by night. In *Mausam* (Gulzar, 1976), the actress Sharmila Tagore plays an innocent village girl, Chanda, and her courtesan daughter, Kajli. In Chapter 5, I discuss the splitting of good dancing and bad dancing and hence virtue and immorality in *Sangeet* (K. Vishwanath, 1992), where Madhuri Dixit plays both the classical-dance-trained Nirmala and her daughter, the *nautanki* performer, Sangeeta.
114. Coorlawala, "The Sanskritized Body," 57.
115. Chakravarty, *National Identity in Indian Popular Cinema (1947–1987)*, 274.
116. Though Champabai is not a Muslim in *Sadhna*, the figuration of the cinematic *tawaif* and the *kotha* is inevitably Islamicate as it harks back to cultural traditions in princely states like Lucknow and Awadh, governed by Muslim rulers.
117. Janaki Nair, *Women and Law in Colonial India: A Social History* (Delhi: Kali for Women, published in collaboration with the National Law School of India University, Bangalore, 1996), 166.
118. Soneji, *Unfinished Gestures: Devadasis, Memory, and Modernity in South India*, 20.
119. Soneji, *Unfinished Gestures: Devadasis, Memory, and Modernity in South India*, 113.
120. Ashish Rajadhyaksha and Paul Willemen. *Encyclopedia of Indian Cinema* (London: British Film Institute, 1999), 350.
121. Ravi Vasudevan, "The Melodramatic Mode and the Commercial Hindi Cinema: Notes on Film History, Narrative, and Performance," *Screen* 30, no. 3 (1989): 50.
122. Vasudevan, "The Melodramatic Mode and the Commercial Hindi Cinema: Notes on Film History, Narrative, and Performance," 50.
123. Vasudevan, "The Melodramatic Mode and the Commercial Hindi Cinema: Notes on Film History, Narrative, and Performance," 50.
124. Veena Talwar Oldenburg, "Lifestyle as Resistance: The Case of the Courtesans of Lucknow," in *Contesting Power: Resistance and Everyday Social Relations in South*

Asia, ed. Douglas E. Haynes and Gyan Prakash (Berkeley: University of California Press, 1991), 48.
125. Oldenburg, "Lifestyle as Resistance: The Case of the Courtesans of Lucknow," 47.
126. Chakravarty, *National Identity in Indian Popular Cinema (1947–1987)*, 304.
127. Chakravarty notes that the film captures a particular ethos of the post-independence era when popular Hindi cinema entertained "the fantasy of the cinema as the agency that would transport a celebrated national artistic tradition to the wider population"; Chakravarty, *National Identity in Indian Popular Cinema (1947–1987)*, 46. Sangita Shresthova observes of the pastiche of classical and folk dance forms in Rosie's two production numbers in the film: "The director's choice to cut between several styles rather than focus on Rosie's mastery in a particular regionally specific dance form attempts to infuse the heroine with a pan-Indian identity, a feature that scholars have identified as a recurring feature in the immediate post-independence cinema"; Sangita Shresthova, "Dancing to an Indian Beat: 'Dola' Goes My Diasporic Heart," in *Global Bollywood: Travels of Hindi Song and Dance*, ed. Sangita Gopal and Sujata Moorti (Minneapolis: University of Minnesota Press, 2008), 249.
128. Majumdar, *Wanted Cultured Ladies Only!: Female Stardom and Cinema in India, 1930s–1950s*, 10.
129. Cinematic *tawaif*s repeatedly masquerade as or are mistaken for brides in films of the period, including *Sadhna*, *Roop Ki Rani Choron Ka Raja*, and *Sunghursh*, among others. While these masquerades are meant, within the narratives, to comment on the inaccessibility of domestic bliss for these women, they unmask as well the normative operations of gender performativity, unveiling the naturalized role for the woman as wife, daughter-in-law, and mother.
130. Amrit Srinivasan, "Why Sadir," http://www.india-seminar.com/2015/676/676_amrit_srinivasan.htm.
131. Oldenburg, "Lifestyle as Resistance: The Case of the Courtesans of Lucknow," 27–28.

Chapter 5

1. Dayanita Singh, "Saroj Khan: Masterji to the Stars," *Live Mint*, Dec 9, 2017, https://www.livemint.com/Leisure/IQfn0XyFZIgAlaW4J5QBzM/Saroj-Khan-Masterji-to-the-stars.html
2. Singh, "Saroj Khan."
3. The Khan-Dixit choreographer-star collaboration spans across *Awara Baap* (Sohanlal Kanwar, 1985), *Dayavan* (Feroz Khan, 1988) *Tezaab* (N. Chandra, 1988), *Ram Lakhan* (Subhash Ghai, 1989), *Tridev* (Rajiv Rai, 1989), *Dil* (Indra Kumar, 1990), *Sailaab* (Deepak Balraaj Vij, 1990), *Thanedaar* (Raj Sippy, 1990), *Beta* (Indra Kumar, 1992), *Khal Nayak* (Subhash Ghai, 1993), *Sahibaan* (Ramesh Talwar, 1993), *Anjaam* (Rahul Rawail, 1994), *Raja* (Indra Kumar, 1995), *Rajkumar* (Pankaj Parashar, 1996), *Prem Granth* (Rajiv Kapoor, 1996), *Koyla* (Rakesh Roshan, 1997), *Wajood* (N. Chandra, 1998), *Gaja Gamini* (M. F. Husain, 2000), *Devdas* (Sanjay Leela Bhansali, 2002), *Gulaab Gang* (Soumik Sen, 2014), and most recently, *Kalank* (Abhishek Varman, 2019).

4. Iyer, "Stardom Ke Peeche Kya Hai?/What Is behind the Stardom? Madhuri Dixit, the Production Number, and the Construction of the Female Star Text in 1990s Hindi Cinema," *Camera Obscura: Feminism, Culture, and Media Studies* 30, no. 3 (90) (2015): 129–159.
5. Saroj Khan choreographed Sridevi's spectacular dances in *Janbaaz* (Feroz Khan, 1986), *Nagina* (Harmesh Malhotra, 1986), *Mr. India* (Shekhar Kapur, 1987), *Chandni* (Yash Chopra, 1989), *Chaalbaaz* (Pankaj Parashar, 1989), *Nigahen* (Harmesh Malhotra, 1989), *Lamhe* (Yash Chopra, 1991), *Khuda Gawah* (Mukul Anand, 1992), and *Roop ki Rani Choron ka Raja* (Satish Kaushik, 1993).
6. While Sridevi is a central figure in defining dance performance in the 1980s and 1990s, this chapter focuses on the Khan-Dixit combine, as they were frequently cited as collaborators, worked on many more films together, and share a similar career trajectory on television in recent decades. Additionally, dance plays a slightly different role in the construction of Sridevi's star text than in Dixit's. Since many of Sridevi's early Hindi films (*Himmatwala* [K. Raghavendra Rao, 1983], *Tohfa* [K. Raghavendra Rao, 1984], etc.) were remakes of South Indian films, in which, by this period, more overtly sexual dancing was part of the performance idiom of the heroine, she was seen as an outsider in terms of her performance and movement vocabulary. Also, comedy plays a much more prominent role in Sridevi's star text than in Dixit's, and many of her famous dance numbers, such as "*Hawa Hawai*" (*Mr. India*, Shekhar Kapur, 1987) and "*Yeh ladki*" (*Chaalbaaz*, Pankaj Parasher, 1989) feature comic dance moves that structure her dancing persona differently. It is worth noting as well that, unlike Dixit's "comeback" film, *Aaja Nachle* (Anil Mehta, 2007), Sridevi's return to acting in *English Vinglish* (Gauri Shinde, 2012) was not dance-focused, and neither did she participate in dance shows on television.
7. Monika Mehta, *Censorship and Sexuality in Bombay Cinema* (Austin: University of Texas Press, 2011), 160.
8. Madhuri Dixit, interview by Usha Iyer, Mumbai, India, June 27, 2013.
9. Madhuri Dixit, interview by Usha Iyer, Mumbai, India, June 27, 2013.
10. *Baaje Payal*, "Baaje Payal: Episode on Madhuri Dixit." Doordarshan, New Delhi, 1998.
11. Nidhi Tuli, *The Saroj Khan Story* (PSBT India, 2012).
12. Tuli, *The Saroj Khan Story*.
13. "I Rehearsed Ek Do Teen for 16 days with Saroj Khan: Madhuri Dixit," *Mumbai Mirror*, August 17, 2012, https://timesofindia.indiatimes.com/entertainment/hindi/bollywood/news/I-rehearsed-Ek-Do-Teen-for-16-days-with-Saroj-Khan-Madhuri-Dixit/articleshow/15528020.cms
14. "I Rehearsed Ek Do Teen for 16 days with Saroj Khan: Madhuri Dixit," *Mumbai Mirror*.
15. Tuli, *The Saroj Khan Story*.
16. Roshmila Bhattacharya, "This Week That Year: 'Ek Do Teen' with Madhuri Dixit," *Mumbai Mirror*, May 18, 2019, https://timesofindia.indiatimes.com/entertainment/hindi/bollywood/news/this-week-that-year-ek-do-teen-with-madhuri-dixit/articleshow/69383802.cms

17. Rajul Hegde, "Picking Bollywood's Favourite Dancing Queens," Rediff.com, November 17, 2010, https://www.rediff.com/movies/slide-show/slide-show-1-saroj-khan-on-her-favourite-bollywood-dancers/20101117.htm#3
18. Jaskiran Kapoor, "The Grand MasterJi," *The Indian Express*, May 4, 2009, http://archive.indianexpress.com/news/the-grand-masterji/454030/0
19. http://madhurimagic.weebly.com/on-madhuri.html
20. For discussions of Dixit's contemporary role as dance guru and reality television judge, see Iyer, "Stardom Ke Peeche Kya Hai?," *Camera Obscura*, and Nandana Bose, *Madhuri Dixit* (London: Bloomsbury, 2019).
21. Tuli, *The Saroj Khan Story*.
22. Ananya Chatterjea, "Training in Indian Classical Dance: A Case Study," *Asian Theatre Journal* 13, no. 1 (1996): 79.
23. Neepa Majumdar, *Wanted Cultured Ladies Only!: Female Stardom and Cinema in India, 1930s–1950s* (Urbana: University of Illinois Press, 2009), 173.
24. Stuti Agarwal, "Madhuri Is Still Superb: Saroj Khan," *Times of India*, May 22, 2013.
25. http://madhurimagic.weebly.com/on-madhuri.html
26. See Chapter 2 for a discussion of body zones and the body-space-movement framework.
27. In her first film as independent choreographer, *Jo Jeeta Wohi Sikandar* (Mansoor Khan, 1992), Farah Khan created a signature vocabulary, with the actor Aamir Khan's slow-motion leaps in the song "*Pehla nasha*" showcasing the young heartthrob's body as a site for ocular, haptic pleasure. As he rises slowly in the tea gardens, plumped with the frisson of a first crush, his body is choreographed as solitary, spectacular, inviting our gaze. This choreography of the male body is significantly amplified in *Om Shanti Om*'s (Farah Khan, 2007) spectacular item number fifteen years later, "*Dard-e-disco*," featuring attention to particular body zones in her choreography of Shah Rukh Khan's moves.
28. Hegde, "Picking Bollywood's Favourite Dancing Queens."
29. Kunal Guha, "Choreographer Saroj Khan: Disappointed to See My Tamma Tamma Go to Dogs," *Ahmedabad Mirror*, December 10, 2017, https://ahmedabadmirror.indiatimes.com/others/sunday-read/choreographer-saroj-khan-disappointed-to-see-my-tamma-tamma-go-to-dogs/articleshow/62001506.cms?utm_source=contentofinterest&utm_medium=text&utm_campaign=cppst (accessed March 25, 2018).
30. Madhuri Dixit, interview by Usha Iyer, Mumbai, India, June 27, 2013.
31. Kareem Khubchandani, "Snakes on the Dance Floor: Bollywood, Gesture, and Gender," *The Velvet Light Trap* 77 (2016): 69–85, 74. See Khubchandani for an in-depth discussion of Dixit and Sridevi's stardom on the cusp of India's economic liberalization, the rise of the choreographer, and how these two dancing heroines' moves proliferate across a range of bodies and sexual identities, especially in *desi* gay dance clubs in the United States and in India.
32. Rupal Oza, *The Making of Neoliberal India: Nationalism, Gender, and the Paradoxes of Globalization* (New York: Routledge, 2012), 2.
33. Oza, *The Making of Neoliberal India*, 156.

34. Quoted in Bhawana Somaaya, Jigna Kothari, and Supriya Mandangarli, "Madhuri Dixit: Had I Really Done All Those Films?," Rediff.com, May 17, 2012, www.rediff.com/movies/slide-show/slide-show-1-birthday-special-revisiting-madhuri-dixit/20120515.htm#1
35. Sangita Gopal, *Conjugations: Marriage and Form in New Bollywood Cinema* (Chicago: University of Chicago Press, 2011), 41.
36. Oza, *The Making of Neoliberal India*, 31.
37. Rajeswari Sunder Rajan, *Real and Imagined Women: Gender, Culture and Postcolonialism* (New York: Routledge, 2003), 131.
38. Bose, *Madhuri Dixit*.
39. Madhuri Dixit, interview by Usha Iyer, Mumbai, India, June 27, 2013.
40. Mazumdar, *Bombay Cinema*, 90.
41. "Baaje Payal: Episode on Madhuri Dixit," 1998.
42. "Baaje Payal: Episode on Madhuri Dixit," 1998.
43. Patsy Nair, "Saroj Khan: Actresses Now Don't Like to Work with Me," Rediff.com, March 29, 2012, https://www.rediff.com/movies/slide-show/slide-show-1-interview-with-choreographer-saroj-khan/20120329.htm.
44. Partha Chatterjee, "A Bit of Song and Dance," in *Frames of Mind*, ed. Aruna Vasudev (New Delhi: UBS, 1995), 215.
45. Madhuri Dixit, interview by Usha Iyer, Mumbai, India, June 27, 2013.
46. For an analysis of how the narrative attempts to rein in the sexual charge of this number, see Mehta, *Censorship and Sexuality*.
47. A significant number of Dixit's most famous production numbers—including "*Ek do teen*," "*Hum ko aaj kal hai intezaar*," "*Main tumhari hoon*" (Sangeet), "*Main Kolhapur se aayi hoon*" (Anjaam), and "*Que sera sera*" (Pukar)—are isolated as stage performances.
48. Examples include "*Dhak dhak karne laga*," "*Main Kolhapur se aayi hoon*," and "*Badan juda hote hain*" (*Koyla*, Rakesh Roshan, 1997).
49. This steady displacement of Dixit's character into the space of fantasy is self-reflexively referenced in Sudhir Mishra's *Dharavi* (1992), where Dixit plays herself, as the superstar "dreamgirl" of the impoverished taxi-driver Rajkaran's (Om Puri) fantasies. In an "art" film marked by realist codes (i.e., featuring no song-and-dance sequences, set in the "real," gritty space of the slum), Dixit's star body stands in for the space of fantasy, and the phantasmic attractions of commercial cinema, including its fantastical dancing bodies.
50. See Mehta, *Censorship and Sexuality in BombayCinema* and Bose, *Madhuri Dixit*.
51. Tuli, *The Saroj Khan Story*.
52. http://madhurimagic.weebly.com/on-madhuri.html
53. Tuli, *The Saroj Khan Story*.
54. Adrienne McLean, *Being Rita Hayworth: Labor, Identity, and Hollywood Stardom* (New Brunswick, NJ: Rutgers University Press, 2004), 142.
55. Laura Mulvey, "Visual Pleasure and Narrative Cinema," in *Film Theory and Criticism: Introductory Readings*, ed. Leo Braudy and Marshall Cohen (New York: Oxford University Press, 1999), 837. Mulvey has famously argued that

mainstream popular cinema highlights a woman's "to-be-looked-at-ness," and in fact "builds the way she is to be looked at into the spectacle itself" (837). While Mulvey acknowledges the potential of spectacle to disrupt narrative coherence and threaten the stability of the narrative system, her emphasis is on the narrative's containment of spectacle through the mechanisms of closure at the end of the film that reassert the status quo.

56. Mehta, *Censorship and Sexuality*, 167.
57. Mulvey. "Visual Pleasure and Narrative Cinema," 838.
58. Mehta, *Censorship and Sexuality*, 167.
59. McLean, *Being Rita Hayworth*, 127.
60. André Lepecki, "The Body as Archive: Will to Re-enact and the Afterlives of Dances," *Dance Research Journal* 42, no. 2 (2010): 28–48, 37.
61. Lepecki, "The Body as Archive," 39.

Epilogue

1. Bollywood dance parties, DJ nights, stage shows, and dance classes across Europe, the United States, and other parts of the world (where Hindi cinema did not traditionally have an audience earlier) are testimony to the predominance of dance in the dissemination of Bollywood.
2. *Tamasha* is a folk theater form from Maharashtra that intersperses dialogue with the dance form *Lavani*, characterized by erotic themes and sensuous dance moves. Bar dancing refers to erotic dance performance to popular film songs by "bargirls" in "dance bars" in urban and semi-urban centers in India. Dance bars, as the name suggests, serve alcohol and feature dancing bargirls. The audience for *Tamasha* and bar dancing is predominantly male. For more on bar dancers, see Morcom, *Illicit Worlds of Indian Dance: Cultures of Exclusion*.
3. Nasreen Rehman with Farah Khan, "Dance in Bombay Cinema," *Marg* 64, no. 4 (June 2013): 65–77, 66.
4. For a thick description of the production ecology of the item number, see Silpa Mukherjee, "Behind the Green Door: Unpacking the Item Number and Its Ecology," BioScope 9, no. 2 (2019): 1–25.
5. Nidhi Tuli, *The Saroj Khan Story* (PSBT India, 2012).
6. Anjana Rajan, "Dance Me No Nonsense," *The Hindu*, March 4, 2010, https://www.thehindu.com/arts/Dance-me-no-nonsense/article16483514.ece.
7. The relationship of Bollywood dance to new body cultures centered on fitness is evident in the immense global popularity of aerobics-style Bollywood dance classes that focus on weight-loss, body-toning, and the like, rather than on learning specific dance skills. See Sangita Shresthova, *Is It All about Hips?: Around the World with Bollywood Dance* (New Delhi: Sage Publishing India, 2011).
8. Neepa Majumdar, *Wanted Cultured Ladies Only!: Female Stardom and Cinema in India, 1930s–1950s* (Urbana: University of Illinois Press, 2009),180.
9. Rehman with Farah Khan, "Dance in Bombay Cinema," 66.

10. Debanjali Biswas. "Whose Dance Is It Anyway?" in *Dancing Mosaic: Issues on Dance Hybridity*, ed. Mohd Anis Md Nor. (Kuala Lumpur: Cultural Centre, University of Malaya and National Department for Culture and Arts, 2012), 194, 197.
11. See discussions of *darshan*, frontality, tableau aesthetics, Ravi Varma, D. G. Phalke, and turn-of-century popular visual culture in Ashish Rajadhyaksha, "The Phalke Era: Conflict of Traditional Form and Modern Technology," in *Interrogating Modernity: Culture and Colonialism in India*, ed. Tejaswini Niranjana, P Sudhir, and Vivek Dhareshwar (Calcutta: Seagull Books, 1993), 47–82; Ravi Vasudevan, *The Melodramatic Public Film Form and Spectatorship in Indian Cinema* (New Delhi: Permanent Black, 2010); Kajri Jain, *Gods in the Bazaar: The Economies of Indian Calendar Art* (Durham, NC: Duke University Press, 2007).
12. See Sangita Gopal and Sujata Moorti, eds., *Global Bollywood: Travels of Hindi Song and Dance* (Minneapolis: University of Minnesota Press, 2008), 25; Kathryn Hansen, "Mapping Melodrama: Global Theatrical Circuits, Parsi Theater, and the Rise of the Social," BioScope 7, no. 1 (2016): 1–30; Madhuja Mukherjee, "The Architecture of Songs and Music: Soundmarks of Bollywood, a Popular Form and Its Emergent Texts," *Screen Sound* 3 (2012): 13.
13. Anjali Arondekar, "In the Absence of Reliable Ghosts: Sexuality, Historiography, South Asia," *Differences* 25, no. 3 (2014): 100.
14. Davesh Soneji, *Unfinished Gestures: Devadasis, Memory, and Modernity in South India* (Chicago: University of Chicago Press, 2012), 11.

Glossary

antara See *mukhda*.

bai or ***baiji*** The common North Indian appellation for professional female musicians and dancers, who were often courtesans that enjoyed princely patronage.

Bhangra A vigorous Punjabi folk dance performed mainly by men.

Bharatanatyam A South Indian classical dance form, among the first to be canonized as "classical" by the Sangeet Natak Akademi (The National Academy for Music, Dance, and Drama). In addition to a vast gestural vocabulary, *Bharatanatyam* is characterized by the *araimandi* (half-squat) stance, and the execution of geometric movements in a given time cycle.

Bollywood Following Madhava Prasad and Ashish Rajadhyaksha's descriptions of the term, in this book Bollywood stands for a specific mode of popular Hindi cinema that developed from the 1990s, characterized by, among other things, family melodramas, big-budget, spectacular song-and-dance sequences, characters who often live outside of India, a conscious display of multinational brand names, and an unmistakable address to a diasporic audience. Following closely on the heels of economic deregulation in India in 1991, Bollywood proceeded to trigger a larger entertainment complex that now includes television, music, advertising, fashion, and new media.

devi The literal English translation of *devi* from Sanskrit/Hindi is "goddess." However, it refers more broadly to a virtuous, respectable, usually married woman.

item girl Female performer in dance numbers known as "item numbers," which bear no relation to the narrative but are inserted purely as spectacular attractions.

Kathak A North Indian classical dance form, one of the eight dance forms canonized as "classical" by the Sangeet Natak Akademi (The National Academy for Music, Dance, and Drama). In addition to a vast gestural vocabulary, it is marked by elaborate footwork and spins of the body.

Kathakali A South Indian classical dance form performed in the state of Kerala, and among the eight canonized classical dance forms. It is predominantly performed by men, and employs specific codes of costume and make-up to depict mythological characters.

Koli A folk dance form performed by fishing communities in Maharashtra.

kotha The performance space of the Islamicate *tawaif*, or courtesan, the *kotha* is a salon that takes on particular architectural features in popular Hindi cinema and is marked by a particular organization of performer and audience.

Lavani A folk dance form from Maharashtra that is characterized by erotic themes and sensuous dance moves.

Manipuri A canonized classical dance form from the North-Eastern state of Manipur that predominantly depicts religious themes, especially the *Raas Lila* or the dance of Krishna and Radha.

Mehfil A performance of poetry, music, or dance before a small, intimate audience.

Mohiniattam Literally translated as "the dance of the enchantress," *Mohiniattam* is a classical dance form from Kerala, performed mainly by women, and marked by fluid, graceful movements.

Mujra A *Kathak*-based dance performance by *tawaif*(s) in the space of the *kotha*. This form was created and popularized in the nineteenth century by *nautch* girls (dancing girls) patronized by Mughal and other noblemen and English soldiers, among others.

mukhda and *antara* In Hindi film songs, the opening stanza is referred to as the *mukhda*. It is the introductory and principal phrase of the composition that, like the chorus in Western music, is repeated after every following stanza. Each of these stanzas, which form the body of the song, is known as the *antara*. The *mukhda* and *antara* are sung by one or more characters, and are often interspersed with instrumental sections.

nattuvanar The male hereditary dance guru, conductor, and choreographer of the *Bharatanatyam* dance form.

nautanki A North Indian folk dance and theater performance tradition. Often in Hindi cinema, *nautanki* is reduced to a generic folk dance performance, frequently of a raunchy nature.

nautch An Anglicized pronunciation and transliteration of the Hindustani word for dance, *naach*. *Nautch* had a pejorative intent and was specially used to designate the dance of the *tawaif*s and the *devadasi*s.

Odissi A canonized classical dance form originating from the state of Odisha in eastern India.

Tamasha A folk theater form from Maharashtra that intersperses dialogue with the dance form, *Lavani*, which is characterized by erotic themes and sensuous dance moves.

Thumri A category of semi-classical music within the North Indian Hindustani classical music system, in which short romantic or religious compositions are set to music. In the nineteenth century, Thumris were predominantly sung by courtesans and were often accompanied by dance.

vamp From the late 1950s to the 1980s, the female figure of the vamp functioned as the archetypal performer of the raunchy song-and-dance sequence in Hindi cinema. As part of a parallel "star system," one with significantly less financial power and social acceptance than that of the heroine, vamps such as Helen, Kalpana Iyer, Bindu, Aruna Irani, and Jayshree T, among others, acted as gangsters' molls, whose participation in a film was often restricted to a "cabaret" performance in a casino/bar/nightclub. The kind of dance they performed (including costume and makeup) marked them as Westernized outsiders, characterized by an unrestrained sexuality, the opposite of the heroine, who was the site of virtue and thus of "Indianness."

Index

For the benefit of digital users, indexed terms that span two pages (e.g., 52–53) may, on occasion, appear on only one of those pages.

Aadmi (1939), 128–29, 171–72
Aasha (1957), 157–58
abhinaya, 1, 9–11, 82–83, 86–87, 155–56, 168, 193–94, *See also* facial expression and movement
Abhinaya (1938), 91–92, 128
Abhinaya Darpana (performance treatise), 9–11, 22, 78–79, 82–85, 164–65, 239n93
Abodh (1984), 183
Abraham, Esther Victoria, 114–15
Abraham, John, 201–2
acting, kinesics of, 162–68
acting/dancing binaries, 162–68, *See also* dancer-actresses
Adshead-Lansdale, Janet, 44–45
Affair in Trinidad (1952), 46
affect
  Abhinaya Darpana on, 165–66
  body-space-movement framework and, 67
  body zones and, 83–86
  cabaret numbers and, 74–75
  dance musicalization and, 11–12, 28, 143–44
  dance training and, 9–11
  as embodied phenomena, 12–13, 46–47, 129–31
  narrative numbers and, 35
  participatory spectatorship and, 44–45
Ajoorie, Srimati. *See* Azurie
alankara (ornamentation), 39–40
Ali, Naushad, 17–18, 119–20
Alibaba (1937), 63–64, 64f, 92–93, 120–24, 123f, 129–31
Alibabavum 40 Thirudargalum (1956), 157–58

Allen, Richard, 68, 128–29
All India Radio ban, 147–48
Altman, Rick, 45–46, 47–48
Aman, Zeenat, 189–90
Amonkar, Kishori, 206
Amrapali (1966), 48–49, 140–41, 157–58, 210n11, 222n53
Anand, Chetan, 76–77
Anand, Dev, 202–3
Anand, Vijay, 74–75, 158–59, 161–62
Andrew, Nell, 14–15
angasuddha, 51–52
Anglo-Indian community, 88–89
Annabelle the Dancer (1895), 14–15
anti-*nautch* movement, 15–17, 21, 70–71, 97, 98–99, 125–26, 128–29, 176
architectures of public intimacy
  Alibaba and, 122–23
  background dancers and, 88–89
  cabaret assemblage and, 71–77
  Court Dancer and, 126–27
  kotha spaces and, 68–71
  spatio-corporeal matrix and, 65–68
Arondekar, Anjali, 143–44
art cinema, 213n55
Arundale, Rukmini Devi
  dance reform and, 94–95, 99–101, 118–19
  "devi" renaming and, 170–71
  gestural genealogies and, 23
  Kalakshetra Foundation of, 105, 146–47, 151
Astaire, Fred, 35–36, 41–42, 47–48
Athaiya, Bhanu, 140–41
authorship
  Azurie and, 136
  Bose and, 93–94, 136

authorship (cont)
   dancer-actresses and, 48–50
   Helen and, 210n10
   Khan and Dixit and, 187–88, 196–97
   star bodies and, 46–47, 64–65
   Vyjayanthimala and, 48–49, 166–67
AVM Productions, 152
Awara (1951), 72*f*, 140–41, 231n118
"Aye hai dilruba," 143–44, 176
Ayodhyecha Raja (1932), 17–18
Azurie, 7–8, 13–14
   authorship and, 136
   in *Bal Hatiya*, 117*f*
   in *Bhen ka Prem*, 113*f*
   career and star text of, 93–94, 112–19, 134–36
   in *Chandrasena*, 116–18, 157–58
   as dance columnist, 118–19
   movement vocabulary lineages and, 4–5, 230n106
   and post-Partition dance advocacy, 134–36
   in *Sonar Sansar*, 115*f*
   spectacle and, 116–18
   transnationalism and, 23, 119–20

Babi, Parveen, 189–90
Bachchan, Amitabh, 199–200, 210–11n17, 216n31
background dancers and spatial practices, 86–90, 116–18, 122–23, 147, 179–80
background songs, 32–33
backstage musicals, 29–30
bai and *devi*, 162–68, 171–72
baijis, 88–89, 147–48, 206
"Bakad bam bam baaje damru," 48–49, 51–54, 80–81
Bal Hatiya (1935), 116, 117*f*
Baran, Timir, 124–25, 132
bazaar cinema, 93–94, 114–15, 119–20, 129–31
Beaster-Jones, Jayson: *Music in Contemporary Indian Film*, 46
beat and rhythm
   Alibaba and, 121–22
   choreomusicology and, 51–54
   in "Piya tu ab toh aa ja," 60
   song picturization and, 46

Begum, Shehzadi, 137, 234n173
belly dancing, 1–3, 19, 82, 93–94, 210n10
Benjamin, Herman, 4–6, 88*f*
bhadralok, 105–7, 124, 134, 227n65, 228n73
bhadramahila
   Court Dancer and, 124–25
   "dance social" genre and, 129–31, 132
   financial independence and, 134
   respectability discourses and, 105–9
   song booklets and, 116
Bhagwan, Master, 211n17, 216n31
bhakti (devotional) dance elements, 99–100, 125–26
Bhangra, 19, 60–61, 219n4
Bhansali, Sanjay Leela, 196–97
Bharatanatyam, 209n2, 211n19
   Azurie and, 135
   body codifications of, 80–82
   film dance influence of, 19
   gentrification and, 78–79, 99–101, 145, 146–47, 152
   Pavolova and, 99
   Rehman (Waheeda) and, 146–47, 151, 155–56
   rhythm and, 53–54
   Tamil cinema and, 236n15
   training in, 105, 145
   Vyjayanthimala and, 9–11, 23–24, 35, 46–47, 51–52, 64–65, 78–79, 141–43, 149, 151, 153, 155–56
Bharathiar, Subramania, 152
Bhaskar, Ira, 68, 128–29
Bhatkande, V. N., 96–97
Bhattacharjya, Nilanjana, 103–5
bhava, 82, 164–65, *See also* affect
Bhosle, Asha, 4–5, 56–57, 59–60, 71–72, 143–44, 206, 235n11
Bhowmick, Kaushik, 109–10, 229n86
Bilwamangal (1919), 15, 16*f*
Biswas, Anil, 147–48
body-space-movement framework, 22
   cabaret numbers and, 71–77
   classical and folk dance in, 78–83
   Khan and Dixit and, 188–90, 198
   kotha spaces and, 69
   reading dance through, 60–65
body zones, 22
   acting/dancing binaries and, 162–63
   affect and, 83–86

INDEX 255

Bollywood, 239n100
  background dancers in, 89
  cinematic past and, 202–4
  item numbers in, 199–202
  male dancers in, 216n31
  spatio-corporeal influences on, 60
  stardom and fandom in, 203–5, 246n1
"*Bol ri kathputli dori*," 35–36, 165–66, 173–75
bols (rhythmic enunciations), 46–47, 53–54
Boogie Woogie (television show), 205
Booth, Gregory, 17–18, 45–46
Bose, Debaki, 114–15
Bose, Modhu
  Aamar Jeeban (My Life), 224n15
  Alibaba and, 120–22
  Calcutta Amateur Players and, 90
  Court Dancer and, 91–92, 126–27
  on Sadhona's stardom, 132–34, 175–76
  social reform discourses and, 111–12
  on Wadia Movietone, 124–25
Bose, Sadhona, 7–8, 13–14
  authorship and, 93–94, 136
  background of, 96, 98
  body-space-movement framework and, 63–64
  class and, 91–93, 94–95, 110–11, 137–38
  "dance social" genre and, 128–32
  female mobility and, 132–35, 137
  film performances by
    Abhinaya (1938), 91–92, 128
    Alibaba, 120–24, 157–58
    Court Dancer, 39–40, 91–93, 98, 124–26, 128, 133, 157–58
    Kumkum the Dancer, 63–64, 91–92, 128, 130f, 131–32
    Shankar Parvati, 108, 131, 133
  Kathak and, 96, 98, 110–11
  Manipuri and, 63–64, 96, 110–11, 211n19
  nationalism and, 112, 136, 137–38
  as pioneer, 94–95
  respectability discourses and, 78–79, 110–11, 112, 137–38
  Shipir Atmakatha (*Autobiography of an Artist*), 94, 118–19, 224n15
  song booklets and, 116
  star text of, 91–93, 94–95, 120–21, 122, 129–32, 133–35, 136, 223n4, 233n157
  transnationalism and, 23
Brahmo Samaj, 96, 227n65 229n19,
Brannigan, Erin, 5–6, 9–11, 49–50, 218n69
Brown, Carol, 65–66, 67–68
Bunty aur Babli (2005), 66–67, 201–2
Burman, R. D., 60
Burman, Sachin Dev, 55–56, 96

cabaret numbers, 22, 59–60, 68, 69–70, 71–77, 88–89, 144,
  See also kotha
Calcutta Amateur Players (C.A.P.), 90, 112, 120–21, 131
camera movement
  Alibaba and, 120–21, 122–23
  cabaret numbers and, 75–76
  Court Dancer and, 126–27
  in *Dr. Vidya*, 139
  Guide and, 159–60
  kotha spaces and, 69–70
Caravan (1971), 59
Carnatic music, 145, 152, 209n1
Carter, Alexandra, 66–67
caste and class
  Alibaba and, 124
  anxieties of gender and, 170–71
  Azurie and, 93–94
  Bose and, 91–93, 94–95, 110–11, 137–38
  Court Dancer and, 129–31
  dance reform and, 70–71, 94–95, 98–99, 100–3, 105, 138, 149, 164–65
  "dance social" genre and, 128–31
  dance training and, 151
  Vyjayanthimala and, 141–43, 145
censorship
  All India Radio ban and, 147–48
  Azurie and, 116–18
  Dixit and Khan and, 24, 182–83, 191–92, 195, 196–97
  film dance and, 110–11
  heroine-vamp binary and, 24–25
cha-cha-cha, 19, 82
Chakraborty, Mithun, 39–40, 205, 210–11n17, 216n31

256   INDEX

Chakravarty, Sumita, 171–72, 235n13, 242n127
Chandra, N., 184, 185–86
Chandrasena (1935), 116–18
"Chane ke khet mein," 186, 188–89, 194–95
Chatterjea, Ananya, 164–65, 187
Chatterjee, Partha, (historian) 170, 224n14
Chatterjee, Partha, (film critic) 41, 194
Chettiar, A. V. Meiyappa, 151, 152
"Chhi Chhi Etta Janjal," 120–21
Chitrapanji, 112–14, 118–19
"Choli ke peeche kya hai," 27–28, 188–89, 191–92, 196–98
Chopra, B. R., 171–72
Chopra, Priyanka, 202–3
choreography
  body-space-movement framework and, 61–62, 65–66, 67–68
  Bollywood and visibility of, 204
  film as phenomenon of, 61–62, 180–81
  Khan and Dixit's articulation of, 181–83, 190–91
  movement vocabularies from, 185–86
  stardom and, 8–9
choreomusicking body
  corporeal history through, 208
  defined, 4–5, 11–12, 22, 54–55
  Khan and, 187–88
  labor and, 11–12, 23–24, 143–44, 153–54
  production numbers and, 54, 59, 141–43, 161, 162
  rehearsal and, 185–86
  Vyjayanthimala and, 141–44
cine-choreography, 60, 73–74, 75–76, 125–27, 161–62, 187–88, 196–97, 218n69, *See also* choreography
cinematography
  aural effects of, 53–54
  body-space-movement framework and, 61–62
  Helen on, 73
  item numbers and, 201
  kotha spaces and, 69–70
  spectacle and, 31–32
  spectatorship and, 44–45
classical dance
  Alibaba and, 124
  body-space-movement framework and, 62–63, 78–83
  canonization of, 70–71, 94–95, 98–99, 138, 149, 164–65
  Court Dancer and, 91–92, 126–27
  film dance training compared to, 186–87
  on group formations, 86–87
  Hindi cinema's representation of, 80–81, 85, 151–62, 165–66
  middle-class appropriation of, 24–25, 78–81, 99–105, 144–45, 206
  physical skill in, 39–40
  Rehman (Waheeda) and, 146–47, 151, 155–56
  Sangeet Natak Akademi seminars and, 144–51
  Vyjayanthimala and, 48–49, 152–53, 165–66
co-choreography, 7–9, 23, 24, 94–95, 139, 181–83
Cohan, Steven, 35–36, 47–48
color film, 157–58
Coomaraswamy, A. K., 78–79
Coorlawala, Uttara Asha, 79, 100–1, 170–71
corporeal histories, 9–14
  Azurie and Bose and, 137–38
  body-space-movement framework and, 62–63
  co-choreography of, 7–9
  Dixit and Khan, 181–82
  occluded figures and, 119–20, 137
  rehearsals/training and, 186–87
  Vyjayanthimala and Helen and, 141–44
costume
  classical dance representations and, 80–81, 100–1, 222n53
  dancer-actress influence on, 140–43
  spectacle and, 31–32, 122–23
Court Dancer (1941), 91–93
  Bose and, 63–64, 98, 124–26, 128, 133, 157–58
  cultural nationalism and, 124–27
  "dance social"- genre and, 128–29
  images from, 65*f*, 92*f*, 125*f*, 127*f*

INDEX 257

Manipuri in, 39–40, 63–64, 85, 125–26, 232n137
Tagore and, 131
courtesan films, 68–71, 111, 144, 209n6, 235n13, 237n56
Cuckoo, 71–72, 72f, 137, 140–41, 216n33

Daag (1952), 33–34
Dance India Dance (television show), 205
dance musicalization, 4–5
  affect and, 11–12, 28, 143–44
  Bollywood and, 204
  corporeal history through, 208
  defined, 11–12, 22, 46–47
  multisensory affects and, 143–44
  production numbers and, 46–48
  star texts and, 132
dancer-actresses, 6–7
  acting/dancing binaries and, 164, 165–66
  authorship and, 48–50
  bai/devi tensions in, 176
  choreomusicology and, 50–52, 55–57
  dance musicalization and, 22, 28, 46–47, 48–50
  "dance social" genre and, 128–31, 133
  gentrification of, 78–79, 105–9, 129–31
  Khan and, 181–83
  melodrama of dance reform and, 168–70
  modes of production influenced by, 46–47, 48–49, 140–41
  pure dance sequences and, 39–40
  representational logics altered by, 165–67
  sounding body of, 56–57
  South Indian identity and, 153–54
  spatial production and, 64–65
  training of, 138, 165–66
"dance social" genre, 128–32
  Bose and, 92–93, 112, 126–27
  cosmopolitan mobilities and, 132–36
  Court Dancer and, 124–27
  melodrama of dance reform and, 168–70
dancing bodies
  background dancers and, 86, 90
  body-space-movement framework for, 60–61, 63–64

  choreomusicology and, 50–55, 56–57
  classical forms and, 81
  dance musicalization and, 47–48
  materiality of, 85–86
  narrative modes interrupted by, 31–32, 131
  participatory spectatorship and, 44–45
  production numbers and, 35–38
  song picturization and, 28
dancing texts, 44–45
dancing women. *See also* female mobility
  affect and, 160
  as agents of spectacle, 40–41
  as background dancers, 88–89
  body zones and, 83
  co-choreography among, 140–41
  cosmopolitanism and, 132–36
  Kathak history and, 70–71
  labor and, 161
  public vs. private spheres and, 168–70, 176, 240–41n111
  social reform discourses and, 114–15, 129–31, 168–70, 176
  spatial configurations for, 38–39, 65–66, 67
Dandiya, 19
De, Esha Niyogi, 102–3
Debi, Chhaya, 110–11
Denishawn Dance Company, 98–99, 103–5
Desai, Leela, 110–11, 233n155
Desmond, Jane, 1–3
devadasis, 211n20, 224n16
  choreomusicking body and, 143–44
  marginalization of, 7–8, 96–97, 99, 100–1, 145, 147–48, 151, 206
  melodrama of dance reform and, 170
  nattuvanars and, 151
  performance repertoire of, 100–1, 207
  upper-class appropriation of, 19–20, 23, 70–71, 98–99, 103–5, 126, 152
Devdas (1955), 140–41, 173–75, 194–95, 196–97
Devi, Janaki, 46–47, 153–54
Devi, Naina, 96
Devi, Ragini, 207
Devi, Sitara, 19–20, 216n33
Devi, Vasundhara, 141–43

Devi, Yadugiri, 141–44, 234–35n4
"*Dhak dhak karne laga*," 182–83, 188–89, 192–93, 195, 196–97
Dickson Experimental Sound Film (1894), 14–15
Dil Chahta Hai (2001), 202
Diler Jigar (1931), 15–18
Dil Toh Pagal Hai (1997), 189–90
Disco Dancer (1982), 39–40
Dixit, Madhuri, 7–8
  background dancers and, 90
  co-choreography and Khan, 8–9, 24, 179–83, 184, 185–88, 193–94
  facial expressions of, 84–85
  film performances by
    Abodh, 183
    "*Choli ke peeche kya hai*," 27–28, 194–95, 197–98
    Dharavi, 245n49
    Dil toh Pagal Hai, 39–40
    "*Ek do teen*," 42, 65–67, 183–85, 192, 194, 204
    Hum Aapke Hain Kaun, 192–93
    Khal Nayak, 194–95
  influence of, 8–9, 24
  Kathak and, 193–94, 211n19
  "Masterji Series" on, 179–81, 180f
  media mobilization, 13–14, 205
  spectatorship and, 44–45
Dodds, Sherril, 50–51
domesticity. See household and domesticity
Don (1978), 199–200, 202
Don: The Chase Begins Again (2006), 199–200, 202
Dr. Vidya (1962), 139–44, 140f, 181–82
dual-star texts, 18–19, 21, 27–28, 55–56, 187–88, See also stardom and star texts
Dutt, Geeta, 71–72, 143–44
Dutt, Guru, 9–11, 155–57, 216n38
Dutt, Sanjay, 196–97
Dutt, Sunil, 33
Dyer, Richard, 45–46

economic deregulation, 21, 198, 239n100
Edison Manufacturing Company, 14–15
editing
  Alibaba and, 120–21, 122–23
  American film musicals and, 45–46
  body-space-movement framework for, 61–62
  item numbers and, 201
  spectacle and, 31–32
  spectatorship and, 44–45
"*Ek do teen*"
  background dancers of, 90
  Dixit and, 183–85, 192, 194
  gendered spaces of, 42, 62–63
  spatio-corporeal matrix of, 65–66
  vamp-heroine figuration and, 65–67, 192
embodiment and acting, 164–66
Erdman, Joan, 98–99, 100–1

facial expression and movement
  acting/dancing binaries and, 162–63
  background dancers and, 86–87
  classical dance and, 82–85
  dancing bodies and, 31–32
  Dixit and, 193–94
  narrative numbers and, 35
  in "*Piya tu ab toh aa ja*," 59
  Rehman and, 155–56
Fairbanks, Douglas, 15–17
Faiz, Faiz Ahmed, 135
fandom, 115–16, 203–5
fashion and fashion models, 66–67
Fearless Nadia, 91–92, 137–38
female mobility, 6–7
  anxieties over, 24–25
  Azurie and, 119–20, 134–37
  Bose and, 132–35, 137
  dance revival and, 103–5
  Khan and, 195–96
  pioneers of, 94–95
femininity See also dancing women; heroines
  Aman and Babi and, 189–90
  Dixit and Khan producing, 182–83, 190, 192, 195–96
  economic globalization and, 191–92
  Mangeshkar and, 219n80
Feuer, Jane, 215n26
film dance. See also Hindi cinema; *specific films and performers*
  attitudes toward, 19–25
  experimentation in, 82

INDEX 259

narrative modes interrupted by, 31–32, 46
participatory spectatorship and, 44–45
spatio-corporeal formations and, 65–68
filmIndia, 118–19
folk dance
background dancers and, 86–87
body-space-movement framework and, 60–61, 62–63, 78–83
Hindi cinema's representation of, 80–81, 147
Republic Day parades and, 146–47
Sanskritization and, 79–80, 102–3
Foster, Susan, 44–45, 232n143
Foucault, Michel, 76–77
Francopolo, T., 96
Fuller, Loie, 14–15, 210n16
Fyzee-Rahamin, Atiya, 112–14

Garba, 19, 102–3
Garland, Judy, 18–19, 85
gaze
in cabaret numbers, 75–76
in narrative vs. production numbers, 35–36, 38–39, 197–98
gender, 6–7
authorship and, 94–95
critical attitudes to film dance and, 21, 41
dance-centered perspective on, 31–32
male/female performance paradigms, 40–42
nationalist dichotomies of, 170
production numbers and, 36–38, 40–42
gesture and gestural genealogies
in *Abhinaya Darpana*, 83
aural dimension of, 53–54
Azurie and, 119–20, 137
body-space-movement framework for, 60–62, 63
from classical and folk dance, 78–83, 86–87, 166–67, 207
co-choreography and, 9
Khan and, 198
in *kotha* spaces, 68–69
methodology in reading, 9–12, 22
in narrative numbers, 34–35

Ghai, Subhash, 185–86, 196–97
ghar/bahir dichotomies, 170–71
Ghoomar, 19
Gidda, 46–47, 153–54
globalization, 191–92, 198
Gohar, Miss, 15
Gopal, Ram, 119–20, 138, 231n116
Gopal, Sangita, 30–31, 38–39, 46, 192
Gopalan, Lalitha, 29–30
Grosz, Elizabeth, 76–77
Gueizelor, Anna Marie. *See* Azurie
Guide (1965), 33–34, 34f, 37f, 158–61, 175–76
Guido, Laurent, 14–15
Gunning, Tom, 14–15, 210n16

Hansen, Kathryn, 131, 232n142
Hassan, Nazia, 189–90
hasta mudras (hand gestures), 85, 103, 126–27, 127f, *See also* gesture and gestural genealogies
Hayworth, Rita, 46, 49–50
Helen, 7–8, 22
authorship and, 210n10
Azurie and, 137
cabaret numbers and, 71–75
film performances by
"*Aye hai dilruba*," 176
Don, 199–200, 202
Dr. Vidya, 139–44, 140f
Gumnaam, 77f
"*Kar le pyaar*," 73–74
"*Muqabla humse na karo*," 1–7, 2f, 8–9
"*O Haseena Zulfanwaali*," 140–41
"*Piya tu ab toh aa ja*," 59–60, 73, 75–76
Smuggler, 74f
Teesri Manzil, 157–58
music influenced by, 56–57
heroine
Bose and, 128–29
cabaret numbers and, 76–77
classical dance and, 151–62
critical attitudes toward, 21
"dance social" genre and, 128–29
Dixit and Khan's co-choreography of, 24, 182–83, 184–85, 187–88, 190–91, 195, 197–98

260 INDEX

heroine (cont)
  "*Ek do teen*" and, 42, 65–67
  melodrama of dance reform and, 168–70, 175–76
  spatial configurations for, 38–39, 62–63, 67
heterotopias, 76–77
Himmatwala (1983), 182–83
Hindi cinema. *See also* song-and-dance sequences
  acting traditions and, 164–65
  aesthetic development of, 29
  attitudes toward dance in, 19–25
  bhadramahila's initiation into, 109–12
  body's centrality to, 32–33
  classical dance representations in, 80–81, 85, 151–62, 165–66
  female star text in, 41–42
  heterogeneous mode of manufacture of, 43–44
  respectability discourses in, 109–12, 116
  Sangeet Natak Akademi seminars on, 147–48
  Sanskritization and, 78–79
  South Indian dancing body and, 153–54
  spaces for staging of dance in, 61
Hindustani music, 54–55, 96–97, 99, 143–44
Hiralal, B., 8–9, 141–43, 147, 153–54, 155–56, 160, 161, 186–87
Hollywood
  Alibaba and, 124
  feminine spectacle in, 40–41
  group choreography in, 86–87
  Hindi cinema influenced by, 19, 88–89, 124
  male dancers in, 41–42
  playback systems and, 18–19
  song-and-dance sequences in, 29, 45–46, 47–48
  sound film and, 17–18
"*Hothon mein aisi baat*," 27–28, 46–47, 161–62
household and domesticity
  bai/devi tensions in, 176
  dancing women and, 168–70, 176, 240–41n111

  in melodrama of dance reform, 171–76
  nationalism and, 170
Hum Aapke Hain Kaun (1994), 192–93
"*Humko aaj kal hai intezaar*," 188–89, 196–97
Hussain, M. F., 191–92

idiogest, 9–11
image-sound hierarchy, 45–46, 55–56
Indian Cinematograph Committee (ICC), 109–10
integrated musicals, 29
intermedial histories, 206–8
Isai Velalar caste, 151
Islam and Islamic dance lineage, 134–36, 151, 155–56, *See also* courtesan films; *tawaifs*
Islamicate, 230n95, 241n116
item girls, 40–41, 43–44, 200, 201–2, 214n14
item numbers
  Bollywood and, 200–2
  defined, 43–44
  Dixit and Khan producing, 182–83, 198
  precedents for, 156–57
Iyer, E. Krishna, 19–20, 98–99, 118–19

Jain, Jyotindra, 146–47
Jatra, 19, 164–65
Jayasimha (1955), 157–58
Jeetendra, 210–11n17, 216n31
Jewel Thief (1967), 74–75, 161–62
Jeyasingh, Shobana, 53–54
Jha, Sachdeva, 226n29, 228n73, 240–41n111
Jhalak Dikhhla Jaa (television show), 205
jhatkas and *matkas*, 24, 43–44, 179–80, 192
Jhingan, Shikha, 18–19, 56–57, 212n41
Jordan, Stephanie, 51–52

Kaikuttikali, 102–3
Kalakshetra Foundation, 100–1, 105, 146–47, 151
Kalarippayattu, 164–65
Kaliya Mardan (1919), 15
Kalpana (4.22), 149
Kamala, Kumari, 145, *See also* Laxman, Kamala

INDEX 261

Kandy dance, 102–3, 122–23
Kapoor, Anil, 42
Kapoor, Kareena, 199–200, 201–2
Kapoor, Karisma, 39–40
Kapoor, Prithviraj, 141–43
Kapoor, Raj, 38–39, 202–3
Kapoor, Rishi, 193–94
Kapoor, Shammi, 1–3, 2*f*, 50–51, 202–3, 211n17, 216n31
Kapse, Anupama, 15, 130–31
Kardar, A.R., 119–20
Kashmir Ki Kali (1964), 50–51
Kathak, 209n6, 211n19
  Azurie and, 135
  body codifications of, 80–82
  Bose and, 96, 98, 110–11
  Dixit and, 193–94, 211n19
  film dance influence of, 19, 84–85
  gentrification and, 146
  kotha spaces and, 69–71
  Rehman and, 155–56
  rhythm and, 53–54
  Vyjayanthimala and, 153–55
Kathakali, 82, 102–3, 146, 165–66, 239n96
Kathputli (1957)
  classical and folk dance movements in, 82
  costume design in, 141–43
  as melodrama of dance reform, 173–75
  narrative numbers in, 35
  production numbers in, 35–36
  Vyjayanthimala and, 36–38, 43, 51–54, 80–81
Katl-e-Aam (1935), 114–15
Kelly, Gene, 41–42
Kerala Kalamandalam, 124–25
Kerkar, Kesarbai, 206
Keskar, B. V., 147–48
Khal Nayak (1993), 194–95, 196–97
Khan, Aamir, 244n27
Khan, Farah, 89–90, 204, 205, 244n27
Khan, Raju, 186–87
Khan, Saroj, 7–8
  authorship and, 196–97
  career of, 181–83, 182*f*, 190–91
  co-choreography and Dixit, 8–9, 24, 179–83, 184, 185–88, 193–94

Devdas and, 196–97
"*Ek do teen*" *and*, 184–85, 204
on item numbers, 201
on Malini's *Bharatanatyam* training, 81–82
"Masterji Series" on, 179–81, 180*f*
media mobilization and, 13–14, 198, 205
Sohanlal and, 141–43
spectatorship and, 44–45
on Vyjayanthimala, 161–62
Khan, Shah Rukh, 27–28, 36–38, 199–200, 201–3
Khanna, Padma, 8–9, 85–86
Khanna, Rajesh, 202–3
Khanum, Khalida Adeeb, 112–14
Khokar, Mohan, 20, 70, 79, 84–85, 147
Khote, Durga, 148
Khubchandani, Kareem, 190–91
kinesics of film acting, 162–68
kinesthetic empathy, 44–45, 75–76, 232n143
kissing and censorship, 111
kotha
  architectures of public intimacy in, 67–71
  background dancers and, 88–89
  historical narratives of, 70–71
  melodrama of dance reform and, 170–73
Kracauer, Siegfried: "The Mass Ornament," 89, 90
Krishna, Gopi, 5–6, 48–49, 147, 216n31
Krishnan, Hari, 236n15
Kuchipudi, 238n64
Kumar, Dilip, 33–34
Kumar, Hemant, 48–49
Kumar, Krishna and Surya, 119–20, 231n118
Kumari, Meena, 8–9, 32–33, 48–49, 69, 85–86, 215–16n30
Kumkum the Dancer (1940), 63–64, 91–92, 128, 130*f*, 131–32
Kurdikar, Mogubai, 206

Laban, Rudolf, 67–68
labor
  body-space-movement framework and, 61–62

labor (cont)
  body zones and, 85–86
  choreographers and, 190–91
  choreomusicking body and, 11–12, 23–24, 143–44, 153–54
  classical dance revival and, 100–1, 103–5, 228n68
  corporeal histories of, 12–13, 206–8
  in *Dr. Vidya*'s co-choreography, 140–41, 143–44
  in Khan and Dixit's co-choreography, 179–81, 187–88
  in melodrama of dance reform, 173–75
  rehearsals and, 185–87
  Rehman and, 160–61
  spatio-corporeal matrix of, 67, 69–70
  stardom produced by, 7–9, 176
  Vyjayanthimala and, 161–62
Ladki (1953), 64–65, 166–67
Lanka Dahan (1917), 15
lasya, 51–52, 159–60
Lavani, 19, 154–55
Laxman, Kamala, 145, 146–47, 151, 152, 153, 173–75
Lefebvre, Henri, 1–3, 61–63, 66–67, 74–75
Lepecki, André, 198
Lewis, Devraj Peter. *See* Raj, P. L.
lip-synchronized songs, 32–33
lokadharmi, 79–80
Lyons, Edwina, 8–9, 85–86, 88*f*, 88–89, 90

Madhubala, 71–72, 85–86
Madhumati (1958), 48–49, 55–56, 141–43, 219n78
Mahapatra, Kelucharan, 79
Maharaj, Lacchu, 147
Mahmood, Talat, 27–28, 33
Majumdar, Neepa, 18–19, 45–46, 109–10, 131, 168–70, 187–88, 203–4
male protagonists and actors
  dancing and, 41–42, 210–11n17, 216n31, 216n33
  Khan and, 182–83
  in song-and-dance sequences, 40–41
  Tezaab and, 42, 184
Malini, Hema, 81–82
Mangeshkar, Lata, 4–5, 51–52, 55–56, 143–44, 206, 235n12

Manipuri, 211n19
  Azurie and, 135
  Bose and, 63–64, 96, 110–11
  in *Court Dancer*, 39–40, 63–64, 85, 125–26, 232n137
  gentrification of, 146
  Tagore and, 102–3
Matondkar, Urmila, 39–40, 202–3
Mazumdar, Ranjani, 65–66, 71–72, 170, 193–94
McLean, Adrienne, 3–4, 18–19, 46, 85–86, 197–98
Meduri, Avanti, 100–1
Meenakshi (1942), 132–33
mehfil, 68–69, 96, 103–5
Mehta, Monika, 184, 197–98
melodrama of dance reform, 23–24, 129–31, 133, 168–76
Menaka, Madame, 119–20, 231n116
Merchant, Vaibhavi, 186–87, 205, 235n6
mise-en-scène
  Alibaba and, 122–23
  production numbers and, 35–36
  spectacle and, 31–32
  spectatorship and, 44–45
mixed-race performers, 88–89, 116–18, 119–20, 137, 230n106
mobility. *See* female mobility
modernity
  Alibaba and, 124
  corporeal histories of, 137–38, 207
  Court Dancer and, 129–31
  "dance social" genre and, 128–29
  in *Dr. Vidya*, 139–44
  models of womanhood and, 170, 192–93
  nationalism and, 124–25, 136, 149
  song-and-dance sequences and, 30–31
modes of production
  background dancers and, 89–90
  cabaret numbers and, 60
  dancer-actress influence on, 46–47, 48–49, 140–41
  in Hindi film vs. Hollywood, 217n41
  spatial construction and, 61–62, 67
Morcom, Anna, 29–30, 240–41n111
Morgan, Daniel, 75–76

movement vocabularies, 13–14
  Alibaba and, 122–23
  cabaret numbers and, 71–73
  censorship and, 24–25
  choreomusicology and, 54–55
  from classical and folk dance, 79, 80–82, 83–85, 86–87
  dance revival and, 99–105
  "Ek do teen" and, 65–67
  Helen and, 140–41
  item numbers and, 201, 202–3
  in Khan and Dixit's co-choreography, 24, 180–82, 187–91
  kotha spaces and, 68–69
  melodrama of dance reform and, 168–70
  narratives engendered through, 168
  Natya Sastra and, 9–11, 82–83
  production numbers and, 35–36
  Shankar and, 103–5
  song choice influenced by, 46–47
  space changed by, 60–62
  textual codification of, 82–83
  Vyjayanthimala and, 140–41, 152, 153–54
mudras. See gesture and gestural genealogies; hasta mudras
mujra, 60, 66–67, 68, 69–71, 84–85, 110–11, 144, 172–73, 219n2
mukhaja abhinaya. See abhinaya; facial expression and movement
Mukherjee, Madhuja, 94
Mulvey, Laura, 40–41, 46, 197–98, 245–246n55
"Muqabla humse na karo," 1–7, 210n11
music composition
  choreomusicology and, 50–52, 54–56
  dance's influence on, 11–12, 22, 28, 43–44, 47–50
  radio's influence on, 94
  Sangeet Akademi seminars and, 147–48
musicking body, 54–56
Muslim cosmopolitanism, 114–15
Muslim courtesan films, 69, 70, 111, 144, 209n6

Nach Baliye (television show), 205
Nadia. See Fearless Nadia
Nagin (1956), 43, 48–49

Nai Duniya (1942), 119–20
Nair, Janaki, 171–72
Nam Iruvar (1947), 146–47, 152
Nandikesvara, 78–79, 83, 211n25
Narayan, R. K., 159
Narayan, Shovana, 70–71
Nargis, 48–49
narrative numbers
  Alibaba and, 120–21
  background dancers and, 86–87
  body-space-movement framework and, 60–61
  choreomusicological approach to, 55–56
  classical dance paradigms in, 82–83
  defined, 33–35
  development of, 144
  Dr. Vidya and, 143–44
  Guide and, 160–61
  interiority and, 45
  musicians in, 88–89
  Rehman and, 155–56
  spatial formations of, 38–39, 69
  spectatorship of, 43
  women's performance circumscribed by, 168–70
narrative. See also narrative numbers
  Alibaba and, 121–22
  Bose and, 128–29
  corporeal histories disrupting, 13–14
  dance/dancer-actor influence on, 46–47, 49–50, 64–65, 126–27
  "dance social" genre and, 128–31
  dancing body's interruption of, 31–32, 217n39
  Dixit and, 194–96
  item numbers and, 200
  Kathak history and, 70–71
  and melodrama of dance reform, 170–72, 173–75
  production numbers and, 35–36
  song-and-dance sequences and, 29–31, 46
  South Indian dancing body and, 153–54
National Commission for Women, 191–92
National Council of the Arts in Islamabad, 135

264 INDEX

nationalism
   Azurie and, 119–20, 136
   Bharatanatyam and, 78–79
   body-space-movement framework and, 60–61
   Bose and, 112, 136, 137–38
   classical dance canonization and, 94–95, 100–1, 105, 145–47
   Court Dancer and, 91–92, 124–25, 126
   "dance social" genre and, 124–27, 132
   Hindu majoritarianism in, 114–15
   Sangeet Akademi seminars and, 144–51
   Shankar and, 149
   Tagore and, 102–3
   Vyjayanthimala and, 153–54
   womanhood and household in, 170, 171–72, 224n14
nattuvanar gurus, 149, 151–52, 155–56, 206, 234–35n4
natya, 82–83
natyadharmi, 79
Natya Sastra (performance treatise)
   authorship of, 211n25, 221n45, 239n92
   Bharatanatyam and, 99
   body zones and, 22, 83
   classical dance canonization and, 78–79, 146, 239n93
   dance training and, 164–65
   on emotions, 226n39
   on group formations, 86–87
   movement vocabularies and, 9–11, 82–83
   on *rasas*, 239n97
   respectability discourses and, 99–100
Nautanki, 19, 164–65, 176, 200, 241n112
nautch, 70–71, 78–79, 97, 98–100, 109–10, 225n26, *See also* anti-*nautch* movement
Nehru, Jawharlal, 146–47
neo-classical, 229n82
Ness, Sally, 9–11, 162–63
New Delhi (1956), 43, 46–47, 48–49, 64–65, 141–43, 153–54
nottusvaram, 100–1, 207
nritya, 83
nrtta, 39–40, 45, 51–54, 82–83, 84–85, 215–16n30
Nutan, 48–49, 55–56

Odissi, 79, 80, 81
Oldenburg, Veena Talwar, 68, 175–76
Omprakash, J., 46–47, 48–49
Om Shanti Om (2007), 27–28, 36–38, 202–3, 244n27
Oriental dance, 98–99, 103–5, 119–20, 138, 149, 207, 231n118
O'Shea, Janet, 66–67
Oza, Rupal, 191–93

Padmini, 145, 149, 239–40n102
Pakeezah (1972), 8–9, 32–33, 69, 85–86, 215–16n30
Pakistan, post-Partition, 134–36, 138
Paluskar, V. D., 96–97
Pandian, M. S. S., 145
Parsi theater, 19, 100–1, 109–10, 124, 131, 164–65, 207
Partition, 134–36, 138
Parwana (1947), 116–18
Patel, Baburao, 118–19, 124–25
Pattammal, D. K., 152
Pavlova, Anna, 23, 94–95, 99, 207
Pawar, Lalita, 15–17
Penn (1953), 152
Phalke, D. G., 15
Phelan, Peggy, 60–61
Pillai, Dandayudapani, 151, 152
Pillai, Swarnavel Eswaran, 152
Pillai, Tiruchandoor Meenaxi Sundaram, 151
Pillai, V. S. Muthuswami, 8–9, 152, 153–54
Pillai, Vazhuvoor Ramiah, 151, 152
playback singers and playback systems. *See also* pre-playback dance
   advent of, 17–19, 212n41
   cabaret numbers and, 71–72
   choreomusicking body and, 54–57, 143–44
   dance musicalization and, 28, 46–47, 213n1
   mobility through, 94
pleasure
   melodrama of dance reform and, 172–73
   production numbers and, 35–36
   rhythm and, 121–22

song-and-dance sequences and, 30–31, 32
Prakash, Chinni, 186–87
Pramila, 114–15
Prasad, Madhava, 239n100, 217n41
Prasad, Vishwambhar, 111
Prem Granth (1996), 179–80, 180*f*
pre-playback dance, 14–19
Prince (1969), 1
production. *See* modes of production
production numbers
  affective architecture and, 165–66
  Alibaba and, 122–23
  Azurie and, 137
  background dancers and, 86–89
  body-space-movement framework for, 61
  Bose and, 92–93
  choreomusicking body and, 54, 141–43, 161, 162
  classical and folk dance movements in, 82
  Court Dancer and, 125–27
  dance musicalization and, 46–48
  defined, 33–34, 35–38
  gaze in, 35–36
  gendering of, 40–42
  image-sound hierarchy in, 45–46
  Khan and Dixit and, 182–83, 188–89, 197–98
  kotha spaces and, 69–70
  melodrama of dance reform and, 168–70, 175–76
  nrtta in, 45
  spatial configuration of, 38–39
  spectatorship and, 43–45
  Vyjayanthimala and, 155–56, 166–67
public dancing. *See also* architectures of public intimacy
  Bose and, 128, 134
  cabaret assemblage and, 71–77
  "dance social" genre and, 128–29
  melodrama of dance reform and, 168–71, 176
  production numbers and, 40–41
  respectability discourses and, 94, 110–11, 176
  stigma of, 99
Pukar (200), 189–90
Punjab Purity Association, 97
pure dance sequences, 39–40, 45, 54, 120–21, 122–23, 159–61
Putcha, Rumya, 234–35n4
Pyaasa (1957), 155–56, 173–75

Raas Lila, 19, 232n137
Raat aur Din (1952), 241n113
Rabadi, Mani, 76–77
Rabindra Nritya Natya, 102–3
Rafi, Mohammed, 4–5, 50–51
Rahaim, Matthew, 54–55, 96–97
Rai, Aishwarya, 66–67, 201–2
Raj, P. L., 4–6
Rajadhyaksha, Ashish, 239n100
Rajagopalachari, C., 155–56
Raja Harishchandra (1917), 15
Rajkumar, Senarik, 96, 124–25
Raj Nartaki (1941). *See Court Dancer* (1941)
Ram, Kalpana, 240n110
Ramamurthy, Priti, 110–11, 138
Raman, M. V., 151
Ramchandra, C., 55–56
Rangeela (1995), 39–40, 202–3
Rani, Devika, 110–11, 137–38
Rao, V. A. K. Ranga, 84–85
Rao, Vidya, 96–97
rasa, 39–40, 82, 239n97
rasika, 20
Ratnam, Mani, 29–30
Rattan (1944), 119–20
Ray, Manmatha, 131
reality TV dance shows, 182–83, 189–90, 203–4, 205
reception. *See* spectatorship and spectatorial engagement
regionality, 24–25, 146–47, 153–54
rehearsal and training
  acting/dancing binaries and, 164
  "*Ek do teen*" and, 184–85
  Rehman and, 9–11, 156–57, 160–61, 162
  Vyjayanthimala and, 151, 161–62
Rehman, Nasreen, 200

266 INDEX

Rehman, Waheeda, 7–8, 23–24
  acting/dancing binaries and, 162–63
  Bharatanatyam and, 146–47,
    151, 155–56
  career of, 156–61
  on dance training, 9–11, 156–57
  film performances of
    Alibabavum 40
      Thirudargalum, 157–58
    Guide, 34f, 155f, 155–56, 158–61,
      175–76, 185–86
    Jayasimha, 157–58
    Muhje Jeene Do, 155–56
    Pyaasa, 155–56, 173–75
    Teesri Kasam, 155–56, 175–76
    "*Yeruvaaka saagaaro ranno
      chinnanna*," 156–57
  in *Guide*, 34f
  melodrama of dance reform and,
    168–70, 175–76
  on narrative numbers, 33–34
  respectability discourses and, 149
  Sanskritization and, 78–79
  South Indian identity of,
    155–56, 158–59
representational space, 61–63
respectability discourses, 210n10
  Alibaba and, 124
  Azurie and, 112–14, 118–20, 137–38
  bhadramahila and, 105–9
  body-space-movement framework
    and, 67
  Bose and, 78–79, 110–11, 112, 137–38
  classical dance and, 78–79, 84–85,
    91–93, 94–95, 99–105
  Court Dancer and, 124–27
  critical attitudes to film dance
    and, 19–21
  "dance social" genre and, 129–31
  Dixit and, 192–93
  melodrama of dance reform
    and, 168–70
  singing and, 96–97
  Vyjayanthimala and, 141–43, 145, 149
Richmond, Scott, 75–76
Rogers, Ginger, 47–48
romantic duets
  body-space-movement framework for,
    60–61, 62–63

  dancer-actress influence on, 49–50
  private space in, 38–39
  representational regimes for, 119–20
Roop Ki Rani Choron Ka Raja (1961), 32–33
Rosenberg, Douglas, 14–15
Roshan, Hritik, 201–2
Roy, Bimal, 162–63

Sadhna (1958), 43, 84–85, 171–73, 241n116
Sadirattam, 19–20, 98–99, 100–1
Sahni, Balraj, 35
Saigal, K. L., 132
St. Denis, Ruth, 23, 94–95, 98–99, 207
Samson, Leela, 125–26
Sangam (1964), 38–39, 76–77
Sangeet (1992), 194–95
Sangeet Natak Akademi, 21, 23–24, 80,
  138, 144–51, 209n2
Sanskritization, 78–79, 99–101, 138,
  145, 171–72
Sarma, Vedantam Jagannatha, 156–57
The Saroj Khan Story (2012), 184, 196–97
Sarrazin, Natalie: *Music in Contemporary
  Indian Film*, 46
Satyam, Vempati, 157–58
Satyavaty, 20
Sayi-Subbulakshmi, 157–58
Schatz, Thomas, 36–38
Seenivasan, 145
Segal, Mohan, 141–43
semi-classical dance, 217n40,
  220n16, 237n55
Sen, Biswarup, 30–31, 38–39
Sen, Keshab Chandra, 96, 97
Sen, Nirmala, 96
Sen, Sadhona. *See* Bose, Sadhona
Sen, Saral Chandra, 96
sexuality
  anti-*nautch* movement and, 97, 99–100
  Azurie and, 116–18
  Dixit and, 84–85, 194–95
  heroine/vamp binary and, 193–94
  respectability discourses and, 168–70
  Tagore and, 102–3
Shabistan (1951), 140–41
Shahjehan (1946), 93–94
Shankar, Uday, 23, 94–95, 99, 103–5,
  104f, 138, 231n118
  on film dance, 149

India Culture Centre of, 141–43, 149
  nationalism and, 149
Shankar Parvati (1943), 108, 131, 133
Shantaram, V., 118–19
Shawn, Ted, 98–99
Sheela, 161
Sheikh Chilli (1942), 93–94
Shetty, Shilpa, 191–92, 202–3
Shiamak Davar Institute for the Performing Arts, 89–90
Shool (1999), 202–3
Shresthova, Sangita, 242n127
silent film, 14–19
Simkie, Madame, 207
Singh, Dayanita: "Masterji Series," 179–81, 180*f*, 186, 196–97
Sitara, 233n155
Smitha, Silk, 43
Sobchack, Vivian, 44–45
"social problem" films, 23–24, 168–70, 171–76
social reform discourses
  bai and *devi* tension of, 176
  Court Dancer and, 125–26, 129–31
  "dance social" genre and, 128–31
  Hindu majoritarianism and, 114–15
  melodrama of dance reform and, 168–76
Sohanlal, B., 141–43, 147, 155–56, 160, 186–87
Sokhey, Leela, 99
Soneji, Davesh, 97, 100–1, 138, 145, 171–72, 224n16, 226n29
song-and-dance sequences. *See also* narrative numbers; production numbers
  Alibaba and, 120–21
  as archives, 115–16
  art cinema and, 213n55
  background dancers/spaces of, 86
  body-space-movement framework for, 62–63
  Bollywood's transformation of, 89, 200–3
  choreomusicological approach to, 50–54
  classical and folk dance in, 80–81, 82–83, 103–5
  dance-centered taxonomy of, 31–33
  dance musicalization and, 28
  emergence of, 94
  narratives and, 29–31, 46
  sound in film and, 17–18
  stardom and, 41–42
song booklets, 115–16, 124–25, 223–224n6, 233n157, *See also specific films*
song picturization
  choreomusicological approach to, 54, 55–56, 57
  dance-centered taxonomy vs., 45–46
  defined, 22, 28, 45–46
song sequences, 222n61
  Alibaba and, 120–21
  song-and-dance sequences compared to, 32–33, 43–44, 45
  spatial configuration of, 38–39
  gender and, 168–70
Sotomayor, Jade Power, 54
sounding body, 56–57
space
  in *Alibaba*, 121–23
  backup dancers and, 86–90
  body-space-movement framework and, 60–65, 67
  in "*Ek do teen*," 66–68
  gendering of, 40–42
  movement vocabularies configuring, 38–39
  in production numbers, 36–38
spatio-corporeal formations
  cabaret numbers and, 73–74
  film dance and, 65–68
  production of, 60, 63–64
special effects, 201
spectacle
  Azurie and, 116–18
  background dancers and, 86, 90
  backstage musicals and, 29
  Bollywood aesthetic and, 203
  critical attitudes toward, 21
  "dance social" genre and, 128–29
  dancing body and, 31–32
  gendering of, 40–41
  item numbers and, 200
  Mulvey on, 245–46n55
  production numbers and, 35–36, 168–70
  repeat viewings and, 43
  spatio-corporeal matrix of, 67

268 INDEX

spectatorship and spectatorial engagement
   cabaret numbers and, 74–76
   classical dance and, 39–40
   dancing bodies' influence on, 27–28, 31–32, 43–45, 46–47
   Khan's choreography and, 189–90
   kotha spaces and, 69–70
   production numbers and, 35–36
   representational space and, 62–63
   somatic engagement in, 44–45
Sridevi, 182–83, 190–91, 243n6
sringara, 99–100
Srinivasan, Amrit, 176
Srinivasan, Priya, 98–99
star bodies, 22
   authorship and, 46–47, 64–65
   labor and, 85–86
   spectacle and, 31–32
stardom and star texts
   of aural performers, 240n108
   Azurie and, 93–94, 112–19, 134–36
   of Bollywood, 202–5
   Bose and, 91–93, 94–95, 120–21, 122, 129–32, 133–35, 136, 223n4, 233n157
   dance-centered perspective on, 31–32, 43
   Dixit and, 189–90
   fandom and, 115–16
   item numbers and, 201–2
   labor and, 7–9
   production numbers and, 36–38
   Rehman and, 156–57, 176
   Vyjayanthimala and, 141–43, 155–56, 176
   wife/household in opposition to, 132–34, 168–70
Stern, Lesley, 240n105
Subramaniam, Arundhathi, 147
Sujata (1959), 27–28, 33, 54
swing dance, 19

Tagore, Rabindranath, 23, 94–95, 102–3, 105, 228n73
Talaash (1969), 73–74
tala suddha, 51–54
Tamasha, 19, 200, 246n2
Tamil and Telugu cinema, 23–24, 145, 151–52, 153–54, 158–59, 168–70, 236n15

tandava, 51–52, 159–60
Tandon, Lekh, 48–49
tatkar (footwork), 53–54, 85–86
tawaif, 211n20, 224n16
   choreomusicking body and, 143–44
   gentrification of, 23, 103–5
   kotha spaces and, 68–69, 70–71
   marginalization of, 7–8, 96–97, 100–1, 147–48, 206
   melodrama of dance reform and, 170
   spatial formations for, 66–67, 88–89
   upper-class appropriation of, 70–71
   Vyjayanthimala and, 154–55
technology
   Court Dancer and, 124–25
   dancer-actress influence on, 12, 48–49
   film music and, 94
   as performance context, 207–8
   playback systems and, 17–19
   spectacle and, 157–58
techno-spectacles, 12
Teesri Kasam (1966), 136, 155–56, 175–76
Teesri Manzil (1966), 157–58
Telugu cinema. *See* Tamil and Telugu cinema
Tezaab (1988), 42, 194–95, See also "*Ek do teen*"
Therukoothu (folk street theater), 145
Thomas, Rosie, 109–10, 114–15
Thumri, 96–97, 98
Tiller Girls, 89
Travancore sisters, 145
Tuli, Nidhi, 184

Uttar Dakshin (1987), 184

vamp
   cabaret and, 71–77, 144
   choreomusicological approach to, 56–57
   in *Dr. Vidya*, 140–41
   "*Ek do teen*" and, 65–67, 192
   item girl compared to, 200, 201–2
   Khan and, 182–83, 193–94
   kotha and, 68
   melodrama of dance reform and, 176
   role of, 40–41
   spatial configurations for, 62–63
Vashi, Nataraj, 119–20

Vasudevan, Ravi, 34–35, 49–50, 128–31, 135–36, 173–75
Vatsyayan, Kapila, 79–82, 84–85, 86–87, 147
Vazhkai (1949), 151–52
Vidyarthi, Govind, 146–47
Viswa-Bharati University, 102–3
Vyjayanthimala, 7–8, 13–14, 23–24
  acting/dancing binaries and, 162–63, 165–67
  authorship and, 48–49, 166–67
  Bharatanatyam and, 9–11, 23–24, 35, 46–47, 51–52, 64–65, 78–79, 141–43, 149, 151, 153, 155–56, 211n19
  body-space-movement framework and, 63–65
  classical/folk binary and, 153–54
  dance musicalization and, 46–47, 48–49
  on dance training, 9–11, 164–65
  film performances by
    Aasha, 157–58
    "*Aye hai dilruba*," 176
    Devdas, 154–55, 162–63, 173–75
    Dr. Vidya, 139–44, 140f
    "*Hoton pe aisi baat*," 27–28
    Jewel Theif, 161–62
    Kathpuli, 35, 36–38, 43, 51–54, 52f, 80–81, 82, 165–66
    Kathputli, 173–75
    Ladki, 166–67
    "*Muqabla humse na karo*," 1–7, 2f, 8–9, 210n11
    Nagin, 157–58
    "*Neel Gagan Ki Chhaon Mein*," 140–41
    New Delhi, 46–47, 153–54
    Pehli Jhalak, 154–55
    Sadhna, 84–85, 154–55, 171–73, 176
    Sangam, 38–39
    Sunghursh, 154–55
    Vazhkai, 152
  Mangeshkar and, 55–56
  melodrama of dance reform and, 168–75
  South Indian identity and, 153–55
  virtuosity of, 43, 48–49

Wadia, Homi, 93–94
Wadia, J. B. H., 91–93, 124–25, 137–38
waltz, 19

Yagnik, Alka, 187–88

Zarina (1932), 111
Zarrilli, Phillip, 164–65